Android Test-Driven Development by Tutorials

By Lance Gleason, Victoria Gonda & Fernando Sproviero

Android Test-Driven Development by Tutorials

By Lance Gleason, Victoria Gonda & Fernando Sproviero

Notice of Rights

Notice of Liability

Trademarks

ISBN: 978-1-950325-41-2

Table of Contents

Book License

Before You Begin

This section tells you a few things you need to know before you get started, such as what you'll need for hardware and software, where to find the project files for this book, and more.

What You Need

To follow along with this book, you'll need the following:

- **Kotlin 1.5.** This book uses Kotlin 1.5 throughout. The examples may work with an earlier version of Kotlin, but they are untested.
- **Android Studio 4.2.1 or later.** Android Studio is the main development tool for Android. You'll need Android Studio 4.2.1 or later for the tasks in this book. You can download the latest version of Android Studio from Android's developer site here: https://developer.android.com/studio.

If you haven't installed the latest version of Android Studio, be sure to do that before continuing with the book. The code covered in this book depends on Android 11, Kotlin 1.5 and Android Studio 4.2.1 — you may get lost if you try to work with an older version.

Book Source Code & Forums

Where to download the materials for this book

The materials for this book can be cloned or downloaded from the GitHub book materials repository:

- https://github.com/raywenderlich/atdd-materials/tree/editions/2.0

Forums

We've also set up an official forum for the book at https://forums.raywenderlich.com/c/books/android-test-driven-development-by-tutorials. This is a great place to ask questions about the book or to submit any errors you may find.

About the Cover

Android Test-Driven Development by Tutorials

Ravens are one of the smartest animals in the world. They can solve puzzles, trick other animals to gain an advantage, and are even better communicators than apes! They're also great planners: Ravens don't leave anything to chance and think ahead to ensure the best chance of success.

Ravens are extremely adaptable and will test new behaviors to stay ahead of other birds. In fact, if ravens could code, they would likely be big fans of test-driven development! Every component of TDD contributes to greater confidence and fewer mistakes, which ensures survival of the fittest, whether you're a bird or a developer.

With Android Test-Driven Development, you'll be the top bird in your flock, with greater confidence and fewer mistakes in your code!

"There are many people who helped to make this book possible. My other half Marlene was the one who initially suggested that I try out for the Ray Wenderlich team. She gave me lots of encouragement and, even before the editors saw my work, edited every chapter to make sure my sentences were coherent. My late mother passed on her love of reading and many creative skills for which I will always be grateful. The many strong women and family members in my life who taught me to live life with honesty and conviction and were encouraging of my work. I owe a debt of gratitude to the Ruby community for teaching me about TDD and infecting me with enthusiasm. I'd also like to thank Ray Wenderlich and the team for giving me the chance to share my love of TDD with the world. Finally, I'd like to thank all of the editors and co-authors of this book. It has been a very rewarding experience working with everybody on the team."

— Lance Gleason

"To my family, friends, and especially my husband, who supported me while writing this book. Tyler, thanks for all your encouragement and patience you gave me as I spent evenings in front of my laptop turning thoughts into words."

— Victoria Gonda

"To my newborn daughter Fiorella and my wife Romina. Thanks for your support and help, examples and discussions about the topics of this book. Yes, she's a developer too, isn't that great? :] Also, to my family, who had to listen repeatedly about what I was writing, and no, they aren't developers!"

— Fernando Sproviero

About the Authors

Victoria Gonda is an author of this book. Victoria is an Android Engineer and technical author. The conferences she has spoken at have been an enjoyable way to connect with the technical community and exchange information with others. She was drawn to programming because of its potential to help people in a meaningful way. In her spare time, Victoria enjoys dancing and curling up with a good book. You can connect with her on Twitter at @TTGonda.

Lance Gleason is an author of this book. Over the years, he has worked in everything from server side development, IoT, wearables, to mobile development. He began his TDD journey as a Ruby developer and has been an Android fan ever since he preordered the G1 in 2008. After a few years of being an Android fan he finally took the plunge into Android development when he became a Google Glass Explorer in 2013. He's had a chance to work on project for organizations ranging from small startups to large companies with millions of users. When he is not writing code, you can find him traveling to interesting places, wine tasting, scuba diving or exploring a new hobby or interest. You can find him on Twitter at @lgleasain.

Fernando Sproviero is an author of this book. He's a mobile developer who works in Buenos Aires, Argentina. He's a graduated software engineer who enjoys learning and discussing about good practices and architecture. He's passionate about Android, iOS and API backend development. You can reach out to him on Twitter @fernandospr or on LinkedIn @fernandosproviero.

About the Editors

Jonathan Wong is the final pass editor of this book. Whether it's Android or iOS, as long as it's mobile, he's interested. Jonathan is a Pluralsight author, YouTuber and is a member of the video team at raywenderlich.com. He's a software engineer in sunny San Diego where he's worked on everything from mobile apps, to front-end Javascript, to server-side development. When he's not taking care of his two kids, three cats, or three chickens, he's usually trying to steal away time for a good run or a good cup of coffee. You can follow him on Twitter at @fattywaffles.

About the Artist

Vicki Wenderlich is the designer and artist of the cover of this book. She is Ray's wife and business partner. She is a digital artist who creates illustrations, game art and a lot of other art or design work for the tutorials and books on raywenderlich.com. When she's not making art, she loves hiking, a good glass of wine and attempting to create the perfect cheese plate.

Section I: Introduction to Test-Driven Development

This section introduces you to Android test-driven development (TDD). If testing or TDD are new concepts to you, we recommend starting here. You'll learn everything from what a test is, why you should test, what you should test, and what you should not test.

You'll then get your feet wet by writing your first Kotlin test, independent of the Android framework, with the principles of TDD. This section lays the foundation for TDD.

Chapter 1: Introduction

By Victoria Gonda

Welcome to the first chapter of this book. If you're curious about learning more about testing on Android, you're in the right place.

In this book, you'll learn about test-driven development (TDD) on Android. You'll do this by working step-by-step in real apps as you increase your testing knowledge.

Whether you're a testing beginner, or ready to bring your testing skills to the next level, this book is for you. By the end, you'll be able to fully apply the TDD process to both your greenfield and legacy apps.

Who is this book for?

This book is intended for Android developers who know at least the basics of the Android framework. You should also know enough about Kotlin that you're comfortable working with it.

Although it's not required, it's helpful to have an understanding of design patterns, dependency injection and app architecture. Whether you're new to testing and TDD, or eager to apply your existing knowledge to your apps, you'll find the information within this book useful.

This book covers everything from the bare basics of testing knowledge to applying that knowledge to existing code using TDD. If any of this interests you, read on!

Note: If you already finished *Android Apprentice*, you're at a great place to start this book. If your knowledge of Android is limited, that book is the perfect place to start. You can find it at https://www.raywenderlich.com/books/android-apprentice.

How to read this book

This book is divided into three sections, each covering a subsection of material. In these chapters, you'll follow along by writing tests while you take on new concepts. Depending on what prior knowledge you're coming in with, you may want to start in a different section or jump around. The sections are as follows:

- **Section 1**: This is where to start if you're new to testing or TDD.
- **Section 2**: If you know the fundamentals of TDD and are ready for some hands-on practice, start here. You'll learn how to follow TDD to add tests to new apps and features. If there's a specific topic in this section that interests you, feel free to jump to it. You'll be directed to a previous chapter if there's anything you need to know that you might have missed.
- **Section 3**: When everything in the previous section looks familiar, you can jump to this section to learn how you can apply your learning to a legacy project.

With that, it's time for a sneak peek of each chapter, so you can choose where to start.

Section 1

Chapter 1: Introduction

You're here now. You're learning what this book covers, and where you should start.

Chapter 2: What Is a Test?

Continue to this chapter to learn about automated testing and why it's important. This is an excellent read if you're new to writing tests or need convincing for why writing tests is important. In this chapter, you'll also learn what you should and should not test, and the importance of code coverage.

Chapter 3: What Is TDD?

This chapter introduces a core concept of this book: **test-driven development**. In it, you'll learn the basics of this software development process and why it's useful. You'll do this by using TDD to create a search URL generating function. Through this hands-on experience, you'll learn some of the tricky things that can come up when testing, and how you can approach them.

Section 2

Chapter 4: The Testing Pyramid

As you might imagine, there are multiple ways to test your app, each having a different focus. In this chapter, you'll learn about the testing pyramid, which describes the types of tests you can write covering different layers of your app, and how many of them you should write. It's a great intro before diving into the specifics in the next chapters.

Chapter 5: Unit Tests

This is the chapter where you'll learn about unit tests, what they are and where you should use them. You'll use JUnit while practicing TDD to add some logic to a new Cocktail app. In this app, you can search for drinks, "favorite" them and play a trivia game. The building blocks you'll learn in this chapter will carry you through the rest of the book.

Chapter 6: Architecting for Testing

The architecture of your project can make or break your testing experience. In this chapter, you'll learn about some of the most common app architectures. Along with this, you'll learn some of the pros and cons of each architecture and how they affect your tests. You'll finish off with some design principles that will help you when you practice the refactor step of TDD.

Chapter 7: Introduction to Mockito

Revisiting the Cocktail app, you'll take your unit tests to the next level using Mockito. You'll learn the basics of how to use mocks and spies to stub behavior to keep unit tests pure, completely independent from other classes. You'll also come away understanding the difference between black-box and white-box testing.

Chapter 8: Integration

This chapter looks at testing how different objects interact or integrate. You'll practice writing integration tests by working on a Wishlist app to keep track of the wishlists of your family and friends. While doing so, you'll learn how to manage your interactions with the Android framework while testing.

Chapter 9: Testing the Persistence Layer

Continuing with the Wishlist app, this chapter teaches you the fundamentals of testing a persistence layer while you build out the database for this app. You'll learn how to handle statefulness in your tests and strategies for creating randomized test data. While working with the RoomDB library, you'll also come across the gray line of testing your code versus testing the library you're using.

Chapter 10: Testing the Network Layer

While HTTP requests can be unpredictable, here, you'll learn how to write predictable network tests while working on an app named Punchline that shows you random jokes to share. You'll learn three different libraries to help you accomplish varying degrees of depth in your testing. With all these libraries, it opens up a discussion about how to choose the right libraries for your project.

Chapter 11: User Interface

Finishing out this section is all about testing your user interface. While adding the visual elements to the Punchline app, you'll learn how to match views, perform actions and make assertions. By having these tests, you'll be able to guard against any future regressions.

Section 3

Chapter 12: Common Legacy App Problems

Launching into this section about testing a pre-existing app, you start by learning some of the common problems you might encounter while doing this. By recognizing some familiar patterns, you'll be prepared to tackle these situations in future chapters. Along the way, you'll learn some reasons why these patterns may have made their way into the code.

Chapter 13: High-Level Testing With Espresso

One of the first tests you might add to a legacy application is an Espresso test. In this chapter, you're tasked with adding features to the Coding Companion Finder app, an app to find a dog or cat to pair program with. Along the way, you'll learn how to set boundaries and set up testing in an existing app.

Chapter 14: Hands-On Focused Refactoring

Refactoring is often used to help make an app more testable and easier to modify. This chapter guides you through refactoring part of the Coding Companion Finder app by writing tests for safety. You'll learn how taking small steps and moving slowly can keep your test suite green as you make changes — even if that means you need to change your tests.

Chapter 15: Refactoring Your Tests

Your tests are code too, and sometimes the first tests you write aren't the quickest or most maintainable. That's why, in addition to working on refactoring the app code, you'll refactor the tests of the Coding Companion Finder app. You'll be able to isolate your tests better, making them less brittle and more helpful.

Chapter 16: Strategies for Handling Test Data

There are many ways to manage test data, and this chapter is perfect for helping you make that decision. By learning the pros and cons of each strategy, you'll be better equipped to decide what's best for your app.

Chapter 17: Continuous Integration & Other Related Tools

Of the many tools you can interact with within the testing world, one type is Continuous Integration (CI) frameworks. In this chapter, you'll explore what it means to have CI for your tests, along with some tools you can use to achieve it. You'll learn the pros and cons of different strategies so you can make the best decision for your team.

Chapter 18: Testing Around Other Components

One of the tricky parts of testing can be around interacting with other libraries and parts of the Android framework. One example you'll see is with permissions. In this chapter, you'll learn how to set boundaries in your test and use strategies for handling these situations, including when it might be better to not spend time on writing tests.

Appendix

Other Related Techniques

This chapter covers some techniques you can use to complement your TDD process. By using these strategies, you can choose how to define what you'll test and build. You can also bridge the gap between technical and non-technical written specifications.

Key points

- There are different places you can start reading this book, depending on what you already know.
- You can jump to the chapters that interest you most.
- Previous chapters are referenced when necessary.

Where to go from here?

You now know what this book is about, so it's time to dive in. Feel free to continue to the next chapter to get started or skip ahead to another chapter on a topic that interests you the most.

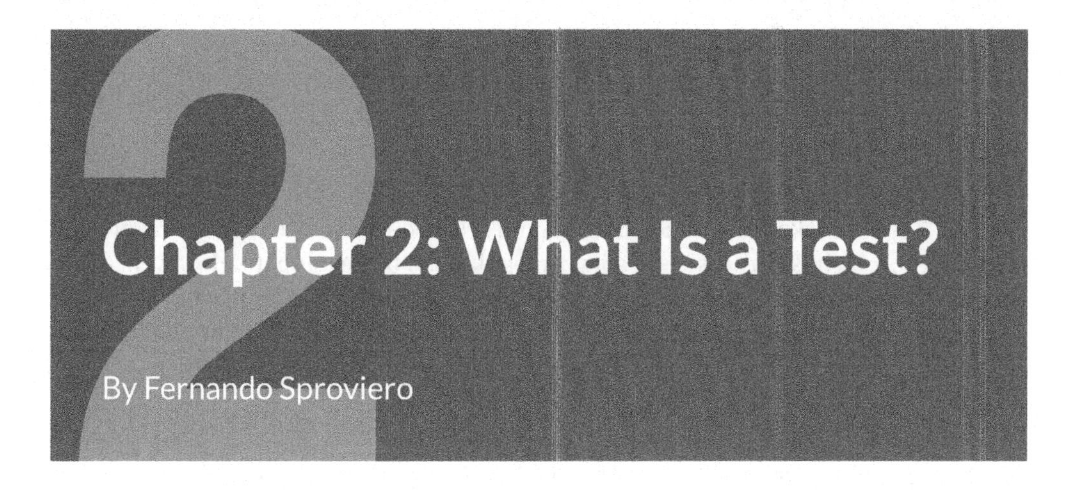

Chapter 2: What Is a Test?

By Fernando Sproviero

A **test** is a manual or automatic procedure used to evaluate if the **System Under Test** (SUT) behaves correctly.

The SUT may be a method, an entire class, a module or even a whole application.

From now on, when mentioning anything related to writing a test this book will be referring to the **automatic** procedure form of a test.

To write a test, you need to understand the feature, specification or requirement of the component you are implementing. That component may be an **Activity**, **Fragment**, **View Model** or several of these components working together. These may come in different forms, such as user stories, use cases or some other kind of documentation.

Testing is an important part of software development. By including tests along with your code, you can ensure that your code works and that later changes to the code won't break it. Tests can give you the peace of mind you need to develop quickly and catch bugs before they're released.

Essentially, there are two approaches to writing tests:

- Write tests **before** you write the feature.
- Write tests **after** you write the feature.

This book primarily focuses on writing tests first versus writing them after a feature has been implemented.

Why should you test?

Writing tests can take more time up front, and it is code you write that the client won't "see", which is why tests are sometimes skipped by developers. However, having tests can speed up development down the road and it presents some advantages.

Change/refactor confidence

You have probably run into a scenario in which you have a section of your application that works correctly before adding new functionality to the application. After adding new functionality, either in **Quality Assurance (QA)** or after it is released to customers you discover that this new functionality broke the previously working section. That is called a **regression**.

Having good, reliable, effective tests would have caught that at the moment the bug was introduced saving time in QA and preventing preventable bugs from making it to your users. Another related scenario is where you have a section of your application that is working correctly, but could use some refactoring to use a new library, break things up to follow a more readable architectural pattern, etc. A good test suite will provide you with the confidence to make those changes without having to do time consuming manual QA regression test cycles to ensure everything is still working correctly.

However, you should always bear in mind that this is not a 100% "insurance". No matter how many tests you write, there could be edge cases that the tests don't catch. Even so, it's absolutely safer to have tests that catch *most* issues than not having them at all!

Usually, you will write tests for the most common scenarios your user may encounter. Whenever someone finds a bug that your tests didn't catch, you should immediately add a test for it.

Documentation

Some companies and developers treat tests as a complementary documentation to explain how the implementation of a feature works. When you have well-written tests, they provide an excellent description of what your code should do. By writing a test, its corresponding implementation and repeating this until a feature is completed, bearing in mind that these tests can be treated as specifications, will help you and your team when a refactor or a modification of the feature is required.

When you're working on a piece of code, you can look at the tests to help you understand what the code does. You can also see what the code *should not* do. Because these are tests rather than a static document, as long as the tests are passing you can be sure this form of documentation is up-to-date!

How to write a test

There are many things to bear in mind when writing a test. You'll understand them by reading this book and practicing writing tests. However, the most important aspects of writing a test are as follows:

- **Naming**: You should give a meaningful name to each test so that it is clearly identifiable in code and in subsequent reports.

For example, consider a quiz game:

```
fun whenAnsweringCorrectly_shouldIncrementCurrentScore() {
  ...
}
```

This test's name represents the state of what you are testing and the expected behavior. This is useful when looking at the report after running a test suite.

- **Short and simple**: You should aim to write tests that focus on a narrow piece of functionality. As a rule of thumb, if your test methods get long, and have multiple **assertion** statements to check conditions of the system, it may be trying to test too many things. In that scenario it may be a good idea to break up that test into multiple, more narrowly focused tests. Take a look at this test:

```
fun whenIncrementingScore_shouldIncrementCurrentScore() {
  val score = Score(0)

  score.increment()

  if (score.current == 1) {
    print("Success")
  } else {
    throw AssertionError("Invalid score")
  }
}
```

The test only has seven lines of code to bring the SUT in the desired state and check the expected behavior.

- **Check one single thing**: Check one thing at a time. If you need to test multiple things, write an additional test similar to the one you've just previously run, but change the **check**:

```
fun
whenIncrementingScore_aboveHighScore_shouldAlsoIncrementHighScor
e() {
  val score = Score(0)

  score.increment()

  if (score.highest == 1) {
    print("Success")
  } else {
    throw AssertionError("Invalid high score")
  }
}
```

As you can see, this test is very similar to the previous one; however, the **check** is different. In the first test, you checked that the score of the quiz game incremented correctly. Now, you check that the *highest score* also increments along with the score.

- **Readable**: Anyone in the team should be able to read and understand what is going on in your test and/or what is the purpose of the test. Consequently, you should pay attention to the naming of each variable or method used and the logic sequence of the test. If you don't, then the tests will become difficult to maintain and keep up-to-date.

What should you test?

You should test code that is related to the logic of your app. This may include code that you have to write to:

- Show the UI and navigate between the screens of your app.
- Make network requests to an API.
- Persist data.
- Interact with device sensors.
- Model your domain.

Having tests for the logic of your application should be your main goal, however, bear also in mind the following:

Code that breaks often

If you have a legacy project without tests, and it breaks often whenever you modify its code, it's useful to have tests for them, so that the next time you make a modification you will be sure that it won't keep breaking.

Code that will change

If you know that some code will be refactored in the near future, tests will be useful here, too, because if you wrote tests for this feature, you can support on them to refactor the code and be sure you don't break anything.

What should you not test?

External dependencies

You should assume that all dependencies (libraries and frameworks, including those from the Android SDK) have been tested. Thus, you shouldn't test functionality of external libraries because the goal is to test things that you control, not a third party tool created by someone else.

> **Note**: In the real world, sometimes some of those dependencies are *not* tested. So, as a rule of thumb, when you have to choose between two or more libraries that have the same functionality, you should go with the one that has tests. This assures you that the features of the library work as expected and that the library developers won't break the features when adding new features and releasing new versions.

Autogenerated code

You shouldn't write tests for autogenerated code. Following the previous principle, it's supposed to be that the library or tool that generates code is tested properly.

When should you not test?

Throwaway/prototype code

Usually, when writing a Minimal Viable Product (MVP), you should focus on just writing the features so the client can get a feeling of what the final product could be.

However, all the stakeholders need to understand that all the code (or almost everything) you wrote will be thrown away. In this case, it doesn't make sense to write any kind of tests.

Code you don't have time to test

This is a controversial topic. Often, developers get stuck in a rut wherein they are fighting fires instead of proactively writing quality code, and they are not given the time to address code quality.

If you are working on a cash-strapped startup, where requirements are changing rapidly, that extra time to test could cause this fledgling company to miss key deadlines, not iterate fast enough, fail to raise it's next round of funding and go out of business.

On a new greenfield project, writing tests can double the amount of time to get features out in the short term. But, as the project gets larger, the tests end up saving time. Writing tests has its benefits; however, it'll take time to write and maintain tests. You and your team will need to make sure that you understand the trade-offs when determining which path you want to take.

A Note on Technical Debt

When you take out a financial loan, you get the benefit of an immediate infusion of cash. But a lender charges you **interest** on the loan in addition to the **principal**, all of which you will need to pay back. If you take on too much debt, you can end up in a situation where it is impossible to pay back the loan. In this case, you might have to declare **bankruptcy**.

Technical debt has many parallels to financial debt. With **technical debt** you make trade offs in your code, such as not writing unit tests, not refactoring, having less stringently quality standards, etc. to get features out quicker. This is analogous to getting a financial cash infusion. But as the code base grows, the lack of tests increase the number of regressions, bugs, time it takes to refactor and QA time. This is analogous to **interest** on a financial loan. In order to pay off that debt you start to add unit tests to your code. That is analogous to paying down the **principal** on a loan. Finally, if too many shortcuts are taken for too long, the project may reach a point where it is more advantageous to scrap the entire project and start with a clean slate. That is the same as declaring **bankruptcy** to get relief from too much financial debt.

Code spikes

At some point, you may find yourself working with a new library or, perhaps, you may realize that you aren't sure how to implement something. This makes it very difficult to write a test first because you don't know enough about how you are going to implement the functionality to write a meaningful failing test. In these instances, a **code spike** can help you figure things out.

A code spike is a throwaway piece of untested code that explores possible solutions to a problem. This code should not be considered **shippable**. Once you have a solution, you will want to delete your spike and then build up your implementation using **TDD**.

What is test coverage?

You can measure how many lines of code of your app have been executed when you run your tests. An app with a high test coverage percentage "suggests" that it works as expected and has a lower chance of containing bugs.

You may have asked yourself how many tests should you write. As mentioned before, you should at least write those that cover the most common scenarios.

In general, you can think of this metric as follows:

$$Test\ Coverage\ \% = \frac{Lines\ of\ code\ called\ by\ the\ test\ suite}{Total\ lines\ of\ code} * 100$$

Criterion

To measure, there are several coverage criterion that you may choose. The most common are:

- **Function/method coverage**: How many functions have been called?
- **Statement coverage**: How many statements of each function have been executed?
- **Branch coverage**: Has each branch in an `if` or a `when` statement been executed?
- **Condition coverage**: Has each subcondition in an `if` statement been evaluated to `true` and also to `false`?

For example, suppose that the following code is part of a feature of your app:

```
fun getFullname(firstName: String?, lastName: String?): String {
  var fullname = "Unknown"
  if (firstName != null && lastName != null) {
    fullname = "$firstName $lastName"
  }
  return fullname
}
```

Having at least one test that calls this function would satisfy the function/method coverage criteria.

If you have a test that calls `getFullname("Michael", "Smith")` you would satisfy the statement coverage criteria, because every statement would be executed.

If you also have a test calling `getFullname(null, "Smith")`, now it complies with branch coverage criteria, because the line inside the `if` is not executed and the previous test that called `getFullname("Michael", "Smith")` executes the line inside the `if` statement.

To satisfy the condition coverage criteria, you need tests that call `getFullname(null, "Smith")` and `getFullname("Michael", null)` so that each subcondition, `firstName != null` and `lastName != null` would evaluate to `true` and `false`.

Tools

There are tools that can assist you to measure the test coverage metric.

JaCoCo (Java Code Coverage Library) is one of them. Don't worry, it handles Kotlin as well!

This library generates a report for you to check which lines were covered by your tests (green) and which ones were not (red or yellow).

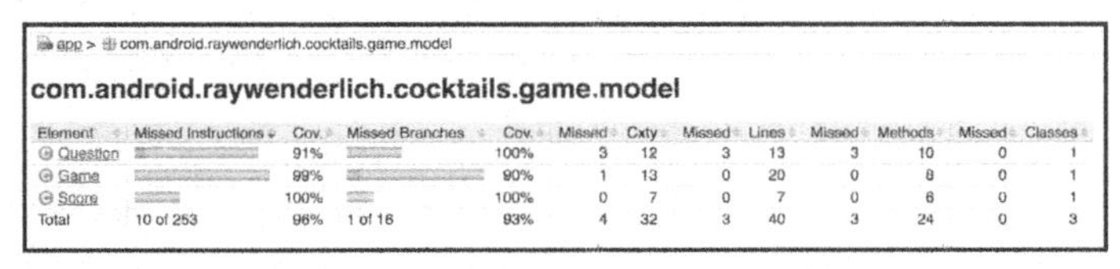

app > com.android.raywenderlich.cocktails.game.model

com.android.raywenderlich.cocktails.game.model

Element	Missed Instructions	Cov.	Missed Branches	Cov.	Missed	Cxty	Missed	Lines	Missed	Methods	Missed	Classes
Question		91%		100%	3	12	3	13	3	10	0	1
Game		99%		90%	1	13	0	20	0	8	0	1
Score		100%		100%	0	7	0	7	0	6	0	1
Total	10 of 253	96%	1 of 16	93%	4	32	3	40	3	24	0	3

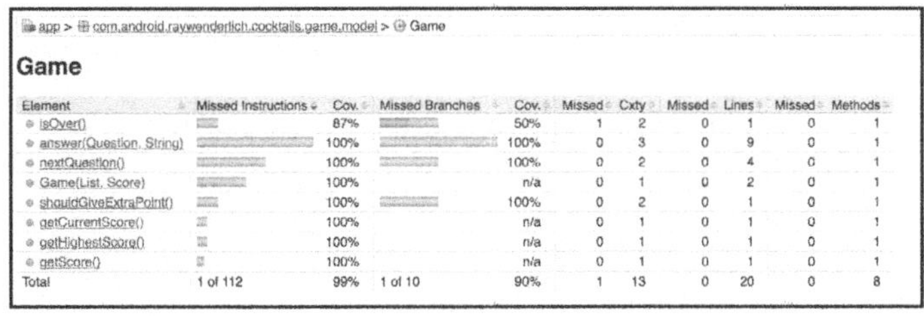

app > com.android.raywenderlich.cocktails.game.model > Game

Game

Element	Missed Instructions	Cov.	Missed Branches	Cov.	Missed	Cxty	Missed	Lines	Missed	Methods
isOver()		87%		50%	1	2	0	1	0	1
answer(Question, String)		100%		100%	0	3	0	9	0	1
nextQuestion()		100%		100%	0	2	0	4	0	1
Game(List, Score)		100%		n/a	0	1	0	2	0	1
shouldGiveExtraPoint()		100%		100%	0	2	0	1	0	1
getCurrentScore()		100%		n/a	0	1	0	1	0	1
getHighestScore()		100%		n/a	0	1	0	1	0	1
getScore()		100%		n/a	0	1	0	1	0	1
Total	1 of 112	99%	1 of 10	90%	1	13	0	20	0	8

```
38. import com.android.raywenderlich.cocktails.common.repository.CocktailsRepository
39. import com.android.raywenderlich.cocktails.common.repository.RepositoryCallback
40.
41. open class CocktailsGameFactoryImpl(private val repository: CocktailsRepository,
42.                                     private val shuffleQuestionsStrategy:
43.                                     (List<Cocktail>) -> List<Cocktail> = { it.shuffled() })
44.   : CocktailsGameFactory {
45.
46.   override fun buildGame(callback: Callback) {
47.     repository.getAlcoholic(object : RepositoryCallback<List<Cocktail>, String> {
48.       override fun onSuccess(cocktailList: List<Cocktail>) {
49.         val questions = buildQuestions(cocktailList, shuffleQuestionsStrategy)
50.
51.         val game = buildGameWithQuestions(questions)
52.         callback.onSuccess(game)
53.       }
54.
55.       override fun onError(e: String) {
56.         callback.onError()
57.       }
58.     })
59.   }
```

Android Studio also comes with a **built-in feature** to run tests with Coverage.

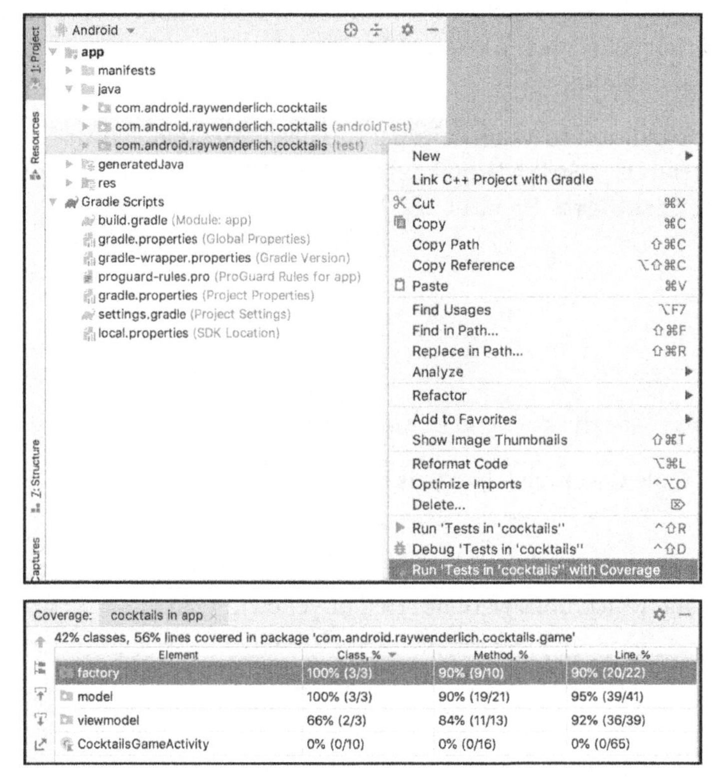

Element	Class, %	Method, %	Line, %
factory	100% (3/3)	90% (9/10)	90% (20/22)
model	100% (3/3)	90% (19/21)	95% (39/41)
viewmodel	66% (2/3)	84% (11/13)	92% (36/39)
CocktailsGameActivity	0% (0/10)	0% (0/16)	0% (0/65)

100% coverage?

In real-world apps, reaching a test coverage of 100%, no matter which criterion you use, is almost impossible to achieve. It often doesn't add value to test all methods, of all the classes, all of the time.

For example, suppose you have the following class:

```
data class Pet(var name: String)
```

You shouldn't write the following test:

```
fun whenCreatingPetWithName_shouldTheNameSetFromTheConstructor()
{
  val aName = "Rocky"
  val aPet = Pet(aName)

  if (aPet.name == aName) {
    print("Success\n")
```

```
    } else {
      throw AssertionError("Invalid pet name")
    }
  }
```

In this case, you are testing a feature (getting and setting a property) of a Kotlin data class that is auto-generated for you!

Test coverage gives you an exact metric of how much of your code has *not* been tested. If you have a low measure, then you can be confident that the code isn't well tested. The inverse however is not true. Having a high measure *is not sufficient* to conclude that your code has been thoroughly tested.

If you try to reach 100% test coverage, you'll find yourself writing meaningless, low-quality tests for the sake of satisfying this goal.

Neither you nor any team member should be obsessed with a test coverage of 100%. Instead, make sure you test the most common scenarios and **use this metric to find untested code** that **should** be tested.

If you feel that writing a particular test is taking too long, you might want to take a step back and evaluate if that test is adding enough value to justify the effort. Also, if a simple fix is causing a lot of changes to your tests, you may need to look at refactoring your tests or implementation to make them less brittle.

At the end of the day, your goal is to create software that provides value to its users. If you are doing TDD well, as your project gets larger, the total amount of effort spent on tests, implementation and QA should be the same or less than if you were creating the same product, with the same level of quality without doing TDD. That said, a project that is doing a good job at TDD may still take more development effort than a project that is not because the project with TDD will have a higher level of quality. The key is finding the right balance for your project.

Key points

- A test is a procedure used to evaluate if a method, an entire class, a module or even a whole application behaves correctly.
- This book focuses on writing tests before implementing the features.
- You should write tests to have confidence when refactoring.
- Tests also act as complementary documentation of the application features.
- The tests you write should be short, simple to read and easy to follow.
- You should only write tests related to the logic of your application.
- You can use test coverage tools to find untested code that should be tested.

Where to go from here?

Congratulations! Now you should understand what a test is, why it matters and the coverage metric.

In the next chapter, you'll find out what Test Driven Development (TDD) is and what the benefits are of writing tests before writing the feature. In the following chapters, you'll also start writing apps with their corresponding tests.

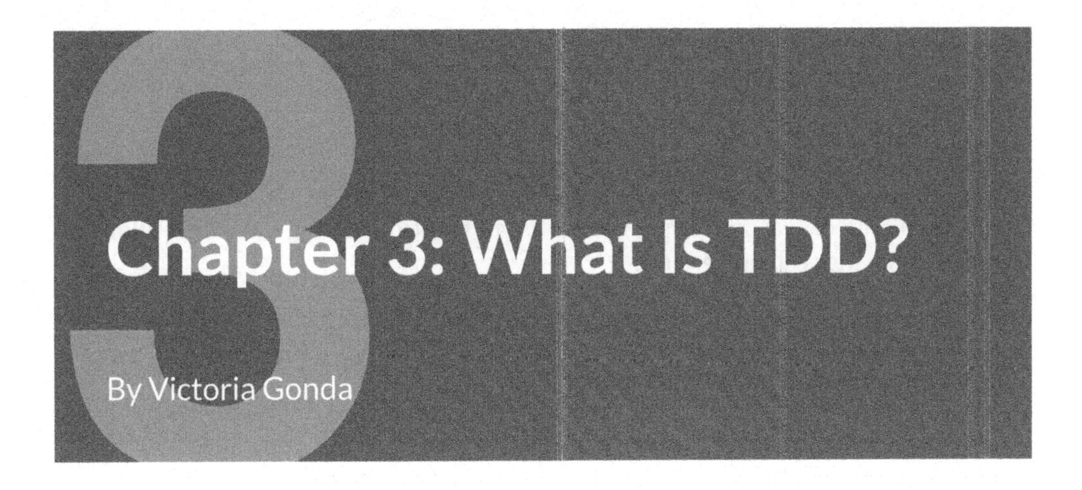

Chapter 3: What Is TDD?

By Victoria Gonda

Once you have decided to add tests to your project, you need to start thinking about *how* and *when* to integrate them into your work. You want to make sure you add tests for any *new* code and the tests you add provide value. You also want to consider how to add tests for *existing code*. Finally, you want to feel confident that the tests you add will catch any regressions in the future.

There are processes for different ways to incorporate tests into your codebase, one of which is **Test-Driven Development**, or **TDD**. In this chapter, you'll learn:

1. The basics of the TDD process.
2. Why TDD is useful.
3. The Red-Green-Refactor steps to practice TDD.
4. Some of the difficulties when learning TDD.

TDD is a process in which you write the tests for the code you are going to add or modify *before* you write the actual code. Because it's a process and not a library, you can apply it to any project, be it Android, iOS, web or anything else.

There are several benefits to this that you'll learn throughout this chapter and this book. Through using the TDD process, you can be confident that any new code has tests and that the code you write adheres to the specification of the tests.

Why is TDD important?

There are plenty of reasons for using TDD as your testing strategy, building upon the benefits of having tests in general:

- **Write intentionally**: Well-written tests describe what your code should do. From the start, you will focus on the end result. Writing these specifications as tests can keep the result from deviating from the initial idea.
- **Automatically document**: When coming to a piece of code, you can look at the tests to help you understand what the code does. Because these are tests — and, again, a process — rather than a static document, you can be sure that this form of documentation is likely up-to-date.
- **Keep maintainable code**: When practicing TDD, it encourages you to pay attention to the structure of your code. You will want to architect your app in a testable way, which is generally cleaner and easier to maintain and read. For example, decoupled classes are easier to set up test classes for, encouraging you to structure your classes this way. Refactoring is also built into this development process. By having this refactoring step built-in, your code can stay squeaky clean!
- **Have confidence in your code**: Tests ensure that your code works the way it should. Because of this, you can have greater confidence that what you wrote is "complete." In addition, with any changes that you make in the future, you can know that you didn't break that functionality as long as the tests you wrote pass.
- **Develop faster**: Using a process that promotes more readable and maintainable code and that acts as self-documentation means you can spend less time trying to understand what the code does when revisiting it and use that time for solving your problem instead. Also, the code you write using the TDD process is less error-prone from the start, so you will need to spend less time on fixing the code down the road.
- **Higher test coverage**: If you're writing tests alongside your code, you're going to have more test coverage over the code. This is important to many organizations and developers.

Getting started

You'll start from scratch using pure Kotlin independent of any framework to learn the steps of TDD. You're not looking at Android or any testing tools here, so you can focus purely on TDD.

Imagine, with a **Wishlist** app — an app in which you can keep track of people's wishlists — that there's a way to select an item and open it in a Google shopping search. For example, say you have a wishlist for your friend, Giuseppe. On this list, you have a gift idea for them, "Tea sampler." When you click on that item it would open up your browser with a Google shopping search for "Tea sampler."

You'll write the tests, and then the code, for a helper function that returns the Google shopping search URL to open in the browser when a list item is tapped.

Start by opening https://play.kotlinlang.org/. This is where you'll write your tests and code. Remove any code inside the `main()` function so you have a place to write your tests:

```
fun main() {
}
```

OK! You're ready to begin! First up: Red-Green-Refactor.

Practicing Red-Green-Refactor

In this chapter, you will learn the basics of the TDD process while walking through the **Red-Green-Refactor** steps. Red-Green-Refactor describes the steps that you follow when practicing the TDD process.

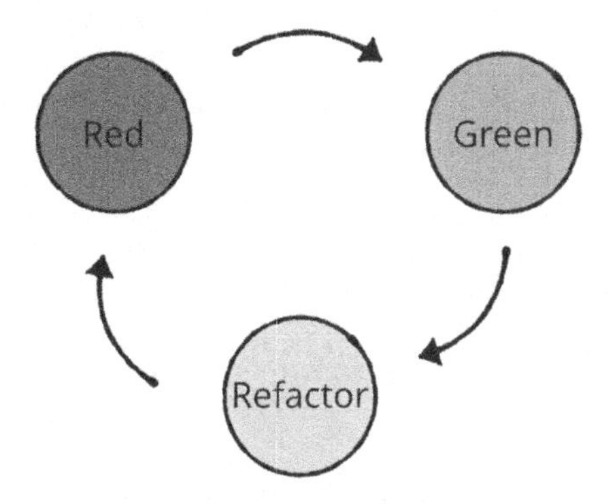

Red: Start any new task by writing a failing (red) test. This is for any new feature, behavior change, or bug fix that doesn't already have a test for what you will be doing. You only write the tests and the bare minimum code to make it compile. Make sure you run the test and see it fail.

Green: Write the minimum code to make the test pass (green). You're not worried about making it pretty or adding any additional functionality at this step. Write the requirements for that test, then run the test to see it pass. Stay here at this step until your test is green.

Refactor: Now is when you can prettify your code, and make any other changes to make sure your code is clean. You know that your changes are safe and correct as long as your tests stay green. Having these tests to ensure the code meets the specifications helps you refactor with confidence.

Red: writing a failing test

Your first test will test that your helper function, `getSearchUrl()`, returns `null` when given a `null` query. Add this code to the `main()` function. There will be a compiler error at `getSearchUrl()` at first until you create that function:

```
// Test getSearchUrl returns null if query is null
// 1
val nullResult = getSearchUrl(null)
if (nullResult == null) {
  // 2
  print("Success\n")
} else {
  // 3
  throw AssertionError("Result was not null")
}
```

Here, you:

1. Call the `getSearchUrl()` function with `null` passed in, storing the result in a variable.

2. If the result correctly equals `null`, print the success.

3. Otherwise, throw an error because it failed.

You need this code to compile in order to run your test, so add this empty function below your `main()` function:

```
fun getSearchUrl(query: String?): String? {
```

```
  return ""
}
```

This is as empty as you can write this function while still allowing it to compile. You may be wondering why you shouldn't add `return null` to the body now. Isn't that the same as writing an empty function? The short answer is, "No."

By including that in the function, the test would pass right away. If there's one thing to never forget about TDD it's that **you always want to see your tests fail**. By seeing it fail, you have confidence that the test is correctly asserting what it should. If you never see the test fail, the test might not be checking for the right thing! If that's the case, it won't fail if something is *actually* wrong. You'll learn more about this in the **False Positives** section of this chapter.

Now that you have eliminated any compiler errors, click the **Run** button to see your test fail!

```
Exception in thread "main" java.lang.AssertionError: Result was not null
   at FileKt.main (File.kt:7)
   at FileKt.main (File.kt:-1)
   at FileKt.main (File.kt:-1)
```

Great! You have a failing test... now to make it pass.

Green: making your test pass

To make the test pass, the function needs to return `null`. Update the body of `getSearchUrl()` to `return null`. Your function should now look like this:

```
fun getSearchUrl(query: String?): String? {
  return null
}
```

Run the test again and see the success message. Congratulations on your first test with TDD!

Writing a second test

You may not need a refactoring step near the start, as the code is still simple. In this case, before moving to the **refactor** step, write one more test to practice the first two **Red** and **Green** steps. This test is to make sure `getSearchUrl()` returns a non-`null` value if a non-`null` `String` is passed in as the query.

Add the following test to the bottom of the `main()` function:

```
// Test getSearchUrl returns not null if query is a string
// 1
val nonNullResult = getSearchUrl("toaster")
if (nonNullResult != null) {
  // 2
  print("Success\n")
} else {
  // 3
  throw AssertionError("Result was null")
}
```

This test is *very* similar to the one you wrote before. You:

1. Call the `getSearchUrl()` function with a `String` passed in, storing the result in a variable.
2. If the result correctly does not equal `null`, print the success.
3. Otherwise, throw an error because it failed.

Run the code again. You will see your first test pass, while your second, new test fails.

```
Success
Exception in thread "main" java.lang.AssertionError: Result was null
   at FileKt.main (File.kt:21)
   at FileKt.main (File.kt:-1)
```

Making it pass

Now, write the minimum amount of code to make your new test pass. Change the body of `getSearchUrl()` to return the query `String`.

```
return query
```

Run the tests, and see them both pass.

False positives

While testing saves you from many pitfalls, some things can go wrong as well, especially when you don't write the test first. One of these is the **false positive**. This happens when you have a test that is passing but really shouldn't be.

To see this, next, test that the URL returned includes the search query. Break the rules a little bit, and add this line to the top of `getSearchUrl()`:

```
val url = "https://www.google.com/search?q=$query"
```

Run your tests to make sure they still pass.

> **Note**: Running your tests often is a habit you want to acquire.

Now, add this test to the bottom of the `main()` function to make sure the result contains the query:

```
// Test getSearchUrl result contains query
// 1
val result = getSearchUrl("toaster")
if (result?.contains("toaster") == true) {
  // 2
  print("Success\n")
} else {
  // 3
  throw AssertionError("Result did not contain query")
}
```

Again, you see this familiar pattern:

1. Call the `getSearchUrl()` function with a `String` passed in, storing the result in a variable.
2. If the result correctly contains the query, print the success.
3. Otherwise, throw an error because it failed.

Run the tests. They pass right away!

Correcting the mistake

Did you catch what is missing? At the start, the desire was to test the returned URL contains the query. If you look closely at `getSearchUrl()`, you'll notice that the URL is never returned! It's the query that the function returns. The test is not asserting what you want to test, because it isn't specific enough.

As a challenge, you can write a test to check for the URL portion of the result. For now, refactor the function to return the URL instead of just the query. The `getSearchUrl()` should now look like this:

```
fun getSearchUrl(query: String?): String? {
  return "https://www.google.com/search?q=$query"
}
```

Run the tests, again.

```
Exception in thread "main" java.lang.AssertionError: Result was not null
   at FileKt.main (File.kt:7)
   at FileKt.main (File.kt:-1)
   at FileKt.main (File.kt:-1)
```

Oh, no! You can't see the result of the new test because the first one (as you probably predicted) is failing now! If you were using a testing framework such as **JUnit**, as you will starting in Chapter 5, "Unit Tests," all the tests would run even if some failed. When JUnit continues running the rest of your tests like this, it helps you to have a comprehensive understanding of what is broken. This is because your well-defined tests will tell you which parts of your code are working, and which are not.

What you know now looking at these results is that the function is no longer returning `null` if the input is `null`. This means you need to update the function so it returns `null` again when given `null` as a parameter while ensuring your newest test is passing. That's next!

Refactor: Updating your code

Now is your chance to refactor the code. You want to change the code to make it better, and fix the failing test, while making sure the rest of the tests pass.

Change the body of `getSearchUrl()` to the following:

```
return query?.let {
  "https://www.google.com/search?q=$query"
}
```

This should now return `null` if the query is `null`, and the URL containing the query otherwise. Run the tests and see them pass to confirm this!

TDD takes practice

While this was a simple example, it shows that there can be some tricky things that show up when testing. It takes practice to learn what works and form good habits. TDD is an art, and to do it well takes a lot of time. It is hard, but worth it.

When starting with TDD, you will make many mistakes. You might change a small piece of functionality that will make half your tests break when the functionality is correct, for example. Or you'll spot false positives. By making these mistakes, you'll grow and learn how to write better tests and better code.

Most projects have too few tests. As you're starting with TDD a good idea is to always add tests, and when in doubt, over test. As you learn and become more confident, you can eliminate tests that are not valuable. Tests are another part of the code you need to maintain, so you can develop judgment about which ones are valuable to continue maintaining.

Challenge

Challenge: Returning the URL

If you want to keep practicing, you can add a test to make sure the URL portion of the search URL is returned. The solution is included in the materials for this chapter. Revert the final two changes you made to the function first so you can watch it fail. Before you start writing this test, the `getSearchUrl()` function should look like this:

```
fun getSearchUrl(query: String?): String? {
  val url = "https://www.google.com/search?q=$query"
  return query
}
```

Key points

- TDD is a process of writing tests before you write your actual code. You can apply TDD to any sort of programming.
- Practicing TDD helps you to code quickly and with intent, document automatically, have confidence your code is maintainable, and have better test coverage.
- TDD follows the Red-Green-Refactor steps.
- This process always starts with writing a failing test. No matter what, you always want to see the test fail.
- Only after you write your test and see it fail do you write your new code or change your existing code.
- You only ever write enough code to make your test pass. If there's more code you need to write, you need another test first.
- You follow up with refactoring to make your code clean and readable.
- Learning to write good tests takes practice.

Where to go from here?

Congrats! You now know how to use TDD with the Red-Green-Refactor steps, and how to apply them to build a simple function. You can find the finished code for this example in the materials for this chapter.

You'll follow this pattern of Red-Green-Refactor for the rest of the book. If you want more practice, you can check out our helpful online tutorial, "Test-Driven Development Tutorial for Android: Getting Started," found here: https://www.raywenderlich.com/7109-test-driven-development-tutorial-for-android-getting-started

Section II: Testing on a New Project

This section dives deep into the art of TDD. You'll learn about the different types of tests that make up the testing pyramid and how to implement all of these different kinds of tests into an app.

You'll learn how to write unit tests, integration tests, and using UI testing to verify your app works as expected end to end.

Chapter 4: The Testing Pyramid

By Fernando Sproviero

Traditionally, software testing was done manually. It consisted of deploying the application to a test environment similar to the real environment but with fake (test) data. The Quality Assurance (QA) members would perform **black-box testing** on it — testing the application without knowing the internals — and raise bug tickets. Then, the developers went back and fixed the bugs.

Even nowadays, without any kind of automation, this is happening on the Android ecosystem. Testing usually consists of compiling the release candidate application, installing it on a physical device or emulator, and passing it to the QA team. The QA members would then follow a test plan, executing their use cases manually to find bugs.

You'll find that automating these repetitive use cases is the way to go. For each use case, you can write one or more automated tests. However, first, you need to understand that there are different kind of tests and how to classify them.

Tests are typically broken into three different kinds:

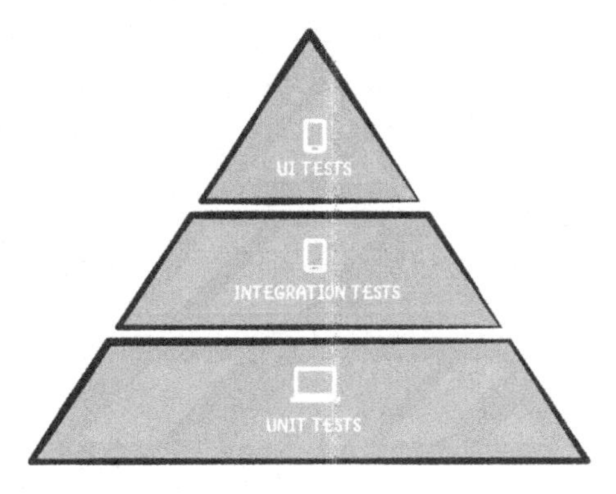

This is **the testing pyramid**, a concept originally explained by Mike Cohn in his book *Succeeding with Agile*. The testing pyramid gives you a way to group different types of tests and gives an understanding of how many tests you should consider on each layer.

You should have lots of small **unit tests**, some **integration** and fewer **UI tests**.

You'll now go through each of the layers.

Unit tests

Unit tests are the quickest, easiest to write and cheapest to run. They generally test one outcome of one method at a time. They are independent of the Android framework.

The **System Under Test** (SUT) is one class and you focus only on it. All dependencies are considered to be working correctly — and ideally have their own unit tests — so they are mocked or stubbed. This way, you have complete control of how the dependencies behave during the test.

These tests are the fastest and least expensive tests you can write because they don't require a device or emulator to run. They are also called **small tests**. To give an example of an **unit test**, consider a game app.

The `Game` class is one of the main classes.

Game
- score: Int - highScore: Int
+ incrementScore()

A common use case is to increment the `score` using a function like `incrementScore()`. Whenever the `score` increments and exceeds the `highscore`, it should also increment the `highscore`. A simple and incomplete definition of the `Game` class can look like this:

```
class Game() {

  var score = 0
    private set

  var highScore = 0
```

```
    private set

  fun incrementScore() {
    // Increment score and highscore when needed
  }
}
```

Therefore, a test that checks this could be as follows:

```
fun shouldIncrementHighScore_whenIncrementingScore() {
  val game = Game()

  game.incrementScore()

  if (game.highScore == 1) {
    print("Success")
  } else {
    throw AssertionError("Score and HighScore don't match")
  }
}
```

If you run this test, you'll see the test doesn't pass. We now have our failing (red) test. You can then fix this to get our passing (green) test by writing the actual method for the Game class:

```
fun incrementScore() {
  score++
  if (score > highScore) {
    highScore++
  }
}
```

Some common libraries for unit testing are **JUnit** and **Mockito**. You'll explore both of these in later chapters.

Google, in its testing fundamentals documentation, also suggests **Robolectric** for local unit tests. Robolectric simulates the Android runtime, it allows you to test code that depends on the framework without using a device or emulator. This means that these tests run fast because they run using just the regular JVM of your computer, just like any other test that uses JUnit and Mockito. However, some may consider Robolectric as an integration testing tool, because it helps you test integrating with the Android framework.

Integration tests

Integration tests move beyond isolated elements and begin testing how things work together. You write these type of tests when you need to check how your code interacts with other parts of the Android framework or external libraries. Usually, you'll need to integrate with a database, filesystem, network calls, device sensors, etc. These tests may or may not require a device or emulator to run; they are a bit slower than unit tests. They are also called **medium tests**.

For a simple example of an **integration test**, think about a Repository class that depends on a JSON parser class that reads from a file. The repository asks the parser to retrieve the data. Then the repository transforms the data to your domain model. You could create a test that given a JSON file verifies that the repository correctly returns the domain data. You would be testing the integration between the repository and the JSON parser.

> **Note**: If you mock the JSON parser and verify only the transformation to your domain model you would be creating a unit test. You should create unit tests for both the repository and also the JSON parser to ensure they work as expected in isolation. Then, you can create integration tests to verify they work together correctly.

Another example could be found in a retail app. You could ensure that the `LoginActivity` is launched whenever the user wants to add a favorite but hasn't signed into the app yet.

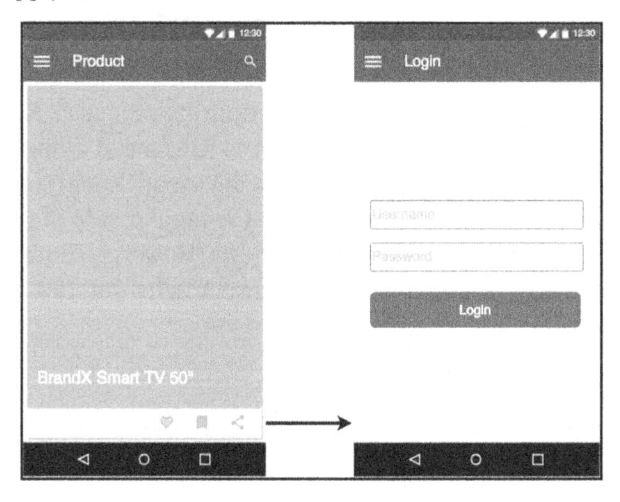

The test could look like this:

```
fun shouldLaunchLogin_whenAddingFavorite() {
  // 1
  val user: User = null
  val detailActivity = createProductDetailActivity(user)
  detailActivity.findViewById(R.id.addFavorite).performClick()

  // 2
  val expectedIntent = Intent(detailActivity,
    LoginActivity::class.java);

  // 3
  val actualIntent = getNextStartedActivity()
  if (expectedIntent == actualIntent) {
    print("Success")
  } else {
    throw AssertionError("LoginActivity wasn't launched")
  }
}
```

Here's what this test does:

1. Creates a new "details" activity, finds the **favorites** button and clicks on it.
2. Creates the expected result: an intent to navigate to the login screen.
3. Checks if the activity that launched is the same as the one expected to be launched.

Although this test deals with activities, you'll see that it doesn't require a screen for them to be rendered.

Another example of integration tests: In a social app, you could check if the list of friends is retrieved correctly from a REST API. Because this automated test will run frequently, you shouldn't use the real production API. Usually, it is replaced with a local or fake testing server. This is to avoid using server quota and because the tests shouldn't alter any production values.

This will also ensure that the tests are repeatable.

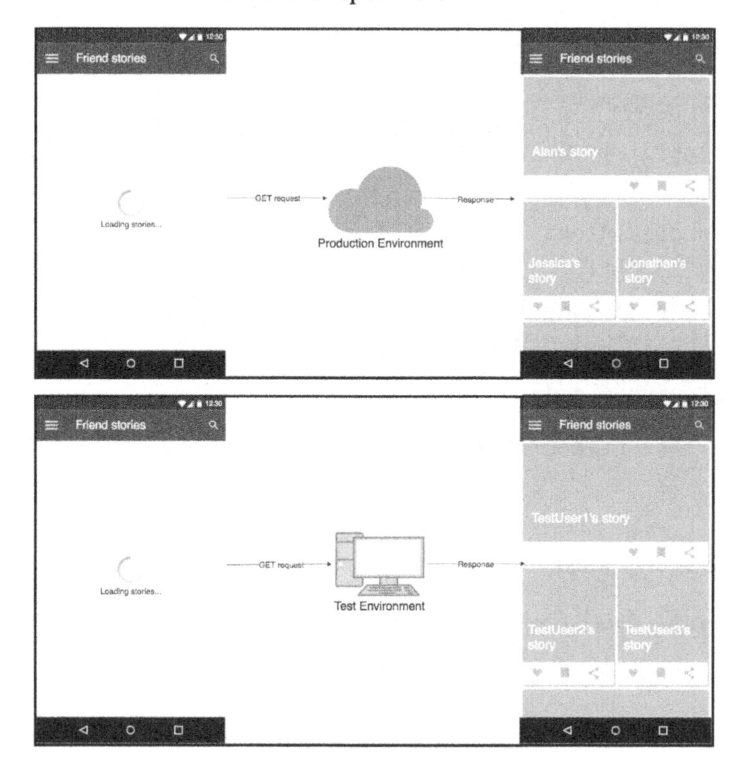

You can still use **JUnit**, **Mockito** and **Robolectric** in integration tests to verify state and behavior of a class and its dependencies as you'll see in later chapters.

Google, in its testing fundamentals documentation, also suggests **Espresso** for medium tests. For example, to perform validation and stubbing of intents or to perform actions on view objects. However, some may consider these kind of tests as UI tests because you would be interacting with UI elements.

UI tests

Finally, every Android app has a User Interface (UI) with related testing. The tests on this layer check if the UI of your application works correctly. They usually test if the data is shown correctly to the user, if the UI reacts correctly when the user inputs something, etc. They are also called **large tests**.

These tests emulate the user behavior and assert UI results. These are the slowest and most expensive tests you can write if you run them on a device or emulator. While these are helpful for testing your interactions on screen, you should limit your UI tests. As in the pyramid diagram, you should perform your tests with unit and integration tests as much as you can.

For a test example of this layer, think of an app with a login screen. You'd like to check that, after logging in, the app shows a `TextView` welcoming the user.

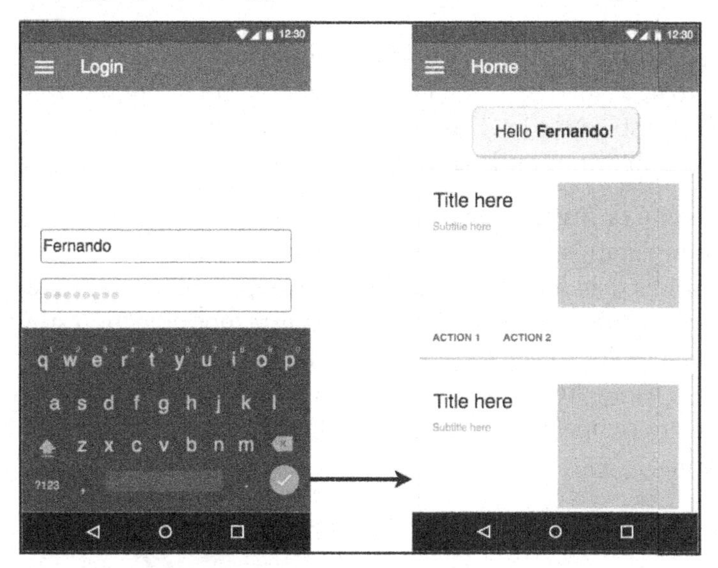

So, the UI test could look like this:

```
fun shouldWelcomeUser_whenLogin() {
  onView(withId(R.id.username)).perform(typeText("Fernando"))
  onView(withId(R.id.password)).perform(typeText("password"))
  onView(withId(R.id.login_button)).perform(click())
  onView(withText("Hello Fernando!"))
    .check(matches(isDisplayed()))
}
```

On Android, a tool suggested by Google for UI testing is **Espresso**. You'll write these kinds of test in later chapters. You could also use Robolectric (since version 4.0) for UI tests to run them without an emulator or a device. However, there are times that you need to run them on an emulator or device. These are called **Android instrumentation tests**.

There's another tool called **UI Automator**. Google recommends it only when you have to do cross-app functional UI testing across system and installed apps.

Distributing the tests

A typical rule of thumb is to have the following ratio among the categories:

- **UI Tests:** 10%
- **Integration Tests:** 20%
- **Unit Tests:** 70%

Google, in its testing fundamentals documentation, suggests these percentages. This doesn't have to be absolutely exact, but it's important to retain the pyramid shape. Remember that tests in the lower layers are easier to maintain and run faster. So you should avoid the following anti-patterns:

- **Ice cream cone or Inverted pyramid**: The team is relying on lots of UI tests, having less integration tests and yet fewer unit tests. This type is commonly found in organizations that don't have a testing culture, or are not encouraging developers to create tests. Usually, a QA team is responsible for testing and, in many cases, they don't even have access to the code repository. In this case, if developers don't create unit and integration tests, no one will. As a result, the QA team will try to compensate by creating tests of the upper layers, forming this anti-pattern.

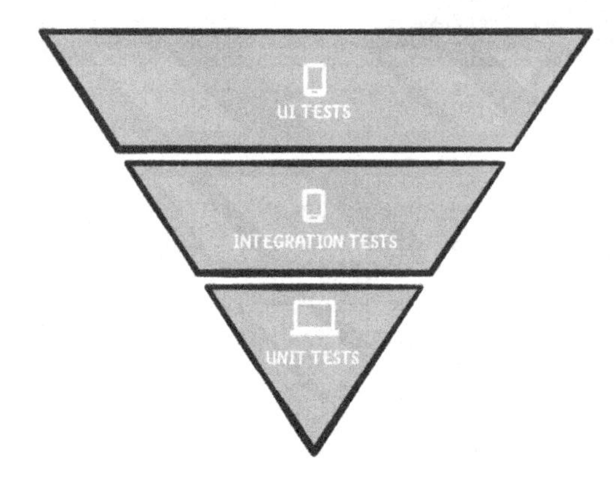

- **Hourglass**: You start writing lots of unit tests, you don't care that much about integration tests and you write many UI tests.

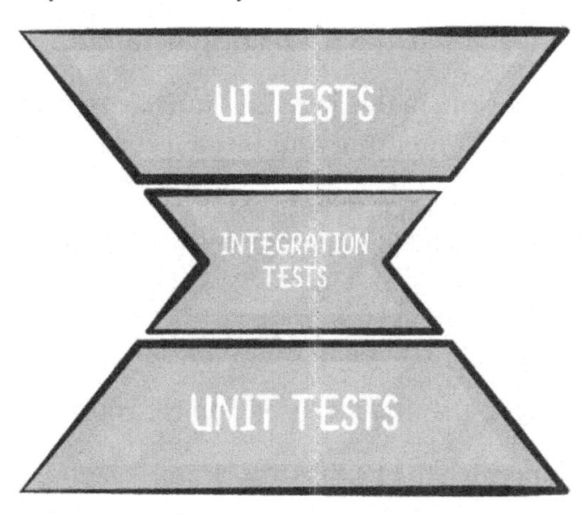

Bear in mind that not following the correct pyramid shape could affect productivity. This is because the test suite will run slower, thus, taking a longer time to provide feedback to the developers.

Key points

- Testing is commonly organized into the **testing pyramid**.
- There are three kinds of tests in this pyramid: **unit, integration and UI** tests. These are also called **small, medium and large** tests, respectively.
- On Android, you can also distinguish between local tests, which run on the JVM and instrumentation tests, which require a device or emulator. Local tests run faster than instrumented tests.
- You'll write tests of different granularity for different purposes.
- The further down you get, the more focused and the more tests you need to write
- Be mindful of how expensive the test is to perform.

Where to go from here?

In the following chapters, you'll start doing TDD by writing each kind of test with the appropriate tools and libraries.

If you want to go deeper on this subject, check the following:

- **Testing Fundamentals**: https://developer.android.com/training/testing/fundamentals#testing-pyramid
- **Unit Tests**: https://youtu.be/pK7W5npkhho?t=111
- **Integration Tests**: https://youtu.be/pK7W5npkhho?t=1915
- **UI Tests**: https://youtu.be/pK7W5npkhho?t=1838
- **The Practical Test Pyramid**: https://martinfowler.com/articles/practical-test-pyramid.html
- **Google Testing Blog - Just Say No to More End-to-End Tests**: https://testing.googleblog.com/2015/04/just-say-no-to-more-end-to-end-tests.html
- ***Succeeding with Agile* book**: https://www.amazon.com/Succeeding-Agile-Software-Development-Using/dp/0321579364

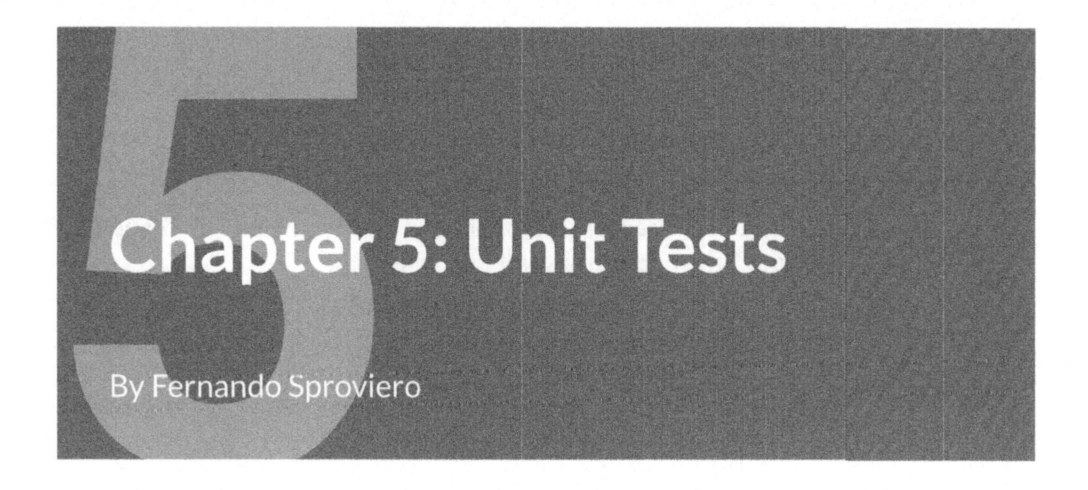

Chapter 5: Unit Tests

By Fernando Sproviero

As mentioned in Chapter 4, “The Testing Pyramid,” **unit tests** verify how isolated parts of your application work. Before checking how things work together, you need to make sure the units of your application behave as expected.

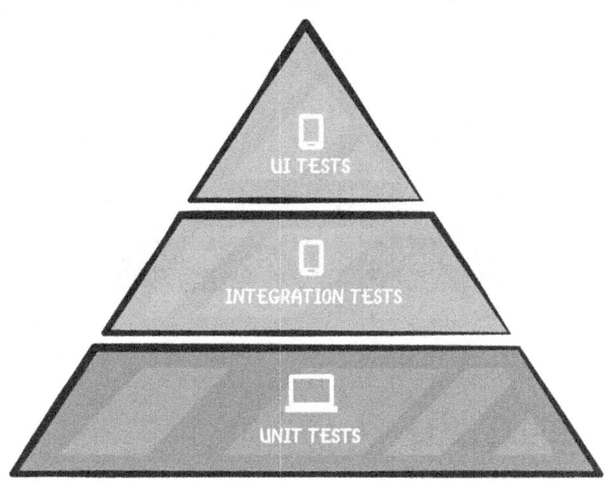

In this chapter, you’ll:

- Learn what unit tests are and what are the best places to use them.
- Write unit tests using the test-driven development (TDD) pattern to learn these concepts in the context of TDD.

Throughout this chapter and Chapter 7, “Introduction to Mockito” you’ll work on an application named **Cocktail Game**. With this application, you’ll have fun with a trivia game about cocktails.

Find the starter project for this application in the materials for this chapter and open it in Android Studio. Build and run the application. You'll see a blank screen.

You'll start writing tests and classes for the application and, by the end of Chapter 7, "Introduction to Mockito," the application will look like this:

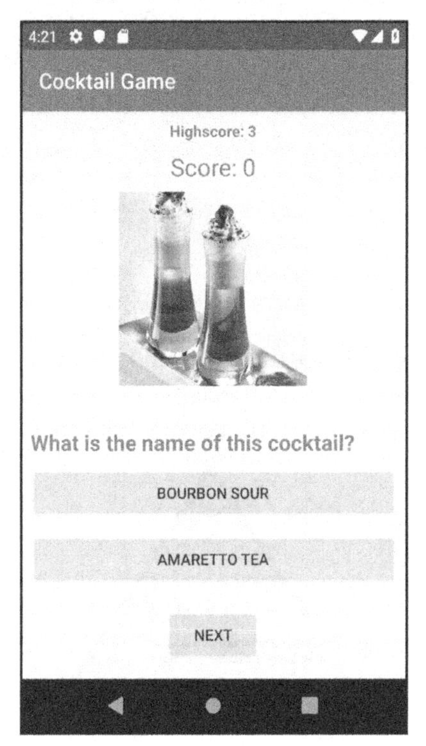

Game Screen

When to use unit tests

Unit tests are the fastest and easiest tests to write. They also are the quickest to run. When you want to ensure that a class or method is working as intended in isolation — this means with no other dependent classes — you write unit tests.

Before writing any feature code, you should first write a unit test for one of the classes that will compose your feature. Afterwards, you write the class that will pass the test. After repeating this procedure, you'll have a completed, testable feature.

Setting up JUnit

You're going to write a unit test for the first class of the cocktail game named `Game`. This first test will be a **JUnit** test, so, open **app/build.gradle** and add the following dependency:

```
dependencies {
  ...
  testImplementation 'junit:junit:4.13.2'
}
```

Notice that it's `testImplementation` instead of `implementation` because you'll use this dependency only when testing. This means that it won't be bundled into the application (APK) that your device or emulator will run.

> **Note**: When creating a new project, you'll find that this dependency is already there. You're adding it here manually for educational purposes.

Creating unit tests

To start, switch to the Project View and open **app ▸ src**. Create a new directory and enter: **test/java/com/raywenderlich/android/cocktails/game/model**. This creates a new test package for your `Game` class. Then, create a file called **GameUnitTests.kt**.

Write the following code:

```
class GameUnitTests {
  // 1
  @Test
  fun whenIncrementingScore_shouldIncrementCurrentScore() {
    // 2
    val game = Game()

    // 3
    game.incrementScore()

    // 4
    Assert.assertEquals(1, game.currentScore)
  }
}
```

> **Note**: When importing `Assert`, you should choose `org.junit.Assert`.

1. Notice the `@Test` annotation. This will tell JUnit that this method is a test.
2. Create an instance of the `Game` class — the one that will be tested.
3. Call the method that you want to test.
4. `assertEquals` verifies that the previous execution modified the `game.currentScore` property to be equal to one. It's important to understand that the first parameter is the **expected value**, and the second parameter is the **actual value**.

There's also the possibility to write a message so that, when the test fails, you'll see this message. For example:

```
Assert.assertEquals("Current score should have been 1",
  1, game.currentScore)
```

Every test has the following steps:

- **Set Up**: You first have a phase where you arrange, configure or set up; in this case, you instantiate a class.
- **Assertion**: You execute the method that you want to test and you assert the result.
- **Teardown**: You want tests to start with the same state each time they are run. Otherwise you might get flaky tests. Sometimes (not in this example), you'll reset the test state after the tests are done running. This is where it would happen.

If you try to compile the test now, you'll get this:

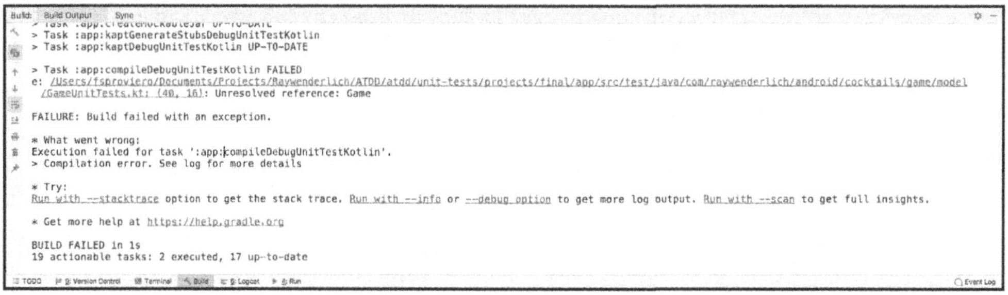

```
Build: Build Output  Sync
> Task :app:kaptGenerateStubsDebugUnitTestKotlin
> Task :app:kaptDebugUnitTestKotlin UP-TO-DATE

> Task :app:compileDebugUnitTestKotlin FAILED
e: /Users/fsproviero/Documents/Projects/Raywenderlich/ATDD/atdd/unit-tests/projects/final/app/src/test/java/com/raywenderlich/android/cocktails/game/model
  /GameUnitTests.kt: (40, 16): Unresolved reference: Game

FAILURE: Build failed with an exception.

* What went wrong:
Execution failed for task ':app:compileDebugUnitTestKotlin'.
> Compilation error. See log for more details

* Try:
Run with --stacktrace option to get the stack trace. Run with --info or --debug option to get more log output. Run with --scan to get full insights.

* Get more help at https://help.gradle.org

BUILD FAILED in 1s
19 actionable tasks: 2 executed, 17 up-to-date
TODO  9: Version Control  Terminal  Build  6: Logcat  4: Run  Event Log
```

Making the test compile

The test won't compile because the `Game` class doesn't exist. So, create the `Game` class under the directory **app ▸ src ▸ main ▸ java ▸ com ▸ raywenderlich ▸ android ▸ cocktails ▸ game ▸ model**. You'll need to create `game` and `model` packages first. In the `Game` class, write the minimum amount of code to make the test compile:

```
class Game() {
  var currentScore = 0
    private set

  fun incrementScore() {
    // No implementation yet
  }
}
```

Running the test

Now, go back to the test, import the `Game` model and you'll see that the test now compiles.

There are several ways to run the tests.

You can click the **Play** button over a test:

```
8      @Test
9      fun whenIncrementingScore_shouldIncrementCurrentScore() {
10         val game = Game()
11
12         game.incrementScore()
13
14         Assert.assertEquals( expected: 1, game.currentScore)
15     }
```

You can also use the shortcut **^ + ⇧ + R**.

Or, if you want to run all the tests (currently you have just one), you can right-click over the **app ▸ src ▸ test ▸ java ▸ com ▸ raywenderlich ▸ android ▸ cocktails ▸ game ▸ model** package and select **Run 'Tests' in 'model'**:

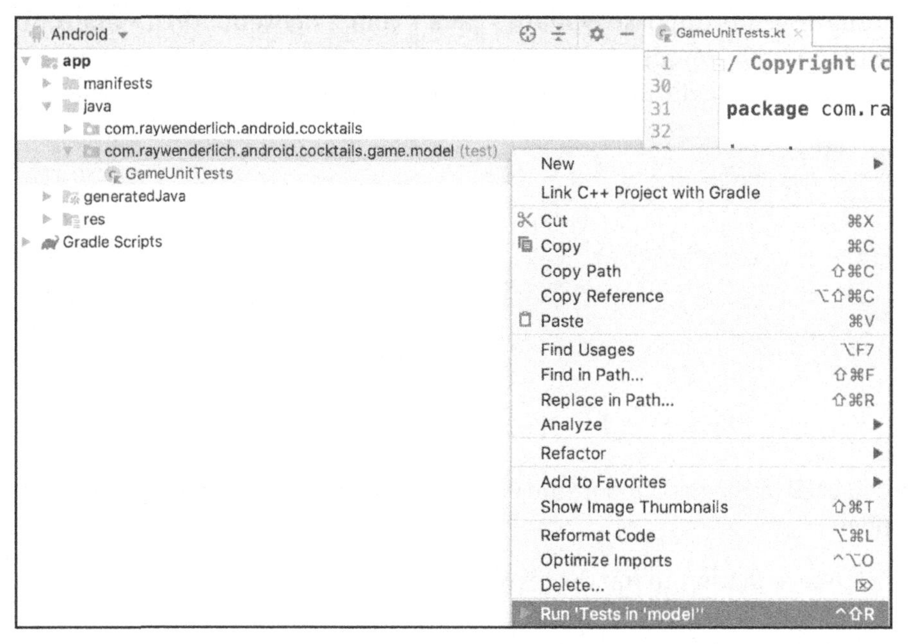

Either way, you should see that it doesn't pass:

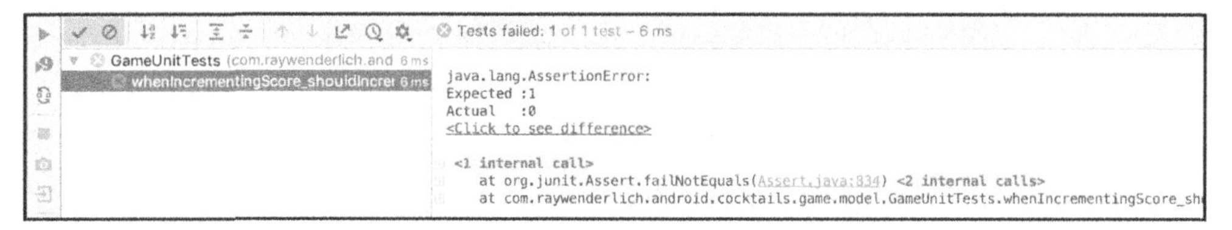

This is because you didn't increment the `currentScore` yet. You'll fix that soon.

You can also open the **Terminal** going to **View ▸ Tool Windows ▸ Terminal** and run the tests from the command line executing:

```
$ ./gradlew test
```

Notice how the expected value is one and the actual value is zero. If we had reversed the order of our expected and actual values in our assertion, this would show up incorrectly.

You'll also see that it generates a report under **/app/build/reports/tests/testDebugUnitTest/index.html**; if you open it in your preferred browser, you'll see the following:

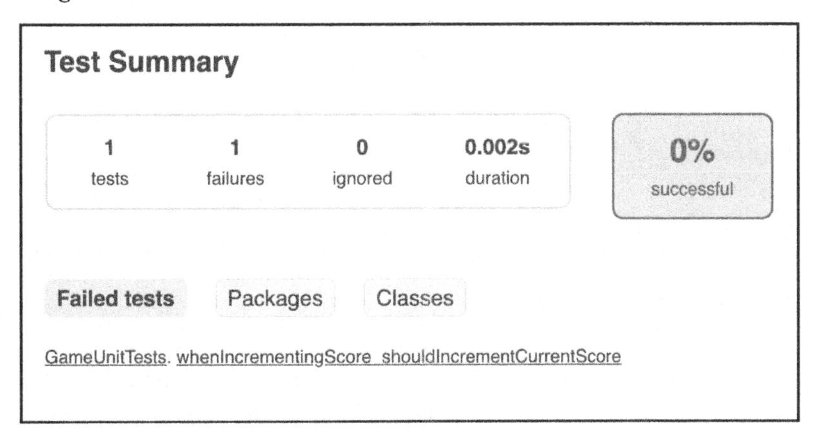

Making the test pass

Modify the Game class to make it pass:

```
class Game() {
  var currentScore = 0
    private set

  fun incrementScore() {
    currentScore++
  }
}
```

Now run the test again and see that it passes.

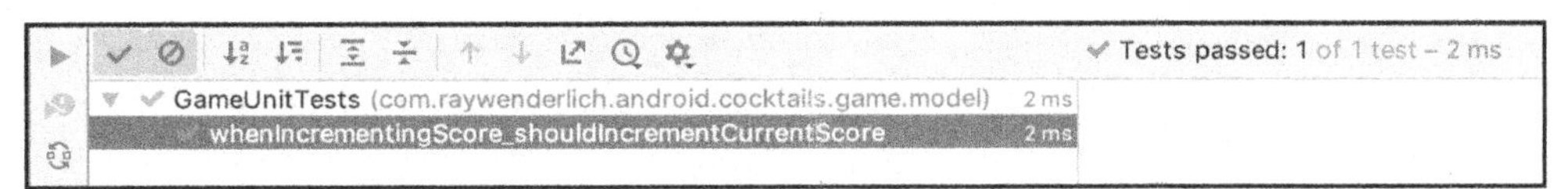

Or if you run the command in the **Terminal**:

```
$ ./gradlew test
```

It'll generate this report:

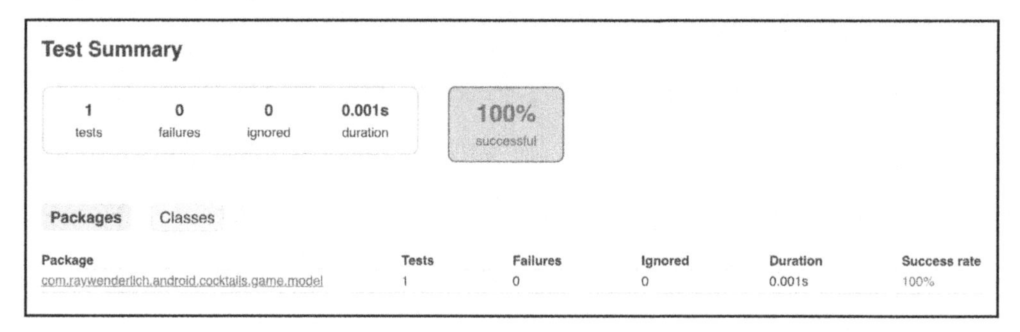

Creating more tests

The game will show a highest score. So, you should add a test that checks that when the current score is above the highest score, it increments the highest score:

```
@Test
fun
whenIncrementingScore_aboveHighScore_shouldAlsoIncrementHighScor
e() {
  val game = Game()

  game.incrementScore()

  Assert.assertEquals(1, game.highestScore)
}
```

Again if you try to compile it'll fail because the `highestScore` property is missing.

So, add the following property to the `Game` class:

```
  var highestScore = 0
    private set
```

Now the test will compile, so run it and watch it fail.

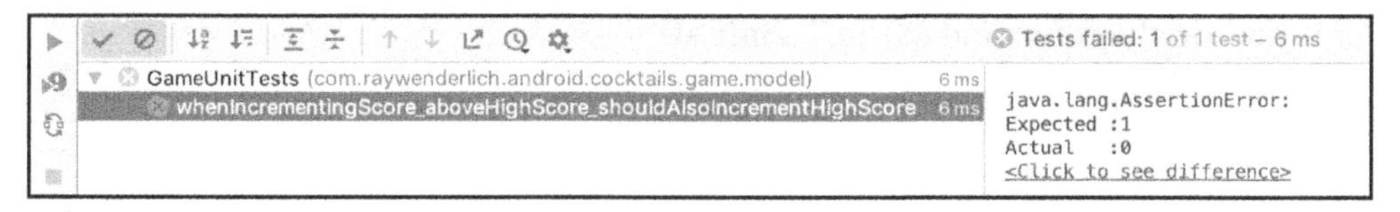

To make it pass, open the `Game` class and modify the `incrementScore()` method as follows:

```
  fun incrementScore() {
    currentScore++
    highestScore++
  }
```

Run the test and you'll see that it passes.

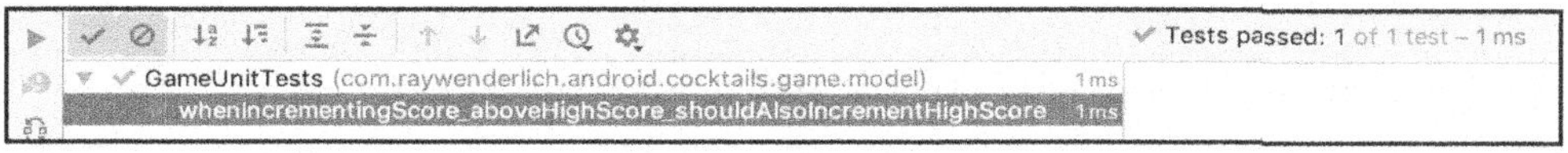

Tests passed: 1 of 1 test – 1 ms
GameUnitTests (com.raywenderlich.android.cocktails.game.model) 1 ms
whenIncrementingScore_aboveHighScore_shouldAlsoIncrementHighScore 1 ms

However, you should also test that, when the highest score is greater than the current score, incrementing the current score won't also increment the highest score, so add the following test:

```
  @Test
  fun
whenIncrementingScore_belowHighScore_shouldNotIncrementHighScore
() {
    val game = Game(10)

    game.incrementScore()

    Assert.assertEquals(10, game.highestScore)
  }
```

Here, the intention is to create a `Game` with a highscore of 10. The test won't compile because you need to modify the constructor to allow a parameter. Because you need to start with a highest score greater than the default, which is 0, you need to alter the constructor like this:

```
class Game(highest: Int = 0) {
```

And change the `highestScore` property to be set to `highest`:

```
 var highestScore = highest
   private set
```

Now, run all the tests and see that the last one doesn't pass. You can use the **green arrow** button on the left-side of the **class** definition.

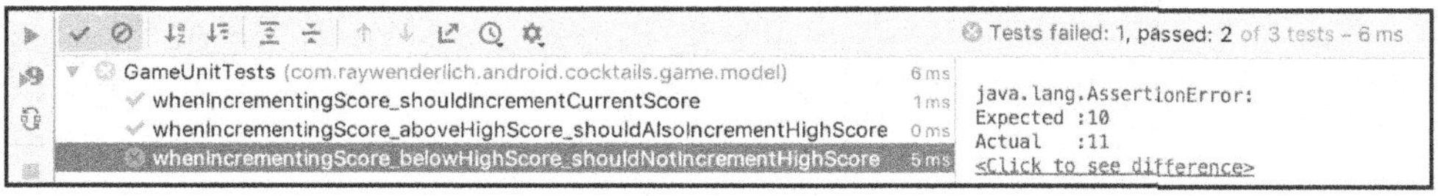

Tests failed: 1, passed: 2 of 3 tests – 6 ms
GameUnitTests (com.raywenderlich.android.cocktails.game.model) 6 ms
whenIncrementingScore_shouldIncrementCurrentScore 1 ms
whenIncrementingScore_aboveHighScore_shouldAlsoIncrementHighScore 0 ms
whenIncrementingScore_belowHighScore_shouldNotIncrementHighScore 5 ms

```
java.lang.AssertionError:
Expected :10
Actual   :11
<Click to see difference>
```

The last one doesn't pass because you're incrementing both the current score and highest score regardless of their values. Fix that by replacing the `incrementScore()` function with the following:

```
fun incrementScore() {
  currentScore++
  if (currentScore > highestScore) {
    highestScore = currentScore
  }
}
```

Build and run the last test to see the satisfying green checkmark.

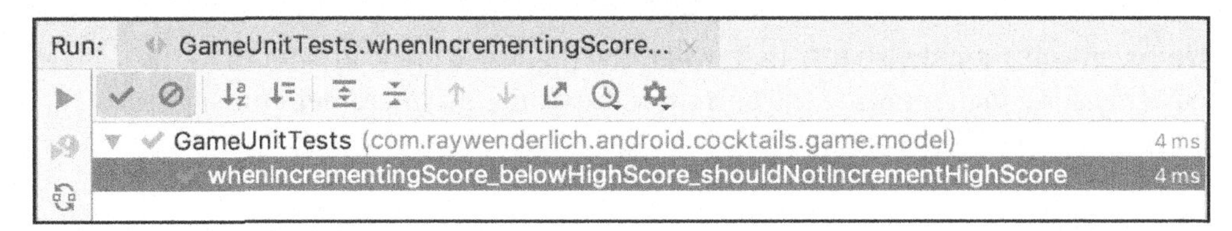

JUnit annotations

For this project, you're creating a trivia game. Trivias have questions, so you'll now create unit tests that model a question with two possible answers. The question also has an "answered" option to model what the user has answered to the question. Create a file called **QuestionUnitTests.kt** in the **app ▸ src ▸ test ▸ java ▸ com ▸ raywenderlich ▸ android ▸ cocktails ▸ game ▸ model** directory.

Add the following code:

```
class QuestionUnitTests {

  @Test
  fun whenCreatingQuestion_shouldNotHaveAnsweredOption() {
    val question = Question("CORRECT", "INCORRECT")

    Assert.assertNull(question.answeredOption)
  }
}
```

Here, you used `assertNull` to check if `question.answeredOption` is `null`.

If you try to run this test it won't compile because the `Question` class doesn't exist.

Create the `Question` class under the directory **app ▸ src ▸ main ▸ java ▸ com ▸ raywenderlich ▸ android ▸ cocktails ▸ game ▸ model** and add the following to make it compile:

```
class Question(val correctOption: String,
               val incorrectOption: String) {
  var answeredOption: String? = "MY ANSWER"
    private set
}
```

Run the test again and watch it fail.

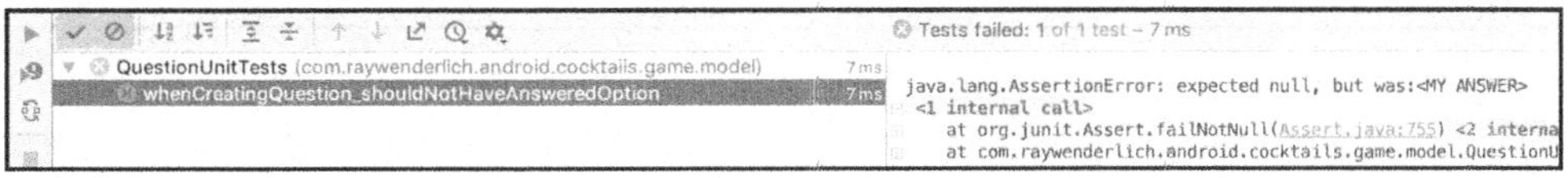

It failed because you hardcoded "MY ANSWER" which is not null.

Modify the `Question` class to the following:

```
class Question(val correctOption: String,
               val incorrectOption: String) {
  var answeredOption: String? = null
    private set
}
```

Run the test again and watch that it now passes.

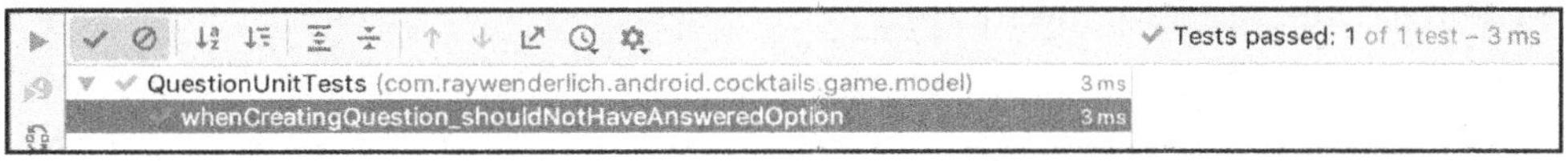

Now, you can add another test:

```
  @Test
  fun whenAnswering_shouldHaveAnsweredOption() {
    val question = Question("CORRECT", "INCORRECT")

    question.answer("INCORRECT")

    Assert.assertEquals("INCORRECT", question.answeredOption)
  }
```

This test will check that, when you add the user's answer to a question, the user's answer is saved in the `answeredOption` property.

You'll get a compilation error since you haven't written the `answer()` method yet.

Add the following to the Question class to make it compile:

```
fun answer(option: String) {
  // No implementation yet
}
```

Now run the test and you'll see that it doesn't pass.

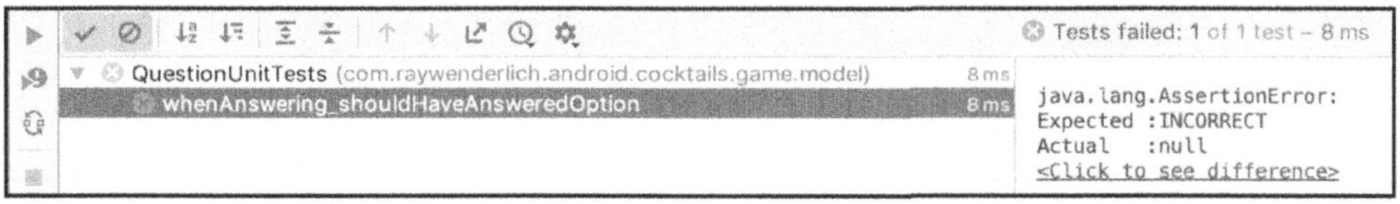

So add the following to the answer() method:

```
fun answer(option: String) {
  answeredOption = option
}
```

Run it and watch that it passes.

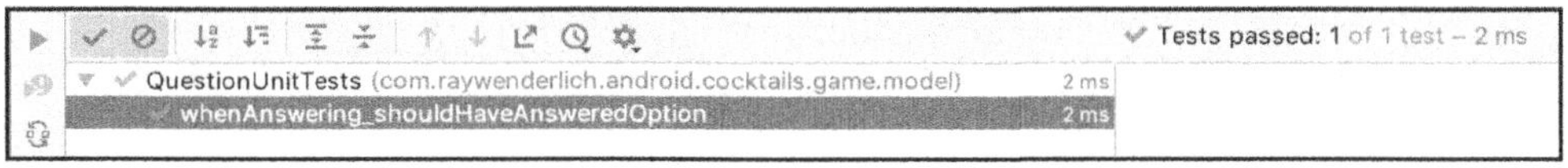

Because you'll need to know if the question was answered correctly, imagine that the answer() method now returns a Boolean. The result would be true when the user answered correctly. Now, add this test:

```
@Test
fun whenAnswering_withCorrectOption_shouldReturnTrue() {
  val question = Question("CORRECT", "INCORRECT")

  val result = question.answer("CORRECT")

  Assert.assertTrue(result)
}
```

Notice, here, that you're using assertTrue. It checks for a Boolean result.

Running this test will get you a compilation error since the answer() method doesn't return a Boolean. Update the Question class so that the answer() method returns a Boolean.

For now, always return `false`:

```
fun answer(option: String): Boolean {
  answeredOption = option

  return false
}
```

Run it and watch it fail.

Tests failed: 1 of 1 test – 6 ms
QuestionUnitTests (com.raywenderlich.android.cocktails.game.model) 6 ms
whenAnswering_withCorrectOption_shouldReturnTrue 6 ms
java.lang.AssertionError <3 internal calls>
at com.raywenderlich.android.cocktails.ga

Fix it temporarily by always returning `true`:

```
fun answer(option: String): Boolean {
  answeredOption = option

  return true
}
```

Run it and watch it pass.

Tests passed: 1 of 1 test – 2 ms
QuestionUnitTests (com.raywenderlich.android.cocktails.game.model) 2 ms
whenAnswering_withCorrectOption_shouldReturnTrue 2 ms

Add the following test:

```
@Test
fun whenAnswering_withIncorrectOption_shouldReturnFalse() {
  val question = Question("CORRECT", "INCORRECT")

  val result = question.answer("INCORRECT")

  Assert.assertFalse(result)
}
```

Run it and see that it fails.

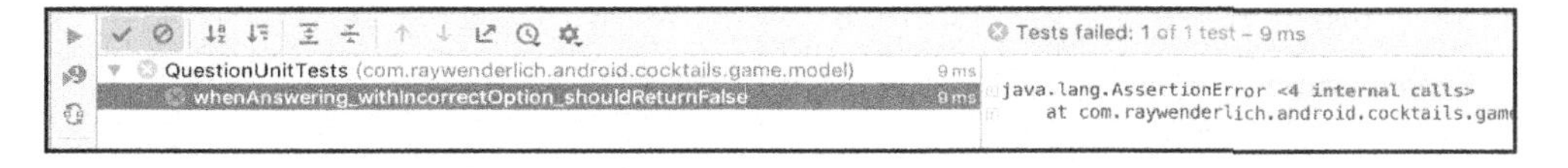

Now that we have tests for when the answer is correct and when the answer is not correct, we can fix the code:

```
fun answer(option: String): Boolean {
  answeredOption = option

  return correctOption == answeredOption
}
```

Run all the `Question` tests and verify they all pass correctly.

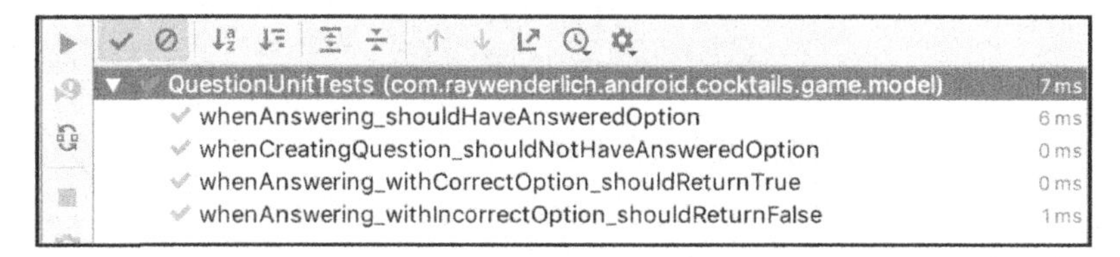

Finally, you should ensure that the `answer()` method only allows valid options. Add this test:

```
@Test(expected = IllegalArgumentException::class)
fun whenAnswering_withInvalidOption_shouldThrowException() {
  val question = Question("CORRECT", "INCORRECT")

  question.answer("INVALID")
}
```

Notice, here, that the `@Test` annotation allows to expect an exception. If that exception occurs, the test will pass. This will save you from writing `try/catch`. If you run the test now, it will fail because the `answer()` method doesn't throw the exception:

```
Run: QuestionUnitTests.whenAnswering_with...
Tests failed: 1 of 1 test – 9 ms
QuestionUnitTests (com.raywenderlich.android.cocktails.game.model) 9 ms
  whenAnswering_withInvalidOption_shouldThrowException 9 ms
"/private/var/folders/bs/2lb00lyn2033x48j7qdjm70r0000gn/T/AppTranslocation/3587F1

java.lang.AssertionError: Expected exception: java.lang.IllegalArgumentException
 <16 internal calls>

Process finished with exit code 255
```

To fix this, modify the `Question` class as follows:

```
fun answer(option: String): Boolean {
  if (option != correctOption && option != incorrectOption)
    throw IllegalArgumentException("Not a valid option")

  answeredOption = option

  return correctOption == answeredOption
}
```

Run the test and watch that it now passes.

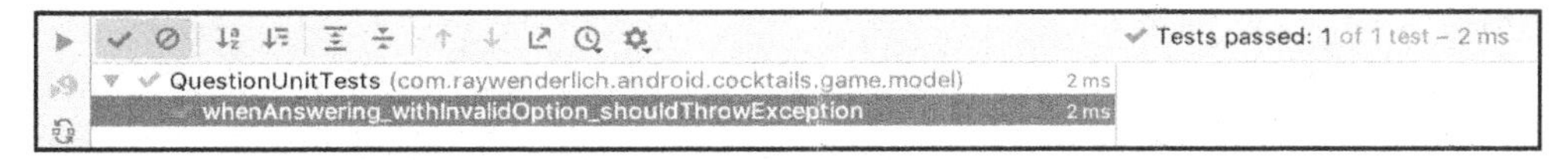

Because later you'll need a property `isAnsweredCorrectly`, open the `Question` class and refactor to the following:

```
val isAnsweredCorrectly: Boolean
  get() = correctOption == answeredOption

fun answer(option: String): Boolean {
  if (option != correctOption && option != incorrectOption)
    throw IllegalArgumentException("Not a valid option")

  answeredOption = option

  return isAnsweredCorrectly
}
```

Run all the tests again to see that everything is still working after the refactor.

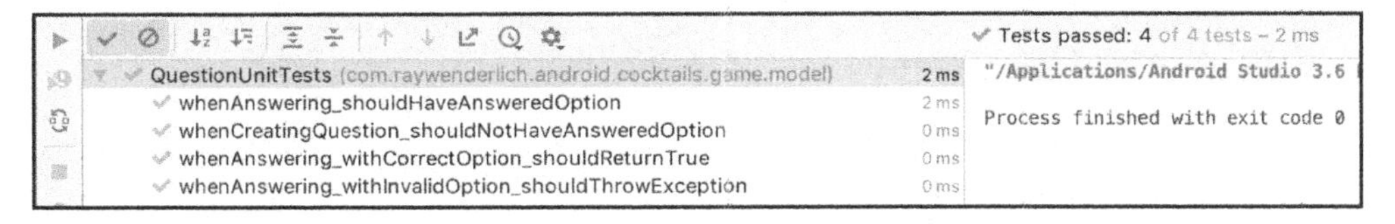

Refactoring the unit tests

Notice that each test repeats this line of code:

```
val question = Question("CORRECT", "INCORRECT")
```

This makes the tests bloated with boilerplate code that makes them hard to read. To improve this, JUnit tests can have a method annotated with **@Before**. This method will be executed before each test and it's a good place to set up objects.

Modify the **QuestionUnitTests** test class, adding the following to the top:

```
private lateinit var question: Question

@Before
fun setup() {
  question = Question("CORRECT", "INCORRECT")
}
```

And remove the repeated line of each test. When you're done, your tests should look like:

```
@Test
fun whenCreatingQuestion_shouldNotHaveAnsweredOption() {
  Assert.assertNull(question.answeredOption)
}

@Test
fun whenAnswering_shouldHaveAnsweredOption() {
  question.answer("INCORRECT")

  Assert.assertEquals("INCORRECT", question.answeredOption)
}

@Test
fun whenAnswering_withCorrectOption_shouldReturnTrue() {
  val result = question.answer("CORRECT")

  Assert.assertTrue(result)
}

@Test
fun whenAnswering_withIncorrectOption_shouldReturnFalse() {
  val result = question.answer("INCORRECT")

  Assert.assertFalse(result)
}

@Test(expected = IllegalArgumentException::class)
fun whenAnswering_withInvalidOption_shouldThrowException() {
  question.answer("INVALID")
}
```

Now, run all the tests again to make sure you didn't break them while refactoring. All tests still pass — great!

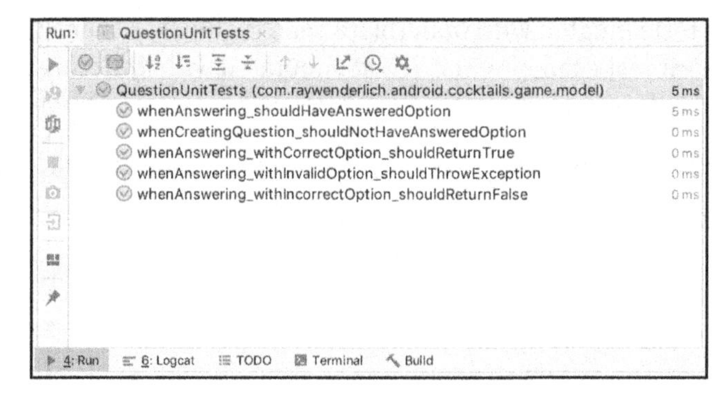

JUnit also has other similar annotations:

- **@After**: The method will be executed after each test. You can use it to tear down anything or reset any objects that you set up in @Before.
- **@BeforeClass**: If you annotate a method with this, it'll be executed only once before all the tests are executed. For example, opening a file, a connection or a database that is shared in all the tests.
- **@AfterClass**: Use this one to execute a method only once after all the tests are executed. For example, closing a file, a connection or a database that is shared in all the tests.

Challenge

Challenge: Testing questions

You have the `Game` and `Question` classes. The `Game` class should contain a list of questions. For now, these are the requirements:

- The game should have a list of questions. It should have a `nextQuestion()` method that returns the next question in from the list.
- When getting the next question, if you've reached the end of the list, the game should return `null`.
- The question should have a `getOptions()` method that returns the correct and incorrect options as a shuffled list, so later you can show them as Buttons. Hint: The method should receive a lambda parameter to sort the list, by default it should be `{ it.shuffled() }` but having a parameter will let you use another one in your test.

Write a test for each one and add the corresponding functionality to the `Game` class progressively to make each test pass.

Remember the TDD procedure: write a test, see it fail, write the minimum amount of code to make it pass and refactor if needed.

Key points

- Unit tests verify how isolated parts of your application work.
- Using JUnit, you can write unit tests asserting results, meaning, you can compare an expected result with the actual one.
- Every test has three phases: set up, assertion and teardown.
- In TDD, you start by writing a test. You then write the code to make the test compile. Next you see that the test fails. Finally, you add the implementation to the method under test to make it pass.

Where to go from here?

Great! You've just learned the basics of unit testing with JUnit. You can check the project materials for the final version of the code for this chapter.

In the next chapter, "Architecting for Testing," you'll learn about good practices and design patterns, that will ensure a good architecture and encourage testability. Afterwards, you'll continue working on this project, creating unit tests using a complementary library called Mockito.

For additional resources, there's a Google library you can use called **Truth**, similar to JUnit. It has a couple of notable benefits:

- More readable test assertions
- Default failure messages

You can check it out, here: https://google.github.io/truth/comparison

Chapter 6: Architecting for Testing

By Fernando Sproviero

Software architecture is a template or blueprint that you can use when building new apps. It defines software elements and their relations. When you create a new app, you need to make some fundamental structural decisions — and those decisions may be difficult to modify once they're implemented.

In this chapter, you'll focus on what it takes to architect an app for testability; specifically, you'll:

- Learn the characteristics of a testable architecture.
- Discover good practices to create a testable architecture.

Why does architecture matter?

To understand why architecture matters, it's essential first to understand what qualifies as a poorly architected app.

A poorly architected app may have all of its logic contained within a single method that consists of many lines; or it may have one large class with too many responsibilities. Both of these scenarios make it impossible to test groups or units of logic independently.

Apps that are architected for testing separate their code into groups of logic using multiple methods and classes to collaborate. With this type of architecture, developers can test each public method and class in isolation.

You also need to consider the effort it takes when adding or modifying an app's features. In TDD, this process starts with creating new tests or modifying existing ones. While it may take some additional time to do this, adding and updating tests shouldn't be a painful process. If it is, you'll eventually stop writing tests and avoid TDD all together. To encourage TDD, it's better to think of a software architecture that encourages and facilitates the creation of tests.

Testing is important for:

- **Communication**: Software architecture establishes a common language between the developers of an app and other members of the team, like managers, QA testers, analysts and designers.

- **Reusable abstraction**: Reusability saves time. Later in the chapter, you'll see that you can reuse patterns within different parts of an app, across different apps as well as on other platforms. You'll also see that you can use architecture patterns to kick-off new projects.

- **Early design decisions**: When you create a new app, one of the first decisions is to decide on the architecture you're going to use. These early design decisions are important because they'll set constraints on your implementation, such as the way your classes will interact and their responsibilities. Early decisions will also organize your codebase a specific way and may even organize the members of your team. For example, on a given architecture, you may divide your team between people who only write domain classes and others who only write visually-related code.

- **Better testing**: By using good architecture from the start or refactoring an existing one, you'll enable the creation of tests that would otherwise be impossible or difficult to write. Also, migrating from an existing architecture to a better one — which is a difficult task, but not impossible — will enable you to migrate slower tests, such as UI or integration tests, to unit tests, which are faster.

To achieve a robust architecture, it's important to know and understand **design patterns** and the **SOLID principles**.

Design patterns

It's not uncommon for developers to encounter the same problems in different projects and platforms, and to solve these problems using similar solutions. Over time, certain developers started formalizing these patterns into templates or solutions that other developers could reuse if they found themselves in a similar context or situation.

Most of the time, these solutions are not specific blocks of code for a specific platform. Instead, they're diagrams, ideas and descriptions of how to proceed when faced with similar circumstances. They tend to show relationships and collaboration between classes. When reviewed carefully, you're able to then take this information and implement solutions in your own language and platform.

These battle-tested and proven patterns can help speed up your development process. Using **design patterns**, which is what this is known as, you avoid searching for solutions that other developers have already solved.

Design patterns are also useful to communicate about software ideas between developers and to help with code readability.

According to the Gang of Four (GoF: Erich Gamma, Richard Helm, Ralph Johnson and John Vlissides) you can classify design patterns into the following categories: **creational**, **structural** and **behavioral**.

Creational

The patterns in the Creational category describe solutions related to object creation.

Singleton

The **Singleton design pattern** specifies that only one instance of a certain class may exist, known as a singleton. Usually, it's possible to access the singleton globally.

Kotlin has the `object` keyword to declare a singleton:

```
object MySingleton {
  private var status = false
  private var myString = "Hello"

  fun validate(): Boolean {
    ...
  }
```

```
  ...
}
```

You can use `MySingleton` by invoking:

```
MySingleton.validate()
```

This line creates the `MySingleton` object. If the object already exists, it uses the existing one, so there's no worry about creating more than one.

Although this might be the easiest pattern to understand and implement, it's important to use caution when using it. For instance, if you have an object that collaborates with `MySingleton`, like this:

```
class MyClass {
  fun methodA() {
    ...
    if (MySingleton.validate()) {
      ...
    }
    ...
  }
}
```

You won't be able to test `methodA()` properly because you're using the actual `MySingleton` object, which means you can't force `validate()` to return `true` or `false`.

Later, you'll learn about a pattern known as dependency injection to deal with this problem. In terms of testing, you should be able to identify a singleton and flag it as code that might need refactoring to test.

Builder

The **Builder design pattern** abstracts the construction of a complex object, joining several parts. For example, think of a restaurant that serves different menus depending on the day.

You might have the following abstract class:

```
abstract class MenuBuilder {
  var menu = Menu()
  abstract fun buildMainDish()
  abstract fun buildDessert()
}
```

You would then implement the builders depending on the day:

```
class DayOneMenuBuilder: MenuBuilder() {
  override fun buildMainDish() {
    // Add day one main dish to the menu
  }
  override fun buildDessert() {
    // Add day one desert to the menu
  }
}

class DayTwoMenuBuilder: MenuBuilder() {
  ...
}
```

You might also have the `Chef` class:

```
class Chef {
  fun createMenu(builder: MenuBuilder): Menu {
    builder.buildMainDish()
    builder.buildDessert()
    return builder.menu
  }
}
```

Notice how `Chef` calls the corresponding methods to build the menu.

This lets you create the menu as follows:

```
val chef = Chef()
val menuBuilder = getDayMenuBuilder()
val menu = chef.createMenu(menuBuilder)
```

In this example, `getDayMenuBuilder()` returns the corresponding `MenuBuilder` depending on the day.

With this implementation, it's easy to test the separated parts. You can test `Chef` to verify that it calls the right methods, and you can also test each class that inherits from `MenuBuilder` by asserting the state of the resulting `Menu`. You'll see how to perform this kind of test in the next chapter.

Effective Java by *Joshua Bloch*, introduced another Builder design pattern, focused on readability. The `AlertDialog.Builder` in Android is an example of this type of pattern:

```
AlertDialog.Builder(this)
  .setTitle("Error!")
  .setMessage("There was an error, would you like to retry?")
```

```
    .setNegativeButton("Cancel", { dialogInterface, i ->
      ...
    })
    .setPositiveButton("Retry", { dialogInterface, i ->
      ...
    })
    .show()
```

The Builder design pattern is useful to avoid an anti-pattern known as a Telescoping Constructor. A Telescoping Constructor consists of a constructor with many parameters where some of them are optional. This is not an issue with Kotlin where you can have default and named parameters.

Dependency Injection

The **Dependency Injection** design pattern is crucial to having a testable architecture.

The following is an example of a class that does *not* use dependency injection. Usually, objects collaborate with other objects. For example:

```
class Vehicle() {
  private val engine = CombustionEngine()

  fun start(): Boolean {
    ...
    return engine.start()
  }
  ...
}
```

When you create a `Vehicle`, it creates, internally, a `CombustionEngine`. You can then use it later to perform some operation. This makes it difficult to properly test `Vehicle` because, for example, you won't be able to test what happens when the engine brakes or when the engine is used for too many hours.

And what happens when you want to use an `ElectricEngine` instead of a `CombustionEngine`?

You can solve these types of problems using the dependency injection design pattern, which describes that collaborators are provided to an object that requires them, instead of this object directly instantiating them internally.

There are two ways to inject dependencies.

The first way is using Constructor Injection, like so:

```
class Vehicle(private val engine: Engine) {
  fun start(): Boolean {
    ...
    return engine.start()
  }
  ...
}
```

In this example, to create a `Vehicle` you need an `Engine`. Here, `Engine` is an interface or an abstract class which lets you inject any implementation (`CombustionEngine` or `ElectricEngine`) provided it complies with the interface or abstract class. So, the creator of the `Vehicle` provides the proper `Engine`.

If you combine the Builder design pattern with the dependency injection design pattern, you end up with something like this:

```
class CombustionVehicleBuilder {
  fun build(): Vehicle {
    val engine = CombustionVehicleEngine()
    ...
    return Vehicle(engine)
  }
}
```

In this example, you aren't injecting the engine here, so you may also want to inject the engine to the builder. You could do that. However, at some point someone or something needs to instantiate the class. Usually, it's the entity that creates objects and provides their dependencies. This entity is known as the injector, assembler, provider, container or factory.

The second way to inject dependencies is by using Property or Method injection:

```
class Vehicle {
  var engine: Engine? = null
  ...
  fun start(): Boolean {
    engine?.let {
      return engine.start()
    }
    return false
  }
  ...
}
```

In this case, you create a `Vehicle` without an `Engine`. You can then set the `Engine` type later.

Dependency injection favors testability because you can inject fake `Engine` objects to test different situations. For example, you can inject a broken `Engine` where its `start()` method returns `false` and asserts that the `Vehicle` won't move.

In Android, **Dagger2** and **Koin** are libraries that help you inject objects.

In Android, `Activity` objects know about the `Application` object, so another way to inject dependencies is to ask them from the `Application` object, for example:

```
class MyActivity : AppCompatActivity() {
  private lateinit var repository: Repository

  override fun onCreate(savedInstanceState: Bundle?) {
    ...
    repository = (application as MyApplication).getRepository()
    ...
  }
}
```

> **Note**: This is sometimes called a Service Locator because you ask a locator object, the app in this example, for other objects, the repository.

The `Application` object might be:

```
class MyApplication : Application() {
  fun getRepository(): Repository {
    val apiService = getApiService()
    val inMemoryService = getInMemoryService()
    return MyRepository(apiService, inMemoryService)
  }
  ...
}
```

Where `MyRepository` implements an interface named `Repository`.

Structural

Structural design patterns ease the design to establish relationships between objects.

Adapter (or Wrapper)

The **Adapter (or Wrapper) design pattern** describes how to let two incompatible classes work together.

For example, in Android, when you have a list of contacts that you want to show in a RecyclerView, the RecyclerView doesn't know how to show objects of the class Contact. That's why you need to use a ContactsAdapter class:

```
class ContactsAdapter(private val contacts: List<Contact>):
  RecyclerView.Adapter<ContactViewHolder>() {

  override fun onCreateViewHolder(viewGroup: ViewGroup,
                                  i: Int): ContactViewHolder {
    val inflater = LayoutInflater.from(viewGroup.context)
    val view = inflater.inflate(
      R.layout.row_contact, viewGroup, false
    )
    return ContactViewHolder(view)
  }

  override fun onBindViewHolder(viewHolder: ContactViewHolder,
                                i: Int) {
    viewHolder.bind(contacts[i])
  }

  override fun getItemCount() = contacts.size

  inner class ContactViewHolder(itemView: View):
    RecyclerView.ViewHolder(itemView) {

    fun bind(contact: Contact) {
      ...
    }
  }
}
```

Here, bind() sets the views (TextView, ImageView, and so on) using the Contact model.

Facade

The **Facade design pattern** defines a high-level interface object which hides the complexity of underlying objects. Client objects prefer using the facade instead of the internal objects because the facade provides a cleaner, easier-to-use interface.

For example, you might have a ProductsRepository class that provides objects of the class Product, like so:

```
class ProductsRepository {
  ...
  fun getProducts(): List<Product> {
    if (isRemoteAvailable) {
      return api.getProducts()
```

```
      } else {
        val localProducts = room.getProducts()
        if (localProducts.isEmpty()) {
          return sharedPrefsManager.getLastProducts()
        } else {
          return localProducts
        }
      }
    }
  }
```

In this example, `getProducts()` grabs the data from a remote server, memory, filesystem, or maybe `SharedPreferences` or `Room`. It's easier to use `ProductsRepository`, which abstracts getting the products from the corresponding source.

Composite

The intent of the **Composite design pattern** is to construct complex objects composed of individual parts, and to treat the individual parts and the composition uniformly.

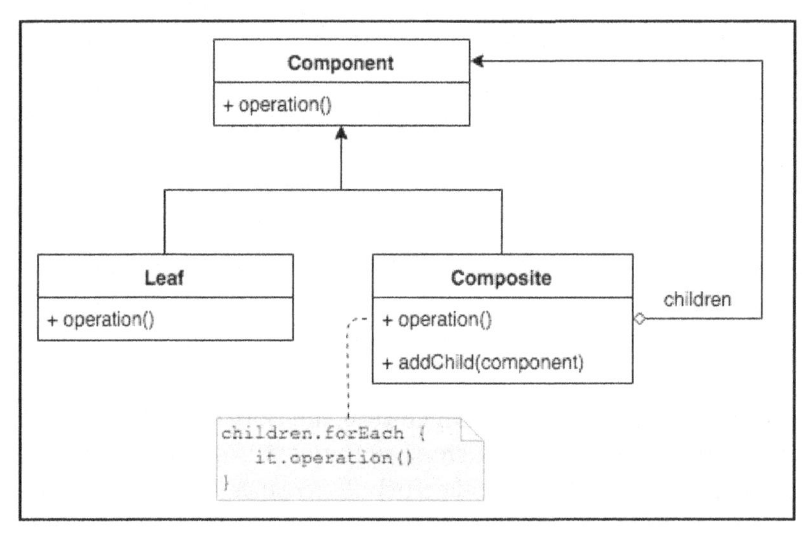

In Android, `View`, `ViewGroup` and the rest of classes that inherit from `View` — like `TextView` and `ImageView` — create a composite pattern because `ViewGroup` inherits from `View`, and contains a list of child `View` objects.

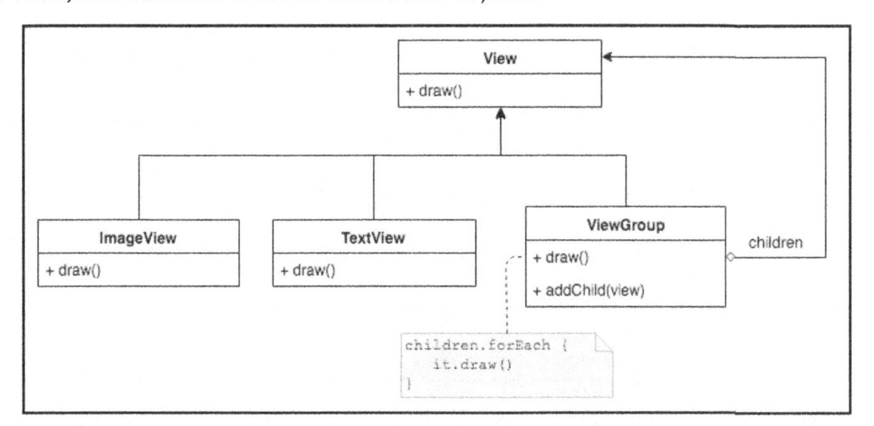

> **Note**: This is not the actual Android implementation; it's simplified for illustration purposes.

When you ask a `ViewGroup` to `draw()`, it iterates through all of its children asking them to `draw()`. A child can be anything that inherits from `View` — even other `ViewGroup` objects.

Behavioral

Behavioral design patterns explain how objects interact and how a task can be divided into sub-tasks among different objects. While creational patterns explain a specific moment of time (the creation of an instance), and structural patterns describe a static structure, behavioral patterns describe a dynamic flow.

Observer

The **Observer design pattern** gives you a way to communicate between objects where one object informs others about changes or actions. There's an **observable** object which you can observe, and there's one or more **observer** objects that you use to subscribe to the observable.

Whenever there's a change in the state of the observable object, it notifies all of its observers.

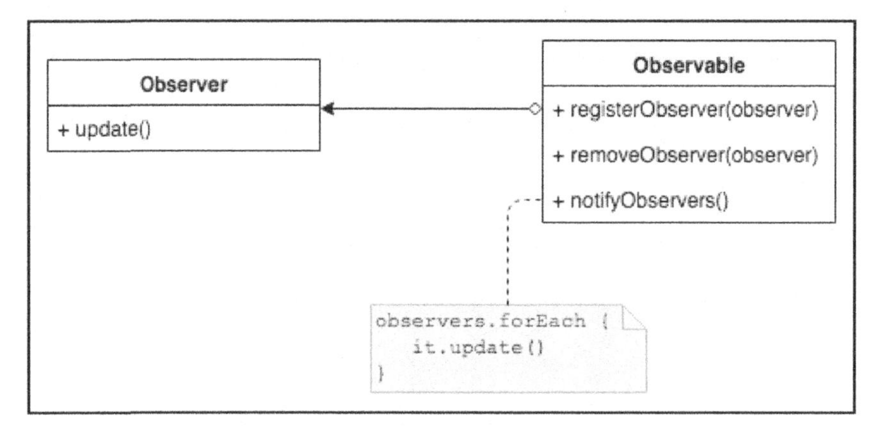

A simple example in Android is to use the `OnClickListener` interface of a button:

```
button.setOnClickListener(object: View.OnClickListener {
  override fun onClick(v: View?) {
    // Perform some operation
  }
})
```

In this case, the observable is the button, and you subscribe to it with an observer, which is the anonymous class that performs some operation when you click the button.

When you use `BroadcastReceiver` objects — or any kind of reactive programming like `LiveData` from *Architecture Components* or the RxKotlin/Android libraries — you're using this pattern. In each case, you subscribe to notifications of some kind of change or event and react to that. When you don't need to observe anymore, you unsubscribe.

Command

The **Command design pattern** describes the encapsulation of an operation without knowing the real content of the operation or the receiver.

A concrete command object knows about the receiver and invokes a method of the receiver. When an invoker calls the execute method of the command object, the command is delegated to the receiver. The invoker only knows about the command interface.

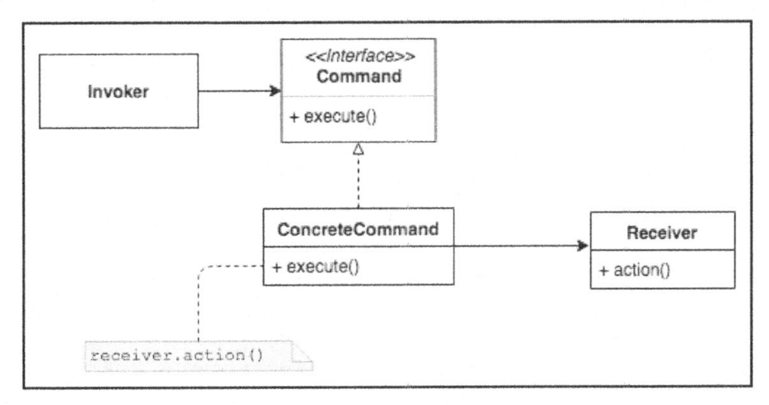

For example, if you have a drawing app where all user interactions are implemented as commands, and you put them in a stack, you can easily implement the undo by popping the commands and executing an `undo()` operation on the command.

Architectural design patterns

There are some other design patterns that may be considered as a fourth category. These are known as **Architectural design patterns**, or **UI Architectural design patterns**.

Architectural design patterns are mostly used in rich clients. In other words, they have some kind of UI, such as Android. Each pattern describes ways to structure and organize your code. You can use them to achieve a robust, stable, **testable**, modular and easy to extend codebase.

MVC

Model-View-Controller (MVC) states that each class you write should be part of one of the following layers:

- **Model**: The data classes that model your business belong to this layer. They usually contain data and business logic. This layer also contains the classes that fetch and create objects of those business classes, networking, caching and handling databases.
- **View**: This layer displays data from the Model. It doesn't contain any business logic.
- **Controller**: The goal of this layer is to connect the objects of the Model and View layers. It gets notified of user interaction and updates the Model. It retrieves data from the Model. It may also update the View when there's a change in the Model.

Ideally, you have separate layers to allow testing them separately.

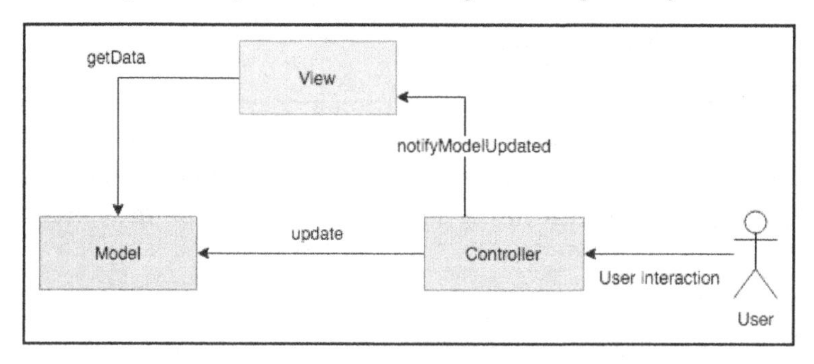

The View knows about the Model, and the Controller has a reference to both the View and the Model.

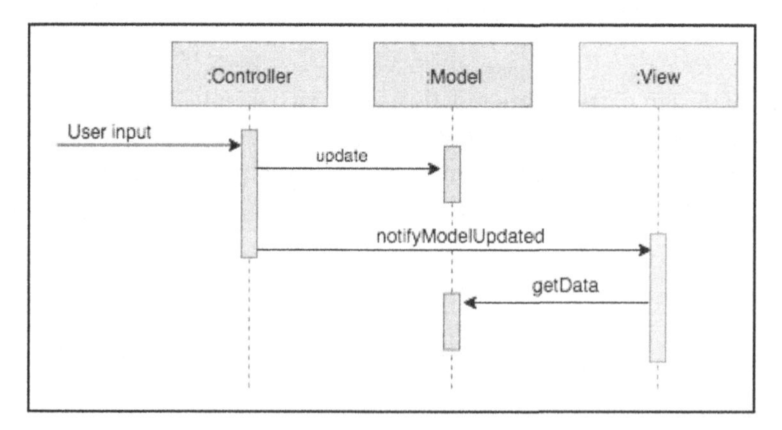

Here's how it works:

Whenever there's user input, it's received by the Controller. The Controller updates the Model, and it also notifies the View that it should update. Finally, the View requests the data from the Model.

In 2011, to apply MVC to Android apps, it was accepted that the Activities, Fragments and custom views were both the View and also the Controller layers because they show the UI and handle user input. The problem with this approach is that you had to unify two layers into one, which goes against the original purpose: To split things into layers, making them independent and testable.

Also, combining View and Controller logic in the Activities, Fragments and custom views makes them larger. This lead to MVC ironically being referred to as **Massive-**View-Controller.

To make it better, this thought was changed. The Activities, Fragments and custom views are just part of the View layer, and any user interaction is delegated to a separate Controller class.

Here's how that works:

1. The View (Activity/Fragment/Custom view) receives the user input.
2. It informs the Controller (a separate class) about it.
3. The Controller updates the Model and notifies the View that should update.
4. Finally, the View requests data from the Model.

However, there's still a problem: The Controller has a reference to the View, which is the Activity, Fragment or custom view, which means it won't be unit testable because you need to create that Activity, Fragment or custom view in the test.

The solution to this problem is to create an interface that the Activity, Fragment or custom view can implement. The Controller will have a reference to the interface instead of the actual Activity, Fragment or custom view.

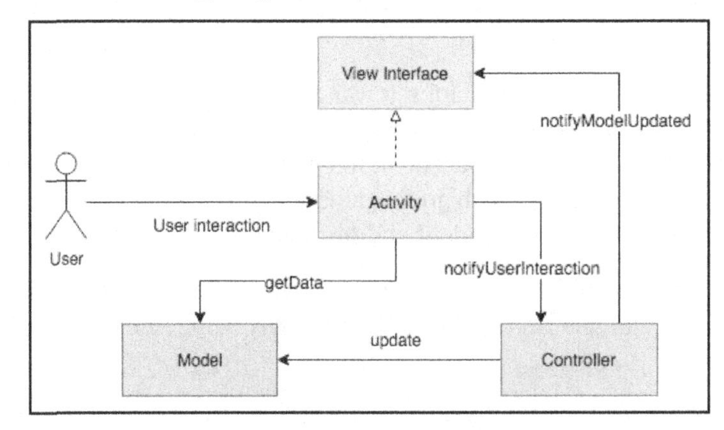

Using this MVC implementation in Android, the Model classes are unit testable, and the Controller classes also are unit testable because they don't extend or use any Android UI classes. For the View classes, you can create UI tests.

This pattern doesn't explicitly state which layer should handle UI logic. For example, if you have the following class, part of the Model layer:

```
data class Address(val street: String,
                   val number: String,
                   val zipCode: String)
```

Suppose in the View layer you need to display it with the following format: `"$number, $street, $zipCode"`. You could do the following in your Activity:

```
addressView.text =
  "${address.street}, ${address.number}, ${address.zipCode}"
```

However, the only way to test this formatting is to create a UI test.

But, if you want to create a unit test, you may instead add a property to the Model, like this:

```
data class Address(val street: String,
                   val number: String,
                   val zipCode: String) {
  val description = "$number, $street, $zipCode"
}
```

Then, in the Activity, you can do this:

```
addressView.text = address.description
```

Now, you could create a unit test for the Model. However, you'd be making the Model dependent on the View layer.

The View simply knows too much: It knows about the Controller and the Model. The Activity, Fragment or custom view knows what to display and how to display it. Even more, if you have a direct reference to the Model, you might be tempted to go directly to the Model to obtain data from an API or database — without going through the correct flow, using the Controller.

The solution is to avoid having a direct reference to the Model. Instead, everything should go through the Controller, and the Controller should handle the UI logic, knowing how to *present* the Model in the View. This is exactly what the next pattern solves.

MVP

Model-View-Presenter (MVP) has these layers:

- **Model**: This is the same as the Model layer from MVC.
- **View**: Displays data presented by the Presenter but doesn't have a reference to the Model. It does, however, have a reference to the Presenter to notify it about user actions.
- **Presenter**: Similar to the Controller from the previous pattern, the Presenter retrieves data from the Model and updates it accordingly. It has UI presentation logic that decides what to display. It notifies the View when a Model has changed. Therefore, it has a reference to the View and the Model.

See the graphic below:

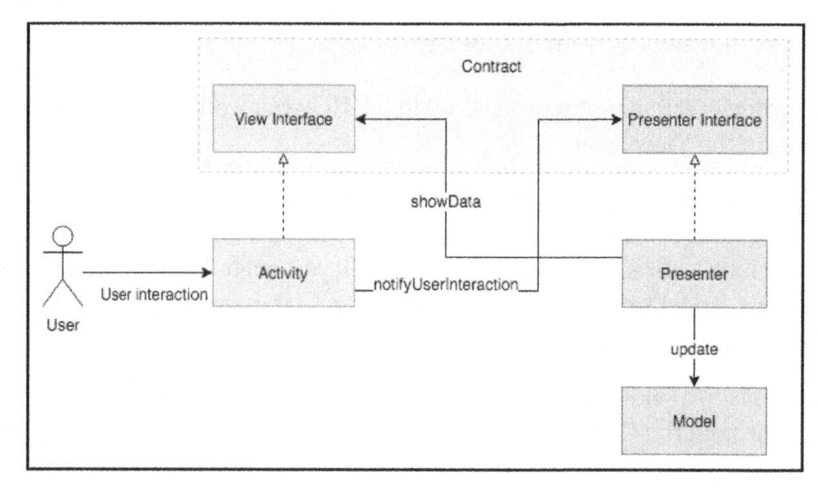

The View layer is composed by the Activities, Fragments or custom views. The View entity notifies the Presenter about user interactions. The Presenter decides if has to fetch something from the Model, updates it, applies UI logic and finally tells the View what to display.

Usually, there's an interface for the View and an interface for the Presenter, and these are written in a single file or package as a sort of contract.

For example, think about a Login flow where you might have the following contract interfaces:

```
interface LoginPresenter {
  fun login(username: String, password: String)
}

interface LoginView {
  fun showLoginSuccess()
  fun showLoginError()
  fun showLoading()
}
```

And the corresponding implementations:

```
class LoginPresenterImpl(
  private val repository: LoginRepository,
  private val view: LoginView): LoginPresenter {

  override fun login(username: String, password: String) {
    view.showLoading()
    repository.login(username, password, object : Callback {
      override fun onSuccess() {
```

```
          view.showLoginSuccess()
        }
        override fun onError() {
          view.showLoginError()
        }
      })
    }
  }

  class LoginActivity: AppCompatActivity(), LoginView {

    private lateinit var presenter: LoginPresenter

    override fun onCreate(savedInstanceState: Bundle?) {
      ...

      loginButton.setOnClickListener {
        presenter.login(usernameEditText.text.toString(),
                        passwordEditText.text.toString())
      }
    }

    override fun showLoginSuccess() { ... }
    override fun showLoginError() { ... }
    override fun showLoading() { ... }
  }
```

Once the View is loaded, you need to show that data has to be fetched from an API. It's common to have an `onLoad()` method in the Presenter called by the View when it's ready, e.g. in Activity's or Fragment's `onResume()`, so that the Presenter starts fetching data from the Model. It's important to also have another method, `onStopLoading()`, in the Presenter to cancel any asynchronous tasks whenever the View is not being shown, e.g. in in Activity's or Fragment's `onPause()`. When using custom views, the analogous methods are `onAttachedToWindow()` and `onDetachedFromWindow()`.

Differences between the MVC and MVP patterns are that in MVP, the View doesn't have a direct reference to the Model, meaning it is loosely-coupled. Instead, the Presenter brings the transformed or simplified Model, ready to be displayed to the View. MVP also proposes that the Presenter should handle everything related to the presentation of the View. In MVC, it's not clear where the UI logic should be, compared to MVP where it's common to put it in the Presenter. Because of this, the Presenter could grow a lot, converting it into another anti-pattern called God-class (you'll learn more about this concept later). It's a good practice to create small classes (e.g. an AddressFormatter) with single responsibilities to have better maintainability and unit testing. These collaborator objects could be injected in the constructor, as explained before.

Because the Presenter talks to a View interface, in production code the Activities, Fragments and custom views implement that interface. But, in your tests, instead of using those Android classes, you could create custom classes that implement the View interfaces and assert that the corresponding methods were called.

For example, using JUnit, if you want to test `login()` of `LoginPresenterImpl` you can create this test:

```
@Test
fun login_shouldShowLoading() {
  var didShowLoading = false

  val testRepository = object: LoginRepository { ... }

  val testView = object: LoginView {
    override fun showLoginSuccess() {}
    override fun showLoginError() {}
    override fun showLoading() { didShowLoading = true }
  }

  val presenter = LoginPresenterImpl(testRepository, testView)

  presenter.login("Foo", "1234")

  Assert.assertTrue(didShowLoading)
}
```

Here, you create a `testRepository` and a `testView`, both implementing their corresponding interfaces. You then instantiate the `LoginPresenterImpl`, passing those test objects. Afterward, you call `login()`. If you implemented everything correctly, it'll call `showLoading()` of your `testView`, and `didShowLoading` gets set to `true` and your test will pass.

> **Note:** In the context of TDD, you should first create this test, and afterward, the corresponding implementation.

MVVM

Model-View-ViewModel (MVVM) contains the following layers:

- **Model**: Same as the Model layer from MVC/MVP.
- **View**: Notifies the ViewModel about user actions. Subscribes to streams of data exposed by the ViewModel.
- **ViewModel**: Retrieves data from the Model and updates it accordingly. Exposes streams of data ready to be displayed, but it doesn't know and doesn't care about who is subscribed to the streams.

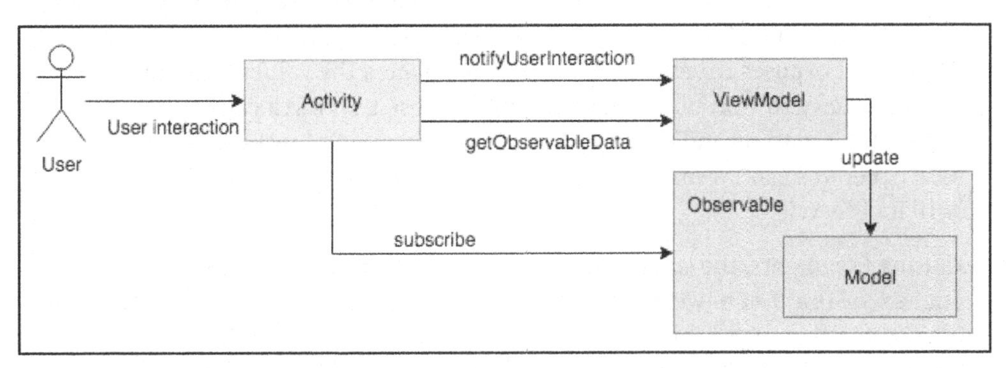

Here, again, the Activities, Fragments and custom views conform the View layer. The interaction between the View and the ViewModel is very similar than the one that had between the View and the Presenter in MVP. The View will notify the ViewModel about user actions, just like it notified the Presenter in MVP, however this time, the ViewModel doesn't have a reference to the View, not even an interface. It just exposes streams of data (Observables), it could be the Model or a transformed-displayable Model.

As you can see, this is an event based approach, where the ViewModel produces data and the View consumes it. The ViewModel doesn't know about the consumer, it just exposes streams of data. The View subscribes and unsubscribes to that data as needed.

The ViewModel layer is composed of classes that don't extend or use any class related to the Android UI framework. Usually, the mechanism of exposing data, observing and updating it, is done using reactive libraries.

The most common are:

- **RxKotlin/Android libraries**: The ViewModel exposes one or more `Observable` objects. The View subscribes to them. When the ViewModel updates the Observable data (the actual Model), the View will react and render the corresponding update. If the views are Activities or Fragments it's important to subscribe in `onResume()` and unsubscribe in `onPause()`. If using a custom view the analogous methods are `onAttachedToWindow()` and `onDetachedFromWindow()`.
- **LiveData + ViewModel from Android Architecture Components**: If your ViewModel classes extend a `ViewModel` class from the Android framework, bear in mind that this class has nothing to do with UI, so it's still unit testable. The ViewModel exposes `LiveData` objects and it updates the values of them. The Activities have to start observing (subscribe) these `LiveData` objects in the `onCreate()` method and doesn't need to stop observing (unsubscribe) because the base `LiveData` class from Android Architecture Components is aware of the Activity lifecycle.

  If using Fragments, the suggested approach is to start observing in the `onCreateView()` or `onViewCreated()` method. For custom views, unfortunately, it's not possible to use this `ViewModel` class from Architecture Components, because it was thought to only work with Activities and Fragments.

For the Login flow example, using ViewModel + LiveData from Android Architecture Components, a possible approach would be:

```
class LoginViewModel(
  private val repository: LoginRepository): ViewModel() {

  private val loginStatus: MutableLiveData<LoginStatus>()

  fun getLoginStatus(): LiveData = loginStatus

  fun login(username: String, password: String) {
    loginStatus.value = LoginStatus.Loading()
    repository.login(username, password, object : Callback {
      override fun onSuccess() {
        loginStatus.value = LoginStatus.Success()
      }
      override fun onError() {
        loginStatus.value = LoginStatus.Error()
      }
    })
  }
}
```

```
sealed class LoginStatus {
  class Error(): LoginStatus()
  class Success(): LoginStatus()
  class Loading(): LoginStatus()
}
```

And the Activity would do the following:

```
class LoginActivity: AppCompatActivity(), LoginView {

  private lateinit var viewModel: LoginViewModel

  override fun onCreate(savedInstanceState: Bundle?) {
    ...
    viewModel = ...

    viewModel.getLoginStatus().observe(this, Observer {
      when(it) {
        is LoginStatus.Loading -> ...
        is LoginStatus.Success -> ...
        is LoginStatus.Error -> ...
      }
    })

    loginButton.setOnClickListener {
      viewModel.login(usernameEditText.text.toString(),
                      passwordEditText.text.toString())
    }
  }
}
```

Suppose that `login()` from the repository returns a data User object, and you need to show that in the UI, you could instead use another approach. Having various LiveData objects exposed, for example, one `LiveData<Boolean>` for the loading state, another one for the error state and another one `LiveData<User>`, in the View you would need to observe them and react accordingly.

Testing `login()` of `LoginViewModel` is similar to the one you saw previously in MVP. In the next chapter, you'll learn more about it.

S.O.L.I.D principles

TDD is closely related to good programming practices. Writing tests before the actual feature makes you think on how the interface of a class will be. Therefore, you'll be exposing only those methods really needed. On the contrary, without using TDD, sometimes you'll find yourself creating a class and exposing methods and properties that you don't need them to be public. Using TDD will also make you think on how the classes will collaborate. After writing several features, while your app grows, there will be times when you realize that things should be refactored. Thanks to having tests you can refactor with confidence.

To complement TDD, the **S.O.L.I.D principles** are a list of principles to build software following good practices, introduced by *Robert C. Martin (Uncle Bob)*, in his *Design Principles and Design Patterns* paper. Though these items are independent from TDD, they both complement each other: while writing a test for a class you'll want to comply with these principles. Also, before writing any test you'll have these principles in mind, so you'll design and write tests and classes accordingly.

Single responsibility (SRP)

Each class should have a **unique objective** or should be **useful for a specific case**. Any logic that is not part of the objective of the class should be the responsibility of some other class. A class that has lots of responsibilities is sometimes called a god class and should be avoided.

You'll often find classes that clearly violate this principle, however, you'll also find that sometimes is not that clear. Whenever you're refactoring or evolving your code you may realize that the class you're modifying starts to have multiple responsibilities.

Thanks to TDD, you may realize a class is becoming a god class when you spot some of the following signs:

- Before adding new functionality for an existing class, you need to add new tests to an existing test suite. If the new tests are not related or don't follow the essence of the existing ones, the functionality violates SRP. For example, think of a Car class that has an associated test class that check the methods `startEngine()`, `accelerate()`, `stopEngine()`. Suppose you need a new feature that drives the car to a place. You may be tempted to open the existing test suite, and write a new test like `testDriveToPlace()` that would check a new method `driveToPlace()` of the `Car` class. You'll realize that this new feature doesn't follow the essence of the class, that it actually should be the responsibility of a new `Driver` class.

- When you have a class A that depends on a class B, and the tests of A start to require you to stub many methods of B, B is turning into a god class. You'll see more about stubbing in a later chapter.

Open-closed

This principle was actually first defined by *Bertrand Meyer* in his book *Object-Oriented Software Construction*.

The software entities of your app: classes, methods, etc. should be open for extension but closed for modification. This means that you should design them in such a way that adding new features or modifying behavior shouldn't require you to modify too much of your existing code but instead add new code or create new classes.

This can be accomplished by:

- Using class inheritance or interfaces and overriding methods.
- Delegating to other classes (dependencies) by using composition and allowing to easily exchange those classes.

For example, suppose you're writing an app for a house architect who tells you that he needs to calculate the total area of each room for a given blueprint of a house. You may end up with the following solution:

```
data class Room(val width: Double, val height: Double)

class ArchitectUtils {
  ...
  fun calculateArea(rooms: List<Room>): Double {
    var total = 0.0
    for (room in rooms) {
      total += room.width * room.height
    }
    return total
  }
}
```

The architect is happy with that, however, the next week comes and he tells you that now he needs to add the area of the yard of the house. The yard could be circular.

You may rename `Room` to `RectangularSpace` and add a `CircularSpace` class, such as:

```
interface Space

data class RectangularSpace(val width: Double, val height:
```

```
Double): Space

data class CircularSpace(val radius: Double): Space

class ArchitectUtils {
  ...
  fun calculateArea(spaces: List<Space>): Double {
    var total = 0.0
    for (space in spaces) {
      if (space is SquareSpace) {
        total += space.width * space.height
      } elseif (space is CircularSpace) {
        total += space.radius * space.radius * Math.PI
      }
    }
    return total
  }
}
```

This code above is violating the principle, because it's not closed for modification, you're always modifying existing code to support new types.

So, to comply with the principle, you should do the following:

```
interface Space {
  fun area(): Double
}

data class RectangularSpace(val width: Double, val height:
Double): Space {
  override fun area() = width * height
}

data class CircularSpace(val radius: Double): Space {
  override fun area() = radius * radius * Math.PI
}

class ArchitectUtils {
  ...
  fun calculateArea(spaces: List<Space>): Double {
    var total = 0.0
    for (space in spaces) {
      total += space.area()
    }
    return total
  }
}
```

As you can see, if you need to support new types, you can just create a new class that implements the `Space` interface with its `area()` method. You won't need to modify anything else! This is what "closed for modification but open for extension" means.

Following this principle will give you a strong code base that almost never changes but enables extension. This is even more noticeable if you're writing a library because you can't change your interface with the clients of your library. In that case, the clients won't need to change anything in their code and at the same time allow them to use new features.

When using TDD, you'll write a new test to check the new feature or change an existing test to verify some behavior that now has to deal with more use cases. While writing the test you may notice that it starts to become too complex. That may be a sign you need to introduce a new class that inherits from the old one or use composition to handle each use case.

Liskov substitution

Also called **design by contract**, was initially introduced by *Barbara Liskov* in a 1987 conference keynote titled *Data abstraction and hierarchy*. Basically, it states that an app that uses an object of a base class should be able to use objects of derived classes without knowing about that and continue working. Therefore, your code should not be checking the subtype. In the subclass you can override some of the parent methods as long as you continue to comply with its semantics and maintain the expected behavior. As you can see, if you respect the contract, the app should continue to work.

A good example, by Uncle Bob (Martin), of a violation of this principle is that in mathematics, a Square is a Rectangle. You may be tempted to implement this having the `Square` class inherit from a `Rectangle` class. Then, anywhere in your code where you expect a `Rectangle`, you could pass a `Square`. The problem is that in a `Rectangle` you can change the width or the height independently, but you cannot do that in a Square. If you want to change the width of a Square, you should override the `setWidth` method to also change the height to the same value. To comply with the essence of a Square, the same would apply if you want to change the height. Therefore, this implementation would be violating the principle because you would be changing the expected behavior defined in the base type, which in this case is a reshapable-rectangle.

In your tests created using TDD, everything that you verified for your base class should also be verified for your new child class.

In the Square/Rectangle example mentioned, by creating your tests first, you would realize that you cannot model a Square inheriting from a Rectangle, because the area tests you write will pass for a Rectangle but not for a Square or vice versa:

```
private const val WIDTH = 4
private const val HEIGHT = 3

private fun assertArea(rectangle: Rectangle) {
  Assert.assertTrue(WIDTH * HEIGHT, rectangle.area())
}

@Test
fun testAreaRectangle() {
  val rectangle = Rectangle()
  rectangle.width = WIDTH
  rectangle.height = HEIGHT

  assertArea(rectangle) // This test will pass
}

@Test
fun testAreaSquare() {
  val square = Square()
  square.width = WIDTH
  square.height = HEIGHT // This will also set square.width to
HEIGHT

  assertArea(square) // Therefore, this test will fail, because
area is 9
}
```

Another example, in this case not violating the principle:

```
interface Repository {
  fun findContactOrNull(id: String): Contact?
}

class InMemoryRepository: Repository {
  private lateinit var cachedContacts: Map<String, Contact>
  ...
  fun findContactOrNull(id: String): Contact? {
    return cachedContacts[id]
  }
}

class SqlRepository: Repository {
  fun findContactOrNull(id: String): Contact? {
    val contact = // Implementation to get it from a SQL DB
    return contact
  }
}
```

As you can see, the base interface declares a method that indicates that it would return a `Contact` object by `id` or `null` if it doesn't find it. Later, the implementations, an in-memory DB and a Sql DB do what they have to do to return the `Contact`. Neither of them change the semantic of the interface. If instead, for example, an implementation removes a contact and then returns it, it would be violating the principle because you wouldn't be maintaining the expected behavior.

Interface segregation

This principle encourages you to create fine grained interfaces that are client specific. Suppose you have a class with a few methods, one part of your app may only need to access a subset of your methods and other part may need to access another subset. This principle encourages you to create two interfaces. Clients should have access to only what they need and nothing more.

For example, suppose you have an app where the user has to register and login to use it. You may have the following interface:

```
interface Membership {
  fun login(username: String, password: String): User
  fun logout(user: User)
  fun register(username: String, password: String)
  fun forgotPassword(username: String)
}
```

You may have a screen that, after login, only deals with showing the user data and enables them to logout.

You may have another screen to register and finally another one to let the user recover their password if it was forgotten.

So instead of all those screens using the fat `Membership` interface, it's better to segregate it into the following interfaces:

```
interface Login {
  fun login(username: String, password: String): User
  fun logout(user: User)
}
```

The screen that handles login and shows user data, enables to logout should use this interface.

```
interface Register {
  fun register(username: String, password: String)
}
```

The screen that handles registration should use this interface.

```
interface Forgot {
  fun forgotPassword(username: String)
}
```

The screen that handles recovering the password should use this last interface.

You may then have a class that implements all of these interfaces if it needs to. But if it doesn't, each screen should use the corresponding interface. Another example where it would be good to segregate interfaces is the following: suppose you're writing an app that will allow you to send a file to a printer, scan a document to use it in your app and send a file to an email address. You may implement it like this:

```
interface Printer {
  fun print(file: File)
  fun scan(): Bitmap
  fun sendTo(file: File, email: String)
}
```

To represent a printer that can do everything, you may have:

```
class FullPrinter: Printer {
  override fun print(file: File) {
    // Implementable logic
  }
  override fun scan(): Bitmap {
    // Implementable logic
  }
  override fun sendTo(file: File, email: String) {
    // Implementable logic
  }
}
```

However, a mobile phone could only implement `scan()` and `sendTo()` so you would have to write:

```
class MobileDevice: Printer {
  override fun print(file: File) {
    throw UnsupportedOperationException()
  }
  override fun scan(): Bitmap {
    // Implementable logic
  }
  override fun sendTo(file: File, email: String) {
    // Implementable logic
  }
}
```

You're forcing the mobile phone to implement methods that it doesn't support. Now you know, you should segregate into the following interfaces:

```
interface Printer {
  fun print(file: File)
}

interface Scanner {
  fun scan(): Bitmap
  fun sendTo(file: File, email: String)
}
```

And implement them accordingly:

```
class FullPrinter: Printer, Scanner {
  override fun print(file: File) {
    // Implementable logic
  }
  override fun scan(): Bitmap {
    // Implementable logic
  }
  override fun sendTo(file: File, email: String) {
    // Implementable logic
  }
}

class Mobile: Scanner {
  override fun scan(): Bitmap {
    // Implementable logic
  }
  override fun sendTo(file: File, email: String) {
    // Implementable logic
  }
}
```

When writing tests using TDD, if your class under test has a dependency, it's easier if you have to stub just the methods of a fine grained interface. TDD enforces writing more client-focused interfaces, because it makes you think from the client perspective — you avoid exposing those methods that won't be used by the client.

Dependency inversion

This principle states that a concrete class A should not depend on a concrete class B, but an abstraction of B instead. This abstraction could be an interface or an abstract class.

For example, think of a Presenter (or ViewModel) that needs to request data from an API. The Presenter (or ViewModel) should require an object that is able to request data from the API. Something like the following:

```
class ApiDataFetcher {
  fun fetch(): Data {
    // Implementation that retrieves data from an API
  }
}

class MyPresenter(private val apiDataFetcher: ApiDataFetcher) {
  fun getData(): Data {
    ...
    return apiDataFetcher.fetch()
  }
  ...
}
```

Here, the presenter is depending on a concrete class, `ApiDataFetcher`. It's not following the dependency inversion principle. What if later you need to fetch the data from `SharedPreferences` or a database using `Room`?

You should rewrite this to comply with the dependency inversion principle:

```
interface DataFetcher {
  fun getData(): Data
}

class ApiDataFetcher: DataFetcher {
  fun fetch(): Data {
    // Implementation that retrieves data from an API
  }
}

class MyPresenter(private val dataFetcher: DataFetcher)
```

Now, when you create the Presenter, you can still pass the `ApiDataFetcher` as a parameter. However, the presenter doesn't know about it, it just depends on an abstraction, the `DataFetcher` interface. So it will be easy to change it to a `SharedPreferencesDataFetcher` or a `RoomDataFetcher` class as long as those classes implement the `DataFetcher` interface.

When writing tests using TDD, instead of passing real collaborators (dependencies) to a class under test, it's easier to pass fake objects that conform to the same interface. These fake objects could be forced to always behave the same to reproduce a specific scenario to test. You'll create this kind of tests in Chapter 7, "Introduction to Mockito."

Key points

- Use software architecture to communicate development standards between team members.
- It's not uncommon to reuse software architecture on different projects.
- When starting a new project, one of the first decisions is to decide on its software architecture.
- Proper software architecture helps with testing.
- Support your software architecture using design patterns and the SOLID principles.
- Design patterns are classified into three categories: creational, structural and behavioral.
- The dependency injection pattern is the key to having a testable architecture.
- There are other user interface design patterns such as MVC, MVP and MVVM.

Where to go from here?

In the next chapter, you'll continue writing tests using **Mockito** and the MVVM architecture that is suggested by Google, which uses `ViewModel` and `LiveData`.

Review the following references to learn more about software architecture:

- Google suggested architecture: https://developer.android.com/jetpack/guide
- *Design Principles and Design Patterns*, by Robert C. Martin, where he introduced the SOLID principles: http://staff.cs.utu.fi/staff/jouni.smed/doos_06/material/DesignPrinciplesAndPatterns.pdf
- *The Principles of Object Oriented Design*, by Robert C. Martin, where he explains the SOLID and other principles: http://www.butunclebob.com/ArticleS.UncleBob.PrinciplesOfOod
- To learn about more design patterns, check the book Design Patterns: Elements of *Reusable Object-Oriented Software*, by the Gang of Four: https://www.oreilly.com/library/view/design-patterns-elements/0201633612/
- *GUI Architectures*, by Martin Fowler: https://www.martinfowler.com/eaaDev/uiArchs.html
- MVC/MVP/MVVM presentation by Florina Muntenescu: https://youtu.be/QrbhPcbZv0I
- Dagger by Tutorials: https://www.raywenderlich.com/books/dagger-by-tutorials

Chapter 7: Introduction to Mockito

By Fernando Sproviero

You'll often find yourself in situations in which you want to write a test for a method of a class that requires collaboration from another class. Unit Tests normally focus on a single class, therefore you need a way to avoid using their actual collaborators. Otherwise, you'd be doing integration testing, which you'll see in Chapter 8, "Integration."

In this chapter, you'll:

- Learn what mocking and stubbing are and when to use these techniques.
- Write more unit tests using the test-driven development (TDD) pattern to continue testing state, and a way to also verify behavior.

Why Mockito?

If you remember from a previous chapter, whenever you create a test, you must:

- First, configure what you're going to test.
- Second, execute the method that you want to test.
- Finally, verify the result by checking the state of the object under test. This is called **state verification** or **black-box testing**. This is what you've done using **JUnit**.

However, to perform state verification, sometimes the object under test has to collaborate with another one. Because you want to focus on the first object, in the configuration phase, you want to provide a **test double** collaborator to your object under test. This fake collaborator is just for testing purposes and you configure it to behave as you want. For example, you could make a mock so that calling a method on it always returns the same hardcoded `String`. This is called **stubbing a method**. You'll use **Mockito** for this.

There's another type of verification called **behavior verification** or **white-box testing**. Here you want to ensure that your object under test will call specific collaborator methods. For example, you may have a repository object that retrieves the data from the network, and before returning the results, it calls a collaborator object to save them into a database. Again, you can use **Mockito** to *keep an eye* on a collaborator and verify if specific methods were called on it.

> **Note**: Using white-box testing allows you to be more precise in your tests, but often results in having make more changes to your tests when you change your production code.

Setting up Mockito

Open the application's build.gradle file and add the following dependency:

```
dependencies {
  ...
  testImplementation 'org.mockito.kotlin:mockito-kotlin:3.2.0'
}
```

Mockito-Kotlin is a wrapper library around Mockito. It provides top-level functions to allow for a more Kotlin-like approach and also solves a few issues with using the Mockito Java library in Kotlin.

Creating unit tests with Mockito

Later, in the UI, you'll show the user a question with two options. You'll want the user to click on one. Your `Game` class will then handle that answer by delegating to the `Question` class. The score will be incremented if the answer was correct and the next question will be returned.

Mocking and verifying

Start by adding the following test to the **GameUnitTests.kt** file:

```
@Test
fun whenAnswering_shouldDelegateToQuestion() {
  // 1
  val question = mock<Question>()
  val game = Game(listOf(question))

  // 2
  game.answer(question, "OPTION")

  // 3
  verify(question, times(1)).answer(eq("OPTION"))
}
```

Note: When importing the `mock`, `verify`, `times` and eq functions, you should choose the option starting with `org.mockito.kotlin.*` to use the functions from the Mockito-Kotlin library, instead of `org.mockito.Mockito.*` which has their own versions of these functions but will give different results as these weren't designed for Kotlin.

In this test:

1. The `answer()` method of `Game` needs a `Question` to know the answer of. It does this by passing a `Question` to its `answer()` method. So you create a **mock** of a `Question`, which you can later verify against.
2. Call the `answer()` method of `Game`, passing the `Question` mock as a parameter.
3. **Verify** the method `answer()` was called on the `Question` mock. You used the `times(1)` **verification mode** to check that the `answer()` method was called exactly one time. You also used the eq **argument matcher** to check that the `answer()` method was called with a `String` equal to `OPTION`.

You can omit `times(1)` as it's the default. So modify the code to the following:

```
verify(question).answer(eq("OPTION"))
```

> **Note**: There are also other verification modes like `never()`, `atLeast()`, `atMost()` and other argument matchers, like `eq()`, `same()`, `any()` that you may use depending on your test.

Try to compile and run the test. You'll see an error because the `Game` class doesn't have the `answer()` method yet.

Open the `Game` class and create the `answer()` method:

```
fun answer(question: Question, option: String) {
  // TODO
}
```

Run the test. You'll see that it doesn't pass:

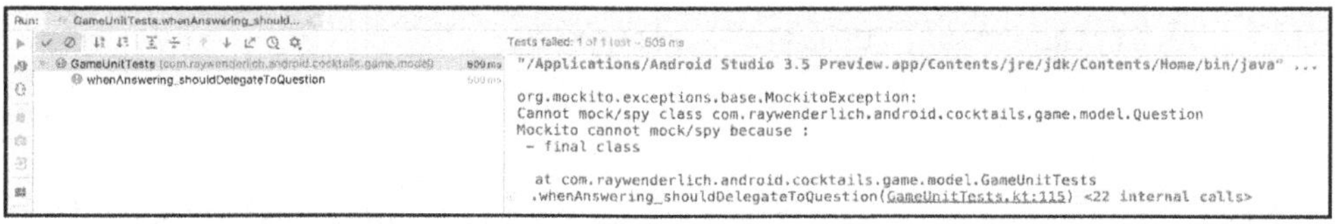
Run: GameUnitTests.whenAnswering_should...
Tests failed: 1 of 1 test – 509 ms
GameUnitTests
whenAnswering_shouldDelegateToQuestion
"/Applications/Android Studio 3.5 Preview.app/Contents/jre/jdk/Contents/Home/bin/java" ...
org.mockito.exceptions.base.MockitoException:
Cannot mock/spy class com.raywenderlich.android.cocktails.game.model.Question
Mockito cannot mock/spy because :
- final class
at com.raywenderlich.android.cocktails.game.model.GameUnitTests
.whenAnswering_shouldDelegateToQuestion(GameUnitTests.kt:115) <22 internal calls>

This is because Kotlin classes and methods are **final** by default. Mockito won't work with final classes/methods out of the box. To fix this you have the following options:

- Use a **mock-maker-inline extension** to allow Mockito mock final classes/methods.
- Add the open keyword to classes and methods that you'll mock.
- Create an interface and have the class implement the interface. Then, just mock the interface (interfaces are open by default).

Using mock-maker-inline extension

- Go to the project window and change to the Project view.
- Create a **resources** directory under **app ▸ src ▸ test**.
- Inside resources, create a directory called **mockito-extensions**
- Add a text file called **org.mockito.plugins.MockMaker**
- Add the text **mock-maker-inline**

See the image below:

Now, you can go back and run the last test you created and see that it still doesn't pass, but this time with another error:

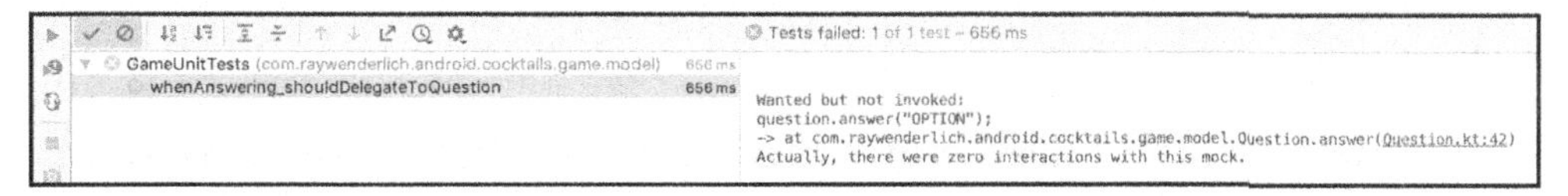

Here it states that it was expecting an invocation to the `answer()` method of the `Question` class.

So now, fix the `answer()` method with the correct implementation:

```
fun answer(question: Question, option: String) {
  question.answer(option)
}
```

Now, run the test and see that it passes:

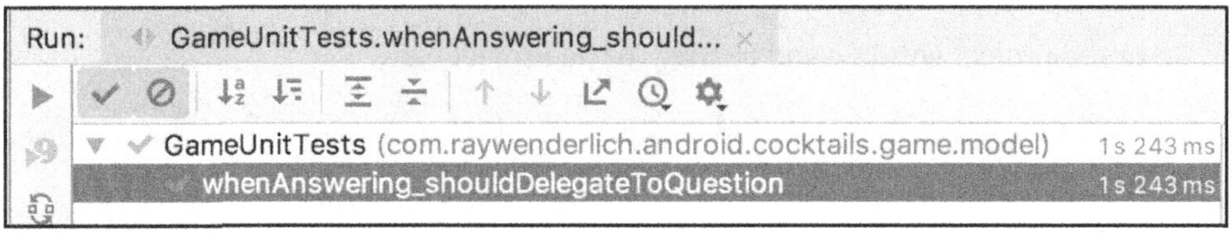

Run: GameUnitTests.whenAnswering_should...
GameUnitTests (com.raywenderlich.android.cocktails.game.model) 1 s 243 ms
whenAnswering_shouldDelegateToQuestion 1 s 243 ms

Stubbing methods

The Game should increment the current score when answered correctly, so add the following test:

```
@Test
fun whenAnsweringCorrectly_shouldIncrementCurrentScore() {
  // 1
  val question = mock<Question>()
  whenever(question.answer(anyString())).thenReturn(true)

  val game = Game(listOf(question))

  // 2
  game.answer(question, "OPTION")

  // 3
  Assert.assertEquals(1, game.currentScore)
}
```

In the above, you:

1. Mocked the `Question` class again. Using **whenever/method/thenReturn** you're **stubbing** the `question.answer()` method to always return `true`. Notice here you used the `anyString()` argument matcher as you don't care which specific `String` you need to stub the call.

> **Note**: You could choose to use a specific `String` matcher here, which would make the test stronger.

2. Call the `answer()` method of `Game`.

3. Check that the game score was incremented.

Run the test, and you will see that it fails. Add the following code to the answer() method of the Game class:

```
fun answer(question: Question, option: String) {
  question.answer(option)
  incrementScore()
}
```

Now, run the test again and you will see that it passes.

You are also going to want to check that it doesn't increment the score when answering incorrectly. To do that, add the following test:

```
@Test
fun whenAnsweringIncorrectly_shouldNotIncrementCurrentScore() {
  val question = mock<Question>()
  whenever(question.answer(anyString())).thenReturn(false)
  val game = Game(listOf(question))

  game.answer(question, "OPTION")

  Assert.assertEquals(0, game.currentScore)
}
```

Here, instead, you are stubbing the answer() method to always return false.

Run the test and you will see that it fails. It's a good thing you checked for that boundary condition! To fix this, replace your answer() method with the following:

```
fun answer(question: Question, option: String) {
  val result = question.answer(option)
  if (result) {
    incrementScore()
  }
}
```

This adds a check to only increment the score if the answer is correct. Now, run both tests and you will see them pass.

Refactoring

Open the Game class. Notice that this class knows about the score and a list of questions. When requesting to answer a question, the Game class delegates this to the Question class and increments the score if the answer was correct. Game could also be refactored to delegate the logic of incrementing the current score and highest score to a new class, Score.

Create a Score class in the same package as the Game class with the following content:

```
class Score(highestScore: Int = 0) {
  var current = 0
    private set

  var highest = highestScore
    private set

  fun increment() {
    current++
    if (current > highest) {
      highest = current
    }
  }
}
```

Now, update the Game class to use this new class:

```
class Game(private val questions: List<Question>,
           highest: Int = 0) {

  private val score = Score(highest)

  val currentScore: Int
    get() = score.current

  val highestScore: Int
    get() = score.highest

  private var questionIndex = -1

  fun incrementScore() {
    score.increment()
  }

  ...
```

Run the tests again and verify that everything is still working.

With that change, take another look at the following unit tests from **GameUnitTests.kt**:

```
@Test
fun whenIncrementingScore_shouldIncrementCurrentScore() {
  val game = Game(emptyList(), 0)

  game.incrementScore()

  Assert.assertEquals(
```

```
    "Current score should have been 1",
    1,
    game.currentScore)
}

@Test
fun
whenIncrementingScore_aboveHighScore_shouldAlsoIncrementHighScor
e() {
  val game = Game(emptyList(), 0)

  game.incrementScore()

  Assert.assertEquals(1, game.highestScore)
}

@Test
fun
whenIncrementingScore_belowHighScore_shouldNotIncrementHighScore
() {
  val game = Game(emptyList(), 10)

  game.incrementScore()

  Assert.assertEquals(10, game.highestScore)
}
```

When calling `game.incrementScore()`, `game.highestScore`, or `game.currentScore` because you refactored to internally delegate to a dependent class, `Score`, you are now performing **integration tests**. You'll see and learn more about them in Chapter 8, "Integration."

In order to keep your tests at the unit level, remove these tests from **GameUnitTests.kt** and create a new file called **ScoreUnitTests.kt** with the following content:

```
class ScoreUnitTests {

  @Test
  fun whenIncrementingScore_shouldIncrementCurrentScore() {
    val score = Score()

    score.increment()

    Assert.assertEquals(
      "Current score should have been 1",
      1,
      score.current)
  }
```

```
  @Test
  fun
whenIncrementingScore_aboveHighScore_shouldAlsoIncrementHighScor
e() {
    val score = Score()

    score.increment()

    Assert.assertEquals(1, score.highest)
  }

  @Test
  fun
whenIncrementingScore_belowHighScore_shouldNotIncrementHighScore
() {
    val score = Score(10)

    score.increment()

    Assert.assertEquals(10, score.highest)
  }
}
```

This gets your tests back to the unit level because you test the methods of the `Score` object without dependent classes.

Run them to check that they pass.

With that refactor, the only method that is still using the `incrementScore()` method in your `Game` class is the `answer()` method. Let's simplify this. Remove the `incrementScore()` method and change the `answer()` method as follows:

```
fun answer(question: Question, option: String) {
  val result = question.answer(option)
  if (result) {
    score.increment()
  }
}
```

Now, because you removed the public `scoreIncrement()` method, the only way to increment the score in your `Game` class is by answering questions.

Next, open **GameUnitTests.kt** and have a look at the following tests:

```
@Test
fun whenAnsweringCorrectly_shouldIncrementCurrentScore() {
  val question = mock<Question>()
  whenever(question.answer(anyString())).thenReturn(true)
  val game = Game(listOf(question))
```

```
    game.answer(question, "OPTION")

    Assert.assertEquals(1, game.currentScore)
  }

  @Test
  fun whenAnsweringIncorrectly_shouldNotIncrementCurrentScore() {
    val question = mock<Question>()
    whenever(question.answer(anyString())).thenReturn(false)
    val game = Game(listOf(question))

    game.answer(question, "OPTION")

    Assert.assertEquals(0, game.currentScore)
  }
```

You may have guessed that now these are integration tests. This is because you are asserting `game.currentScore` that internally depends on a `Score` class from your refactor. To convert them to unit tests, you will need to change them to verify that the `increment()` method on the `Score` class was or wasn't called. To do that, replace them with the following:

```
  @Test
  fun whenAnsweringCorrectly_shouldIncrementCurrentScore() {
    val question = mock<Question>()
    whenever(question.answer(anyString())).thenReturn(true)
    val score = mock<Score>()
    val game = Game(listOf(question), score)

    game.answer(question, "OPTION")

    verify(score).increment()
  }

  @Test
  fun whenAnsweringIncorrectly_shouldNotIncrementCurrentScore() {
    val question = mock<Question>()
    whenever(question.answer(anyString())).thenReturn(false)
    val score = mock<Score>()
    val game = Game(listOf(question), score)

    game.answer(question, "OPTION")

    verify(score, never()).increment()
  }
```

You'll see that it doesn't compile now, because you're passing a list of questions and a score to the `Game` class constructor, but it doesn't support that yet.

To fix that, open your Game class and change the constructor to the following:

```
class Game(private val questions: List<Question>,
           val score: Score = Score(0)) {
```

Once that is done, remove the old score, currentScore and highestScore properties as they are not needed anymore. Your modified Game class should be the following:

```
class Game(private val questions: List<Question>,
           val score: Score = Score(0)) {

  private var questionIndex = -1

  fun nextQuestion(): Question? {
    if (questionIndex + 1 < questions.size) {
      questionIndex++
      return questions[questionIndex]
    }
    return null
  }

  fun answer(question: Question, option: String) {
    val result = question.answer(option)
    if (result) {
      score.increment()
    }
  }
}
```

Run the tests and everything should now pass. Congratulations, you have successfully refactored your tests and kept them at the unit level!

Verifying in order

To save and retrieve the high score, you'll need to add functionality to a repository. From the **Project** view, create a new package **common ▸ repository** under **app ▸ src ▸ test ▸ java ▸ com ▸ raywenderlich ▸ android ▸ cocktails**. Create a new file called **RepositoryUnitTests.kt** and add the following code:

```
class RepositoryUnitTests {

  @Test
  fun saveScore_shouldSaveToSharedPreferences() {
    val api: CocktailsApi = mock()
    // 1
    val sharedPreferencesEditor: SharedPreferences.Editor =
        mock()
```

```
    val sharedPreferences: SharedPreferences = mock()
    whenever(sharedPreferences.edit())
      .thenReturn(sharedPreferencesEditor)
    val repository = CocktailsRepositoryImpl(api,
            sharedPreferences)

    // 2
    val score = 100
    repository.saveHighScore(score)

    // 3
    inOrder(sharedPreferencesEditor) {
      // 4
      verify(sharedPreferencesEditor).putInt(any(), eq(score))
      verify(sharedPreferencesEditor).apply()
    }
  }
}
```

Going over each step in turn:

1. You're going to save the score into the `CocktailsRepository` using `SharedPreferences`, so you need to mock this dependency and instruct to return an `Editor` mock whenever an editor is requested.

2. Execute the `saveHighScore()` method.

3. Use `inOrder` to check that the subsequent verifications are executed in the exact order.

4. Verify that the score is saved correctly.

In order for this code to compile, add a `saveHighScore()` method to your `CocktailsRepository` interface.

```
interface CocktailsRepository {
  ...
  fun saveHighScore(score: Int)
}
```

Then modify your `CocktailsRepositoryImpl` constructor to take in `SharedPreferences` as a parameter and override the `saveHighScore()` method:

```
class CocktailsRepositoryImpl(
    private val api: CocktailsApi,
    private val sharedPreferences: SharedPreferences)
  : CocktailsRepository {

  override fun saveHighScore(score: Int) {
    // TODO
  }
```

Run the test and see that it fails. To fix it, add the following code to the `CocktailsRepositoryImpl` class:

```
private const val HIGH_SCORE_KEY = "HIGH_SCORE_KEY"

class CocktailsRepositoryImpl(
    private val api: CocktailsApi,
    private val sharedPreferences: SharedPreferences)
  : CocktailsRepository {

  ...

  override fun saveHighScore(score: Int) {
    val editor = sharedPreferences.edit()
    editor.putInt(HIGH_SCORE_KEY, score)
    editor.apply()
  }
```

This is adding logic to your `saveHighScore` method to save it in `sharedPreferences`. Run the test again it will pass.

You are also going to want to have a way to read the high score from the repository. To get started, add the following test:

```
  @Test
  fun getScore_shouldGetFromSharedPreferences() {
    val api: CocktailsApi = mock()
    val sharedPreferences: SharedPreferences = mock()

    val repository = CocktailsRepositoryImpl(api,
        sharedPreferences)

    repository.getHighScore()

    verify(sharedPreferences).getInt(any(), any())
  }
```

Next, add the `getHighScore()` method to `CocktailsRepository` and `CocktailsRepositoryImpl`:

```
interface CocktailsRepository {
  ...
  fun getHighScore(): Int
}
```

```
class CocktailsRepositoryImpl(
    private val api: CocktailsApi,
    private val sharedPreferences: SharedPreferences)
  : CocktailsRepository {

  ...

  override fun getHighScore(): Int = 0
```

Run the test, see it fail, and then add the following code to the `CocktailsRepositoryImpl` class to see it pass:

```
  override fun getHighScore()
    = sharedPreferences.getInt(HIGH_SCORE_KEY, 0)
```

If you look at these two tests, you may notice that you have some code that is repeated in both of them.

Let's DRY this up by refactoring your `RepositoryUnitTests` so that it looks like the following:

```
class RepositoryUnitTests {
  private lateinit var repository: CocktailsRepository
  private lateinit var api: CocktailsApi
  private lateinit var sharedPreferences: SharedPreferences
  private lateinit var sharedPreferencesEditor:
SharedPreferences.Editor

  @Before
  fun setup() {
    api = mock()
    sharedPreferences = mock()
    sharedPreferencesEditor = mock()
    whenever(sharedPreferences.edit())
      .thenReturn(sharedPreferencesEditor)

    repository = CocktailsRepositoryImpl(api, sharedPreferences)
  }

  @Test
  fun saveScore_shouldSaveToSharedPreferences() {
```

```
    val score = 100
    repository.saveHighScore(score)

    inOrder(sharedPreferencesEditor) {
      verify(sharedPreferencesEditor).putInt(any(), eq(score))
      verify(sharedPreferencesEditor).apply()
    }
  }

  @Test
  fun getScore_shouldGetFromSharedPreferences() {
    repository.getHighScore()

    verify(sharedPreferences).getInt(any(), any())
  }
}
```

Run the tests again to check everything is still working.

Spying

Suppose you want to only save the high score if it is higher than the previously saved high score. To do that, you want to start by adding the following test to your `RepositoryUnitTests` class:

```
  @Test
  fun saveScore_shouldNotSaveToSharedPreferencesIfLower() {
    val previouslySavedHighScore = 100
    val newHighScore = 10
    val spyRepository = spy(repository)
    doReturn(previouslySavedHighScore)
        .whenever(spyRepository)
        .getHighScore()

    spyRepository.saveHighScore(newHighScore)

    verify(sharedPreferencesEditor, never())
        .putInt(any(), eq(newHighScore))
  }
```

In this test you are stubbing the `getHighScore()` method but you also need to call the real `saveHighScore()` method on the same object, which is a real object, `CocktailsRepositoryImpl`. To do that you need a **spy** instead of a mock. Using a **spy** will let you call the methods of a real object, while also tracking every interaction, just as you would do with a mock. When setting up spies, you need to use **doReturn/whenever/method** to stub a method. Try running the test and you will see that it fails.

To make the test pass, modify the `saveHighScore()` method of the `CocktailsRepositoryImpl` so that it is as follows:

```
override fun saveHighScore(score: Int) {
  val highScore = getHighScore()
  if (score > highScore) {
    val editor = sharedPreferences.edit()
    editor.putInt(HIGH_SCORE_KEY, score)
    editor.apply()
  }
}
```

Run the test again and it will pass.

In order to make games for a user, you'll need a factory to build a `Game` with questions, which will map the cocktails returned by the API. Create a **CocktailsGameFactoryUnitTests.kt** file under **app ▸ src ▸ test ▸ java ▸ com ▸ raywenderlich ▸ android ▸ cocktails ▸ game ▸ factory**. Add the following code:

```
class CocktailsGameFactoryUnitTests {

  private lateinit var repository: CocktailsRepository
  private lateinit var factory: CocktailsGameFactory

  @Before
  fun setup() {
    repository = mock()
    factory = CocktailsGameFactoryImpl(repository)
  }

  @Test
  fun buildGame_shouldGetCocktailsFromRepo() {
    factory.buildGame(mock())

    verify(repository).getAlcoholic(any())
  }
}
```

With this test, you are checking that `buildGame` is calling `getAlcoholic` from the repository.

Create the following interface and class to make it compile, under **app ▸ src ▸ main ▸ java ▸ com ▸ raywenderlich ▸ android ▸ cocktails ▸ game ▸ factory**:

```
interface CocktailsGameFactory {

  fun buildGame(callback: Callback)

  interface Callback {
```

```
    fun onSuccess(game: Game)
    fun onError()
  }
}
```

```
class CocktailsGameFactoryImpl(
    private val repository: CocktailsRepository)
  : CocktailsGameFactory {

  override fun buildGame(callback:
CocktailsGameFactory.Callback) {
    // TODO
  }
}
```

Run the test and see that it fails. To make the test pass, add the following code to the `buildGame()` method:

```
  override fun buildGame(callback:
CocktailsGameFactory.Callback) {
    repository.getAlcoholic(
        object : RepositoryCallback<List<Cocktail>, String> {
          override fun onSuccess(cocktailList: List<Cocktail>) {
            // TODO
          }

          override fun onError(e: String) {
            // TODO
          }
        })
  }
```

This is adding a call to the `getAlcoholic` method with stubbed callbacks for `onSuccess` and `onError`. Run the test again and it will pass.

Stubbing callbacks

Create a new test that verifies that the callback is called when the repository returns successfully with a list of cocktails in **CocktailsGameFactoryUnitTests.kt**:

```
  private val cocktails = listOf(
      Cocktail("1", "Drink1", "image1"),
      Cocktail("2", "Drink2", "image2"),
      Cocktail("3", "Drink3", "image3"),
      Cocktail("4", "Drink4", "image4")
  )

  @Test
```

```
fun buildGame_shouldCallOnSuccess() {
  val callback = mock<CocktailsGameFactory.Callback>()
  setUpRepositoryWithCocktails(repository)

  factory.buildGame(callback)

  verify(callback).onSuccess(any())
}

private fun setUpRepositoryWithCocktails(
  repository: CocktailsRepository) {
  doAnswer {
    // 1
    val callback: RepositoryCallback<List<Cocktail>, String>
      = it.getArgument(0)
    callback.onSuccess(cocktails)
  }.whenever(repository).getAlcoholic(any())
}
```

In `setUpRepositoryWithCocktails`, you are using `doAnswer` to stub the `repository.getAlcoholic()` method to always return success with a list of cocktails. The `doAnswer` closure returns an `InvocationOnMock` type, with which you can spy on its arguments. You then get the first argument of the method (which is the callback), and call `onSuccess()` on it.

Run the test and it will fail. Now, modify the code to the `onSuccess` callback of the `buildGame()` so that `buildGame()` looks like the following:

```
  override fun buildGame(callback:
CocktailsGameFactory.Callback) {
    repository.getAlcoholic(
        object : RepositoryCallback<List<Cocktail>, String> {
          override fun onSuccess(cocktailList: List<Cocktail>) {
            callback.onSuccess(Game(emptyList()))
          }

          override fun onError(e: String) {
            // TODO
          }
        })
  }
```

Run your test again and it will pass. Now, let's do the same with the `onError` case to ensure you test the error path as well as success. First, add the following test:

```
@Test
fun buildGame_shouldCallOnError() {
  val callback = mock<CocktailsGameFactory.Callback>()
  setUpRepositoryWithError(repository)
```

```
    factory.buildGame(callback)

    verify(callback).onError()
  }

  private fun setUpRepositoryWithError(
    repository: CocktailsRepository) {
    doAnswer {
      val callback: RepositoryCallback<List<Cocktail>, String>
        = it.getArgument(0)
      callback.onError("Error")
    }.whenever(repository).getAlcoholic(any())
  }
```

Here `setUpRepositoryWithError()` is stubbing the `getAlcoholic()` method to always answer with an error. Run the test and it will fail.

Now, add the following implementation to the `onError` callback of your `buildGame` function so that `buildGame` looks like the following:

```
  override fun buildGame(
        callback: CocktailsGameFactory.Callback
    ) {
    repository.getAlcoholic(
        object : RepositoryCallback<List<Cocktail>, String> {
          override fun onSuccess(cocktailList: List<Cocktail>) {
            callback.onSuccess(Game(emptyList()))
          }

          override fun onError(e: String) {
            callback.onError()
          }
        })
  }
```

Run the test and it will pass.

The following tests are similar to what you've been writing, they ensure that `CocktailsGameFactoryImpl` builds a `Game` using the high score and maps the list of `Cocktail` objects to `Question` objects. They are here to give you more practice, but if you are really anxious to move on you can skip to the next section "Testing ViewModel and LiveData".

Create the following tests that verify the factory creates a `Game` using the `repository.getHighScore()` method:

```
  @Test
  fun buildGame_shouldGetHighScoreFromRepo() {
    setUpRepositoryWithCocktails(repository)
```

```
    factory.buildGame(mock())

    verify(repository).getHighScore()
  }

  @Test
  fun buildGame_shouldBuildGameWithHighScore() {
    setUpRepositoryWithCocktails(repository)
    val highScore = 100
    whenever(repository.getHighScore()).thenReturn(highScore)

    factory.buildGame(object : CocktailsGameFactory.Callback {
      override fun onSuccess(game: Game)
        = Assert.assertEquals(highScore, game.score.highest)

      override fun onError() = Assert.fail()
    })
  }
```

As you should always do, run the tests once to make sure that they fail. To make them pass, modify your `buildGame()` method so that it is as follows:

```
  override fun buildGame(callback:
CocktailsGameFactory.Callback) {
    repository.getAlcoholic(
        object : RepositoryCallback<List<Cocktail>, String> {
          override fun onSuccess(cocktailList: List<Cocktail>) {
            val score = Score(repository.getHighScore())
            val game = Game(emptyList(), score)
            callback.onSuccess(game)
          }

          override fun onError(e: String) {
            callback.onError()
          }
        })
  }
```

Run the tests and they will pass.

Now, create the following test that verifies the factory creates a `Game` mapping a list of cocktails to a list of questions:

```
  @Test
  fun buildGame_shouldBuildGameWithQuestions() {
    setUpRepositoryWithCocktails(repository)

    factory.buildGame(object : CocktailsGameFactory.Callback {
      override fun onSuccess(game: Game) {
        cocktails.forEach {
          assertQuestion(game.nextQuestion(),
```

```
                it.strDrink,
                it.strDrinkThumb)
          }
        }

        override fun onError() = Assert.fail()
      })
    }

    private fun assertQuestion(question: Question?,
                               correctOption: String,
                               imageUrl: String?) {
      Assert.assertNotNull(question)
      Assert.assertEquals(imageUrl, question?.imageUrl)
      Assert.assertEquals(correctOption, question?.correctOption)
      Assert.assertNotEquals(correctOption,
              question?.incorrectOption)
    }
```

Here, you are asserting that the image of the question that will be shown in the UI corresponds to the cocktail image, the correct option corresponds to the name of the drink, and also that the incorrect option is not the name of the drink.

If you run this, the test will not compile, so add the `imageUrl` property to the `Question` class:

```
class Question(val correctOption: String,
               val incorrectOption: String,
               val imageUrl: String? = null) {
...
```

Now run the test, which compiles but now fails. To make it pass, replace your `buildGame()` method with the following:

```
override fun buildGame(callback: CocktailsGameFactory.Callback)
{
  repository.getAlcoholic(
      object : RepositoryCallback<List<Cocktail>, String> {
        override fun onSuccess(cocktailList: List<Cocktail>) {
          val questions = buildQuestions(cocktailList)
          val score = Score(repository.getHighScore())
          val game = Game(questions, score)
          callback.onSuccess(game)
        }

        override fun onError(e: String) {
          callback.onError()
        }
      })
}
```

```
private fun buildQuestions(cocktailList: List<Cocktail>)
  = cocktailList.map { cocktail ->
      val otherCocktail
          = cocktailList.shuffled().first { it != cocktail }
      Question(cocktail.strDrink,
          otherCocktail.strDrink,
          cocktail.strDrinkThumb)
    }
```

This adds in a `buildQuestions` method that creates a series of questions for the list of cocktails. This is called in your `onSuccess` callback in `buildGame` with the result passed to `Game`. Run the test again and it will pass.

Testing ViewModel and LiveData

To update the UI with questions, the score, and also to enable the user to interact with the question options, you're going to use `ViewModel` and `LiveData` from Android Architecture Components.

To get started, add the following dependency in your **build.gradle** within the app module:

```
dependencies {
  ...
  testImplementation 'androidx.arch.core:core-testing:2.1.0'
}
```

Next, create a package called **viewmodel** under **app ▸ src ▸ test ▸ java ▸ com ▸ raywenderlich ▸ android ▸ cocktails ▸ game**. Now, create a **CocktailsGameViewModelUnitTests.kt** file under this **viewmodel** directory you just created with the following code:

```
class CocktailsGameViewModelUnitTests {
  @get:Rule
  val taskExecutorRule = InstantTaskExecutorRule()
}
```

You may have noticed `@get:Rule`. This is a **test rule**. A test rule is a tool to change the way tests run, sometimes adding additional checks or running code before and after your tests. Android Architecture Components uses a background executor that is asynchronous to do its magic. `InstantTaskExecutorRule` is a rule that swaps out that executor and replaces it with synchronous one. This will make sure that, when you're using `LiveData` with the `ViewModel`, it's all run synchronously in the tests.

Now that you have your test scaffolding, add the following to your test file:

```
private lateinit var repository: CocktailsRepository
private lateinit var factory: CocktailsGameFactory
private lateinit var viewModel: CocktailsGameViewModel
private lateinit var game: Game
private lateinit var loadingObserver: Observer<Boolean>
private lateinit var errorObserver: Observer<Boolean>
private lateinit var scoreObserver: Observer<Score>
private lateinit var questionObserver: Observer<Question>

@Before
fun setup() {
  // 1
  repository = mock()
  factory = mock()
  viewModel = CocktailsGameViewModel(repository, factory)

  // 2
  game = mock()

  // 3
  loadingObserver = mock()
  errorObserver = mock()
  scoreObserver = mock()
  questionObserver = mock()
  viewModel.getLoading().observeForever(loadingObserver)
  viewModel.getScore().observeForever(scoreObserver)
  viewModel.getQuestion().observeForever(questionObserver)
  viewModel.getError().observeForever(errorObserver)
}
```

In the above:

1. Your ViewModel will require a `CocktailsRepository` to save the highscore and a `CocktailsGameFactory` to build a game. These are dependencies, so you need to mock them.
2. You'll use a `Game` mock to stub some of its methods and verify you call methods on it.
3. You need a few mocked observers because the Activity will observe `LiveData` objects exposed by the `ViewModel`. In the UI, you'll show a loading view when retrieving the cocktails from the API and an error view if there's an error retrieving the cocktails, score updates and questions. Because there's no lifecycle here, you can use the `observeForever()` method.

Note: Ensure to import `androidx.lifecycle.Observer`.

To make the test compile, create a class under **app ▸ src ▸ main ▸ java ▸ com ▸ raywenderlich ▸ android ▸ cocktails ▸ game ▸ viewmodel** called **CocktailsGameViewModel** with the following content:

```
class CocktailsGameViewModel(
    private val repository: CocktailsRepository,
    private val factory: CocktailsGameFactory) : ViewModel() {

  private val loadingLiveData = MutableLiveData<Boolean>()
  private val errorLiveData = MutableLiveData<Boolean>()
  private val questionLiveData = MutableLiveData<Question>()
  private val scoreLiveData = MutableLiveData<Score>()

  fun getLoading(): LiveData<Boolean> = loadingLiveData
  fun getError(): LiveData<Boolean> = errorLiveData
  fun getQuestion(): LiveData<Question> = questionLiveData
  fun getScore(): LiveData<Score> = scoreLiveData
}
```

Next, add the following methods to **CocktailsGameViewModelUnitTests.kt**:

```
  private fun setUpFactoryWithSuccessGame(game: Game) {
    doAnswer {
      val callback: CocktailsGameFactory.Callback =
              it.getArgument(0)
      callback.onSuccess(game)
    }.whenever(factory).buildGame(any())
  }

  private fun setUpFactoryWithError() {
    doAnswer {
      val callback: CocktailsGameFactory.Callback =
              it.getArgument(0)
      callback.onError()
    }.whenever(factory).buildGame(any())
  }
```

You'll use these methods to stub the `buildGame()` method from the `CocktailsGameFactory` class.

Now, add the following test:

```
@Test
fun init_shouldBuildGame() {
  viewModel.initGame()

  verify(factory).buildGame(any())
}
```

Here, you're verifying that calling `initGame` on the ViewModel will call `buildGame` from the factory.

Finally, add the corresponding implementation to your `CocktailsGameViewModel` to make the test compile:

```
fun initGame() {
  // TODO
}
```

Run the test and it will compile but won't pass.

To make it pass, replace `initGame()` in `CocktailsGameViewModel` with the following:

```
fun initGame() {
  factory.buildGame(object : CocktailsGameFactory.Callback {
    override fun onSuccess(game: Game) {
      // TODO
    }

    override fun onError() {
      // TODO
    }
  })
}
```

Run the test again and it will pass.

You are going to want to show a loading view and remove the error view while building the game. To get started with that, add the following tests to **CocktailsGameViewModelUnitTests.kt**:

```
@Test
fun init_shouldShowLoading() {
  viewModel.initGame()

  verify(loadingObserver).onChanged(eq(true))
}
```

```
@Test
fun init_shouldHideError() {
  viewModel.initGame()

  verify(errorObserver).onChanged(eq(false))
}
```

In both tests, you verify that `initGame` publishes the correct data. When the program posts a value to a `LiveData`, the object calls `onChanged()` with the value. This is the function you are checking for.

> **Note**: There are multiple ways you can verify the result. For example, instead of using `verify(loadingObserver).onChanged(eq(true))`, you could replace it with `Assert.assertTrue(viewModel.getLoading().value!!)` instead to achieve the same result. This alternative compares the last value of the `LiveData` to the expected one instead of making sure a method was called with that data.

As always, you run your new tests to ensure that they fail. To fix them, modify your `initGame()` method by adding the following two lines as follows:

```
fun initGame() {
  loadingLiveData.value = true
  errorLiveData.value = false
  factory.buildGame(...)
}
```

Run the tests again and they will pass.

You are also going to want to show the error view and stop showing the loading view when there's a problem building the game. To get started add the following tests:

```
@Test
fun init_shouldShowError_whenFactoryReturnsError() {
  setUpFactoryWithError()

  viewModel.initGame()

  verify(errorObserver).onChanged(eq(true))
}

@Test
fun init_shouldHideLoading_whenFactoryReturnsError() {
  setUpFactoryWithError()
```

```
    viewModel.initGame()

    verify(loadingObserver).onChanged(eq(false))
  }
```

Run the tests to ensure that they fail. To fix them, modify your `onError()` callback in `initGame()` as follows:

```
  override fun onError() {
    loadingLiveData.value = false
    errorLiveData.value = true
  }
```

Run the tests and check that they pass.

Another scenario that you will want to cover is to hide the error and loading views when the factory builds a game successfully. To get started, add these tests:

```
  @Test
  fun init_shouldHideError_whenFactoryReturnsSuccess() {
    setUpFactoryWithSuccessGame(game)

    viewModel.initGame()

    verify(errorObserver, times(2)).onChanged(eq(false))
  }

  @Test
  fun init_shouldHideLoading_whenFactoryReturnsSuccess() {
    setUpFactoryWithSuccessGame(game)

    viewModel.initGame()

    verify(loadingObserver).onChanged(eq(false))
  }
```

Here, you check the error is set to `false` two times. The first `false` value is before calling the repository to build the game, and the second one is set when the game couldn't be built because of an error.

Run the tests to ensure that they fail. To fix these tests, modify your `onSuccess()` callback in `initGame` as follows:

```
  override fun onSuccess(game: Game) {
    loadingLiveData.value = false
    errorLiveData.value = false
  }
```

Run the tests again and they will pass.

Another requirement is to show the score when the game is built. Start by adding the following test:

```
@Test
fun init_shouldShowScore_whenFactoryReturnsSuccess() {
  val score = mock<Score>()
  whenever(game.score).thenReturn(score)
  setUpFactoryWithSuccessGame(game)

  viewModel.initGame()

  verify(scoreObserver).onChanged(eq(score))
}
```

Run it to make sure it doesn't pass. Now, modify your `onSuccess()` callback in `initGame()` as follows:

```
override fun onSuccess(game: Game) {
  loadingLiveData.value = false
  errorLiveData.value = false
  scoreLiveData.value = game.score
}
```

Run the test and check that it passes.

You are going to want to show the first question when the game is built. Start by adding this test:

```
@Test
fun init_shouldShowFirstQuestion_whenFactoryReturnsSuccess() {
  val question = mock<Question>()
  whenever(game.nextQuestion()).thenReturn(question)
  setUpFactoryWithSuccessGame(game)

  viewModel.initGame()

  verify(questionObserver).onChanged(eq(question))
}
```

Run it to make sure that if fails. Now, modify the `onSuccess()` callback of `initGame` as follows:

```
override fun onSuccess(game: Game) {
  loadingLiveData.value = false
  errorLiveData.value = false
  scoreLiveData.value = game.score
  questionLiveData.value = game.nextQuestion()
}
```

Run the test and make sure that it passes.

You are going to want to show the next question when calling `nextQuestion`. Once again, you will start by adding a test as follows:

```
@Test
fun nextQuestion_shouldShowQuestion() {
  val question1 = mock<Question>()
  val question2 = mock<Question>()
  whenever(game.nextQuestion())
      .thenReturn(question1)
      .thenReturn(question2)
  setUpFactoryWithSuccessGame(game)
  viewModel.initGame()

  viewModel.nextQuestion()

  verify(questionObserver).onChanged(eq(question2))
}
```

Here, you can see you're stubbing the `nextQuestion()` method from a `Game` to first return `question1` and then `question2`.

To make it compile add the `nextQuestion()` method method to your ViewModel as follows:

```
fun nextQuestion() {
  // TODO
}
```

Now run your test to make sure that it fails. To fix it, replace your `nextQuestion()` with the following implementation:

```
fun nextQuestion() {
  game?.let {
    questionLiveData.value = it.nextQuestion()
  }
}
```

Then, inside your `onSuccess()` in `initGame()` modify it as follows:

```
override fun onSuccess(game: Game) {
  loadingLiveData.value = false
  errorLiveData.value = false
  scoreLiveData.value = game.score
  this@CocktailsGameViewModel.game = game
  nextQuestion()
}
```

Finally, add the game variable to the class:

```
private var game: Game? = null
```

Now, run your test and it will pass.

You have one more piece of functionality to implement. Answering a question should delegate to the `answer()` method of the `Game`, save the high score and show the next question and score — in that order. Start off by adding this test:

```
@Test
fun
answerQuestion_shouldDelegateToGame_saveHighScore_showQuestionAn
dScore() {
  val score = mock<Score>()
  val question = mock<Question>()
  whenever(game.score).thenReturn(score)
  setUpFactoryWithSuccessGame(game)
  viewModel.initGame()

  viewModel.answerQuestion(question, "VALUE")

  inOrder(game, repository, questionObserver, scoreObserver) {
    verify(game).answer(eq(question), eq("VALUE"))
    verify(repository).saveHighScore(any())
    verify(scoreObserver).onChanged(eq(score))
    verify(questionObserver).onChanged(eq(question))
  }
}
```

Notice, here, that you're using `inOrder()` again to check the methods are called exactly in the specified order.

Add the `answerQuestion()` method, to make it compile:

```
fun answerQuestion(question: Question, option: String) {
}
```

Now, run the test to make sure that it fails. Finally, add the corresponding implementation:

```
  fun answerQuestion(question: Question, option: String) {
    game?.let {
      it.answer(question, option)
      repository.saveHighScore(it.score.highest)
      scoreLiveData.value = it.score
      questionLiveData.value = question
    }
  }
```

Run the test and check it passes.

Mockito annotations

Instead of calling the `mock()` and `spy()` methods, you can use annotations. For example, open **RepositoryUnitTests.kt** and modify the class definition, variable definitions and setup functions to look like the following:

```
@RunWith(MockitoJUnitRunner::class)
class RepositoryUnitTests {
  private lateinit var repository: CocktailsRepository
  @Mock
  private lateinit var api: CocktailsApi
  @Mock
  private lateinit var sharedPreferences: SharedPreferences
  @Mock
  private lateinit var sharedPreferencesEditor:
      SharedPreferences.Editor

  @Before
  fun setup() {
    whenever(sharedPreferences.edit())
      .thenReturn(sharedPreferencesEditor)

    repository = CocktailsRepositoryImpl(api, sharedPreferences)
  }
```

> **Note**: Be sure to import `org.mockito.junit.MockitoJUnitRunner` when asked.

The `@RunWith(MockitoJUnitRunner::class)` annotation is to instruct that you are going to write tests using Mockito. Now, you can annotate using `@Mock` every property that you'll later use as mocks. Notice that in the `setup()` method, you removed the calls to `mock` for each property.

Run the tests and they will still pass.

You've been doing a lot of work getting logic correct in your app. To see it work in the UI, un-comment the commented implementation in **CocktailsGameActivity.kt**, **CocktailsGameViewModelFactory.kt** and **CocktailsApplication.kt** and run the app.

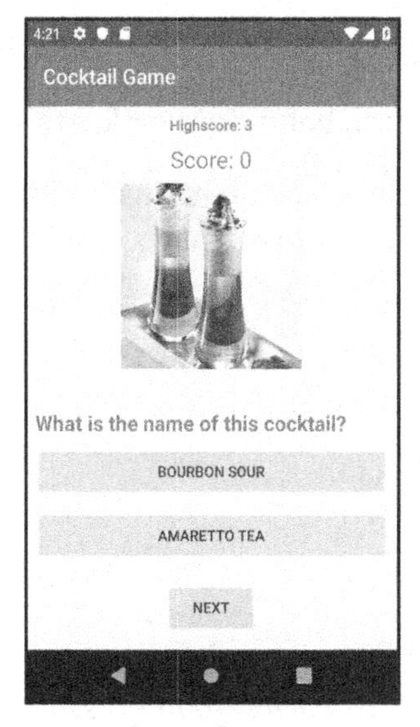

Game Screen

You now have a well-tested working cocktail game with the help of TDD.

Challenge

Challenge: Writing another test

- When answering incorrectly three times, it should finish the game.
- When answering correctly three times sequentially, it should start giving double score.

Write a test for each one, and add the corresponding functionality progressively to make each test pass.

Key points

- With **JUnit** you can do **state verification**, also called **black-box testing**.
- With **Mockito** you can perform **behavior verification** or **white-box testing**.
- Using a mock of a class will let you stub methods simulate a particular situation in a test. It'll also verify if one or more methods were called on that mock.
- Using a spy is similar to using a mock, but on real instances. You'll be able to stub a method and verify if a method was called just like a mock, but also be able to call the real methods of the instance.
- Remember: Red, Green, Refactor

Where to go from here?

Awesome! You've just learned the basics of unit testing with Mockito.

Check the materials for the final and challenge versions of the code of this chapter.

Check the following references to know more about the topic:

- *Test Double Patterns* by Gerard Meszaros: http://xunitpatterns.com/Test%20Double%20Patterns.html
- *Mocks Aren't Stubs* by Martin Fowlder: https://martinfowler.com/articles/mocksArentStubs.html

Chapter 8: Integration

By Victoria Gonda

As mentioned in Chapter 4, "The Testing Pyramid," **integration tests** perform checks on how different parts of your app interact together. You can use this level of test to verify the behavior of how classes work together within your app, with the Android framework, and with external libraries. It's the next level up from unit tests.

Unit tests are great for ensuring that all your individual pieces work. Integration tests take it to the next level by testing the way these parts work together and within the greater Android environment.

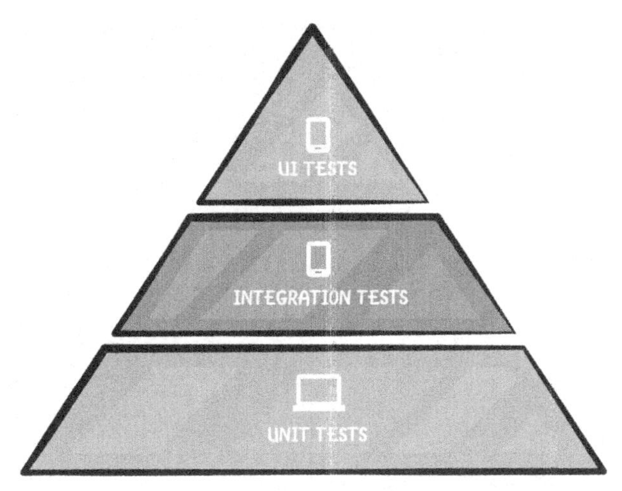

In this chapter, you'll:

- Learn what an integration test is and where are the best places to use them.
- Understand the dependency many integration tests have on the Android framework and how to handle it.
- Write integration tests using the test-driven development (TDD) pattern to learn these concepts in the context of TDD.

Getting started

To learn TDD with integration tests, you'll work on a **Wishlist** app. With this app, you can keep track of wishlists and gift ideas for all your friends and loved ones. You will continue working on this app in the next chapter.

Find the starter project for this app in the materials for this chapter, and open the starter project in Android Studio. Build and run the app. You'll see a blank screen with a button to add a list on the bottom. Clicking the button, you see a field to add a name for someone's wishlist. Enter all you want right now, but it won't save yet. You'll be able to see it when you finish the implementation. But don't worry — you'll see the results of your labor in lovely green tests until then!

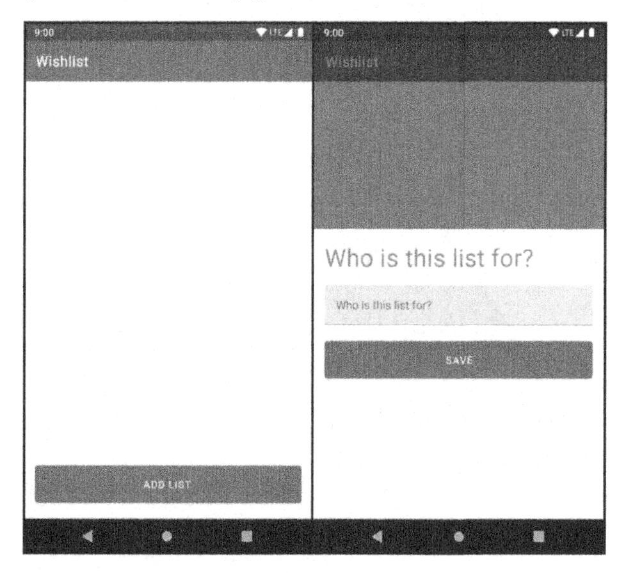

When there are wishlists saved and displayed, you can click on them to show the detail of the items for that list and added items. You will write tests for the `ViewModel` of this detail screen in this chapter.

In the end, this is what the app will look like:

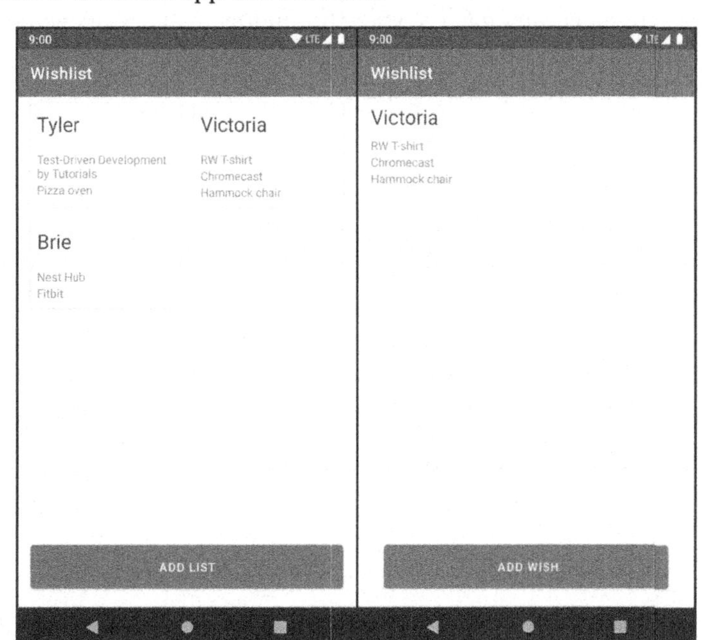

Explore the files in the app for a moment. The ones you need to be familiar with in this chapter are:

- **DetailViewModel.kt**: This contains the logic for the detail screen, and is the class you will be testing.
- **Repository.kt**: This is the interface for the data repository in this app.
- **RepositoryImpl.kt**: This is the implementation of the `Repository` interface.

When to use integration tests

Integration tests tend to be slower than unit tests, but quicker than UI tests. Because of this, you want to first put everything you can into unit tests. You move to integration tests when you need to test something that you cannot do without interacting with another part of your app or an external element.

Generally, when you want to create a unit test but can't test it in isolation, you want to use an integration test. Sometimes you can get away with extracting the logic out so it can be unit tested (and is preferable), but the integration test is inevitable at times.

While balancing the lean towards more unit tests, you also need to rely on integration tests to make sure each of your thoroughly tested units works well together with others. If your database works perfectly, as does your view model, it's still useless if the code linking them fails!

Testing with the Android framework

One of the most frequent dependencies that force you to use an integration test is the Android framework. This does not necessarily mean it uses the screen; it can be any component of the SDK. When your code ends up interacting with Android, you can't get away with unit tests. For example, in this chapter, you'll test the integration of the `ViewModel` down to the database. Because this test relies on other parts of the app, you need an integration test.

Once you implement the database in the next chapter, it will also rely on the Android framework. Because of that, you'll write this test as if it uses the Android framework already.

> **Note**: You may know that it is possible to test a `ViewModel` as a unit test. You saw an example in Chapter 7, "Introduction to Mockito." For this exercise, you are specifically testing the `ViewModel` in an integration fashion — testing that it works with its dependencies rather than mocking them. If you want to see an example of how to test a similar `ViewModel` as a unit test, take a look at **MainViewModelTest.kt** in the project for this chapter.

When running tests that require the Android framework you have two options:

1. Run them on an Android device or emulator.
2. Use **Robolectric**.

Robolectric is a framework that allows you to run Android-dependent tests in a unit-test way. It creates a sandbox in which to run your tests; the sandbox acts like an Android environment with Android APIs. A benefit to using Robolectric is that it's faster, running on the JVM. Using a device/emulator, however, more accurately shows how your code will behave when installed onto a device, having more Android features.

This chapter will show you how to use either a device/emulator or Robolectric. However, note that the final sample project is taking the emulator approach.

Creating a test class

Create a file called **DetailViewModelTest.kt** in the directory **app ▸ src ▸ androidTest ▸ java ▸ com ▸ raywenderlich ▸ android ▸ wishlist**. The key here is that it mimics the location of **DetailViewModel.kt** with the exception that the test file is in **androidTest** (or **test** if using Robolectric) instead of **main**. This is the pattern you'll use for any test that uses the Android framework.

Using the Create Test shortcut

There's also a shortcut to create test files as an alternative to manually creating them. Open **DetailViewModel.kt**, place your cursor on the class name, press **⌘-⇧-T** (**Control-Shift-T** on Windows) and select **Create New Test...**. Android Studio then shows you a dialog to create this file for you.

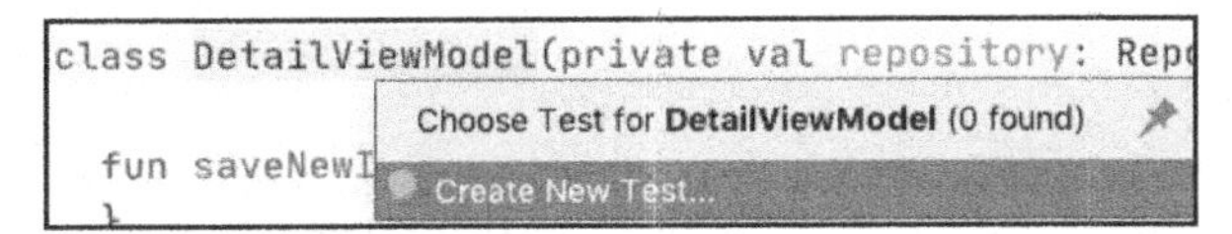

Select **Ok** to accept the defaults, then, select the **androidTest** option (or **test** when using Robolectric for writing a unit test), and the editor does the rest.

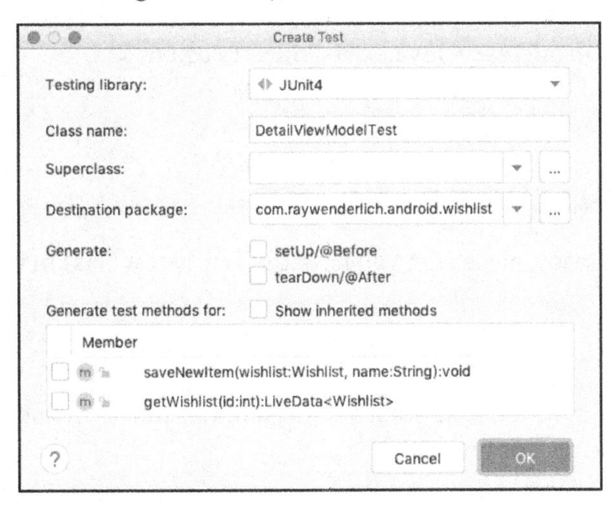

And then:

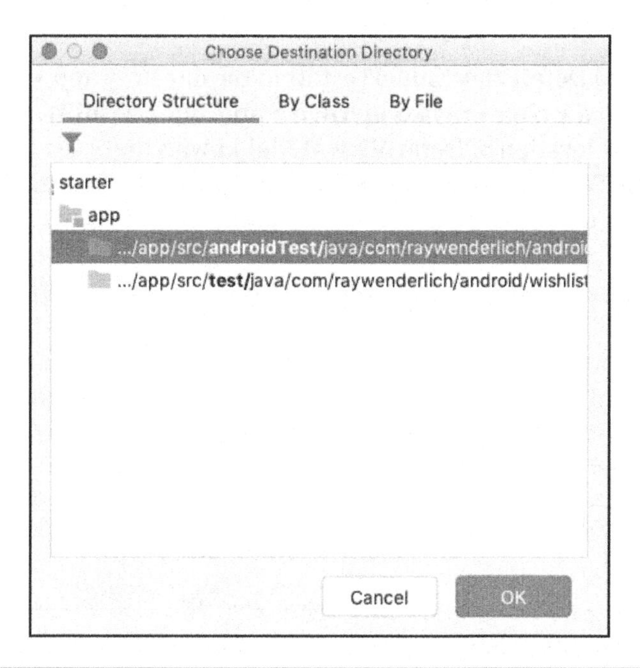

Note: If you do not see the option to choose a destination directory, make sure **app ▸ src ▸ androidTest ▸ java** exists, then try again.

Setting up the test class

If it's not there already, make sure you have the empty test class in your file:

```
class DetailViewModelTest {
}
```

Great! Now, make sure you have what you need to run your `ViewModel` test. Add the following test rule to your test class:

```
@get:Rule
var instantTaskExecutorRule = InstantTaskExecutorRule()
```

This is the same `TestRule` you used in Chapter 7, "Introduction to Mockito" to make sure that when you're using `LiveData` with the `ViewModel` it's all run synchronously in the tests.

Two more tasks before you're able to write a test: 1. You need an instance of the `DetailViewModel` to perform the tests on; 2. You'll need the dependency to create it. Add the following to your test class:

```
// 1
private val wishlistDao: WishlistDao =
    Mockito.spy(WishlistDaoImpl())
// 2
private val viewModel =
    DetailViewModel(RepositoryImpl(wishlistDao))
```

In the above, you:

1. Create a spy of `WishlistDao` to use to create the `Repository` dependency for the `DetailViewModel`. You're using Mockito to create the spy, as described in Chapter 7, "Introduction to Mockito." You could mock the repository here, instead, but in this example, you will test their interaction. To see an example of what a test would look like with the `Repository` mocked, take a look at **MainViewModelTest.kt**.
2. Create a `DetailViewModel`, with a `RepositoryImpl` created from your spy.

Using Robolectric

If you want to use Robolectric to run your tests, make sure your test is using **test** in the package structure instead of **androidTest**.

> **Note**: The materials included for this chapter use the device/emulator approach rather than use Robolectric. All Robolectric steps are optional and are there to help you if you're interested in using the library.

Then, add the following code within the `andorid` block in **app ▸ build.gradle**:

```
testOptions {
  unitTests.includeAndroidResources = true
}
```

This ensures that you can use Android resources in your unit tests.

Then, add the Robolectric dependency within the `dependencies` block in the same file:

```
testImplementation 'org.robolectric:robolectric:4.5-alpha-3'
testImplementation 'androidx.test.ext:junit:1.1.2'
```

This adds both the Robolectric and AndroidX Test APIs. As of Robolectric 4.0, Robolectic is compatible with these Android testing libraries, as you'll see in a moment.

> **Note**: You're using an alpha version of Robolectric because Robolectric 4.4 only supports up to SDK 29, and at the time of this writing, Robolectric 4.5 is in alpha stages.

Gradle sync to apply your changes.

In **DetailViewModelTest.kt**, right above the class declaration add:

```
@RunWith(AndroidJUnit4::class)
```

This test runner will delegate to the appropriate runner to run Android tests. In this case, it will delegate to the `RobolectricTestRunner`.

Writing a failing integration test

In the fashion of TDD, write some tests before adding the implementation of `DetailViewModel`. Starting with the `saveNewItem()` function, write a test that verifies that saving a new item calls the database using the Data Access Object (DAO):

```
@Test
fun saveNewItemCallsDatabase() {
  // 1
  viewModel.saveNewItem(Wishlist("Victoria",
      listOf("RW Android Apprentice Book", "Android phone"), 1),
      "Smart watch")
  // 2
  verify(wishlistDao).save(any())
}
```

Here, you:

1. Call the `saveNewItem()` function with data. You can use your name and wishes if you like!

2. Verify that `saveNewItem()` called the `save()` function on the DAO using the same technique learned in Chapter 7, "Introduction to Mockito."

This is an example of a "white-box test" that you learned about in Chapter 7, "Introduction to Mockito".

Build and run your test to see it fail. You'll need an emulator running or a device attached for the Android test to run on.

```
Wanted but not invoked:
wishlistDao_Impl.save(
<any com.raywenderlich.android.wishlist.Wishlist>
);
-> at com.raywenderlich.android.wishlist
  .persistance.WishlistDao_Impl.save(Unknown
  Source:34)
Actually, there were zero interactions with this
  mock.
```

This error is saying that the `save()` function was never called on the `wishlistDao`. You know what you need to do to make it pass — keep moving on!

Making the test pass

Next step! The function needs to call `save()` on the DAO (and *only* call `save()`). Add the following to `saveNewItem()` in `DetailViewModel`:

```
repository.saveWishlistItem(Wishlist("", listOf()))
```

Run the test, and see it pass.

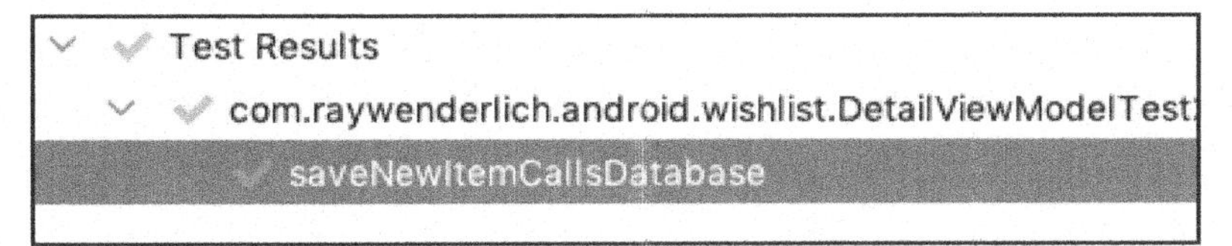

Testing the wishlist's save functionality

Repeat the TDD pattern for three more tests:

1. One similar to the above test that makes sure `saveNewItem()` saves the correct data.
2. One that `getWishList()` calls the database using the DAO.
3. One that ensures correct data returns when calling `getWishList()`.

Add the first test to your test class:

```
@Test
fun saveNewItemSavesData() {
  // 1
  val wishlist = Wishlist("Victoria",
      listOf("RW Android Apprentice Book", "Android phone"), 1)
  // 2
  val name = "Smart watch"
  viewModel.saveNewItem(wishlist, name)

  // 3
  val mockObserver = mock<Observer<Wishlist>>()
  // 4
  wishlistDao.findById(wishlist.id)
      .observeForever(mockObserver)
  verify(mockObserver).onChanged(
      wishlist.copy(wishes = wishlist.wishes + name))
}
```

With this test, you:

1. Create a new wishlist.
2. Create a new item name for the list and call `saveNewItem()`.
3. Create a mock `Observer` to use as you've done in Chapter 7, "Introduction to Mockito."
4. Query the database and ensure that the wishlist you saved returns, signaling it saved correctly. When the program posts a value to a `LiveData`, the object calls `onChanged()` with the value. This is the function you are checking for.

It's the same pattern: creating test data as your setup, calling the function, then verifying the result.

Build and run the test to make sure it fails before modifying the `DetailViewModel` to make it pass.

```
Argument(s) are different! Wanted:
observer.onChanged(
Wishlist(receiver=Victoria, wishes=[RW Android
  Apprentice Book, Android phone, Smart watch],
  id=1)
);
-> at com.raywenderlich.android.wishlist
  .DetailViewModelTest.saveNewItemSavesData
  (DetailViewModelTest.kt:54)
Actual invocation has different arguments:
observer.onChanged(
Wishlist(receiver=, wishes=[], id=1)
);
```

It's the expected error you see. The function called `save()`, but it saved the wrong thing!

Once you see that it's failing, change the body of `saveNewItem()` to make it pass:

```
repository.saveWishlistItem(
    wishlist.copy(wishes = wishlist.wishes + name))
```

> **Note**: You may be wondering why you're making a copy of the wishlist here instead of mutating it. This is to follow the safety of immutability. You can learn more about this in "Functional Programming for Android Developers" https://medium.freecodecamp.org/functional-programming-for-android-developers-part-2-5c0834669d1a.

Run it again to see it pass.

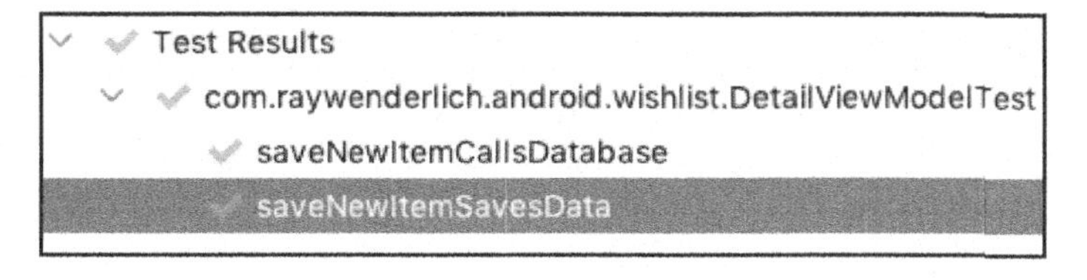

Testing the database queries

Add the next test to ensure that `getWishlist()` calls the database:

```
@Test
fun getWishListCallsDatabase() {
  viewModel.getWishlist(1)

  verify(wishlistDao).findById(any())
}
```

This looks very similar to your first test in this class. Run it and see it fail.

```
Wanted but not invoked:
wishlistDao_Impl.findById(
<any java.lang.Integer>
);
-> at com.raywenderlich.android.wishlist
  .persistance.WishlistDao_Impl.findById(Unknown
  Source:38)
Actually, there were zero interactions with this
  mock.
```

There's the message that says you need to implement that call to the `wishlistDao`.

Once you've run your failing test, change the code in `getWishList()` to make it pass:

```
return repository.getWishlist(0)
```

Run all the tests that you've written in this chapter. Hooray! All three tests are passing!

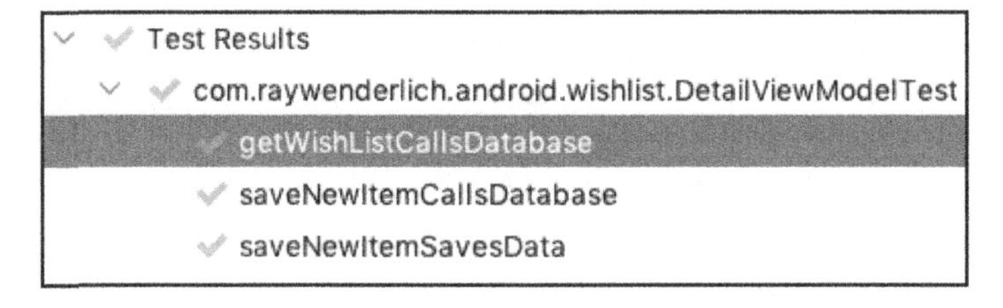

Testing the data returned

Your last test in this chapter is to make sure `getWishlist()` returns the correct data. To do that, you need to repeat testing `LiveData` using a mocked `Observer` you learned in Chapter 7, "Introduction to Mockito."

Add this final test to your test class:

```
@Test
fun getWishListReturnsCorrectData() {
  // 1
  val wishlist = Wishlist("Victoria",
      listOf("RW Android Apprentice Book", "Android phone"), 1)
  // 2
  wishlistDao.save(wishlist)
  // 3
  val mockObserver = mock<Observer<Wishlist>>()
  viewModel.getWishlist(1).observeForever(mockObserver)
  // 4
  verify(mockObserver).onChanged(wishlist)
}
```

Taking each part in turn:

1. Again, you set up your test data.
2. Save a wishlist to the database to be retrieved later in this test.
3. Create a `mockObserver`, mocking a lifecycle `Observer`. You use this observer to `observeForever()` on the `LiveData` that `getWishlist()` returns.
4. Verify that the function published the correct data.

Run your test to make sure it fails.

```
Argument(s) are different! Wanted:
observer.onChanged(
Wishlist(receiver=Victoria, wishes=[RW Android
  Apprentice Book, Android phone], id=1)
);
-> at com.raywenderlich.android.wishlist
  .DetailViewModelTest
  .getWishListReturnsCorrectData
  (DetailViewModelTest.kt:77)
Actual invocation has different arguments:
observer.onChanged(
null
);
```

Attempt to invoke observeForever on a null object reference

This error says that `getWishlist()` is returning `null`! Sure, you mocked it, but only when you use an id of `1`, the id you're passing into `getWishlist()`. If you look in the `DetailViewModel`, right now there is a `0` hardcoded in for the id. Change the body of the `getWishlist()` function to use the id that's passed in:

```
return repository.getWishlist(id)
```

Run the test again. You can do this by clicking on the **Run Test** button near the name of the test class.

```
class DetailViewModelTest
```

All green! Great job!

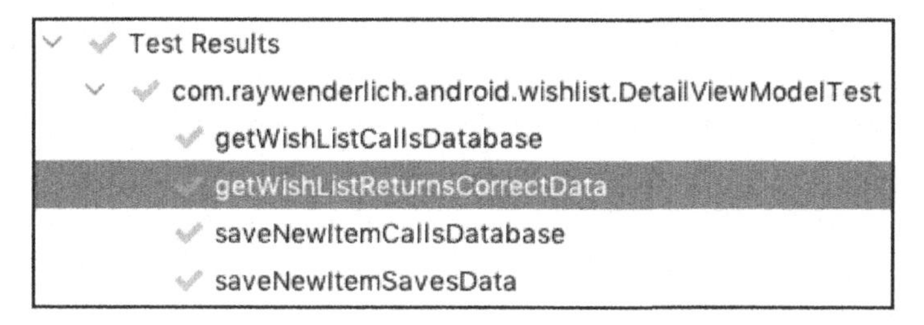

Refactoring

Now that you have green tests for `DetailViewModel` and how it interacts with `LiveData` and the database, you can refactor with confidence.

Take a look at `saveNewItem()` in `DetailViewModel`. It's doing a bit of work to format the `Wishlist` for saving:

```
fun saveNewItem(wishlist: Wishlist, name: String) {
  repository.saveWishlistItem(
      wishlist.copy(wishes = wishlist.wishes + name))
}
```

One could argue that this responsibility belongs to the repository. Why not perform that refactoring!

There are three files you need to change to refactor this, and it won't compile until you've done all three.

1. In `DetailViewModel` change the contents of `saveNewItem()` to be:

```
repository.saveWishlistItem(wishlist, name)
```

2. In the `Repository` interface, change the `saveWishlistItem()` signature to this:

```
fun saveWishlistItem(wishlist: Wishlist, name: String)
```

3. In `RepositoryImpl`, change the body of `saveWishlistItem()` to have the logic you deleted from the `DetailViewModel`, and the signature to match the interface:

```
override fun saveWishlistItem(
  wishlist: Wishlist,
  name: String
) {
  wishlistDao.save(
    wishlist.copy(wishes = wishlist.wishes + name))
}
```

Run the tests to make sure nothing broke during the refactor.

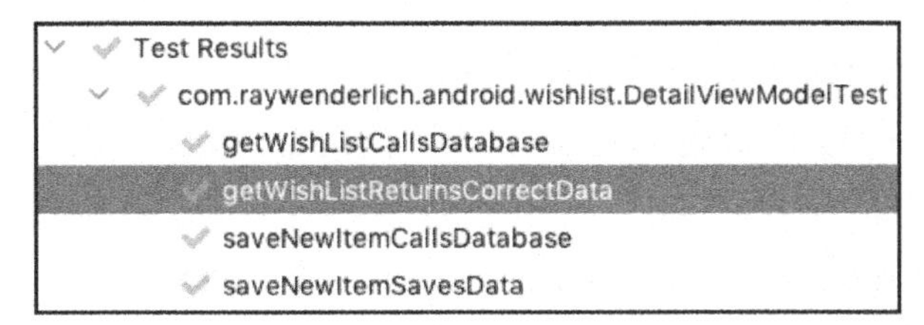

It didn't — congratulations!

Running the app

After all your hard work, you can see your app in action! Build and run the app, and play around with creating wishlists. In the next chapter, you'll be able to add items.

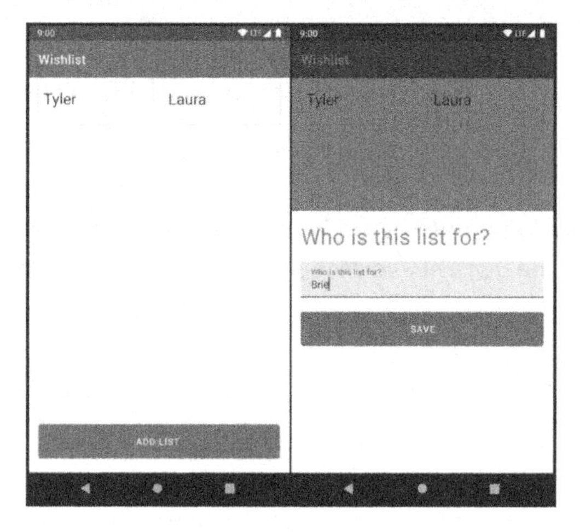

Key points

- Integration tests verify the way different parts of your app work together.
- They are slower than unit tests, and should therefore only be used when you need to test how things interact.
- When interacting with the Android framework you can rely on an Android device or emulator, or use Robolectric.
- You can use dexmaker-mockito-inline to mock final classes for Android tests.

Where to go from here?

You can find the final version of the code in this chapter in the chapter materials.

If you want to continue exploring integration tests in this app, take a look at **MainViewModelTest.kt** at the tests already written there.

There's much more that you can do with integration tests than `ViewModel` tests. In Chapter 9, "Testing the Persistence Layer," you'll learn how you can test your persistence layer, and Chapter 10, "Testing the Network Layer," introduces the network layer.

For more about integration testing, you can look at the Android documentation:

- https://developer.android.com/training/testing/fundamentals#medium-tests
- https://developer.android.com/training/testing/integration-testing/

Chapter 9: Testing the Persistence Layer

By Victoria Gonda

In most apps you'll build, you will store data in one way or another. It might be in shared preferences, in a database, or otherwise. No matter which way you're saving it, you need to be confident it is always working. If a user takes the time to put together content and then loses it because your persistence code broke, both you and your user will have a sad day.

You have the tools for mocking out a persistence layer interface from Chapter 7, "Introduction to Mockito." In this chapter you will take it a step further, testing that when you interact with a database, it behaves the way you expect.

In this chapter you will learn:

- How to use TDD to have a well-tested RoomDB database.
- Why persistence testing can be difficult.
- Which parts of your persistence layer should you test.

> **Note**: It is helpful, but not necessary to have a basic understanding of RoomDB. To brush up on the basics, check out our tutorial, "Data Persistence with Room": https://www.raywenderlich.com/69-data-persistence-with-room.

Getting started

To learn about testing the persistence layer you will write tests while building up a RoomDB database for the Wishlist app. This app provides a place where you can keep track of the wishlists and gift ideas for all your friends and loved ones.

To get started, find the starter project included for this chapter and open it up in Android Studio, or continue with the project from Chapter 8, "Integration."

Build and run the app. You'll see a blank screen with a button to add a list on the bottom. Clicking the button, you see a field to add a name for someone's wishlist. You can add a name, but it will be gone next time you open the app! You will implement the persistence layer to save the wishlist in this chapter.

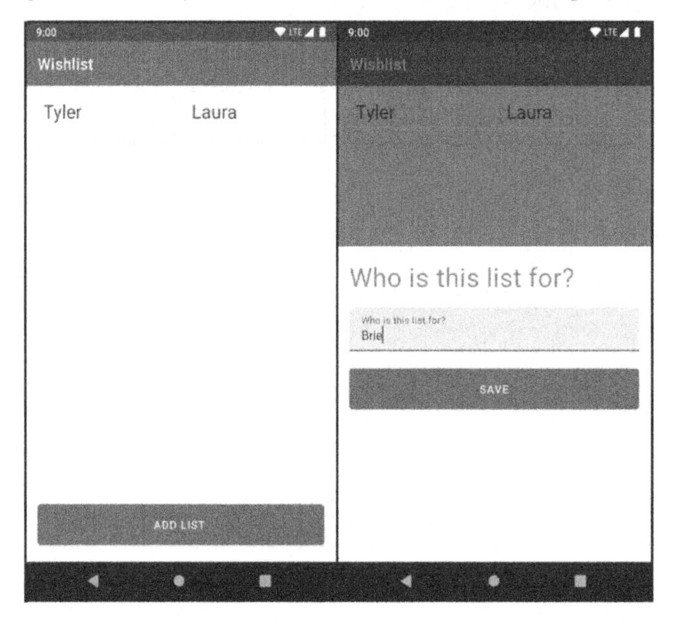

When there are wishlists saved and displayed, you can click on them to show the detail of the items for that list, and add items. By the end of this chapter, this is what the app will look like:

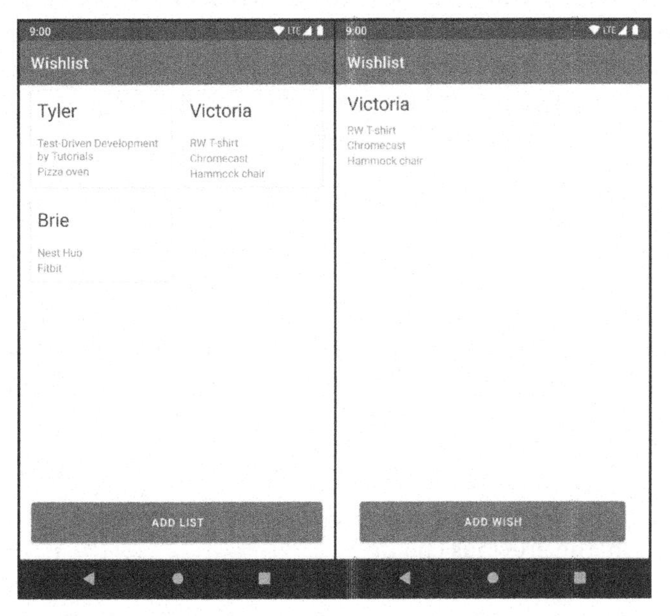

Time to get familiar with the code.

Exploring the project

There are a couple of files you should be familiar with before getting started. Open these files and take a look around:

- **WishlistDao.kt**: Is the database access object. You will work on defining the database interactions in this class. This is also the class you will write your tests for. Notice that right now the Dao interactions are stubbed out in `WishlistDaoImpl`.
- **RepositoryImpl.kt**: This class should be familiar to you from Chapter 8, "Integration." It's the repository that hooks your app up with the database.
- **KoinModules.kt**: This handles the dependency injection for the app, specifying how to create any dependencies.
- **StringListConverter.kt**: This is a helper object to convert lists of `Strings` to a single `String` and back again to store in the database.

Setting up the test class

As with any test, the first thing you need to do is create the file. Create **WishlistDaoTest.kt** in **app ▸ src ▸ androidTest ▸ java ▸ com ▸ raywenderlich ▸ android ▸ wishlist ▸ persistence**. In it, create an empty class with the `@RunWith` annotation. The import you want for `AndroidJUnit4` is `androidx.test.ext.junit.runners.AndroidJUnit4`:

```
@RunWith(AndroidJUnit4::class)
class WishlistDaoTest {
}
```

In this context, the test runner facilitates loading your test package and the app under test onto a device or emulator, running your tests, and reporting the results. You might recall from the Robolectric discussion in the previous chapter that it can also delegate to Robolectric.

> **Note**: You can use Robolectric for this test, too, if you follow the instructions to set it up from the previous chapter.

Continuing your set up, add the following test rule to your test class:

```
@get:Rule
var instantTaskExecutorRule = InstantTaskExecutorRule()
```

Android Architecture Components uses an asynchronous background executor to do its work. `InstantTaskExecutorRule` is a rule that swaps out that executor and replaces it with a synchronous one. This will make sure that, when you're using `LiveData`, it's all run synchronously in the tests.

You also need to create the properties to hold your `WishlistDatabase` and `WishlistDao`. Add these properties to your test class now:

```
private lateinit var wishlistDatabase: WishlistDatabase
private lateinit var wishlistDao: WishlistDao
```

The `WishlistDao` is what you are performing your tests on. To create an instance of this class, you'll need an instance of the `WishlistDatabase` first. You will initialize these in a `@Before` block in a moment.

Setting up the database

Right now, the `WishlistDao` has a fake implementation so it would compile for the previous chapter. Because you want to use a real DAO with a real database in this chapter, you need to set that up. Take a moment to make the following changes. Note that the app will not compile until all the following steps are complete.

Start by opening **WishlistDatabase.kt** and add the following abstract method:

```
abstract fun wishlistDao(): WishlistDao
```

This tells the Database to look for and build the `WishlistDao`.

Then, open **WishlistDao.kt** and annotate the interface with `@Dao` to round out the connections. Leave the fake implementation for now so the app can compile. You'll swap it out for your real one at the end of this chapter.

Using an in-memory database

One of the challenges that make writing persistence tests difficult is managing the state before and after the tests run. You're testing saving and retrieving data, but you don't want to end your test run with a bunch of test data on your device or emulator. How can you save data while your tests are running, but ensure that test data is gone when the tests finish? You could consider erasing the whole database, but if you have your own non-test data saved in the database outside of the tests, that would delete too.

Tests must be repeatable. This means you should be able to run a test multiple times with the same result. There's also a requirement that one test cannot influence the outcome of another. What if you're testing for an empty database but there are items left over from another test? You will need to clear data between tests.

You can solve this problem by using an **in-memory database**. RoomDB luckily provides a way to easily create one. Add this to your test class:

```
@Before
fun initDb() {
  // 1
  wishlistDatabase = Room.inMemoryDatabaseBuilder(
      ApplicationProvider.getApplicationContext(),
      WishlistDatabase::class.java).build()
  // 2
  wishlistDao = wishlistDatabase.wishlistDao()
}
```

1. Here you're using a RoomDB builder to create an in-memory `WishlistDatabase`. Compare this to the database creation you'll add to **KoinModules.kt** at the end of this chapter. Information stored in an in-memory database disappears when the tests finish, solving your state issue.
2. You then use this database to get your `WishlistDao`.

> **Note**: If you're using Robolectric, add `.allowMainThreadQueries()` before your `.build()`.

Almost done setting up! After your tests finish, you also need to close your database. Add this to your test class:

```
@After
fun closeDb() {
  wishlistDatabase.close()
}
```

Now you're ready to start writing tests.

Writing a test

Test number one is going to test that when there's nothing saved, `getAll()` returns an empty list. This is a function for fetching all of the wishlists from the database. Add the following test, using the imports `androidx.lifecycle.Observer` for `Observer`, and `org.mockito.kotlin.*` for `mock()` and `verify()`:

```
@Test
fun getAllReturnsEmptyList() {
  val testObserver: Observer<List<Wishlist>> = mock()
  wishlistDao.getAll().observeForever(testObserver)
  verify(testObserver).onChanged(emptyList())
}
```

This tests the result of a `LiveData` response similar to how you wrote your tests in Chapter 7, "Introduction to Mockito." You create a mock `Observer`, observe the `LiveData` returned from `getAll()` with it, and verify the result is an empty list.

Everything looks pretty good, so try to run the test.

Oh no! There's a compiler error.

```
/persistance/WishlistDao.java:10: error: An abstract DAO method must be annotated with one and only one of the
following annotations: Insert,Delete,Query,Update,RawQuery
    public abstract androidx.lifecycle.LiveData<java.util.List<com.raywenderlich.android.wishlist.Wishlist>> getAll();
                                                                                                              ^
```

An abstract DAO method must be annotated with one and only one of the following annotations

Hmmm. The next minimum thing to make this test run is to add a `@Query` annotation. Add an empty query annotation to `getAll()`:

```
@Query("")
```

Try running it with this change. If you are familiar with RoomDB, you may know what's coming.

```
/persistance/WishlistDao.java:11: error: Must have exactly 1 query in the value of @Query or @DatabaseView
    public abstract androidx.lifecycle.LiveData<java.util.List<com.raywenderlich.android.wishlist.Wishlist>> getAll();
                                                                                                              ^
```

Must have exactly 1 query in the value of @Query

The compiler enforces that you include a query in the parameter. That means the next step is to fill in the query as simply as possible. Fill in your query with the following:

```
@Query("SELECT * FROM wishlist")
```

Finally, RoomDB requires all the abstract methods in the DAO class to have annotations, so go ahead and add the following incorrect annotations to the other two methods.

```
@Query("SELECT * FROM wishlist WHERE id != :id")
fun findById(id: Int): LiveData<Wishlist>

@Delete
fun save(vararg wishlist: Wishlist)
```

Run your test and it finally compiles! But… it's passing. When practicing TDD you always want to see your tests fail first. You never saw a state where the test was compiling and failing. You were so careful to only add the smallest bits until it compiled. RoomDB made it hard to write something that didn't work. Maybe the real question is "Should you be testing this?" The answer to this question is important.

Knowing not to test the library

The fact that RoomDB made it hard to write a failing test is a clue. When your tests align closely with a library or framework, you want to be sure you're testing **your** code and not the third-party code. If you really want to write tests for that library, you might be able to contribute to the library, if it's an open-source project. ;]

Sometimes this is a gray line to try to find, and it's one of the things that makes testing persistence difficult. It's a part of your code that likely relies heavily on a framework.

It's a balance to test that your interactions with the framework or library are correct without testing the library itself. Watch out for cases like these and use your best judgment. Over time you'll gain intuition on which tests are valuable, and what tests are better left to the library's contributors.

In this case, it's not up to you to test the RoomDB framework. It's those writing RoomDB's responsibility to make sure that when the database is empty, it returns nothing. Instead, you want to test that your logic, your queries, and the code that depends on them are working correctly.

With that in mind, you can move on to test other database interactions.

Testing an insert

With any persistence layer, you need to be able to save some data and retrieve it. That's exactly what your next test will do. Add this test to your class:

```
@Test
fun saveWishlistsSavesData() {
  // 1
  val wishlist1 = Wishlist("Victoria", listOf(), 1)
  val wishlist2 = Wishlist("Tyler", listOf(), 2)
  wishlistDao.save(wishlist1, wishlist2)

  // 2
  val testObserver: Observer<List<Wishlist>> = mock()
  wishlistDao.getAll().observeForever(testObserver)

  // 3
  val listClass =
      ArrayList::class.java as Class<ArrayList<Wishlist>>
  val argumentCaptor = ArgumentCaptor.forClass(listClass)
  // 4
  verify(testObserver).onChanged(argumentCaptor.capture())
```

```
  // 5
  assertTrue(argumentCaptor.value.size > 0)
}
```

Here you:

1. Create a couple of wishlists and save them to the database. At this point `save()` does not exist yet, so there will be an error.
2. Use your mock `testObserver` again to call `getAll()`.
3. Create an `ArgumentCaptor` to capture the value in `onChanged()`. Using an `ArgumentCaptor` from Mockito allows you to make more complex assertions on a value than `equals()`.
4. Use `verify` method to capture the argument passed to the `onChanged()` method.
5. Test that the result from the database is a non-empty list. At this point you care that data was saved and not *what* was saved, so you're checking the list size only.

Great! Remember, this is currently the `save()` function you have in `WishlistDao`:

```
@Delete
fun save(vararg wishlist: Wishlist)
```

You need to have a database interaction annotation for this to compile, as you learned earlier in this chapter. You also want to see this test failing, so you're using the wrong one, `@Delete`. Run your test and see it fail.

```
junit.framework.AssertionFailedError <3 internal calls>
at com.raywenderlich.android.wishlist.persistence.WishlistDaoTest.saveWishlistsSavesData(WishlistDaoTest.kt:54)
```

AssertionFailedError

You know the drill, time to make this test green!

Making your test pass

This one is simple enough to make it pass. Just change the `@Delete` annotation with an `@Insert`. Your `save()` signature should now look like this:

```
@Insert(onConflict = OnConflictStrategy.REPLACE)
fun save(vararg wishlist: Wishlist)
```

Using `OnConflictStrategy.REPLACE` allows the database to override an entry that already exists.

Run your tests, and they should all be green.

Testing your query

Now that you have a way to save data in your database, you can test your `getAll()` query for real! Add this test:

```
@Test
fun getAllRetrievesData() {
  val wishlist1 = Wishlist("Victoria", emptyList(), 1)
  val wishlist2 = Wishlist("Tyler", emptyList(), 2)
  wishlistDao.save(wishlist1, wishlist2)

  val testObserver: Observer<List<Wishlist>> = mock()
  wishlistDao.getAll().observeForever(testObserver)

  val listClass =
      ArrayList::class.java as Class<ArrayList<Wishlist>>
  val argumentCaptor = ArgumentCaptor.forClass(listClass)
  verify(testObserver).onChanged(argumentCaptor.capture())
  val capturedArgument = argumentCaptor.value
  assertTrue(capturedArgument
      .containsAll(listOf(wishlist1, wishlist2)))
}
```

This is almost the same as your previous test except for the final line. In that line, you're testing that the list result contains the *exact* wishlists you expect.

Build and run your tests. It may come as a surprise, but they failed! Why is that? Insert a debugger breakpoint on the assertion line and inspect the `capturedArgument` at that point when you run it again, using the debugger. Huh! Somehow there is a list with an empty string in it.

```
capturedArgument = {ArrayList@13298} size = 2
  0 = {Wishlist@13329} "Wishlist(receiver=Victoria, wishes=[], id=1)"
    id = 1
    receiver = "Victoria"
    wishes = {ArrayList@13334} size = 1
      0 = ""
```

Good investigating! You found the bug *before* it reached production. Time to solve the problem.

Fixing the bug

How could this happen? `StringListConverter` holds the key. Take a look at the object. In `stringToStringList()`, when there is an empty `String` saved in the database, as is the case for an empty list, the split function used returns a list with an empty string in it! Now that you know the problem, you can solve it.

Replace the body of `stringToStringList()` with:

```
if (!string.isNullOrBlank()) string.split("|").toMutableList()
else mutableListOf()
```

Now run those tests again and see them pass!

> **Note**: All over while testing you'll be performing verifications that rely heavily on the `equals()` method to perform comparisons. `containsAll()` is one of them. Much of the time in these cases you are looking for data equality (the properties of both objects are the same) rather than object equality (they reference the same object in memory). Because of this, you want to make sure your `equals()` performs the way you expect. In Kotlin, this is often as simple as making your class a `data class`. This overrides `equals()` and `hashcode()` for you to compare the properties. Take caution for the times where this isn't enough! For example, Kotlin may not compare `Lists` the way you expect. For that reason `equals()` and `hashcode()` are overridden for `Wishlist` in this app. You can see this in **Wishlist.kt**.

Testing a new query

Moving on. In your database you also need the ability to retrieve an item by id. To create this functionality, start by adding a test for it:

```
@Test
fun findByIdRetrievesCorrectData() {
  // 1
  val wishlist1 = Wishlist("Victoria", emptyList(), 1)
  val wishlist2 = Wishlist("Tyler", emptyList(), 2)
  wishlistDao.save(wishlist1, wishlist2)
  // 2
  val testObserver: Observer<Wishlist> = mock()

wishlistDao.findById(wishlist2.id).observeForever(testObserver)
  verify(testObserver).onChanged(wishlist2)
}
```

Here, you:

1. Create and save some wishlists, same as your other tests.
2. Query for a specific wishlist, `wishlist2`, and verify the result is correct.

As a reminder, this is what you have in `WishlistDao`:

```
@Query("SELECT * FROM wishlist WHERE id != :id")
fun findById(id: Int): LiveData<Wishlist>
```

Notice it's intentionally incorrect. It's searching for a wishlist where the id is **not** the given id. This is again to make sure you see a failing test.

Run that test and verify it really does fail.

```
Argument(s) are different! Wanted:
observer.onChanged(
Wishlist(receiver=Tyler, wishes=[], id=2)
);
-> at com.raywenderlich.android.wishlist.persistence.WishlistDaoTest
  .findByIdRetrievesCorrectData(WishlistDaoTest.kt:87)
Actual invocation has different arguments:
observer.onChanged(
Wishlist(receiver=Victoria, wishes=[], id=1)
);
```

Arguments are different

Making the test pass

It's the last time you'll do it in this chapter: make that test green! All you need to do is remove that not (!) from the query. It should now look like this:

```
@Query("SELECT * FROM wishlist WHERE id = :id")
```

Ready? Run your tests to see them all pass.

Creating test data

You have a working database with reliable tests but there's more that you can do. There is something you can do to also help save setup time as you write other tests. This tool is called **test data creation**.

If you look at the tests you've written in this chapter, as well as Chapter 8, "Integration," you see many lines where you're manually creating a `Wishlist`. Not only is this tedious, but you're only testing that your code works for that specific `Wishlist`.

One way to abstract this work and make your data random is by using a **Factory**. A Factory object will create instances of your data class with random values for the properties. This will make your tests stronger and easier to write!

Start by creating a `WishlistFactory` object in your test directory. As this is specific to your persistence right now, a good place to put it is **app ▸ src ▸ androidTest ▸ java ▸ com ▸ raywenderlich ▸ android ▸ wishlist ▸ persistence ▸ WishlistFactory.kt**:

```
object WishlistFactory {
}
```

If you use this in other places as well, you can move this Factory to a more convenient location. Since you're only using it in this one test right now, this location works great.

You need a way to create random values for your data class properties. A simple way to do this is to create helper methods to create them, one for each type of property you need. Again, you could place these in a reusable location, but because you're only using them here right now, they can share the `WishlistFactory`.

In your `Wishlist` you need two types of data: `String` and `Int`. Add these methods to your `WishlistFactory`:

```
// 1
private fun makeRandomString() = UUID.randomUUID().toString()
// 2
private fun makeRandomInt() =
    ThreadLocalRandom.current().nextInt(0, 1000 + 1)
```

These are simple, built-in ways to create random values. You can use similar ways to create helpers for `Long`, `Boolean`, etc.

Now, to finish the Factory, add a method to create a `Wishlist`:

```
fun makeWishlist(): Wishlist {
  return Wishlist(
      makeRandomString(),
      listOf(makeRandomString(), makeRandomString()),
      makeRandomInt())
}
```

You use the random value methods you just created to set the properties, knowing you will likely have a completely different `Wishlist` every time you create one. They won't look anything like what's on *your* wishlist, but they will be unique. Well, the `Wishlist` won't have what you want unless you want a UUID for your birthday.

Using a Factory in your test

You now have an easy way to create test data, so why not use it? Refactor your tests so that each time you create a `Wishlist`, you use the factory instead. It should look like this in each of your tests:

```
val wishlist1 = WishlistFactory.makeWishlist()
val wishlist2 = WishlistFactory.makeWishlist()
```

So clean! Run your tests to make sure they still pass.

Hooking up your database

You now have beautiful, tested database interactions, so surely you want to see them in action! Before you run the app, open up **KoinModules.kt** and change `single<WishlistDao> { WishlistDaoImpl() }` to:

```
single {
  Room.databaseBuilder(
      get(),
      WishlistDatabase::class.java, "wishlist-database"
  )
      .allowMainThreadQueries()
      .build().wishlistDao()
}
```

All this is doing is hooking up dependency injection to use your real database rather than your fake DAO. You're ready to build and run the app!

Play around with your fully functioning app! Create some Wishlists and add some items to them. You'll always know the perfect gift to give now.

See the results:

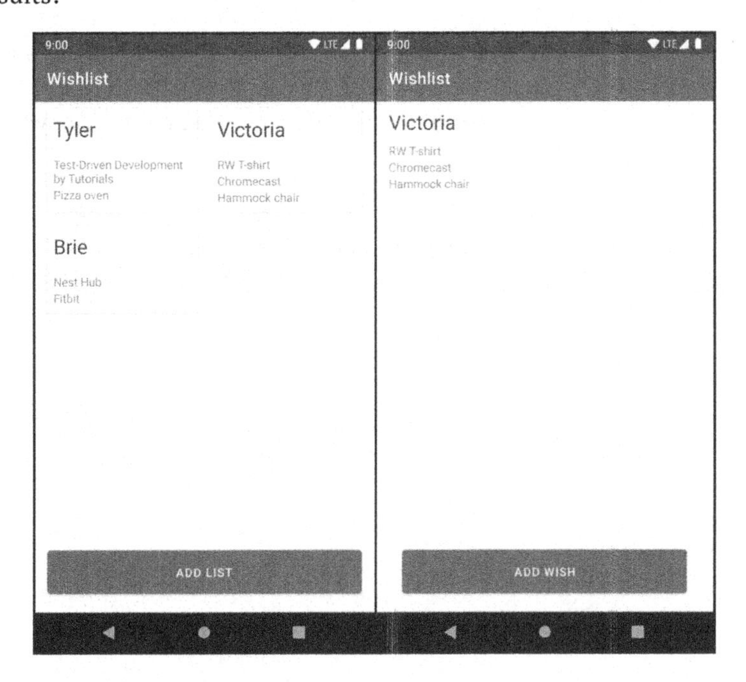

Optional: Updating your integration test

The integration test, `DetailViewModelTest`, that you wrote in the last chapter is still using the fake DAO implementation. Wouldn't it be great to use the real one and delete the fake one?

Open **DetailViewModelTest.kt** and replace the initialization of the `WishlistDao` with the following:

```
private val wishlistDao: WishlistDao = Mockito.spy(
    Room.inMemoryDatabaseBuilder(
        ApplicationProvider.getApplicationContext(),
        WishlistDatabase::class.java)
        .allowMainThreadQueries()
        .build().wishlistDao())
```

This swaps out the fake with the real one! No more imposters here. Go ahead and delete `WishlistDaoImpl`.

> **Note**: In the above block, `allowMainThreadQueries()` is only required if you're using Robolectric.

Using Dexmaker

One final thing. The `WishlistDao` implementation that RoomDB provides is a final class, which means you can't spy on it using Mockito. While in Chapter 7, "Introduction to Mockito" you used the mock-maker-inline extension, you cannot use that in Android tests.

> **Note**: If you're using Robolectric, add `testImplementation "org.mockito:mockito-inline:3.2.0"` as a dependency instead of the below Dexmaker.

You'll use Dexmaker (https://github.com/linkedin/dexmaker) to accomplish this.

> There are other options for mocking final classes in your Android tests you can look into if you prefer:
>
> - **MockK**: https://mockk.io/
> - **DexOpener**: https://github.com/tmurakami/dexopener

Start by adding the following dependency to **app ‣ build.gradle**:

```
androidTestImplementation 'com.linkedin.dexmaker:dexmaker-
mockito-inline:2.28.1'
```

Then, because they include duplicate resources, delete these dependencies:

```
androidTestImplementation 'org.mockito:mockito-android:3.10.0'
```

You're all set! Now, run `DetailViewModelTest` to see your nice green tests.

Handling stateful tests

In this chapter, you learned hands-on how to handle the statefulness of your tests using an in-memory database. You need this set up and tear down to write reliable, repeatable persistence tests, but how do you handle it when you're using something other than RoomDB for your persistence?

Unfortunately, many libraries don't have these convenient, built-in testing helpers.

Some do, such as Realm, but often you're left in the dust. In these cases, you're usually left to clear the persisted data before each test. When doing this, make sure your testing device doesn't have any data you want to keep for that app!

Key points

- Persistence tests help keep your user's data safe.
- Statefulness can make persistence tests difficult to write.
- You can use an **in-memory database** to help handle stateful tests.
- You need to include both set up (`@Before`) and tear down (`@After`) with persistence tests.
- Be careful to test your code and not the library or framework you're using.
- Sometimes you need to write "broken" code first to ensure that your tests fail.
- You can use **Factories** to create test data for reliable, repeatable tests.
- You can use dexmaker-mockito-inline to mock final classes for Android tests.
- If the persistence library you're using doesn't have built-in strategies for testing, you may need to delete all persisted data before and after each test.

Where to go from here?

You now know how to get started testing your persistence layer in your app. Keep these strategies in mind whenever you're implementing this layer.

As with all of programming, there are often many ways to do the same thing. For another example of how to test RoomDB, take a look at "Room DB: Advanced Data Persistence" https://www.raywenderlich.com/5686-room-db-advanced-data-persistence. You may even start to think about how you can use the strategy in this tutorial for the tests you wrote in Chapter 8, "Integration." ;]

For an example of how to test an SQLite database, take a look at "Testing persistence in the Android ecosystem" https://blog.novoda.com/testing-persistence-in-the-android-ecosystem/.

Moving on to an equally important layer, in the next chapter, Chapter 10, "Testing the Network Layer," you'll learn strategies for testing code that relies on API network calls.

Chapter 10: Testing the Network Layer

By Victoria Gonda

You live in a time of the internet, and it's likely that your app does, too. Most apps connect to an API over the network in one way or another, giving them a **network layer**. As this is often a critical part of your app, it stands to reason that you should test it. This is what you'll learn to test in this chapter! Along the way you'll learn:

- Tools for testing your network layer.
- How to provide reliable test data.
- Important things to know about maintaining network layer tests.

One thing to consider when testing your interaction with data across a network is that, when running your automated tests, you don't *actually* want to make a network call. Network calls are unpredictable. A call can fail because of the network connection, the server, the internet service provider, and so on. You can't always know the state of any of these components. You need your tests to be **repeatable** and **predictable**, so this dependency on a wobbly network won't work, here.

There are tools that you can use to test your network layer without hitting the network, which is what you will focus on in this chapter. You will look at three tools to add to your testing toolbox:

- **MockWebserver** to mock the responses from network requests
- **Mockito** to mock your API responses
- **Faker** for data creation

Getting started

In this chapter, you will work on the network layer for an app called **Punchline**. This is an app that will show you a new, random joke every time you press a button. To start, find the starter project in the materials for this chapter and open it in Android Studio.

Run the app, but you won't see much yet:

There will be no UI for you to play with until the end of Chapter 11, "User Interface." Until then, you'll see your progress made in the form of green tests for the network layer!

The Punchline app has a single call to the network: the one that fetches a random joke. You will test this request three times, each using a different tool. There are a couple of files that you should have on hand before you get started with your tests:

- **JokeService.kt**: This is the **Retrofit** service that you will declare your network requests in.
- **Repository.kt**: This file defines `RepositoryImpl`. It's the glue that connects the network layer with the rest of the app.
- **Joke.kt**: Your `Joke` data model lives here. You can see that it has values for the ID and joke.

> **Note**: It is helpful, but not required, to have a familiarity with Retrofit for this chapter. To learn more, go to "Android Networking Tutorial: Getting Started" https://www.raywenderlich.com/6994782-android-networking-with-kotlin-tutorial-getting-started.

Creating your test file

You can't write tests without a place to put them! First off, create your test file. Create **JokeServiceTest.kt** in **app ▸ src ▸ test ▸ java ▸ com ▸ raywenderlich ▸ android ▸ punchline** without a class declaration. You'll put all three of your test classes in this file for easy comparison. Notice that this test is under **test** and not **androidTest**. That's right, you don't need the Android framework to test your network layer when using these tools! They'll run nice and fast. You can also use MockWebServer in your Android tests if there's a place you want to use it in an integration test in your apps.

Investigating the API

Most of the Retrofit boilerplate is already set up for you. You can peek at **KoinModules.kt** if you're interested in seeing that setup. What you care about before you test is the specific endpoint you are testing and implementing.

When interfacing with a network, you often have the endpoints and responses prescribed for you. Even if you are helping with or have a say in how they look, they ultimately live outside your app. Just as you often do in your own apps, you have API specifications to stick to here.

The call you are implementing is rather simple. You make a call to `"random_joke.json"`, and get a JSON response back. The JSON looks as follows:

```
{
  "id":17,
  "joke":"Where do programmers like to hangout? The Foo Bar.",
  "created_at":"2018-12-31T21:08:53.772Z",
  "updated_at":"2018-12-31T21:36:33.937Z",
  "url":"https://rw-punchline.herokuapp.com/jokes/17.json"
}
```

You only care about the first two properties for this example — `"id"` and `"joke"` — and will ignore the rest.

Now you have all the knowledge you need to get started with your test writing!

Using MockWebServer

The first tool you will learn is **MockWebServer**. This is a library from **OkHttp** that allows you to run a local HTTP server in your tests. With it, you can specify what you want the server to return and perform verifications on the requests made.

The dependency for MockWebServer is already added to the project for you. You can see it in **app ▸ build.gradle** as:

```
testImplementation "com.squareup.okhttp3:mockwebserver:3.12.0"
```

To start, you need a test class. Add this empty class to your test file:

```
class JokeServiceTestUsingMockWebServer {
}
```

Setting up MockWebServer

MockWebServer has a test rule you can use for your network tests. It is a scriptable web server. You will supply responses to it and it will return them on request. Add the rule to your test class:

```
@get:Rule
val mockWebServer = MockWebServer()
```

Now, you'll set up your `JokeService` to test. Because you're using Retrofit, you'll use a `Retrofit.Builder` to set it up. Add the following to your test class:

```
private val retrofit by lazy {
  Retrofit.Builder()
      // 1
      .baseUrl(mockWebServer.url("/"))
      // 2
      .addCallAdapterFactory(RxJava2CallAdapterFactory.create())
      // 3
      .addConverterFactory(GsonConverterFactory.create())
      // 4
      .build()
}
```

In that code, you:

1. Set the `baseUrl` on the builder using the `mockWebServer`. This is required when using Retrofit. Because you're not hitting the network, "/" is perfectly valid, here.
2. Add a call adapter. Using an RxJava call adapter allows you to return RxJava streams in your `JokeService`, helping you handle the asynchronous nature of the network calls. Don't worry; you don't need to be an RxExpert to keep going!
3. Add a converter factory. This is so you can use `Gson` to automatically convert the JSON to a nice Kotlin object, `Joke`.
4. Build it!

You then use `retrofit` to create your `JokeService`! Add this code:

```
private val jokeService by lazy {
  retrofit.create(JokeService::class.java)
}
```

You're all set to start scripting and testing!

Running the MockWebServer

Your `JokeService` should have a function, `getRandomJoke()`, that returns a random joke. To handle the asynchronous nature of network calls, you will use RxJava. If you're not familiar with RxJava, this is all you need to know:

- `getRandomJoke()` will return a `Single` of type `Joke`.
- Parties will subscribe to this `Single` and receive an event when it **emits** a `Joke`.
- RxJava brings a lot of power, but, for the sake of this exercise, you can think of it as a way to perform a **callback**.

This test for `getRandomJoke()` will be called `getRandomJokeEmitsJoke()` to match the described functionality. Add the test function to your class:

```
@Test
fun getRandomJokeEmitsJoke() {
}
```

There's nothing in it yet but run the test anyway. There's some interesting output in the console.

```
Feb 27, 2019 8:32:27 PM okhttp3.mockwebserver.MockWebServer$2 execute
INFO: MockWebServer[64726] starting to accept connections
Feb 27, 2019 8:32:27 PM okhttp3.mockwebserver.MockWebServer$2
  acceptConnections
INFO: MockWebServer[64726] done accepting connections: Socket is closed
```

The MockWebServer starts up at the beginning of your test and closes at the end. Anywhere in-between the beginning and end, you can script requests, make those requests to get the response and perform verifications.

Scripting a response

Now that you have MockWebServer set up to receive requests, it's time to script something for it to return!

There are two ways to set up the JSON to script a response. One way is to pull in the JSON from a file. This is a great option if you have a long expected response or you have a real response from a request that you want to copy and paste in. You won't use this first way in this chapter, but know that you can place this JSON in a ***.json** file under **app ▸ src ▸ test ▸ resources**, then use `getJson("file/path.json")` from MockWebServer to fetch it. For example, if you had an **app ▸ src ▸ test ▸ resources ▸ joke ▸ random_joke.json**, you would call `getJson("joke/random_joke.json")`.

Because it's such a short response and because it will allow you to dynamically build it, you will create your JSON `String` in your test file.

Start by creating a property with a JSON string at the class level:

```
private val testJson = """{ "id": 1, "joke": "joke" }"""
```

Notice the use of triple quotes to create raw strings. By using raw strings for your JSON `Strings`, you don't need to worry about escaping characters such as the quotes around the JSON properties.

You have to admit, this JSON is pretty boring, but later you'll spice it up! For now, it's time to learn how to use this JSON to script a response!

Add this to your empty getRandomJokeEmitsJoke() test:

```
// 1
mockWebServer.enqueue(
    // 2
    MockResponse()
        // 3
        .setBody(testJson)
        // 4
        .setResponseCode(200))
```

Going over these step-by-step:

1. Use the mockWebServer that you created before to enqueue a response.
2. You enqueue a response by building and passing in a MockResponse object.
3. Use the testJson that you created as the body of the response.
4. Set the response code to 200 — success!

There are many other things you can set on this MockResponse to test different situations. For example, you can set headers and use throttleBody() to simulate a slow network!

One other thing to note, as the name suggests, you can enqueue multiple responses in a row to return with each new request. This could be helpful when you have an integration test that hits multiple different endpoints and combines the results.

Writing a MockWebServer test

Phew! With all that set up, it's finally time to finish writing your test. Add these two lines to the bottom of getRandomJokeEmitsJoke(). There will be an error at getRandomJoke() because you haven't created it yet:

```
// 1
val testObserver = jokeService.getRandomJoke().test()
// 2
testObserver.assertValue(Joke("1", "joke"))
```

Here, you:

1. Call `getRandomJoke()` on your `jokeService`. By chaining `test()` you get a `TestObserver` that you can use to verify the value of the `Single` that `getRandomJoke()` returns.
2. Verify that the value that returns is a `Joke` object with the same values you placed in the `testJson` and enqueued with `MockWebServer`.

Next step of the TDD process: Write *just enough* code so you can compile and run your test. Add `getRandomJoke()` to the `JokeService` interface with a return value of `Single<Joke>`:

```
fun getRandomJoke(): Single<Joke>
```

> **Note**: When you're writing tests and need to create a method, property, etc. that doesn't exist yet, you can use the shortcut **Option-Return** on Mac or **Alt-Enter** on Windows to pop up a dropdown with options to auto-create it for you.

Build and run your test! As you may have expected if you went through Chapter 9, "Testing the Persistence Layer," and have some familiarity with Retrofit, you'll get an error that Retrofit requires an HTTP method annotation for your new method:

```
java.lang.IllegalArgumentException: HTTP method annotation
  is required (e.g., @GET, @POST, etc.).
   for method JokeService.getRandomJoke
```

Your goal is to make this run, so next, you add an annotation! Add the `@GET` annotation to your `JokeService` method:

```
@GET("https://raywenderlich.com")
fun getRandomJoke(): Single<Joke>
```

The `@GET` annotation requires a path or URL. When you pass in a full URL like `"https://raywenderlich.com"` it uses that URL, but if you pass in a path like `"joke.json"` it uses the base URL appended with `"joke.json"` for the URL. To make sure you see your test fail, you're passing in a full URL. Remember, right now you have a response enqueued for any endpoint given with the base URL, so giving it something without the base URL will return an empty response.

Run it and see it fail:

```
Expected :Joke(id=1, joke=joke) (class: Joke)
Actual   :[] (latch = 0, values = 0, errors = 1,
  completions = 0)
```

That's no joke! No wonder, you're calling the wrong URL. Update the parameter so the test can pass:

```
@GET("joke.json")
```

Run it, and you're all green!

Refactoring your test

You may feel like there's a code-smell in the way you're hard coding the values for the ID and joke. Thankfully, you can change that! Because you're creating the JSON `String` in the test, you can create it the way you like. Make a constant for the ID and the joke. By putting them outside the test class at the file level you'll be able to use them in your other tests too:

```
private const val id = "6"
private const val joke =
    "How does a train eat? It goes chew, chew"
```

> **Note**: Think about how you might use a factory such as in Chapter 9, "Testing the Persistence Layer" to make these random values for each test.

Now use these values to update your `testJson`:

```
private val testJson = """{ "id": $id, "joke": "$joke" }"""
```

And your test assertion:

```
testObserver.assertValue(Joke(id, joke))
```

Run your test, and it should still pass!

Maintaining test data

You just set up some test data and wrote some tests. Now, imagine the JSON response had many more properties and you had more endpoints to test. Then, imagine the format of the response changed. Maybe instead of `joke` as a `String`, it contained an object with different translations of the joke. You need to make sure you update your tests with this change when it happens. If you don't test the new type of response, your tests are no longer accurate.

This is one of the difficulties of network tests: How do you make your tests reliable and maintainable? Do you keep a file of your responses and swap it whenever there's a change? Do you dynamically create your responses? This will differ depending on your needs and may change as you figure out what's right for your app. You'll learn even more about this in Chapter 16, "Strategies for Handling Test Data"

Testing the endpoint

You may be having some doubts about that last test. If it will pass with any endpoint with the same base URL, what is it testing? Is it testing that the response is correctly parsed into a `Joke` object? While it's important to know your data is represented correctly, `MockWebServer` does help you test the endpoint too! Next you'll add a test that the endpoint is correct.

Add the following test to your test class:

```
@Test
fun getRandomJokeGetsRandomJokeJson() {
  // 1
  mockWebServer.enqueue(
      MockResponse()
          .setBody(testJson)
          .setResponseCode(200))
  // 2
  val testObserver = jokeService.getRandomJoke().test()
  // 3
  testObserver.assertNoErrors()
  // 4
  assertEquals("/random_joke.json",
      mockWebServer.takeRequest().path)
}
```

Here's what's happening:

1. Enqueue the response, same as before.
2. Call `getRandomJoke()` as before, getting a reference to a TestObserver.
3. You can also use the `testObserver` to make sure there were no errors emitted.
4. Here's what you're writing this for! You can use the `mockWebServer` to get the path that was requested to compare it to what you expect. There are many other things other than the request path you can test this way!

Run the test, and you're right! It fails!

```
Expected :/random_joke.json
Actual   :/joke.json
```

Update the `@GET` annotation once more to make this pass:

```
@GET("random_joke.json")
```

Build and run your test. It passes! You now know your `JokeService` uses the correct endpoint. That's all you'll use of `MockWebServer` for this chapter, but you can see how it is a powerful and robust tool for testing network requests! But what if you don't need that much detail? That's what you'll learn how to do next.

Mocking the service

Depending on your app and your team, it may be enough to know that the service methods are available and you're using them correctly. This can be done using `Mockito`, which you first learned in Chapter 7, "Introduction to Mockito." In this test you will also be concerned with `getRandomJoke()`, but your test will worry more about its interaction with the repository.

To start, create a new test class to write your `Mockito` tests in. This class can be in the same file as your `MockWebServer` test if you like:

```
class JokeServiceTestMockingService {
}
```

You technically don't need to put your new tests in a new test class (as long as the test methods themselves have different names). However, by creating this separate class, it helps keep the topics divided and allows you to run the new tests without the server running behind them.

Next, you need to set up your test subject. Add this to your `JokeServiceTestMockingService` class. When prompted, import `org.mockito.kotlin.mock`:

```
private val jokeService: JokeService = mock()
private val repository = RepositoryImpl(jokeService)
```

Here, you're mocking the `JokeService`, which you then pass into the constructor of `RepositoryImpl`.

Now, the test you've been waiting for! Add this test method:

```
@Test
fun getRandomJokeEmitsJoke() {
  // 1
  val joke = Joke(id, joke)
  // 2
  whenever(jokeService.getRandomJoke())
      .thenReturn(Single.just(joke))
  // 3
  val testObserver = repository.getJoke().test()
  // 4
  testObserver.assertValue(joke)
}
```

Here, you:

1. Create the `Joke` object to use in this test. Notice that it's using the constant ID and joke you set up while writing the MockWebServer tests.
2. Set up your `JokeService` mock to return a `Single` with that `Joke` when `getRandomJoke()` is called.
3. The signature of `getJoke()` on the repository also returns a `Single`. Use the same `TestObserver` strategy you used before here.
4. Assert that the repository's `getJoke()` emits the same `Joke` that comes from the `JokeService` you mocked.

You can see this is testing the interactions with the network layer instead of the network calls themselves.

Run your test and see it fail:

```
Expected :Joke(id=6, joke=How does a train eat? It goes
  chew, chew) (class: Joke)
Actual   :[] (latch = 0, values = 0, errors = 1,
  completions = 0)
```

What else now but to make it pass! Open up **Repository.kt**. Change the body of `getJoke()` in `RepositoryImpl` to be the following:

```
return service.getRandomJoke()
```

Now, you're calling the `JokeService` as expected. Run that test and see it pass this time!

With this strategy, you can't (and don't need to) test for the endpoint. That means you get to move onto the next tool to learn!

Using Faker for test data

Throughout this chapter, you've been using the same boring old test data:

```
private const val id = "6"
private const val joke =
    "How does a train eat? It goes chew, chew"
```

This is quite a change from the last chapter when you learned to use Factories to create random test data! How would you like to learn another way to generate test data? Now's the time! Your test will look very similar to the one you just wrote, but with more fun test data.

One library that helps with this is **Faker**. With this library, you can generate data from names and addresses to *Harry Potter* and *Hitchhiker's Guide to the Galaxy*. You can see the full list at https://github.com/DiUS/java-faker#fakers. The library is already added to the project for you. You can see it in **app ▸ build.gradle** as:

```
testImplementation 'com.github.javafaker:javafaker:0.16'
```

To get started, add a test class to your file just as before:

```
class JokeServiceTestUsingFaker {
}
```

Then, your setup is like the one for the last test with one addition:

```
var faker = Faker()
private val jokeService: JokeService = mock()
private val repository = RepositoryImpl(jokeService)
```

You include an instance of `Faker` to use to create your test data this time.

Final test for this chapter! Add this to your new test class:

```
@Test
fun getRandomJokeEmitsJoke() {
  val joke = Joke(
      faker.idNumber().valid(),
      faker.lorem().sentence())

  whenever(jokeService.getRandomJoke())
      .thenReturn(Single.just(joke))
  val testObserver = repository.getJoke().test()

  testObserver.assertValue(joke)
}
```

Everything is the same as the last test you write except for the creation of your `Joke` object at the start. For this, you're using `faker`, which you instantiated above. Many of the `Faker` methods return an object that's part of the library. It's from these objects that you can get a value. For example, the `IdNumber` object that's returned from `idNumber()` has methods to get both valid and invalid IDs, as well as other forms of ID such as SSN.

Play around with what values you can get from Faker for your `Joke`. You don't need to stick with the ID and Lorem ipsum prescribed here.

Run the test, and it passes! Of course, that's because you implemented this feature with the previous test. Take the responsibility to revert the changes you made so you can see this test fail.

Deciding what tools to use

You've learned so many tools in this chapter and the previous chapters. How do you decide which to use? When is a unit test best or when is it time for an integration test? Hopefully, you're starting to think about how you can mix and match some of these things, such as how you used both Faker and Mockito for your last test.

There are some patterns, many of which you see in this book, that guide your testing decisions. There are also some restrictions from the libraries themselves on how they can be used. Ultimately, you have to figure out what works best for your needs and your team.

Don't be afraid to try out new things or think again when something isn't working. Where are the holes in your tests where you aren't catching the bugs? What tests are brittle and hard to maintain? On the other hand, what tests have been consistently saving you from deploying buggy code? Watching for these things will help you grow to understand how to make testing work for your app.

Key points

- To keep your tests repeatable and predictable, you shouldn't make real network calls in your tests.
- You can use MockWebServer to script request responses and verify that the correct endpoint was called.
- How you create and maintain test data will change depending on the needs for your app.
- You can mock the network layer with Mockito if you don't need the fine-grained control of MockWebServer.
- By using the Faker library you can easily create random, interesting test data.
- Deciding which tools are right for the job takes time to learn through experiment, trial, and error.

Where to go from here?

You've come so far! From unit tests to integration, testing so many parts of your apps. You still have a very important part to learn how to test: the User Interface! All the things you've been learning are leading up to this point. In Chapter 11, "User Interface," you'll learn how to automate those clicks on your screen and to verify what the user sees.

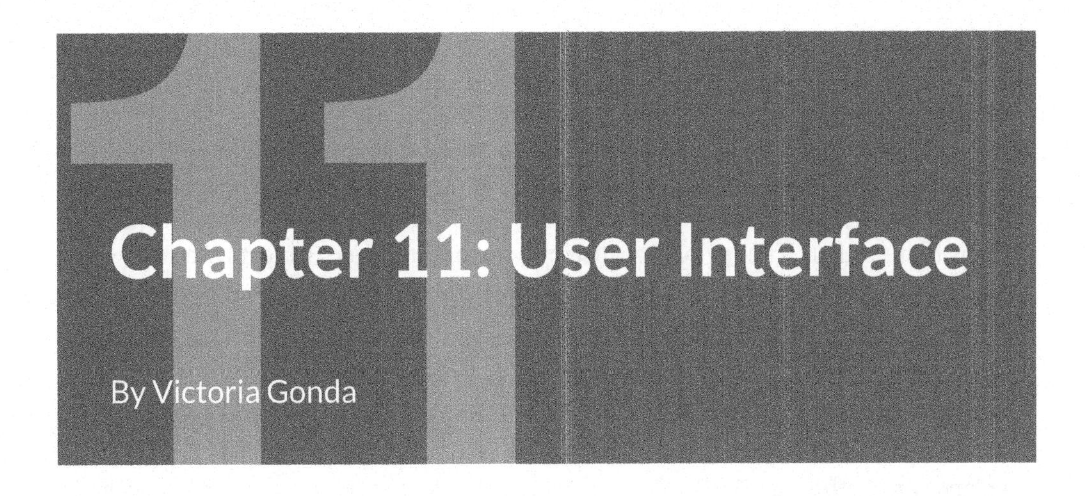

Chapter 11: User Interface

By Victoria Gonda

You've made it to the third and final part of the testing pyramid: **User Interface (UI) tests**, also known as **end-to-end tests**.

Almost all Android apps have a UI, and subsequently, an essential layer for testing. UI testing generally verifies two things:

1. That the user sees what you expect them to see.
2. That the correct events happen when the user interacts with the screen.

With UI tests, you can automate some of the testing you might otherwise need to do with tedious, manual click-testing. A step up from integration tests, these test your app most holistically.

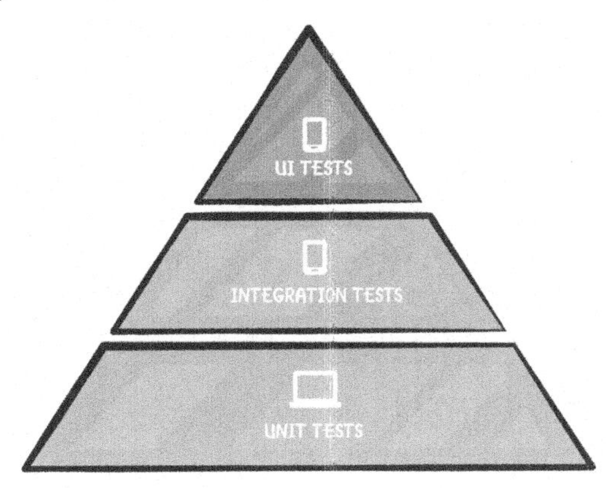

Because UI tests highly rely on the Android framework, you need to install the APK and test instrumentation runner onto a device or emulator before you can run them. Once installed, you can run the tests that use the screen to display and perform actions that verify the behavior. Because of the work involved, UI tests are the slowest and most expensive to run, which means you're less likely to run them, losing the benefit of quick feedback.

> **Note**: With AndroidX Test, it's possible to run these tests without a device or emulator and instead run them with Robolectric. This chapter will not elaborate on the specifics as the technique is the same as described in Chapter 8, "Integration."

Following the TDD process requires running your tests frequently while building, so you won't want to lean too heavily on UI tests. The length of time it takes to run them will increase the time it takes to write them. Test the logic you need to test with UI tests and push what you can into integration or unit tests. A good rule of thumb is the **10/20/70** split mentioned in Chapter 4, "The Testing Pyramid," which explains that 10% of your tests should be UI tests. The idea is that you test for the main flows, putting whatever logic you can into classes that you can verify using a faster test.

Introducing Espresso

The main library used for testing the UI on Android is **Espresso**. Manually click-testing all parts of your app is slow and tedious. With Espresso, you can launch a screen, perform view interactions and verify what is or is not in view. Because this is common practice, Android Studio automatically includes the library for you when generating a new project.

> **Note**: Google's motivation behind this library is for you "to write concise, beautiful and reliable Android UI tests."

Getting started

In this chapter, you'll continue working on the Punchline Joke app that you worked on in Chapter 10, "Testing the Network Layer." This is an app that shows you a new, random joke each time you press a button.

Open the project where you left off in Android Studio, or find the starter project in the materials for this chapter and open that.

Build and run the app. There's not much to see yet because it's your job to add the UI in this chapter.

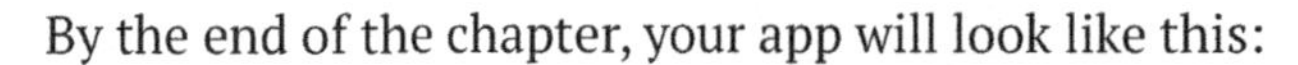

By the end of the chapter, your app will look like this:

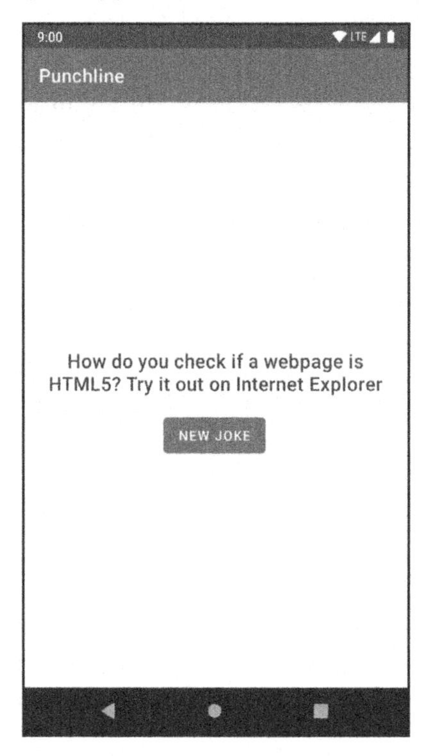

Getting familiar with the project

In this chapter, you'll write tests and implementation for `MainActivity`. Find the following files, so you're all set to go:

- **activity_main.xml**: This is the layout file. At the moment, it's sparse, but it won't be when you're done with it.
- **MainActivity.kt**: This file is where you set up the view. Notice in `onCreate()` that it's subscribing to `LiveData`, and then handling the results in `render()`. It's using `UiModel` to hold the data that you need to display.

Using Espresso

As is the case when generating a new project in Android Studio, the dependency for Espresso is already included for you.

Open **app ▸ build.gradle**, and you'll see the following testing dependency alongside the other testing dependencies:

```
androidTestImplementation 'androidx.test.espresso:espresso-core:
3.3.0'
```

This is the primary library that you'll be using in this chapter. You'll be using this alongside some of the libraries and techniques you used from previous chapters.

You're all set to go now, so it's time to dive in!

What makes up Espresso?

There are three main classes you need to know when working with Espresso: `ViewMatchers`, `ViewActions` and `ViewAssertions`:

- **`ViewMatchers`**: Contain methods that Espresso uses to find the view on your screen with which it needs to interact.
- **`ViewActions`**: Contain methods that tell Espresso how to automate your UI. For example, it contains methods like `click()` that you can use to tell Espresso to click on a button.
- **`ViewAssertions`**: Contain methods used to check if a view matches a specific set of conditions.

Setting up the test class

To get started, inside **app ▸ src ▸ androidTest ▸ java ▸ com ▸ raywenderlich ▸ android ▸ punchline**, create a file named **MainActivityTest.kt**. Add to it, an empty test class using `androidx.test.ext.junit.runners.AndroidJUnit4` and `org.koin.test.KoinTest` for imports:

```
@RunWith(AndroidJUnit4::class)
class MainActivityTest: KoinTest {
}
```

You should be familiar with `AndroidJUnit4` from previous chapters. You're extending from `KoinTest` because this project uses the **Koin** dependency injection framework. You don't need to know much about Koin to see the power of using dependency injection to help with your UI tests.

Using dependency injection to set mocks

In previous chapters, you used Mockito mocks to stub out some functionality. For example, when you didn't want to hit the network layer. In many of these cases, you can introduce these mocked classes by passing them through the constructor. But how would you do that for an Activity? You don't have the same luxury, because the Android framework instantiates the class for you. This is why dependency injection is helpful when it comes to testing.

In this test, you'll mock the repository so that you're not hitting the network layer. This helps with speed and stability.

In **KoinModules.kt**, a Retrofit service is defined which you need to override. This Koin test rule will allow you to do this using Mockito. Add it to the top of **MainActivityTest.kt**:

```
@get:Rule
val mockProvider = MockProviderRule.create { clazz ->
  Mockito.mock(clazz.java)
}
```

By using `declareMock()`, you're overriding the provided dependency injection `Repository` with a **Mockito** mock.

You'll need a reference to this repository so that you can stub methods onto it later. Luckily, Koin will deliver it to you — all you need to do is ask. Add this property to your class, importing `org.koin.test.inject`:

```
private val mockRepository: Repository by inject()
```

By delegating the property instantiation to `inject()`, this sets `mockRepository` to the mock that Koin passes to the `ViewModel` used in the Activity.

One last thing to set up before writing tests. You'll use the **Faker** library you learned in Chapter 10, "Testing the Network Layer" to generate random test data.

Add the property code to prepare this:

```
private var faker = Faker()
```

Great! Now you're all set up for writing tests.

Writing a UI test

This Joke app has a button that makes a new joke appear, so the first test you'll add checks if this button is visible. Following the usual pattern, this test will have set up, actions and verifications.

Start with the setup. Create a new test function with the following stub:

```
@Test
fun onLaunchButtonIsDisplayed() {
  declareMock<Repository> {
    whenever(getJoke())
        .thenReturn(Single.just(Joke(
            faker.idNumber().valid(),
            faker.lorem().sentence())))
  }
}
```

Here, you're stubbing out the repository so that you don't hit the network layer. It's building on the skills you learned in the previous chapters using Mockito to stub a function that returns an RxJava `Single`. You're also using Faker to generate random test data for you. Have fun with the different values you can generate. Just make sure the type is correct for creating your `Joke`.

Next, you need to open the activity and perform your verification. Add these lines to the bottom of your new test. Use the suggested `androidx.test.espresso.*` imports, and know that `buttonNewJoke` will be unresolved in the beginning:

```
// 1
ActivityScenario.launch(MainActivity::class.java)
// 2
onView(withId(R.id.buttonNewJoke))
    .check(matches(isDisplayed()))
```

There are a few new things here, so here's how it works:

1. You use `ActivityScenario` to launch `MainActivity`. This comes from the **AndroidX Test** library imported as `androidx.test.ext:junit:1.1.2` in the **app ▸ build.gradle** file. Here, you're only using it for one thing, but you can use `ActivityScenario` for several things, including driving the Activity's lifecycle state.
2. This is where you use the Espresso library. You're passing the `ViewMatcher`, `withId()`, to `onView` to find the view with the ID `buttonNewJoke`. You haven't created it yet, so there's an error here. Then, you're using the `ViewAssertion` `matches()` to assert that this view is also matched by the `ViewMatcher` `isDisplayed()`.

You can almost run this test, but you need to write enough code to make it compile. Add the button to **activity_main.xml**, inside the `ConstraintLayout` tag:

```
<Button
    android:id="@+id/buttonNewJoke"
    android:layout_width="wrap_content"
    android:layout_height="wrap_content"
    android:visibility="gone"
    />
```

Android Studio might complain that you haven't added constraints yet, but now's not the time to make it pretty. You're adding just enough code to make it compile and run. Notice that you did include `android:visibility="gone"`. This is so you can see the test fail first, which lets you know that your test is working.

Before you run your test, turn off animations on your testing device. Whether it's an emulator or physical device you're working with, go to **Settings ▸ Developer options** and set all of the following to **off**:

- Window animation scale.
- Transition animation scale.
- Animator duration scale.

While you're there, make sure you have "Don't keep activities" **disabled**; otherwise, the `ActivityScenario` cannot run.

Build and run the test. Android Studio might prompt you to pick a device on which to run the test, so take your pick. After you run it, you'll see a long error that includes something like this:

```
Expected: is displayed on the screen to the user
Got: "AppCompatButton{id=2131165226, res-name=buttonNewJoke...
```

This indicates the test found a button with the ID `buttonNewJoke`, but it's not being displayed. It's an easy fix to make it pass. Remove the visibility attribute from the XML:

```
android:visibility="gone"
```

Run the test again, and it passes. You can now move on to making sure the joke shows up.

> **Note**: If you're snooping through all of the Android Studio options, you may notice there's a **Record Espresso Test** option.
>
> Yes, you can use this to automatically create Espresso tests by clicking through your app and entering details into a wizard. However, the result is brittle, hard-to-read tests. While it can be useful for setting up the starting boilerplate or learning how to match something you're unsure of, it's best to avoid using it.

Testing for text

When the app is first launched, you expect to see the first joke. In this test, you'll make sure there's a view that displays that joke right away.

Add this test to your test class:

```
@Test
fun onLaunchJokeIsDisplayed() {
  // 1
  val joke = Joke(
      faker.idNumber().valid(),
      faker.lorem().sentence())
  declareMock<Repository> {
```

```
        whenever(getJoke())
            .thenReturn(Single.just(joke))
    }
    // 2
    ActivityScenario.launch(MainActivity::class.java)
    onView(withId(R.id.textJoke))
        .check(matches(withText(joke.joke)))
}
```

This test is similar to the first test with some small but significant differences:

1. You're keeping a reference to the `Joke` you're creating to stub the repository. You want to know what the joke was later, to make sure it's on the screen.
2. This verification uses many of the same elements you saw before, but this time you're using `withText()` instead of `isDisplayed()` to match the text of the joke. `withText()` accepts both a `String` literal and a `String` reference ID.

Deciding which Matcher to use

Did you notice how many autocomplete options appeared after you typed "with" of `withText()` or `withId()`? With so many options, how do you know which to choose?

First, you must watch for **accuracy** and **brittleness**. Then, make sure what you're matching can only match the one view you want to test.

This could tempt you to be very specific, but you also want to make sure your tests aren't breaking with any little change to the UI. For example, what if you're matching with the `String` literal `"Okay"` and it's later changed to `"OK"` and then changed again to `"Got it"`? You'd have to update the test with each change.

This is why matching using IDs is common. Once you have an ID set, it's likely the only view on-screen with that ID and unlikely to frequently change — unless it's a collection.

Here's Google's handy Espresso Cheat Sheet for possible Matchers, Actions and Assertions: https://developer.android.com/training/testing/espresso/cheat-sheet

You're almost ready to run this test. There's no view with the ID `textJoke` yet, so add that to the XML immediately below your button:

```
<TextView
    android:id="@+id/textJoke"
    android:layout_width="wrap_content"
    android:layout_height="wrap_content"
    />
```

Once again, you have the bare minimum to make it compile and run. Everything will be scrunched into the corner, but don't worry, you'll fix that soon.

Run the test, and you'll see an error similar to before:

```
Expected: with text: is "Dolores quia consequatur quos."
Got: "AppCompatTextView{id=2131165357, res-name=textJoke, text=,
```

It found the right view, but there's no text. Because it's failing, you know you're following the right TDD steps.

Open **MainActivity.kt** and find `showJoke()`. `render()` already calls this for you when a `Joke` is loaded, so you don't need to worry about the logic, only the UI (which makes sense with this being a chapter about UI testing).

With everything set up, all you need to do is connect the data to the view. Add this line to `showJoke()` using the suggested synthetic import:

```
binding.textJoke.text = joke.joke
```

Run your test to make sure it passes.

Refactoring

Run the app to see how it's looking so far. It may not be pretty, but it sure is testable!

Now that you have some UI tests in place, you can take a break from test writing and do some refactoring in **activity_main.xml**.

Add these attributes to the `TextView`:

```
style="@style/TextAppearance.MaterialComponents.Headline6"
android:gravity="center_horizontal"
android:padding="16dp"
app:layout_constraintBottom_toTopOf="@+id/buttonNewJoke"
app:layout_constraintEnd_toEndOf="parent"
app:layout_constraintStart_toStartOf="parent"
app:layout_constraintTop_toTopOf="parent"
app:layout_constraintVertical_chainStyle="packed"
```

Add these to the `Button`:

```
android:text="@string/new_joke"
app:layout_constraintBottom_toBottomOf="parent"
app:layout_constraintEnd_toEndOf="parent"
```

```
app:layout_constraintStart_toStartOf="parent"
app:layout_constraintTop_toBottomOf="@id/textJoke"
```

This adds a little style, along with some descriptive text and constraints. Run it again to see the changes.

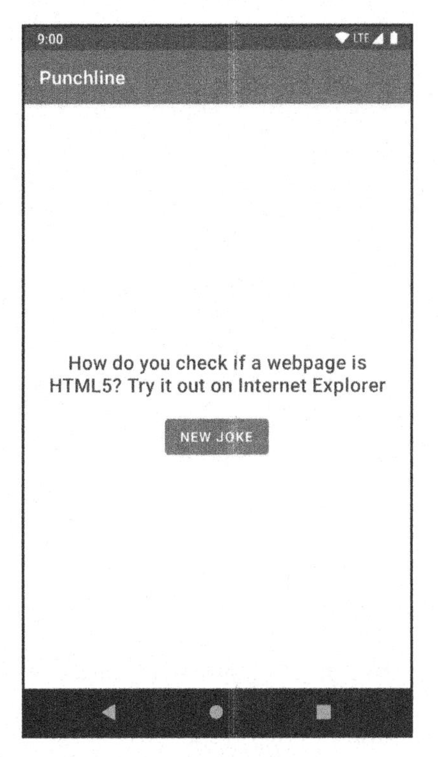

Run your tests to make sure everything still works.

> **Note**: Feel free to modify the view to make it look the way you want. Just make sure you don't break your tests while you do it.

Regression testing

It's relatively easy to keep things from breaking when you're working with a simple UI like this. But these tests are extremely helpful when you're working with a complicated UI with nested, reused views. Because you want to limit your UI tests, you may fall into a pattern of introducing **regression tests**.

Regression tests are tests that you add when something goes wrong. You can start by adding a couple of tests for the happy path in the UI layer. If you find something that's broken, write a test for it to make sure it doesn't break, or regress, again. You can use this at any layer of the testing pyramid, and it might look like this when paired with TDD:

1. Something broke, a bug is reported, or there's a crash.
2. You write a test for the expected behavior that broke. Likely, there's not already a test for this; otherwise, it would have caught the issue ahead of time.
3. Fix the issue. Do what you need to do to fix the bug, make the test pass, and keep all other tests green.
4. You now have a regression test to make sure the same issue doesn't come up again. No zombie bugs coming back to life here.

These types of tests are especially helpful when working with legacy systems that aren't well tested. It's a way to start introducing valuable tests alongside your fixes. While you're in there writing the regression test, you might take a few minutes to add other tests for vulnerable nearby areas.

Performing an action

There's one more behavior to test and implement for this app: When a user taps the button, a new joke should appear. This is the final and most complex test you'll write for this chapter, so you'll write it in two steps.

Add this test to your test class:

```
@Test
fun onButtonClickNewJokeIsDisplayed() {
  // 1
  val joke = Joke(
      faker.idNumber().valid(),
      faker.lorem().sentence())
  // 2
  val jokeQueueAnswer = object: Answer<Single<Joke>> {
    val jokes = listOf(
        Joke(
            faker.idNumber().valid(),
            faker.lorem().sentence()),
        joke
    )
    var currentJoke = -1
```

```
    override fun answer(invocation: InvocationOnMock?):
Single<Joke> {
       currentJoke++
       return Single.just(jokes[currentJoke])
    }
  }
  // 3
  declareMock<Repository> {
    whenever(getJoke())
        .thenAnswer(jokeQueueAnswer)
  }
}
```

This is a longer one, so take it step-by-step:

1. Create the joke you want to see after the button is pressed.
2. Create a Mockito `Answer`. This allows you to create a more complex response. In this case, you're queuing jokes for each request because you want a *new* joke when the button is pressed.
3. Use that `Answer` to mock out `getJoke()`

Great! Now you can finish up your test. Add this to the bottom:

```
ActivityScenario.launch(MainActivity::class.java)
// 1
onView(withId(R.id.buttonNewJoke))
    .perform(click())
// 2
onView(withId(R.id.textJoke))
    .check(matches(withText(joke.joke)))
```

1. This is where you use a `ViewAction` for the first time. You locate the view using a `ViewMatcher`, then pass in the `ViewAction` `click()` to `perform()` to perform that action.
2. Finally, verify the new joke is shown in the `TextView`.

Phew! That was a lot. Everything is already compiling, so go ahead and run your test. You'll see a familiar error:

```
Expected: with text: is "Error ut sed doloremque qui."
Got: "AppCompatTextView{id=2131165357, res-name=textJoke, ...
     text=Laudantium et quod dolor.,
```

It looks like the new joke never showed up! That's because nothing is happening when you click the button. Don't worry, you can fix that.

In `MainActivity`, add this click listener to the bottom of `onCreate()`:

```
binding.buttonNewJoke.setOnClickListener {
  viewModel.getJoke()
}
```

Again, all of the logic is already there for you to fetch the new joke. Call `showJoke()` when it's finished. Run your test to see it pass.

You made it! You finished Punchline with fully functioning UI tests. Run your app and play around with it.

You can now refactor the UI and make it as visually appealing as you'd like. Just remember to run the tests periodically. Oh yeah, and do your best to remember the jokes — you may need them for your next party! :]

Using sharedTest (optional)

In Chapter 8, "Integration," you learned that you could run Android tests on either a device or locally using Robolectric. For this to work, your test must be in the correct **test/** or **androidTest/** directory. With a small configuration change and a new **sharedTest/** directory, you'll be able to run your tests both ways *without* needing to move the file.

> **Note**: If you drag and drop a test from **test/** or **androidTest/** into **sharedTest/**, Android Studio might have some problems running it because of caching issues.

The first step to setting up shared tests is modifying **app ▸ build.gradle** so that it pulls the shared tests into the **test/** and **androidTest/** source sets. Add this to the `android` block of **app ▸ build.gradle**:

```
sourceSets {
  String sharedTestDir = 'src/sharedTest/java'
  test {
    java.srcDir sharedTestDir
  }
  androidTest {
    java.srcDir sharedTestDir
  }
}
```

You then need to make sure that any libraries you use in your tests are in your `dependencies` list with both `androidTestImplementation` and `testImplementation`. To save you some work, this is done for you. You'll see the duplicates if you open **app ▸ build.gradle**. Just remember to do a Gradle Sync while you're there.

The only thing left is learning how to run your shared tests. By default, you don't have the local vs. device control you want. You can only run the shared tests as Android tests. There are two ways you can get this control:

- Running the tests from the **command line**.
- Creating a **run configuration**.

Add this small test to **sharedTest/** in a newly created file named **JokeTest.kt**. This way you'll have something to run:

```
class JokeTest {

  private val faker = Faker()

  @Test
  fun jokeReturnsJoke() {
    val title = faker.book().title()
    val joke = Joke(faker.code().isbn10(), title)

    assert(title == joke.joke)
  }
}
```

To be honest, that was a bit of a joke! :]

Running tests from the command line

Using gradle, running your tests from the command line is easy. Open a terminal and navigate to the root directory of your project, or use the terminal view in Android Studio.

Run the following command:

```
./gradlew test
```

This runs all of the tests you have in **test/** *and* **sharedTest/**. You can use this even if you don't have shared tests as it will run the tests you have in **test/** only.

Now, try running this one:

```
./gradlew connectedAndroidTest
```

Likewise, this one will run the tests you have in **androidTest/** and **sharedTest/**. This also works if you don't have any shared tests.

Creating a run configuration

Android Studio also supports creating run configurations, which are presets you create and run that inform Android Studio of how you want things to run.

To start, select **Edit Configurations...** from the run drop-down.

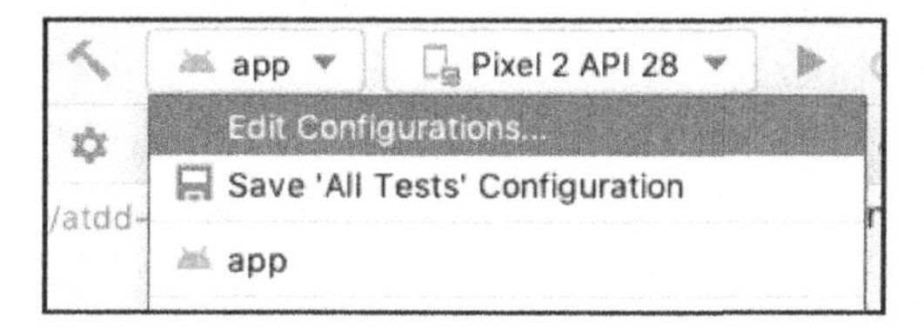

Then, select "+" to create a new run configuration, selecting **Android JUnit** for the type.

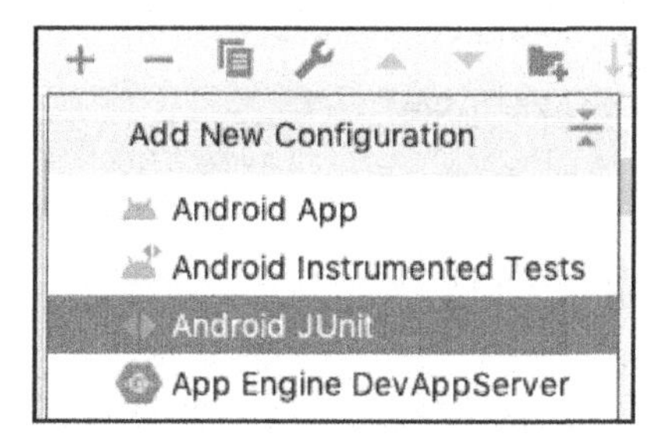

You now have a few things to fill out in the editor:

- **Name**: Pick a name that makes sense to you. Something like **Robolectric Shared Tests** works well.
- **Test kind**: Select "All in directory" to run all of your tests. You can change this to be more specific if you want even more control over which tests run.
- **Directory**: Select the path to **src/** if you want to run both **test/** and **sharedTest/**, or **sharedTest/** if you only want to run the ones in that directory.
- **Use classpath of module**: Select **app** here.
- Click **OK**.

As demonstrated below:

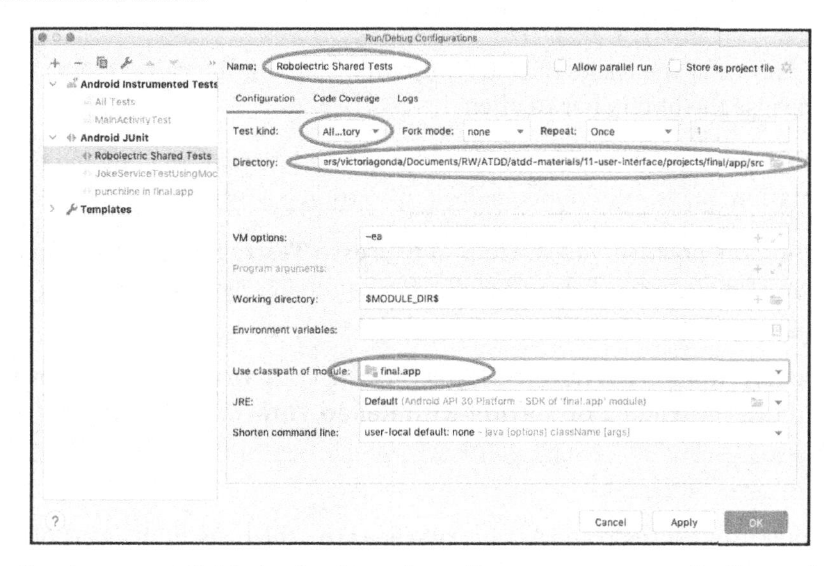

This option is now available in the drop-down if you want to run all of your shared tests with Robolectric from Android Studio.

Key points

- UI tests allow you to test your app end-to-end without having to manually click-test your app.
- Using the Espresso library, you're able to write UI tests.
- You can run Android tests on a device and locally using Roboelectric.

Where to go from here?

Now that you know the basics of UI testing with Espresso, you can explore and use everything else the library has to offer.

You can find out about Espresso's helper libraries and more by reading their documentation: https://developer.android.com/training/testing/espresso/

If you want more practice, you can look at **Espresso Testing and Screen Robots: Getting Started**: https://www.raywenderlich.com/949489-espresso-testing-and-screen-robots-getting-started

To take your UI tests to the next level, you can learn how to use **Kakao** for even more elegant UI tests by reading **UI Testing with Kakao Tutorial for Android: Getting Started**: https://www.raywenderlich.com/1505688-ui-testing-with-kakao-tutorial-for-android-getting-started

This chapter uses Espresso and `ActivityScenario`, which are both a part of **AndroidX Test**. To learn more about this suite of testing libraries, you can watch **Getting Started with AndroidX Test**: https://vimeo.com/334519652

Finally, if you've adopted Jetpack Compose in your app, you can apply TDD there, too! Learn how to test Compose in this codelab, then practice applying your TDD skills. https://developer.android.com/codelabs/jetpack-compose-testing

This is the end of this section, and you've learned a lot about how to test new apps and features. But what if you're working on an existing app? In the next section, you'll learn some techniques for working with legacy code.

Section III: TDD on Legacy Projects

Now that you have an understanding of TDD and have different tools at your disposal, you'll learn how to apply these techniques to projects that weren't created using TDD and do not have sufficient test coverage. You'll work through Furry Coding Companion Finder on your way to becoming a TDD guru.

Chapter 12: Common Legacy App Problems

By Lance Gleason

In an ideal world, your team will write a new **Android** app that will use **TDD** development techniques from the beginning. In this world, your app will have great test coverage, an architecture that is set up for **TDD**, and code with a high level of quality. Because of that, the team will be very confident in its ability to fearlessly refactor the code, and they will ship code regularly.

In the real world, many, if not most, apps have technical debt that you will need to work around. In this chapter, you will learn about some of the more common issues you will run into with legacy applications. Then, in subsequent chapters, you will learn how to address these when working on legacy projects.

A brief history of TDD in Android

While there are many technical aspects that affect **TDD** on a platform, the culture surrounding the development community has a big impact on its adoption.

Android was first released on the **G1** in **2008**. In those days, the primary development language was **Java** and, as a result, many early developers came from other Java domains, such as server-side development. At that point, **TDD** as we know it today had only been around for nine years and was just beginning to see adoption in some software development communities and organizations. During that time, the **Rails** framework, which was four years old, arguably had the largest percentage of projects being developed using TDD. This was due, in part, because many signatories of the **Agile Manifesto** were evangelizing it.

Java was 12 years old at that time and pre-dated TDD. It had become a mature technology that large conservative enterprises were using to run mission-critical software. As a result, most Java developers, with the exception of those who were working at cutting edge Agile development shops, were not practicing TDD.

This enterprise Java development culture affected the early days of Android development. Unlike Rails, the initial versions of Android supported testing as more of an afterthought, or not at all. As a result, most new Android developers had not come from an environment where testing was important or even known; it was not a primary concern of the framework and most developers focused on learning how to write apps, not on testing. During those early days, many of the concepts we take for granted today were just beginning to be developed. Over time the platform evolved, devices became more powerful, and apps became more complex.

Eventually, tools like **Robolectric** and **Espresso** were introduced and refined. TDD became more of an accepted practice among Android developers. But even today, it is not uncommon to be at an Android developer meetup where fewer than half of the developers in the audience are actively writing tests or practicing TDD on a daily basis.

Lean/XP technical practice co-dependency

TDD is one of the key development practices of **Lean/XP**.

Before Lean/XP became popular, most development organizations used a **Waterfall** development approach with steps that often provided marginal value for projects.

Some traits of a Waterfall project include:

1. All known requirements for the entire project (i.e., a project that will take months of development effort) are gathered and written in a requirements document before coding begins.
2. Certain documents, such as software architecture design documents, are often created after the requirements have been created, but before development begins.
3. Test plans need to be created before testing begins.

While all of this sounds logical in theory, in reality:

1. At some point, usually mid-project, new requirements are discovered that require a change.
2. If the project is really strict with its process (usually the exception), it must modify all artifacts upstream and downstream. This leads to a project timeline that is extended.
3. If the business cannot afford to have the timeline slip because of the process (again, what usually happens), phases are skipped, the documents end up not reflecting the reality of the project, and the project gradually becomes chaotic.

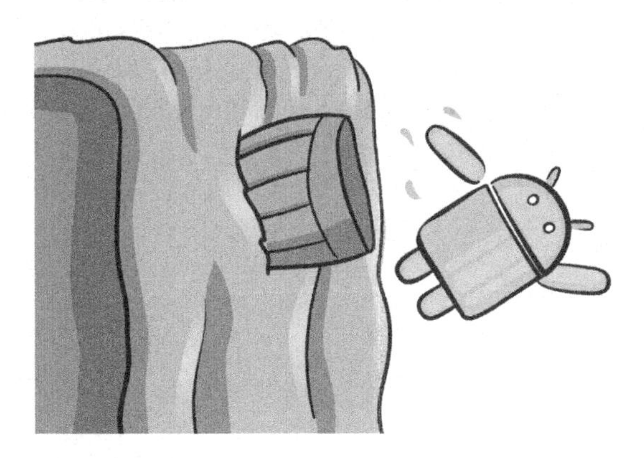

Lean/XP fun historical facts

In software, the techniques we use were built on the shoulders of the giants, often from other industries. TDD/XP has roots in manufacturing through a subset of **Six Sigma techniques**, which are called **Lean**. To learn more about Lean, XP and its relationships, this *Wikipedia* article on Lean software development is a great place to start: https://en.wikipedia.org/wiki/Lean_software_development.

Lean, as the word implies, eliminated many of the unnecessary aspects of the development process and only kept the things that were deemed necessary. The practices that are kept are often highly interdependent. Because of this, if one practice is not followed, another one becomes more difficult or may not be done as well. For example, TDD is a critical component for doing continuous deployment. When an app is developed with TDD principles at the unit and integration layer, the practice guides the project towards better architecture.

Let's explore some of the **co-dependent** legacy code issues.

No unit or integration tests

This is the biggest issue you will likely run into when working on a legacy project. It happens for a variety of reasons. The project may be several years old and the development team may have chosen not to write unit tests. For example, it is not uncommon to find teams with technically strong Android developers who do not know how to write tests. Of course, if you are on a team that does not know how to practice TDD, this book would make a great gift, especially for holidays, birthdays or "just because." :]

Difficult to test architecture

One of the reasons why **MVVM**, **MVP** and **MVI** are popular is because they tend to drive a structure that is easier to test. But, if the app was initially developed without any unit tests, it is likely there is no coherent architecture. While you may get lucky with a design that is testable, it is more common to find an untested app with an architecture that is, in fact, difficult to test.

Components that are highly coupled

When an app's components are highly **coupled**, they are highly interdependent.

For example, let's say that you want to be able to search for any pets that share traits with a specific pet — in this case you will use the name of the pet. One implementation might look like this:

```
class Cat(
  val queenName: String,
  val felineFood: String,
  val scratchesFurniture: Boolean,
  val isLitterTrained: Boolean)

class Dog(
  val bestFriendName: String,
  val food: String,
  val isHouseTrained: Boolean,
  val barks: Boolean)

fun findPetsWithSameName(petToFind: Any): List<Any> {
  lateinit var petName: String
  if (petToFind is Cat){
    petName = petToFind.queenName
  } else if (petToFind is Dog) {
    petName = petToFind.food
  }
  return yourDatabaseOrWebservice.findByName(petName)
}
```

The functionality that should be truly unique to the `findPetsWithSameName` method is the call to the `yourDatabaseOrWebservice.findByName()` call. But, this method also has code to get data from these objects before doing a find on them. To test this, you could write a test that only creates an instance of a **Cat** and passes it into the method. For example, let's say that you have a cat named **Garfield** and your test data has two other animals with the same name. Your test would look something like this:

```
@Test
fun `find pets by cats name`() {
  val catNamedGarfield = Cat("Garfield", "Lasagne", false,
false)
  assertEquals(2, findPetsWithSameName(catNamedGarfield).size)
}
```

This test will pass. The problem is that there is a bug in your implementation, because the code for the dog is retrieving the search name from the wrong field. To get full code coverage, and find this issue, you need to write an additional test that also passes in a **Dog**. There is also a boundary condition that has not been addressed if someone passes in different class, like a **Lion**:

```
@Test
fun `find pets by dogs name`() {
  val dogNamedStay = Dog("Stay", "Blue Buffalo", false, false)
  assertEquals(5, findPetsWithSameName(dogNamedStay).size)
}

@Test
fun `find pets by lions name`() {
  val lionNamedButterCup = Lion("Buttercup", "Steak", false,
false)
  assertEquals(2, findPetsWithSameName(lionNamedButterCup).size)
}
```

In total, you needed three unit tests for this method. A less coupled implementation might look like this:

```
open class Pet(var name: String, var food: String)

class Cat(
  name: String,
  food: String,
  var scratchesFurniture: Boolean,
  var isLitterTrained: Boolean): Pet(name, food)

class Dog(
  name: String,
  food: String,
  var isHouseTrained: Boolean,
  var barks: Boolean): Pet(name, food)

fun findPetsWithSameName(petToFind: Pet): List<Pet> {
  return yourDatabaseOrWebservice.findByName(petToFind.name)
}
```

With the new version of this code, you only need to write one test to test the functionality of `findPetsWithSameName(petToFind: Pet)`:

```
@Test
fun `find pets by cats name`() {
  val catNamedGarfield = Cat("Garfield", "Lazagne", false,
false)
  assertEquals(2, findPetsWithSameName(catNamedGarfield).size)
}
```

You could refine this test further to mock a **pet**, taking away any dependency on implementations of **Cat**. Highly coupled code can also lead to situations where one component changes or you do a small refactoring in one area that leads to large changes throughout the app (or even the tests). While an app's architecture doesn't guarantee that this won't happen, the less consistent the architecture, the more likely you are to see this.

Components with low cohesion

One important tenant for **Object-Oriented Design** is to have components that focus on doing one thing well. This is also referred to as **cohesion**. For example, let's say you have a class called **Car**:

```
class Car {
  val starter = Starter()
  val ignition = Ignition()
  val throttle = Throttle()
  val engineTemperature = Temperature()
  var engineRPM = 0
  var oilPressure = 0
  var steeringAngle = 0L
  var leftDoorStatus = "closed"
  var rightDoorStatus = "closed"

  fun startCar() {
    ignition.position = "on"
    starter.crank()
    engineRPM = 1000
    oilPressure = 10
    engineTemperature = 60
  }

  fun startDriving() {
    if(leftDoorStatus.equals("closed") &&
        rightDoorStatus.equals("closed")) {
      steeringAngle = 0L
      setThrottle(5)
    }
```

```
    }

    private fun setThrottle(newPosition: Int) {
      if (ignition.position.equals("on") && engineRPM > 0 &&
          oilPressure > 0) {
        throttle.position = newPosition
        engineRPM = newPosition * 1000
        oilPressure = newPosition * 10
      }
    }

}
```

For this implementation, you have two publicly callable methods, `startCar()` and `startDriving()`:

- `startCar()` method: Turns on the ignition, cranks the starter and updates the status of the **engine RPM**, **oil pressure** and **engine temperature**.
- `startDriving()` method: Checks that the doors are closed, sets the **steering wheel** to an angle of **0** and calls a private method called `setThrottle()` that begins to move the car.

`setThrottle()` has to check that the ignition position is **on** and that the `engineRPM` and `oilPressure` are above **0**. If they are, it sets the throttle position to the value passed in, and sets the engine RPM and oil pressure to a multiplier of the **throttle position**.

With a car, you could have multiple engine choices. For example, your current car runs on fuel, but what if you wanted to switch the current car out for an electric one? Things such as the `engineRPM` and `oilPressure` would not be needed — these are really details of the engine. As a result of this, your class currently has **low cohesion**.

Since this is an incomplete car, before it'll be usable, you will need to add things such as brakes and tires, which will make `Car` a very big (and complex) class.

Now, take a look at the same example with **high cohesion**:

```
class Engine {
  val starter = Starter()
  val ignition = Ignition()
  val throttle = Throttle()
  val engineTemperature = Temperature()
  var engineRPM = 0
  var oilPressure = 0

  fun startEngine() {
    ignition.position = "on"
    starter.crank()
    engineRPM = 1000
    oilPressure = 10
  }

  fun isEngineRunning(): Boolean {
    return ignition.position.equals("on") && engineRPM > 0 &&
        oilPressure > 0
  }

  fun setThrottle(newPosition: Int) {
    if (isEngineRunning()) {
      throttle.position = newPosition
    }
  }
}

class Car {
  val engine = Engine()
  var steeringAngle = 0L
  var leftDoorStatus = "closed"
  var rightDoorStatus = "closed"

  fun startCar() {
    engine.startEngine()
  }

  fun startDriving() {
    if (leftDoorStatus.equals("closed") &&
        rightDoorStatus.equals("closed")) {
      steeringAngle = 0L
      engine.setThrottle(5)
    }
  }
}
```

Here, you have the same functionality, but classes have more of a single purpose.

If you've been in enough legacy code-bases, you will run across components like the first example in which you have large classes that are doing a lot of different things. The more lines of code that a class has, the more likely it is to have low cohesion.

Reliance on Internal Constructors

Imagine that you were writing a unit test for the `Car` class above and wanted to test that class in isolation. The current implementation is written in a way where it would be very difficult to pass in a mock or spy for an `Engine`. The good news is that there is an easy fix for this by refactoring `Car` with an optional constructor parameter:

```
class Car(val engine = Engine()) {
  var steeringAngle = 0L
  var leftDoorStatus = "closed"
  var rightDoorStatus = "closed"

  fun startCar() {
    engine.startEngine()
  }

  fun startDriving() {
    if (leftDoorStatus.equals("closed") &&
        rightDoorStatus.equals("closed")) {
      steeringAngle = 0L
      engine.setThrottle(5)
    }
  }
}
```

Use of Singletons

Imagine that you used a singleton to create your `Engine` class with the following implementation.

```
class Engine private constructor() {

  private object HOLDER {
    val INSTANCE = Engine()
  }

  companion object {
    val instance: Engine by lazy { HOLDER.INSTANCE }
  }

  val starter = Starter()
  val ignition = Ignition()
  val throttle = Throttle()
```

```
    val engineTemperature = Temperature()
    var engineRPM = 0
    var oilPressure = 0

    fun startEngine() {
      ignition.position = "on"
      starter.crank()
      engineRPM = 1000
      oilPressure = 10
    }

    fun isEngineRunning(): Boolean {
      return ignition.position.equals("on") && engineRPM > 0 &&
          oilPressure > 0
    }

    fun setThrottle(newPosition: Int) {
      if (isEngineRunning()) {
        throttle.position = newPosition
      }
    }
  }

  class Car {
    val engine = Engine.instance
    var steeringAngle = 0L
    var leftDoorStatus = "closed"
    var rightDoorStatus = "closed"

    fun startCar() {
      engine.startEngine()
    }

    fun startDriving() {
      if (leftDoorStatus.equals("closed") &&
          rightDoorStatus.equals("closed")) {
        steeringAngle = 0L
        engine.setThrottle(5)
      }
    }
  }
```

Since `Engine` is only created once this can result in flaky unit tests. The solution is the same as the one for internal constructors.

```
  class Car(val engine = Engine.instance) {
    var steeringAngle = 0L
    var leftDoorStatus = "closed"
    var rightDoorStatus = "closed"

    fun startCar() {
      engine.startEngine()
```

```
    }

    fun startDriving() {
      if (leftDoorStatus.equals("closed") &&
          rightDoorStatus.equals("closed")) {
        steeringAngle = 0L
        engine.setThrottle(5)
      }
    }
  }
```

Now when you are testing this class you can pass in a mock or spy for your `Engine`.

Other legacy issues

A large codebase with many moving parts

Many legacy systems, over time, become large apps that do a lot of things. They may have hundreds of different classes, several dependencies, and may have had different developers — with different development philosophies — working on the project. Unless you were the original developer on the project, there will be sections of the app code that you don't fully understand. If you are new to the project, you may be trying to figure out how everything works.

One common **anti-pattern** is have a developer that is new to a project get familiar with it by adding tests to an untested component of the application. That is a bad idea because, in order to write a meaningful test, you need to understand what the expected behavior of the component is that you are testing. A better approach is to add tests to features, modifications and bug fixes along with related components as you are working on the system.

Your sample projects for this book will not be large, but you will be using the same approach that you will want to use for large projects — namely, focusing on one section of the app and working through the others over time.

Complex/large dependent data

In some domains, you may have an app that creates and consumes a large amount of data. Those projects may have a large number of models with several unique data fields. Taming this beast as you test can easily look like a insurmountable task, so stay tuned for tricks on how to address this.

Libraries/components that are difficult to test

A lot of libraries and components have very important functionality that are easy to use, but did not consider automated **unit tests** as part of the design. One example is using **Google Maps** in a project with custom map markers. If you had to create this functionality, you would have to write a lot of code. But, integration tests can be very challenging. In some instances, the best solution may be not to test these components because the value added by the tests are lower than the effort to create tests.

Google Location Services Components are another example of this. Stay tuned for an example where we look at ways to work around these kinds of libraries.

Old libraries

This happens a lot: A developer needs to add functionality to an app. Instead of reinventing the wheel, they use a library from the Internet. Time passes and the library version included with the app is not updated. If you are lucky, the library is still being supported and there are no breaking changes when you update it.

The library has a new version with breaking changes

If a library version in a project has not been updated in a few years, and it is being actively maintained, there is a good chance that a new version with breaking changes has been introduced.

Issues that may introduce include:

1. Features you currently use may have been removed.
2. You may have a significant number of touch-points in the app that require a significant amount of refactoring.
3. Core functionality may have changed.

Even if you used TDD with the initial version of the library, there is not much you can practically do to prevent this, outside of timing when you do your upgrade.

The library is no longer being maintained

This happens for a variety of reasons, including:

1. It was an open-source side project for a developer who ended up getting busy with other endeavors.
2. A new library or approach has been developed, which leads to projects migrating from the old library.
3. If a company created the library, they may have gone out of business or stopped supporting a product.

If the library is open source, you could decide to take over maintenance of it. Alternatively you will need to migrate to a new library. If your app already has a lot of unit tests, this will break them as you add support for the new library.

Wrangling your project

The app is working well with no tests

After seeing all of the issues you can run into with a legacy project, you may be asking if you should start to add tests to the project. If you plan on continuing to maintain a project for a while, the short answer is yes, but with a few caveats.

1. If your project has more than one developer, TDD will not add as much value to the project unless the entire development team is dedicated to practicing it.
2. Unless your project is small, the first passes at TDD will take a non-trivial amount of effort to set up.
3. Rome wasn't built in a day; neither will your test suite.
4. You probably will not have the luxury of stopping new feature development for several months to add test coverage to your entire project.

You consider rewriting the entire app

This can be a very tempting option when working with a legacy app, especially if you were not the original author. If your app is small or truly a mess, that may be the best solution. But, if your project is large, and you are planning on keeping most of these features, however tempting a rewrite may be, it could be a job-killing move.

Most legacy apps have a significant number of undocumented features and edge cases. For these projects, a rewrite will often take several months. In addition to that, the business will likely want to maintain the existing app and add new features to it. While a rewrite may still be the best solution, before heading down that path, a better option would be to break the app up into components and refactor things a component at a time. This is called the **Strangler pattern**.

Lore has it that the Strangler pattern got its name from a vine called **the strangler vine**. These vines seed themselves in fig trees. Over time, they grow into their own plants surrounding and killing the tree. Likewise, you components will surround the initial implementation, eventually killing off the original one.

Key points

- Lean and Extreme Programming have a lot of interdependencies.
- Many legacy applications have little or no automated tests.
- Lack of automated tests can make it difficult to get started with TDD and may require getting started with end-to-end Espresso tests.
- Rewriting a legacy application should generally be considered as a last resort option.

Where to go from here?

Beyond the techniques you will be learning in this book, the book *Working Effectively With Legacy Code* by Michael Feathers does a great job of talking about legacy code problems. You can check out this book at https://www.oreilly.com/library/view/working-effectively-with/0131177052/.

Chapter 13: High-Level Testing With Espresso

By Lance Gleason

For many — arguably most — legacy projects, it is easier (and often provides quicker wins) by starting with UI tests using Espresso.

There are a number of reasons for this, including:

1. Most non-TDD apps have not been decomposed for testability.

2. If you are new to the project and it is fairly large, it can take you a while to get your head around the architecture of the system as a whole.

3. UI tests test the large parts of the app working together.

A holistic approach allows you to get functionality of the app under test before making code changes. This gives you a number of quick wins, including:

1. The ability to get a section of the app under test before adding features or refactoring the code.

2. Quickly getting the benefits of automated testing, even if you do not have time to start to make architectural changes.

3. Providing you with test coverage for when you do start to refactor your code for testability at a lower level.

Getting started

To explore UI tests, you are going to work on an app called **Coding Companion Finder**.

The story

This app was created by a developer who practices pair programming, in which two developers work side by side on a problem at the same time. This technique has a number of benefits, including helping to improve the quality of the software you are working on. Unfortunately, this person often works from home where it may not always be possible to have a human partner to pair up with.

Other developers have been in the same situation, and they had developed a technique called purr programming, in which a human development pair is substituted with a cat. The developer loved cats, adopted one, began to regularly purr program, and noticed that the quality of their software written at home dramatically improved. Beyond the benefits of pair programming, the developer also gained a loving companion, and soon realized that it could be used with dogs as well. Whenever the developer was at meetup groups or work, they'd tell friends about the benefits of purr programming and a related practice called canine coding.

One day, when the developer was at the pet store, they noticed that a local pet shelter was hosting an "Adopt a Pet" day and immediately thought: "What if there was an app to help match fellow programmers to these pets?" They decided to partner with the shelter to create the Coding Companion Finder.

The app has been successful at placing companions into loving homes, but many pets are still without homes and many developers have yet to discover this technique. After getting feedback from users, the shelter has some ideas for the app, but the original developer is too busy, so they have reached out to you!

Setting up the app

This app uses an API from a website called **Petfinder**, which requires a developer key.

To get started, go to the Petfinder registration page at https://www.petfinder.com/user/register/ and create a new account.

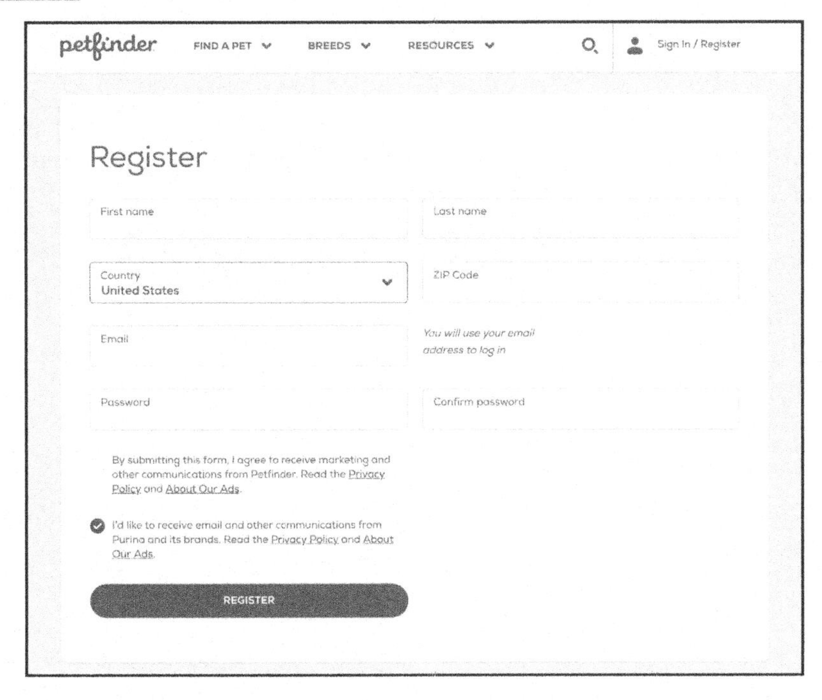

If you are not in the US, Canada or Mexico, choose the **United States** for your location and **30354** as your **zipcode**. Once your account is created, go here https://www.petfinder.com/developers/, log in, and click **GET AN API KEY**.

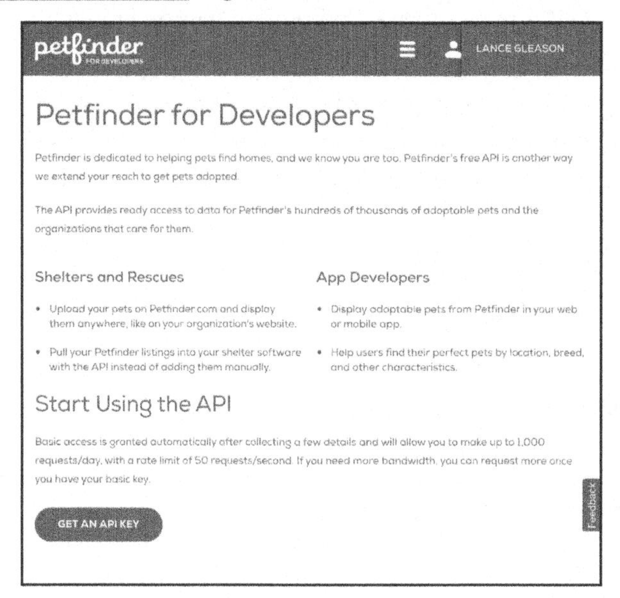

Create a API key by entering a **Application Name**, **Application URL**, accept the **Terms of Service** and click the **GET A KEY** button.

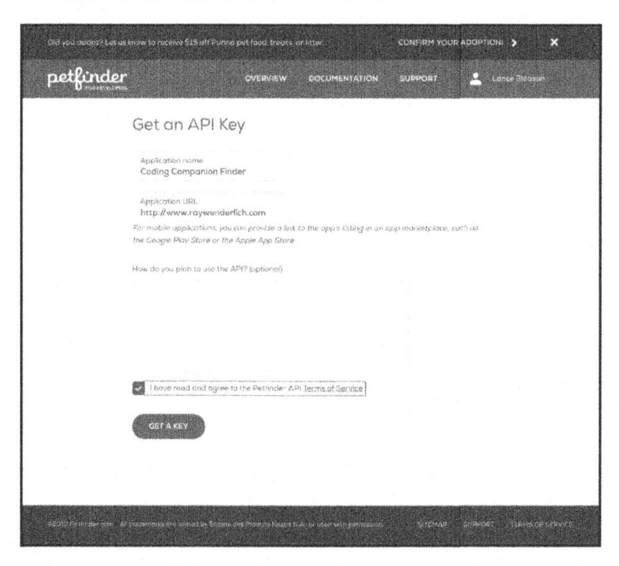

Once you request a key, you will be redirected to a page that will show you an **API Key** and an **API Secret**. Copy the API key value.

Now, import the starter project and open up **MainActivity.kt**. At the top of this file you will see the following:

```
val apiKey = "replace with your API key"

val apiSecret = "replace with your API secret"
```

Replace the string with the key that you've just copied. Run the app.

A tour of the app

The app will briefly present you with a splash screen; then, if you pasted in the correct key, it will bring up a page showing you a **Featured Companion**.

Tap on **Find Companion**. You will be taken to a search screen where you can search for companions in the United States, Canada or Mexico. Enter a location and tap the **FIND** button to find companions close to that location. Then, tap on one of them to see more information about a companion.

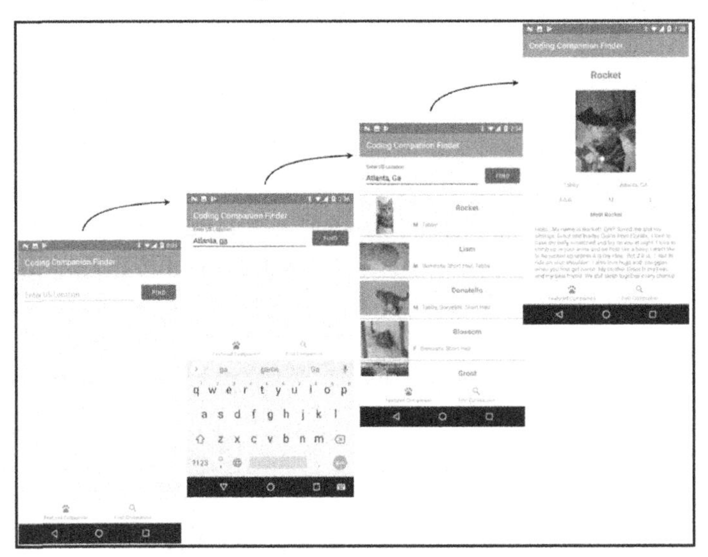

Your first assignment

Users have really liked the app, but it is difficult to find the contact information for a companion in the details screen. As your first task, the shelter has asked you to add contact information to the companion details screen.

Understanding the app architecture

Before adding tests and features, you need to understand how the app is put together. Open up the starter project and open the app level **build.gradle**. In addition to the normal Kotlin and Android dependencies, you have the following:

```
// Glide
implementation("com.github.bumptech.glide:glide:4.12.0") {
  exclude group: "com.android.support"
}
kapt 'com.github.bumptech.glide:compiler:4.12.0'

// carouselview library
implementation "com.synnapps:carouselview:0.1.5"
```

```
// retrofit
implementation "com.squareup.okhttp3:logging-interceptor:3.14.9"
implementation 'com.squareup.retrofit2:retrofit:2.9.0'
implementation 'com.squareup.retrofit2:converter-gson:2.9.0'
```

Our project depends on **Glide**, **Carouselview** and **Retrofit**. Now, open up **MainActivity.kt**. In your **onCreate** method, you will see the following:

```
if (petFinderService == null) {
    val logger = HttpLoggingInterceptor()
    logger.level = HttpLoggingInterceptor.Level.BODY
    val client = OkHttpClient.Builder()
        .addInterceptor(logger)
        .connectTimeout(60L, TimeUnit.SECONDS)
        .readTimeout(60L, TimeUnit.SECONDS)
        .addInterceptor(AuthorizationInterceptor(this))
        .build()

    petFinderService = Retrofit.Builder()
        .baseUrl("http://api.petfinder.com/v2/")
        .addConverterFactory(GsonConverterFactory.create())
        .client(client)
        .build().create(PetFinderService::class.java)
}
```

This sets up Retrofit with a hard-coded URL. Looking at **onResume**, you will see a few more hints about how things come together:

```
val navHostController = Navigation.findNavController(this,
  R.id.mainPetfinderFragment)

val bottomNavigation =
  findViewById<BottomNavigationView>(R.id.bottomNavigation)

NavigationUI.setupWithNavController(bottomNavigation,
navHostController)
```

This is using the **Jetpack Navigation Library** to set up your **BottomNavigationView** and hook it up to a fragment element in your **activity_main.xml** layout. Open up that file and you will see the following:

```
<androidx.fragment.app.FragmentContainerView
    android:id="@+id/mainPetfinderFragment"
    android:name="androidx.navigation.fragment.NavHostFragment"
    android:layout_width="match_parent"
    android:layout_height="0dp"
    app:defaultNavHost="true"
    app:layout_constraintBottom_toTopOf="@id/bottomNavigation"
    app:layout_constraintEnd_toEndOf="parent"
```

```
    app:layout_constraintStart_toStartOf="parent"
    app:layout_constraintTop_toTopOf="parent"
    app:navGraph="@navigation/nav_graph"
    />

<com.google.android.material.bottomnavigation.BottomNavigationVi
ew
    android:id="@+id/bottomNavigation"
    android:layout_width="match_parent"
    android:layout_height="wrap_content"
    app:layout_constraintBottom_toBottomOf="parent"
    app:layout_constraintEnd_toEndOf="parent"
    app:layout_constraintStart_toStartOf="parent"
    app:layout_constraintTop_toTopOf="parent"
    app:layout_constraintVertical_bias="1"
    app:menu="@menu/bottom_navigation_menu"/>
```

Your **BottomNavigationView** has a menu that is set up in **bottom_navigation_menu.xml** and your **fragment** references a **navGraph** with:

```
app:navGraph="@navigation/nav_graph"
```

Now, open up **bottom_navigation_menu.xml** and you will see the following:

```
<menu xmlns:android="http://schemas.android.com/apk/res/android"
  xmlns:app="http://schemas.android.com/apk/res-auto">

  <item
    android:id="@id/randomCompanionFragment"
    android:enabled="true"
    android:icon="@drawable/ic_featured_pet_black_24dp"
    android:title="@string/featured_pet"
    app:showAsAction="ifRoom" />

  <item
    android:id="@id/searchForCompanionFragment"
    android:enabled="true"
    android:icon="@drawable/ic_search_black_24dp"
    android:title="@string/find_pet"
    app:showAsAction="ifRoom" />
</menu>
```

This is populating your bottom menu items. Finally open up **nav_graph.xml** and you will see the following navigation definition:

```
<navigation
  xmlns:android="http://schemas.android.com/apk/res/android"
  xmlns:app="http://schemas.android.com/apk/res-auto"
  xmlns:tools="http://schemas.android.com/tools"
  android:id="@+id/nav_graph"
```

```
    app:startDestination="@id/randomCompanionFragment">

    <fragment
      android:id="@+id/randomCompanionFragment"

  android:name="com.raywenderlich.codingcompanionfinder.randomcomp
  anion.RandomCompanionFragment"
      android:label="fragment_random_pet"
      tools:layout="@layout/fragment_random_companion"/>
    <fragment
      android:id="@+id/searchForCompanionFragment"

  android:name="com.raywenderlich.codingcompanionfinder.searchforc
  ompanion.SearchForCompanionFragment"
      android:label="fragment_search_for_pet"
      tools:layout="@layout/fragment_search_for_companion"/>
  </navigation>
```

The call to `NavigationUI.setupWithNavController` matches the ID of your menu items with the IDs of your `nav_graph` and instantiates either your **randomCompanionFragment** or **searchForCompanionFragment** depending on which menu item you select.

When you have multiple screens in your app, there are three main ways that you might choose to do it:

1. **Multiple activities, one for each screen.** When your user navigates to another screen, a new activity is shown.
2. **One activity with multiple fragments.** When you user navigates to a new screen, you show a new fragment.
3. A hybrid of #1 and #2.

Because this is using the Jetpack Navigation Component, it probably is going to be using a one-activity, multiple-fragment approach.

To verify that, take a look at your project view.

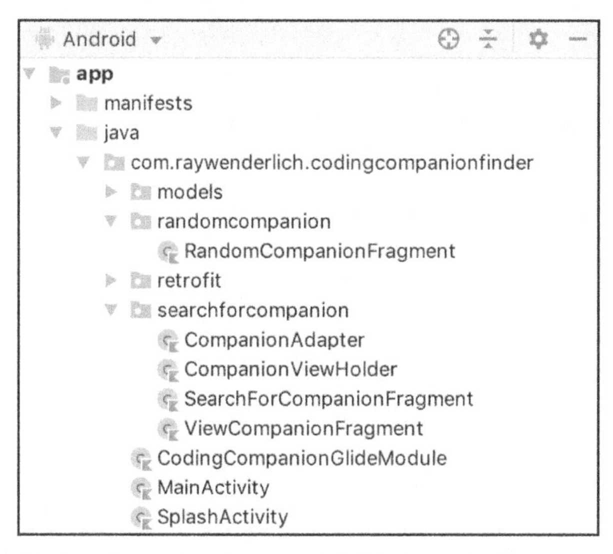

Other than one additional activity that is used for the splash screen, that assumption appears to be correct. Since you're going to be working on the search functionality, open up **SearchForCompanionFragment.kt** and have a look around.

```
override fun onActivityCreated(savedInstanceState: Bundle?) {
  view?.findViewById<MaterialButton>(R.id.searchButton)?.setOnClickListener { it: View!
    try {...} catch (e: Exception) {...}
    searchForCompanions()
  }

  super.onActivityCreated(savedInstanceState)
}
```

In your `onActivityCreated` method, you are using `findViewById` to get a reference to your search button. This probably means that the app does not use data binding or a helper library such as **Butterknife** to get references to objects in your view.

```
override fun onActivityCreated(savedInstanceState: Bundle?) {
  view?.findViewById<MaterialButton>(R.id.searchButton)?.setOnClickListener { it: View!
    try {...} catch (e: Exception) {...}
    searchForCompanions()
  }

  super.onActivityCreated(savedInstanceState)
}
```

When the search button is tapped, a call is made to a local method called `searchForCompanions()`.

```
private fun searchForCompanions() {
  val companionLocation = view?.findViewById<TextInputEditText>(R.id.searchFieldText)?.text.toString()
  val noResultsTextView = view?.findViewById<TextView>(R.id.noResults)
  val searchForCompanionFragment = this
```

At the top of this method are additional `findViewById` calls.

```
GlobalScope.launch {
  accessToken = (activity as MainActivity).accessToken
  (activity as MainActivity).petFinderService?.let { petFinderService ->
    val getAnimalsRequest = petFinderService.getAnimals(accessToken, location = companionLocation)

    val searchForPetResponse = getAnimalsRequest.await()
    if (searchForPetResponse.isSuccessful) {
      searchForPetResponse.body()?.let {
        GlobalScope.launch(Dispatchers.Main) {
          if (it.animals.size > 0) {
            noResultsTextView?.visibility = INVISIBLE
            viewManager = LinearLayoutManager(context)
            companionAdapter = CompanionAdapter(it.animals, searchForCompanionFragment)
            petRecyclerView = view?.let {
              it.findViewById<RecyclerView>(R.id.petRecyclerView).apply {
                layoutManager = viewManager
                adapter = companionAdapter
              }
            }
          } else {...}
        }
      }
    } else {...}
  }
}
```

This is calling your `PetFinderService` which is provided by **Retrofit**.

```
GlobalScope.launch {
  accessToken = (activity as MainActivity).accessToken
  (activity as MainActivity).petFinderService?.let { petFinderService ->
    val getAnimalsRequest = petFinderService.getAnimals(accessToken, location = companionLocation)

    val searchForPetResponse = getAnimalsRequest.await()
    if (searchForPetResponse.isSuccessful) {
      searchForPetResponse.body()?.let {
        GlobalScope.launch(Dispatchers.Main) {
          if (it.animals.size > 0) {
            noResultsTextView?.visibility = INVISIBLE
            viewManager = LinearLayoutManager(context)
            companionAdapter = CompanionAdapter(it.animals, searchForCompanionFragment)
            petRecyclerView = view?.let {
              it.findViewById<RecyclerView>(R.id.petRecyclerView).apply {
                layoutManager = viewManager
                adapter = companionAdapter
              }
            }
          } else {...}
        }
      }
    } else {...}
  }
}
```

The results are then passed into a `CompanionAdapter` that is part of a RecyclerView.

In summary, your app has the following traits:

1. It does not follow a **MVC**, **MVP**, **MVVM**, or **MVI** type of pattern.
2. Looking at the app as a whole, it has one main external dependency on the **Petfinder** service.
3. Like many legacy apps, it has some coding/architectural issues that you will need to work around to get it under test.

Determining your system boundaries

When you are adding automated testing to an app using Espresso, you want to have tests that are repeatable and fast. Using Espresso, you are performing a form of integration testing, but you still need to have some system boundaries for your tests. The boundary determines what you are testing and allows you to control the inputs to your app.

A rule of thumb when writing Espresso tests is to not have tests that make network requests or access external resources. In the case of your app, your boundary is the Petfinder service. Pets are constantly being added and removed from the service, and some calls, such as the one for a featured pet, provide different data every time you call it. Beyond the network latency, those changes would make it very difficult to create meaningful repeatable tests. As you get the app under test, you will be adding a mock of this to address that.

Preparing your app for testing

To get started, open your app level **build.gradle** file and add the following:

```
androidTestImplementation "androidx.test:rules:1.3.0"
androidTestImplementation "androidx.test.ext:junit:1.1.2"
androidTestImplementation "android.arch.navigation:navigation-testing:1.0.0-alpha08"
androidTestImplementation 'com.squareup.okhttp3:mockwebserver:3.12.0'
androidTestImplementation "androidx.test.espresso:espresso-contrib:3.3.0"
```

This is adding libraries for rules, junit, navigation-testing, mockwebserver and espresso-contrib.

Next, rename **ExampleInstrumentedTest** in the **androidTest** source set to be **FindCompanionInstrumentedTest**.

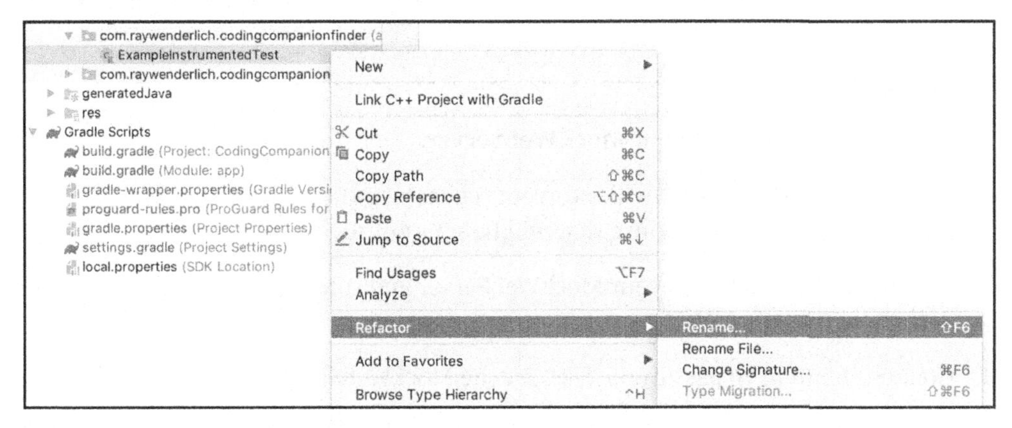

Now, paste the following into your renamed test class:

```
lateinit var testScenario: ActivityScenario<MainActivity>

companion object {

  private lateinit var startIntent: Intent

  // 1
  val server = MockWebServer()

  // 2
  val dispatcher: Dispatcher = object : Dispatcher() {

    @Throws(InterruptedException::class)
    override fun dispatch(
      request: RecordedRequest
    ): MockResponse {
      return CommonTestDataUtil.dispatch(request) ?:
        MockResponse().setResponseCode(404)
    }
  }

  @BeforeClass
  @JvmStatic
  fun setup() {
    // 3
    server.setDispatcher(dispatcher)
    server.start()

    // 4
```

```
      startIntent =
        Intent(ApplicationProvider.getApplicationContext(),
          MainActivity::class.java)
      startIntent.putExtra(MainActivity.PETFINDER_URI,
        server.url("").toString())
    }
  }
```

This is doing the following:

1. Creating an instance of your **MockWebServer**.
2. Creating a dispatcher that will intercept requests to the MockWebServer and respond with a MockResponse that will be sent out to the server.
3. Passing the dispatcher to your MockWebServer and starting it when the class is first instantiated.
4. Creates an intent to pass in the URL for the MockWebServer.

Fix all the required imports, selecting `okhttp3.mockwebserver.Dispatcher` as the import for the `Dispatcher` if you get multiple options. There is an "unresolved reference" error with `CommonTestDataUtil`.

To fix that, create a new file in your **androidTest** directory called **CommonTestDataUtil.kt**, and paste in the following:

```
object CommonTestDataUtil {
  fun dispatch(request: RecordedRequest): MockResponse? {
    when (request.path) {
      else -> {
        return MockResponse()
          .setResponseCode(404)
          .setBody("{}")
      }
    }
  }
}
```

This is the beginning of a helper method that will look at the request coming in, and respond based on the request parameters. Don't worry about the warning that the `when` clause can be simplified for now. The code still won't compile with an error on `MainActivity.PETFINDER_URI`. We'll fix that in the next section.

Adding test hooks

MockWebServer spins up a local web server that runs on a random port on an Android device. In order to use it, your app will need to point your Retrofit instance at this local server instead of the one at petfinder.com. Since your app sets up Retrofit in your `MainActivity`, you are going to add some logic to allow this to be passed in.

Open open **MainActivity.kt** and look for the following:

```
        petFinderService = Retrofit.Builder()
            .baseUrl("http://api.petfinder.com/v2/")
            .addConverterFactory(GsonConverterFactory.create())
            .client(client)
            .build().create(PetFinderService::class.java)
    }
```

Replace it with the following:

```
        val baseUrl = intent.getStringExtra(PETFINDER_URI) ?:
          "http://api.petfinder.com/v2/"

        petFinderService = Retrofit.Builder()
            .baseUrl(baseUrl)
            .addConverterFactory(GsonConverterFactory.create())
            .client(client)
            .build().create(PetFinderService::class.java)
    }
```

This checks the intent for a value stored under `PETFINDER_URI`, and if one is present uses it instead of your hard-coded URI.

Now, add the following to the top of the class:

```
  companion object {
    val PETFINDER_URI = "petfinder_uri"
    val PETFINDER_KEY = "petfinder_key"
  }
```

This creates two constants for your `Intent` keys.

Finally, paste the following into the top part of your `onCreate` function:

```
intent.getStringExtra(PETFINDER_KEY)?.let{
  apiKey = it
}
```

This looks for an API key being passed into your `MainActivity` via an `Intent`, and if there is one, sets your key to that value instead of your hard-coded one.

Adding legacy tests

When adding tests to a legacy app with no test coverage, the first step is to add tests around the functionality where you are going to be adding a feature.

To get started, you are going to add tests around the "search for companion" section of your app. When you first start the app, you are taken to the **Featured Companion** page.

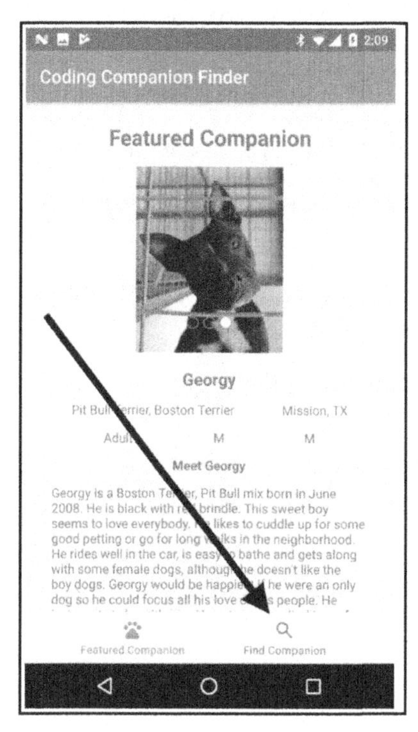

Pressing the **Find Companion** button takes you to the find page:

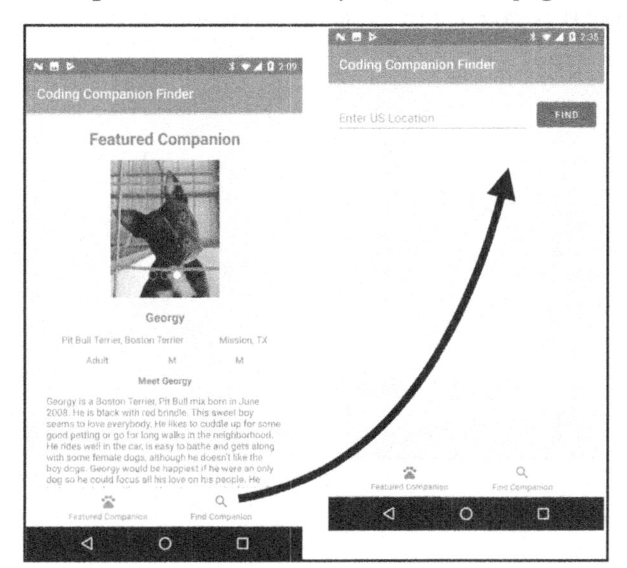

For your first test, you are going to open up the app, press the **Find Companion** bottom item and verify that you are on the “Find Companion” page.

To get started, make sure that the app is running on your device and use the **Layout Inspector** in your Android Studio **Tools** menu to get a snapshot of the screen.

Now, highlight that menu item to find the ID of that menu item:

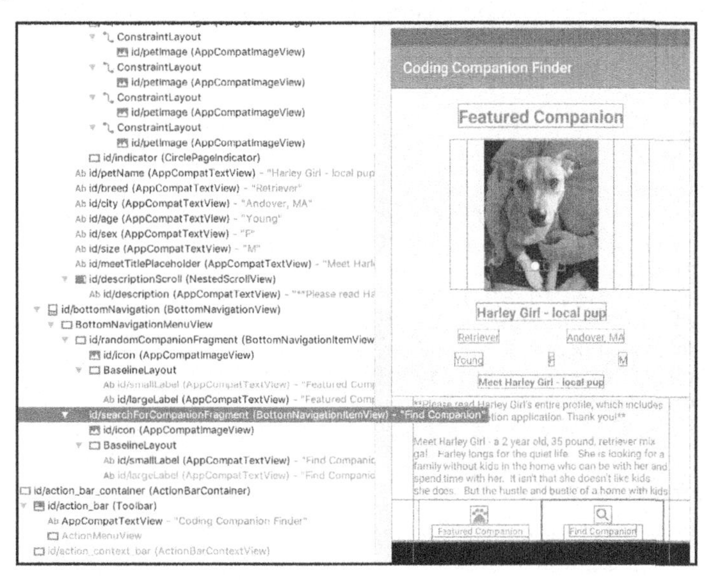

Your `SearchForCompanionFragment` is the entry point for your search page. It has a view called **`fragment_search_for_companion`**. Open it up and get the ID of your **Find** button:

```
    <com.google.android.material.button.MaterialButton
      android:id="@+id/searchButton"
      android:layout_width="wrap_content"
      android:layout_height="wrap_content"
      android:text="Find"
      app:layout_constraintBottom_toBottomOf="@+id/searchField"
      app:layout_constraintEnd_toEndOf="parent"
      app:layout_constraintStart_toEndOf="@id/searchField"
      app:layout_constraintTop_toTopOf="@id/searchField" />
```

Next, look for the ID of your text input field:

```
      <com.google.android.material.textfield.TextInputEditText
        android:id="@+id/searchFieldText"
        android:layout_width="match_parent"
        android:layout_height="wrap_content"
        android:hint="Enter US Location"
        android:textColor="@color/primaryTextColor" />
```

Putting this all together, when you enter the app, you are going to click on a button with an ID of **`searchForCompanionFragment`**. Then, you will check that items with the ID of **`searchButton`** and **`searchFieldText`** are visible, in order to verify that your app does indeed go to the next screen.

Open up your **`FindCompanionInstrumentedTest`** and paste in the following function:

```
@Test
fun
pressing_the_find_bottom_menu_item_takes_the_user_to_the_find_pa
ge() {
  testScenario = ActivityScenario.launch(startIntent)
  onView(withId(R.id.searchForCompanionFragment))
    .perform(click())
  onView(withId(R.id.searchButton))
    .check(matches(isDisplayed()))
  onView(withId(R.id.searchFieldText))
    .check(matches(isDisplayed()))
  testScenario.close()
}
```

Add all the imports, picking `androidx.test.espresso.assertion.ViewAssertions.matches` when presented with choices for the `matches()` method.

Next, run the test by clicking the **green arrow** on the left of the code — and you should have green (passing) test!

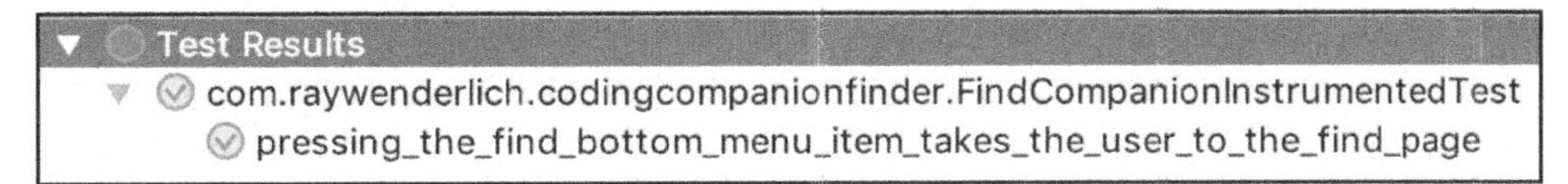

> **Note**: You may have noticed that you are not really mocking anything required for the Featured Companion screen. This is because you are not testing this screen, and it is not necessary to populate data for it to test your Find Companion screen.

Now that you have a passing test, you are going to want to have a basic test to exercise performing a search and tapping on a result.

Understanding your API

Your `SearchForCompanionFragment` is making a call to your `getAnimals` function in your `PetFinderService` when you tap the **Find** button, which is implemented like this using **Retrofit**:

```
@GET("animals")
suspend fun getAnimals(
    @Header("Authorization")  accessToken: String,
    @Query("limit") limit: Int = 20,
    @Query("location") location: String? = null
) : Response<AnimalResult>
```

That call passes in a `accessToken` and `location`. The `accessToken` is retrieved via a **OAUTH** call to a `oauth2/token` endpoint passing in the apiKey and apiSecret you received when you registered for the Petfinder API. In order to mock out this test data, you are going to need to figure out what real data might look like! The calls to `getAnimals` happen to be GET requests, and the data returned is in a JSON format. But in order to test out the calls, you will need to make a POST call to get your accessToken and then pass that in the header of your GET request.

To get an idea of how the data looks, you can use a tool such as Postman, found here https://www.getpostman.com/, to explore the Petfinder documents located here https://www.petfinder.com/developers/v2/docs/.

Looking at the output from Postman with the list of pets contracted, you will see a list with 20 animals.


```
{
    "animals": [...],
    "pagination": {
        "count_per_page": 20,
        "total_count": 230898,
        "current_page": 1,
        "total_pages": 11545,
        "_links": {
            "next": {
                "href": "/v2/animals?location=30318&page=2"
            }
        }
    }
}
```


For your test, you will only need to have one or two pets. Each pet record will also have several photos.


```
"photos": [
    {
        "small": "https://dl5zpyw5k3jeb.cloudfront.net/photos/pets/44544502/1/?bust=1556211130&width=100",
        "medium": "https://dl5zpyw5k3jeb.cloudfront.net/photos/pets/44544502/1/?bust=1556211130&width=300",
        "large": "https://dl5zpyw5k3jeb.cloudfront.net/photos/pets/44544502/1/?bust=1556211130&width=600",
        "full": "https://dl5zpyw5k3jeb.cloudfront.net/photos/pets/44544502/1/?bust=1556211130"
    },
    {
        "small": "https://dl5zpyw5k3jeb.cloudfront.net/photos/pets/44544502/2/?bust=1556211144&width=100",
        "medium": "https://dl5zpyw5k3jeb.cloudfront.net/photos/pets/44544502/2/?bust=1556211144&width=300",
        "large": "https://dl5zpyw5k3jeb.cloudfront.net/photos/pets/44544502/2/?bust=1556211144&width=600",
        "full": "https://dl5zpyw5k3jeb.cloudfront.net/photos/pets/44544502/2/?bust=1556211144"
    }
],
```


These photos reference URLs on the web. For the time being, you are not going to test the photo loading and are going to want to have records without photos. A relatively straight-forward way to do this is to copy the fully expanded formatted text into a text file, edit out the data you don't want, and save it.

To save you some time, we have included a file called **search_30318.json** in **app/src/androidTest/assets**.

`SearchForCompanionFragment` uses a `RecyclerView` to display the list of results. Open the **CompanionViewHolder.kt**. At the bottom of this file, you will see:

```
private fun setupClickEvent(animal: Animal){
  view.setOnClickListener {
    val viewCompanionFragment = ViewCompanionFragment()
```

```
    val bundle = Bundle()
    bundle.putSerializable(ViewCompanionFragment.ANIMAL, animal)
    viewCompanionFragment.arguments = bundle
    val transaction =
      fragment.childFragmentManager.beginTransaction()
    transaction.replace(R.id.viewCompanion,
      viewCompanionFragment).addToBackStack("companionView")
      .commit()
  }
}
```

When you tap on a companion in that list, a `ViewCompanionFragment` is created, and the `Animal` object for that record is passed into it via `Bundle` arguments.

Now open your `ViewCompanionFragment` and you will see that the only data inputs for this fragment are via the `arguments` Bundle. So you do not have to mock out any other calls!

```
animal = arguments?.getSerializable(ANIMAL) as Animal
```

Setting up your mock data

Now that you have the data from your API, you are going to need to tell your test `Dispatcher` how to retrieve it in order to mock out the API response. Open **CommonTestDataUtil.kt** and add in the following:

```
@Throws(IOException::class)
private fun readFile(jsonFileName: String): String {
  val inputStream = this::class.java
    .getResourceAsStream("/assets/$jsonFileName")
      ?: throw NullPointerException(
          "Have you added the local resource correctly?, "
              + "Hint: name it as: " + jsonFileName
      )
  val stringBuilder = StringBuilder()
  var inputStreamReader: InputStreamReader? = null
  try {
    inputStreamReader = InputStreamReader(inputStream)
    val bufferedReader = BufferedReader(inputStreamReader)
    var character: Int = bufferedReader.read()
    while (character != -1) {
      stringBuilder.append(character.toChar())
      character = bufferedReader.read()
    }
  } catch (exception: IOException) {
    exception.printStackTrace()
  } finally {
```

```
      inputStream.close()
      inputStreamReader?.close()
    }
    return stringBuilder.toString()
  }
```

This is opening up your file, reading it, and returning it as a string. Next, replace your `dispatch` function with the following:

```
  fun dispatch(request: RecordedRequest): MockResponse? {
    return when (request.path) {
      "/animals?limit=20&location=30318" -> {
        MockResponse().setResponseCode(200)
          .setBody(readFile("search_30318.json"))
      }
      else -> {
        MockResponse().setResponseCode(404).setBody("{}")
      }
    }
  }
```

This is adding a `when` condition for the request that is made when you do a search for the zipcode **30318**.

Writing your next test

For this test, you are going to perform a search, click on a result, and see details for the companion you tapped on.

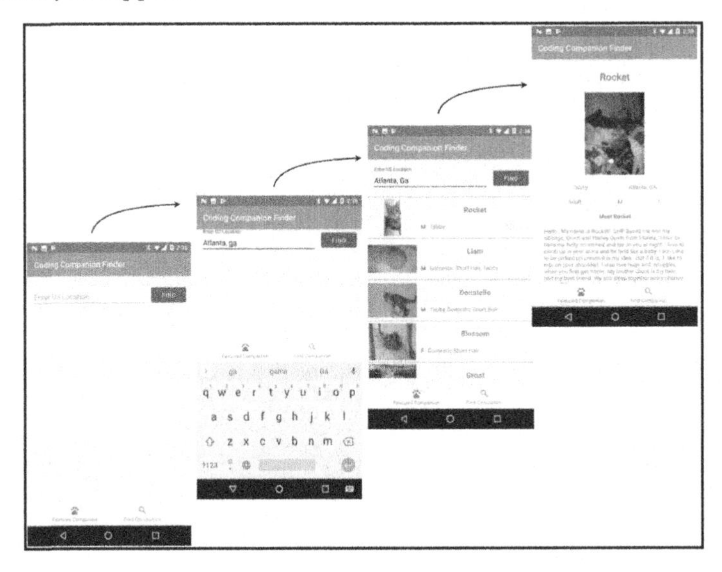

Open up **FindCompanionInstrumentedTest.kt** and add the following:

```
@Test
fun
searching_for_a_companion_and_tapping_on_it_takes_the_user_to_th
e_companion_details() {
  testScenario = ActivityScenario.launch(startIntent)
  // 1
  onView(withId(R.id.searchForCompanionFragment))
    .perform(click())

  // 2
  onView(withId(R.id.searchFieldText))
    .perform(typeText("30318"))
  onView(withId(R.id.searchButton))
    .perform(click())

  // 3
  onView(withId(R.id.searchButton))
    .check(matches(isDisplayed()))

  // 4
  onView(withText("KEVIN")).perform(click())

  // 5
  onView(withText("Rome, GA")).check(matches(isDisplayed()))
  testScenario.close()
}
```

Here is what this is doing:

1. Clicks the bottom menu item to find a companion.
2. Enters 30318 in `searchTextField` and clicks the "Find" button.
3. It makes sure that you are still on the Find Companion screen.
4. Clicks on the record for a cat named KEVIN.
5. Verifies that you are on the new page by looking for a data item that was not in the list of items. In this case, the city of Rome, GA.

Now run the test.

```
▼ Test Results
  ▼ ⊖ com.raywenderlich.codingcompanionfinder.FindCompanionInstrumentedTest
      ⊖ searching_for_a_companion_and_tapping_on_it_takes_the_user_to_the_companion_details
```

```
Started running tests

androidx.test.espresso.NoMatchingViewException: No views in hierarchy found matching: with text: is "Rocket"
```

Unfortunately, something is not right. It is not finding results for your search.

IdlingResources

When using Espresso, your test suite is running in a different thread from your app. While there are some things related to the lifecycle of your activity that Espresso will be aware of, there are other things that it is not. In your case, in order to make your tests and test data readable, you are putting your data in a separate JSON file that needs to be read in. While this is not a big hit on the performance of your tests, a file read is slower than the execution time of your Espresso statements.

Because of this, Espresso is evaluating your statement to press the button for Rocket the cat before your app has finished reading in the data and populating your RecyclerView. One clumsy-but-effective way to work around this is to put a `Thread.sleep(5000)` before the command for the button press.

There are, however, a number of problems with that idea, including:

- Your tests may not need the amount of time you specified on a device, and will thus run slower than needed.
- Your tests may need more time than you specified on other devices which makes them unreliable.

This is where **IdlingResource** comes in. The idea behind using `IdlingResource` is to create a mechanism that allows you to send a message to Espresso telling it that the app is busy doing something and another message to tell it when it is done. That way your test is only waiting for a longer running command when it actually should.

To get started, create a new Kotlin file in your test directory called **SimpleIdlingResource.kt** and enter the following:

```
class SimpleIdlingResource : IdlingResource {

  // 1
  @Nullable
  @Volatile
  private var callback: IdlingResource.ResourceCallback? = null

  // 2
  // Idleness is controlled with this boolean.
  var activeResources = AtomicInteger(0)

  override fun getName(): String {
    return this.javaClass.name
  }

  // 3
  override fun isIdleNow(): Boolean {
```

```
    return activeResources.toInt() < 1
  }

  override fun registerIdleTransitionCallback(
    callback: IdlingResource.ResourceCallback
  ) {
    this.callback = callback
  }

  // 4
  fun incrementBy(incrementValue: Int) {
    if (activeResources.addAndGet(incrementValue) < 1 &&
        callback != null) {
      callback!!.onTransitionToIdle()
    }
  }
}
```

This class is an implementation of the `IdlingResource` interface. There is a lot going on here, so let's break it down:

1. Setting up a `ResourceCallback` reference to tell Espresso when it is transitioning to idle.
2. Creating a counter to keep track of the current active resources.
3. Returns the idling status based on the number of active resources.
4. Increments the active resources count by the number passed in and transitions to idle if this new value is less than 1.

Now that you have your `SimpleIdlingResource`, you are going to need a way to trigger it when something happens. You could move this to your app code, call it from there, and access it from your test. But, there is a way that is a little bit cleaner using **EventBus**.

EventBus is a library that makes it easy to subscribe to and publish messages. If you haven't used it before you can learn all about it at https://github.com/greenrobot/EventBus.

To get started, add the following to your app level build.gradle:

```
implementation 'org.greenrobot:eventbus:3.1.1'
```

`EventBus` posts and receives messages as data objects (often called Plain Old Java Objects, or POJOs in Java). These objects need to be in your app. Under **com.raywenderlich.codingcompanionfinder** in the main source set, create a new package called **testhooks**. In that package, create a Kotlin file called **IdlingEntity.kt**, and add the following content:

```
data class IdlingEntity(
  var incrementValue: Int = 0,
  var resetValue: Boolean = false
)
```

Next, open your **`MainActivity`** and add the following:

```
// 1
@Subscribe
fun onEvent(idlingEntity: IdlingEntity) {
  // noop
}

// 2
override fun onStart() {
  super.onStart()
  EventBus.getDefault().register(this)
}

// 3
override fun onStop() {
  super.onStop()
  EventBus.getDefault().unregister(this)
}
```

This is doing three things:

1. Adding a subscription, which is required for the EventBus library to work.
2. Registering this class with `EventBus` when the activity starts.
3. Unregistering this class with `Eventbus` when the activity stops.

Now, open your **`SearchForCompanion`** fragment in the **searchforcompanion** package and go to your `searchForCompanions` function. Add a post command to increment your Idling resources before you call your petfinder service:

```
EventBus.getDefault().post(IdlingEntity(1))
```

And another to decrement it once it is done with the call:

```
EventBus.getDefault().post(IdlingEntity(-1))
```

Your final method should look like this:

```
private fun searchForCompanions() {
  val companionLocation = view?
    .findViewById<TextInputEditText>(R.id.searchFieldText)
    ?.text.toString()
  val noResultsTextView = view?
    .findViewById<TextView>(R.id.noResults)
  val searchForCompanionFragment = this

  GlobalScope.launch {
    accessToken = (activity as MainActivity).accessToken
    (activity as MainActivity).petFinderService
      ?.let { petFinderService ->
      // increment the IdlingResources
      EventBus.getDefault().post(IdlingEntity(1))
      val getAnimalsRequest = petFinderService
        .getAnimals(accessToken, location = companionLocation)

      val searchForPetResponse = getAnimalsRequest.await()

      if (searchForPetResponse.isSuccessful) {
        searchForPetResponse.body()?.let {
          GlobalScope.launch(Dispatchers.Main) {
            if (it.animals.size > 0) {
              noResultsTextView?.visibility = INVISIBLE
              viewManager = LinearLayoutManager(context)
              companionAdapter = CompanionAdapter(it.animals,
                searchForCompanionFragment)
              petRecyclerView = view?.let {
                it.findViewById<RecyclerView>(
                  R.id.petRecyclerView
                ).apply {
                  layoutManager = viewManager
                  adapter = companionAdapter
                }
              }
            } else {
              noResultsTextView?.visibility = VISIBLE
            }
          }
        }
      } else {
        noResultsTextView?.visibility = VISIBLE
      }
      // Decrement the idling resources.
      EventBus.getDefault().post(IdlingEntity(-1))
    }
  }
}
```

You're almost there! Open up your **FindCompanionInstrumentedTest.kt** and add a line to create a `SimpleIdlingResource` as a property at the class level:

```
private val idlingResource = SimpleIdlingResource()
```

Now add a subscribe function to receive increment/decrement calls:

```
@Subscribe
fun onEvent(idlingEntity: IdlingEntity) {
  idlingResource.incrementBy(idlingEntity.incrementValue)
}
```

Next, in `searching_for_a_companion_and_tapping_on_it_takes_the_user_to_the_companion_details()`, add these two lines after you launch your activity:

```
EventBus.getDefault().register(this)
IdlingRegistry.getInstance().register(idlingResource)
```

This registers your test class with `EventBus` and registers the idling resources. Finally, add these two lines at the end of that function before `testScenario.close()`:

```
IdlingRegistry.getInstance().unregister(idlingResource)
EventBus.getDefault().unregister(this)
```

Your final function should look like this:

```
@Test
fun
searching_for_a_companion_and_tapping_on_it_takes_the_user_to_th
e_companion_details() {
  testScenario = ActivityScenario.launch(startIntent)

  // eventbus and idling resources register
  EventBus.getDefault().register(this)
  IdlingRegistry.getInstance().register(idlingResource)
  onView(withId(R.id.searchForCompanionFragment))
    .perform(click())
  onView(withId(R.id.searchFieldText))
    .perform(typeText("30318"))
  onView(withId(R.id.searchButton)).perform(click())
  onView(withId(R.id.searchButton))
    .check(matches(isDisplayed()))
  onView(withText("KEVIN")).perform(click())
  onView(withText("Rome, GA")).check(matches(isDisplayed()))

  // eventbus and idling resources unregister.
  IdlingRegistry.getInstance().unregister(idlingResource)
```

```
    EventBus.getDefault().unregister(this)
    testScenario.close()
  }
```

Run your tests and everything will be green.

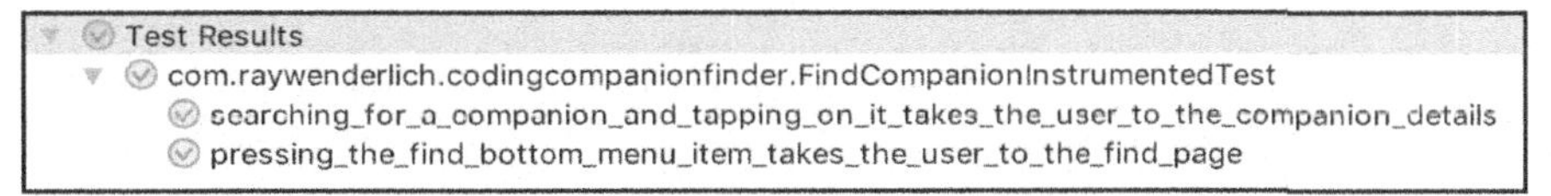

Now that you have all of this in place, it's time to add the shelter information to your companion details page. The test for this will be very similar to the last test you added. You are going to go to your Find Companion page, search by a location, select a companion, and then verify that the contact information is correct. The only difference will be what you are checking for.

DRYing up your tests

One term you will hear when someone speaks about software as a craft is writing **DRY** code. DRY stands for **Do Not Repeat Yourself**. In practical terms, this means that you should try to avoid multiple lines of duplicate code in your app.

This is also a good thing to do with tests. That said, your tests, if you are doing TDD well, provide a form of documentation for the code. If drying up your tests makes it easier to maintain your tests and makes them more readable, by all means do it, but if a particular effort to dry out the tests doesn't add a significant maintainability benefit, or makes them more difficult to read, it may be better not to do that refactor.

Looking at your current tests, you have the following code at the beginning of both:

```
testScenario = ActivityScenario.launch(startIntent)
```

You also have the following at the end of both:

```
testScenario.close()
```

The common code at the beginning of both tests can be moved to a common **@Before** method and will make both tests more readable by moving common set-up information out of the individual tests.

To get started, add the following method to your test class:

```
@Before
fun beforeTestsRun() {
  testScenario = ActivityScenario.launch(startIntent)
}
```

The **@Before** annotation tells the test suite to run that function before every test. Now, add the following method:

```
@After
fun afterTestsRun() {
  testScenario.close()
}
```

Next, remove the following from your `pressing_the_find_bottom_menu_item_takes_the_user_to_the_find_page()` and `searching_for_a_companion_and_tapping_on_it_takes_the_user_to_the_companion_details()` tests:

```
testScenario = ActivityScenario.launch(startIntent)
```

And:

```
testScenario.close()
```

Finally, run the tests and everything will still be green.

Test Results
com.raywenderlich.codingcompanionfinder.FindCompanionInstrumentedTest
searching_for_a_companion_and_tapping_on_it_takes_the_user_to_the_companion_details
pressing_the_find_bottom_menu_item_takes_the_user_to_the_find_page

Your next test is going to use the `IdlingRegistry`. Having that run before your `pressing_the_find_bottom_menu_item_takes_the_user_to_the_find_page` will not affect that test. It will also make `searching_for_a_companion_and_tapping_on_it_takes_the_user_to_the_companion_details` and your next test more readable. Move the following two lines from `searching_for_a_companion_and_tapping_on_it_takes_the_user_to_the_companion_details` to the end of the `beforeTestRun()` function:

```
EventBus.getDefault().register(this)
IdlingRegistry.getInstance().register(idlingResource)
```

Next, cut the following two lines from the end of `searching_for_a_companion_and_tapping_on_it_takes_the_user_to_the_companion_details`:

```
IdlingRegistry.getInstance().unregister(idlingResource)
EventBus.getDefault().unregister(this)
```

And add them to the beginning of your `afterTestRun()` function.

Finally, run the tests and make sure everything is green.

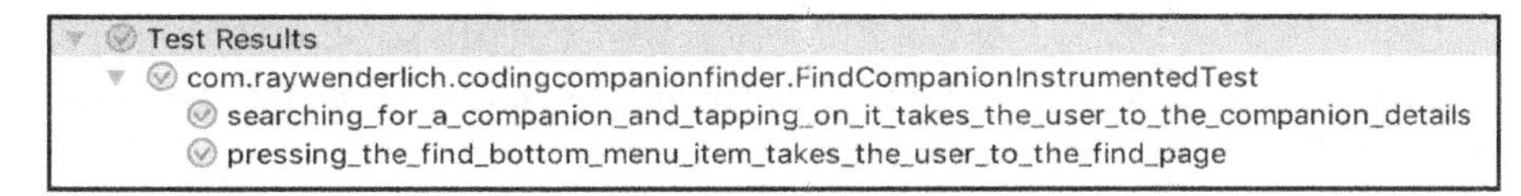

Your next test is going to share a lot of steps with `searching_for_a_companion_and_tapping_on_it_takes_the_user_to_the_companion_details`. So lets refactor some common functionality.

First, cut the following lines from `searching_for_a_companion_and_tapping_on_it_takes_the_user_to_the_companion_details`:

```
onView(withId(R.id.searchForCompanionFragment))
  .perform(click())
onView(withId(R.id.searchFieldText))
  .perform(typeText("30318"))
onView(withId(R.id.searchButton)).perform(click())
onView(withId(R.id.searchButton))
  .check(matches(isDisplayed()))
onView(withText("KEVIN")).perform(click())
```

Next, paste them into a new function:

```
private fun find_and_select_kevin_in_30318(){
  onView(withId(R.id.searchForCompanionFragment))
    .perform(click())
  onView(withId(R.id.searchFieldText))
    .perform(typeText("30318"))
  onView(withId(R.id.searchButton)).perform(click())
  onView(withId(R.id.searchButton))
    .check(matches(isDisplayed()))
  onView(withText("KEVIN")).perform(click())
}
```

Now, add a call to your new function in
searching_for_a_companion_and_tapping_on_it_takes_the_user_to_the_companion_de
tails:

```
@Test
fun
searching_for_a_companion_and_tapping_on_it_takes_the_user_to_th
e_companion_details() {
  find_and_select_kevin_in_30318()
  onView(withText("Rome, GA")).check(matches(isDisplayed()))
}
```

Finally, run the tests and make sure everything is still green — it is important to check your refactors haven't accidentally broken anything.

Test Results
com.raywenderlich.codingcompanionfinder.FindCompanionInstrumentedTest
searching_for_a_companion_and_tapping_on_it_takes_the_user_to_the_companion_details
pressing_the_find_bottom_menu_item_takes_the_user_to_the_find_page

Writing your failing test

Now, it is time to write your failing test – which you will implement afterwards. For this new test, you are going to check to make sure that you can view the correct phone number and email address when you view the details for Rocket.

To get started, add the following test:

```
@Test
fun
verify_that_companion_details_shows_a_valid_phone_number_and_ema
il() {
  find_and_select_kevin_in_30318()
  onView(withText("(706) 236-4537"))
    .check(matches(isDisplayed()))
  onView(withText("adoptions@gahomelesspets.com"))
    .check(matches(isDisplayed()))
}
```

Now, run the test and make sure that it fails.

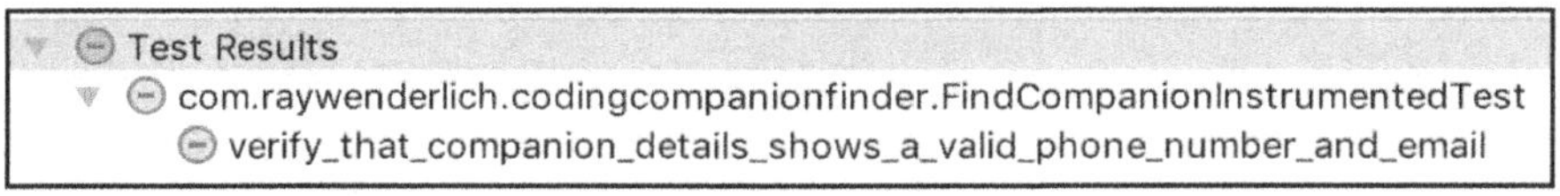

Test Results
com.raywenderlich.codingcompanionfinder.FindCompanionInstrumentedTest
verify_that_companion_details_shows_a_valid_phone_number_and_email

Next, open **fragment_view_companion.xml** and replace this:

```
<androidx.appcompat.widget.AppCompatTextView
  android:id="@+id/breed"
  android:layout_width="wrap_content"
  android:layout_height="wrap_content"
  android:text="@string/breed_placeholder"
  app:layout_constraintBottom_toTopOf="@+id/age"
  app:layout_constraintEnd_toStartOf="@id/city"
  app:layout_constraintStart_toStartOf="parent"
  app:layout_constraintTop_toBottomOf="@+id/petCarouselView" />

<androidx.appcompat.widget.AppCompatTextView
  android:id="@+id/city"
  android:layout_width="wrap_content"
  android:layout_height="wrap_content"
  android:text="@string/city_placeholder"
  app:layout_constraintBottom_toBottomOf="@id/breed"
  app:layout_constraintEnd_toEndOf="parent"
  app:layout_constraintStart_toEndOf="@+id/breed"
  app:layout_constraintTop_toTopOf="@+id/breed" />

<androidx.appcompat.widget.AppCompatTextView
  android:id="@+id/age"
  android:layout_width="wrap_content"
  android:layout_height="wrap_content"
  android:text="@string/age_placeholder"
  app:layout_constraintBottom_toTopOf="@id/meetTitlePlaceholder"
  app:layout_constraintEnd_toStartOf="@id/sex"
  app:layout_constraintStart_toStartOf="parent"
  app:layout_constraintTop_toBottomOf="@id/breed" />
```

With:

```
<androidx.appcompat.widget.AppCompatTextView
  android:id="@+id/breed"
  android:layout_width="wrap_content"
  android:layout_height="wrap_content"
  android:text="@string/breed_placeholder"
  app:layout_constraintBottom_toTopOf="@+id/email"
  app:layout_constraintEnd_toStartOf="@id/city"
  app:layout_constraintStart_toStartOf="parent"
  app:layout_constraintTop_toBottomOf="@+id/petCarouselView" />

<androidx.appcompat.widget.AppCompatTextView
  android:id="@+id/city"
  android:layout_width="wrap_content"
  android:layout_height="wrap_content"
  android:text="@string/city_placeholder"
  app:layout_constraintBottom_toBottomOf="@id/breed"
  app:layout_constraintEnd_toEndOf="parent"
  app:layout_constraintStart_toEndOf="@+id/breed"
```

```
    app:layout_constraintTop_toTopOf="@+id/breed" />

  <androidx.appcompat.widget.AppCompatTextView
    android:id="@+id/email"
    android:layout_width="wrap_content"
    android:layout_height="wrap_content"
    android:text="email placeholder"
    android:textStyle="bold"
    app:layout_constraintBottom_toTopOf="@+id/age"
    app:layout_constraintEnd_toStartOf="@id/telephone"
    app:layout_constraintStart_toStartOf="parent"
    app:layout_constraintTop_toBottomOf="@+id/breed" />

  <androidx.appcompat.widget.AppCompatTextView
    android:id="@+id/telephone"
    android:layout_width="wrap_content"
    android:layout_height="wrap_content"
    android:text="telephone placeholder"
    android:textStyle="bold"
    app:layout_constraintBottom_toBottomOf="@id/email"
    app:layout_constraintEnd_toEndOf="parent"
    app:layout_constraintStart_toEndOf="@+id/email"
    app:layout_constraintTop_toTopOf="@+id/email" />

  <androidx.appcompat.widget.AppCompatTextView
    android:id="@+id/age"
    android:layout_width="wrap_content"
    android:layout_height="wrap_content"
    android:text="@string/age_placeholder"
    app:layout_constraintBottom_toTopOf="@id/meetTitlePlaceholder"
    app:layout_constraintEnd_toStartOf="@id/sex"
    app:layout_constraintStart_toStartOf="parent"
    app:layout_constraintTop_toBottomOf="@id/email" />
```

Next, open **ViewCompanionFragment.kt** and add the following to the `populatePet()` function:

```
populateTextField(R.id.email, animal.contact.email)
populateTextField(R.id.telephone, animal.contact.phone)
```

Finally, run your tests and everything should be green.

```
Test Results
  com.raywenderlich.codingcompanionfinder.FindCompanionInstrumentedTest
    verify_that_companion_details_shows_a_valid_phone_number_and_email
    searching_for_a_companion_and_tapping_on_it_takes_the_user_to_the_companion_details
    pressing_the_find_bottom_menu_item_takes_the_user_to_the_find_page
```

Congratulations! Your app is under test and the shelter has a new feature that will help them to place more coding companions!

Key points

- When working with a legacy app, start by abstracting away external dependencies.
- Don't try to get everything under test at one time.
- Focus your testing efforts around a section you are changing.
- MockWebServer is a great way to mock data for Retrofit.
- When getting a legacy app under test you will probably end up needing to use IdlingResources.
- DRY out your tests when it makes them more readable.
- Don't try to refactor a section of your legacy app until it is under test.

Where to go from here?

You've done a lot of work in this chapter! If you want to take some of these techniques further, try writing some tests around more scenarios in the app. You can also try your hand at adding additional features to the app. To see what is available with the API check out the Petfinder API documentation at https://www.petfinder.com/developers/api-docs.

Digging deeper, in the next chapter, Chapter 14, "Hands-On Focused Refactoring," you will begin to explore how you can use TDD and refactoring side-by-side.

Chapter 14: Hands-On Focused Refactoring

By Lance Gleason

In the last chapter, you had a chance to:

1. Get familiar with the Coding Companion app.
2. Add tests around the search functionality.
3. Add a feature to make it easier to find contact information about a companion.

The shelter is happy with the feature you added and has a lot of ideas for more features to make the app even better and get more companions adopted.

Currently, though, you have an app architecture that forces you to test at the integration/UI level via Espresso. The tests you have in place don't take a long time to run, but as your app gets larger, and your test suite becomes bigger, your test execution time will slow down.

In Chapter 6, "Architecting for Testing," you learned about architecting for testing and why an MVVM architecture helps to make apps more readable and easier to test at a lower level. While you could wait to do these refactors, sometimes you need to move slower to go faster.

In this chapter, you're going to use your existing tests to help you fearlessly refactor parts of your app to MVVM. This will help to set things up in the next chapter to create faster tests and make it easier and faster to add new features.

Getting started

To get started, open the final app from the previous chapter or open the starter app for this chapter. Then, open **FindCompanionInstrumentedTest.kt** located inside the **androidTest** source set.

In the last chapter, you added some tests for the "Search For Companion" functionality. You can find this test inside **FindCompanionInstrumentedTest.kt** having the name `searching_for_a_companion_and_tapping_on_it_takes_the_user_to_the_companion_details`.

This test does the following:

1. It starts the app's main activity, which takes the user to the **Random Companion** screen; this screen is backed by `RandomCompanionFragment`.

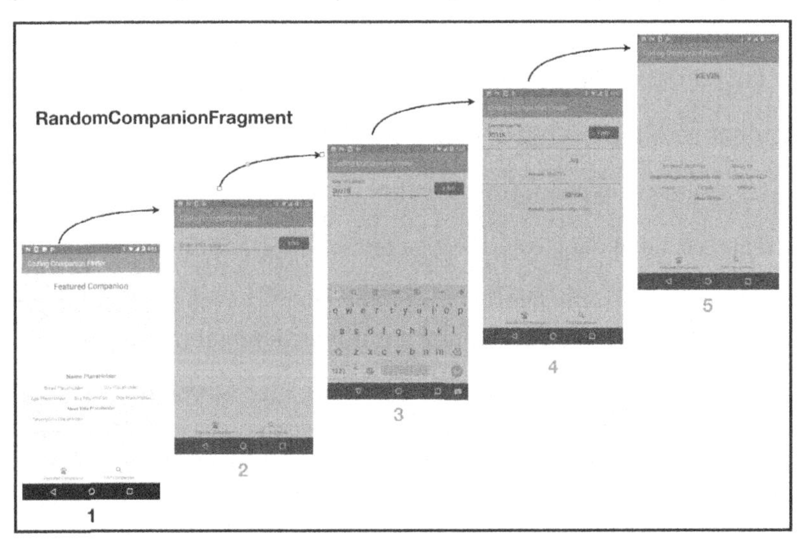

2. Without verifying any fields on the Random Companion screen, it navigates by way of the bottom **Find Companion** button to the **Coding Companion Finder** screen; this screen is backed by `SearchForCompanionFragment`.

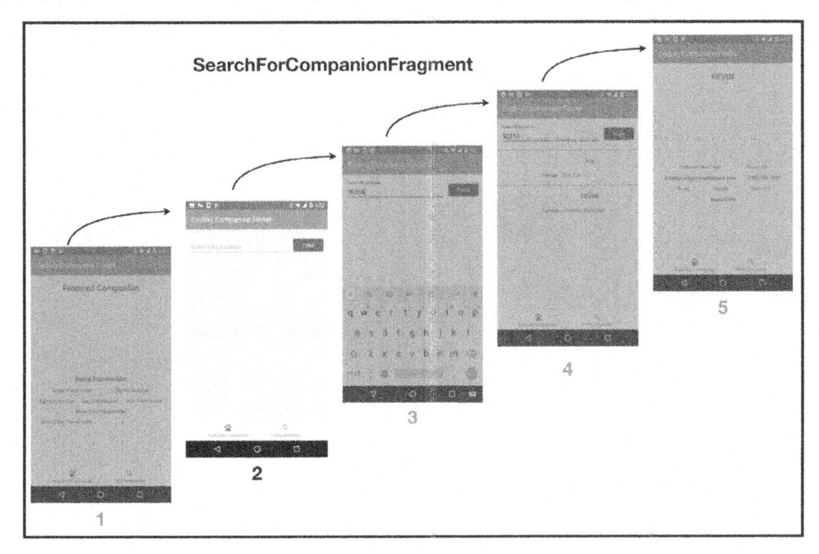

3. Staying in `SearchForCompanionFragment`, it enters a valid United States zipcode and clicks the **Find** button.

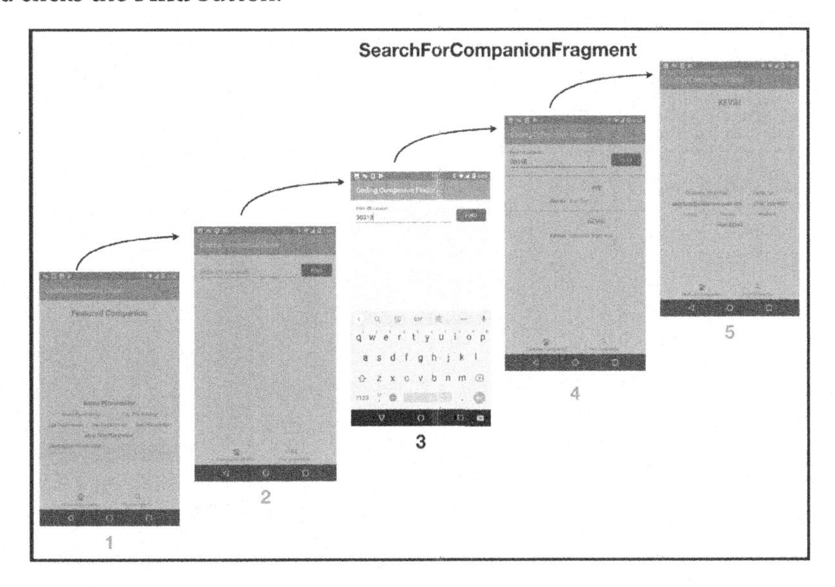

4. Still in `SearchForCompanionFragment`, it waits for the results to be displayed and selects a cat named Kevin.

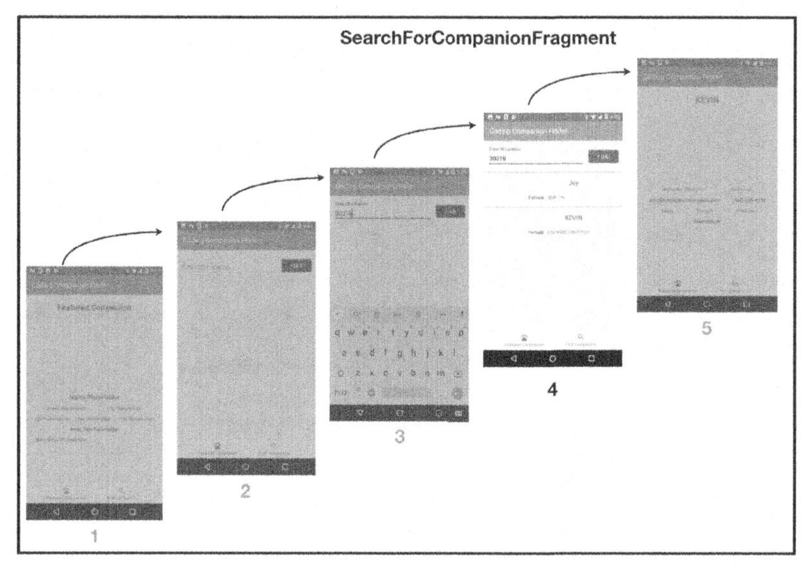

5. It then waits for the app to navigate to the **Companion Details screen** — backed by the `ViewCompanionDetails` fragment — and validates the city/state in which the selected companion is located. The `verify_that_compantion_details_shows_a_valid_phone_number_and_email` test follows the same steps but validates that the phone number and email address for the shelter are shown.

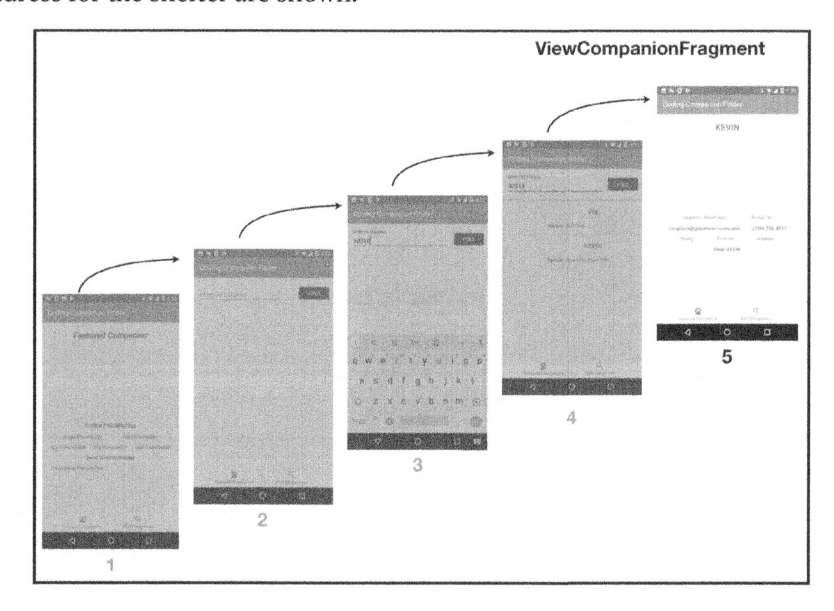

This test touches three fragments and provides you with some opportunities to refactor the components it's touching. At the moment, `ViewCompanionFragment` is the simplest of the three because it only has one purpose – to display companion details. Therefore, you'll start by refactoring this test.

Adding supplemental coverage before refactoring

You already have some testing around the "Search For Companion" functionality, including `ViewCompanionFragment`. Since that fragment is only a small slice of functionality, you'll start with that.

Before you start to refactor, you need to make sure you have tests around everything that you're changing. This helps to ensure that your refactoring doesn't accidentally break anything. Because you're changing things to an MVVM architecture, you're going to touch all of the data elements this fragment displays.

Looking at the two tests that test this screen, in **FindCompanionsInstrumentedTest.kt**, you'll see the following:

```
@Test
fun
searching_for_a_companion_and_tapping_on_it_takes_the_user_to_th
e_companion_details() {
  find_and_select_kevin_in_30318()
  onView(withText("Rome, GA")).check(matches(isDisplayed()))
}

@Test
fun
verify_that_companion_details_shows_a_valid_phone_number_and_ema
il() {
  find_and_select_kevin_in_30318()
  onView(withText("(706) 236-4537"))
    .check(matches(isDisplayed()))
  onView(withText("adoptions@gahomelesspets.com"))
    .check(matches(isDisplayed()))
}
```

This is testing some of the fields in the View Companion details, but not all of them. Because Espresso tests are slow, it's better to add these checks to one of your existing tests.

In this case, you're going to use `searching_for_a_companion_and_tapping_on_it_takes_the_user_to_the_companion_details`, so paste the following to the end of that test:

```
onView(withText("Domestic Short
Hair")).check(matches(isDisplayed()))
onView(withText("Young")).check(matches(isDisplayed()))
onView(withText("Female")).check(matches(isDisplayed()))
onView(withText("Medium")).check(matches(isDisplayed()))
onView(withText("Meet KEVIN")).check(matches(isDisplayed()))
```

Your test will now look like this:

```
@Test
fun
searching_for_a_companion_and_tapping_on_it_takes_the_user_to_th
e_companion_details() {
  find_and_select_kevin_in_30318()
  onView(withText("Rome, GA")).check(matches(isDisplayed()))
  onView(withText("Domestic Short
Hair")).check(matches(isDisplayed()))
  onView(withText("Young")).check(matches(isDisplayed()))
  onView(withText("Female")).check(matches(isDisplayed()))
  onView(withText("Medium")).check(matches(isDisplayed()))
  onView(withText("Meet KEVIN")).check(matches(isDisplayed()))
}
```

Run it, and you'll see the following:

```
▼ Test Results                                                                              3 s 763 ms
    com.raywenderlich.codingcompanionfinder.FindCompanionInstrumentedTest                  3 s 763 ms
      searching_for_a_companion_and_tapping_on_it_takes_the_user_to_the_companion_details  3 s 763 ms
```

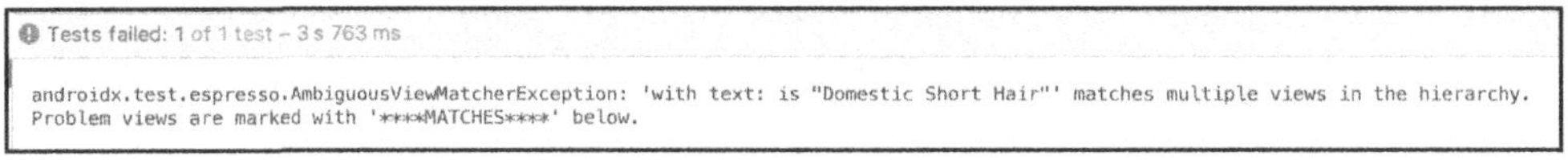

```
Tests failed: 1 of 1 test – 3 s 763 ms

androidx.test.espresso.AmbiguousViewMatcherException: 'with text: is "Domestic Short Hair"' matches multiple views in the hierarchy.
Problem views are marked with '****MATCHES****' below.
```

According to this message, the view hierarchy has more than one field with text containing "Domestic Short Hair".

Refactoring for testability

With Espresso tests, you'll often run into a scenario where you have a matcher for an element that ends up matching more than one element in the view hierarchy. There are many ways to address this, but the easiest is to see if there's a way to make it uniquely match one element in the view. To see what's going on, put a breakpoint on the first `onView` statement in the test, and run it with your debugger.

Looking at the app screen, you'll see the following:

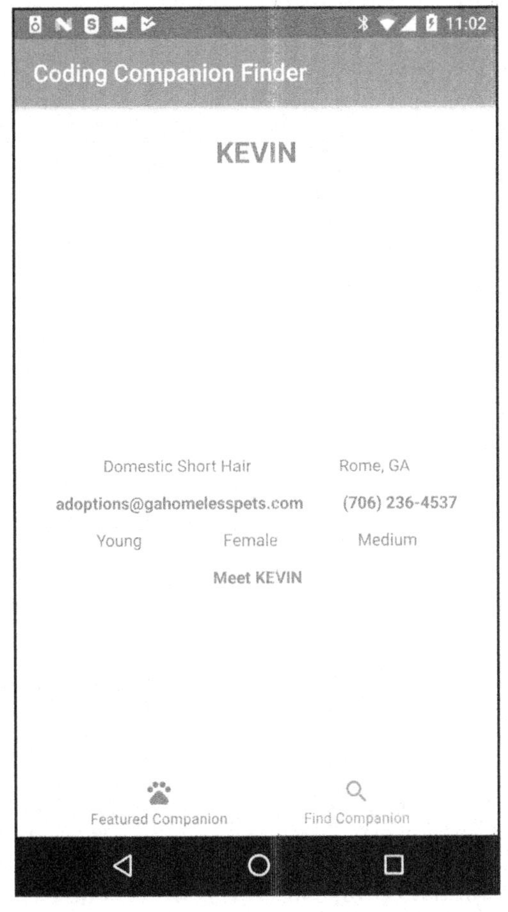

The screen only displays "Domestic Short Hair" once. So, what's happening here?

The `CompanionViewHolder` holds some clues. Look at `setupClickEvent` in this View Holder, and you'll see the following line:

```
transaction.replace(R.id.viewCompanion,
viewCompanionFragment).addToBackStack("companionView").commit()
```

Click on **R.id.viewCompanion** to find it in your view, and you'll see that it is displaying `viewCompanionFragment` in a `FrameLayout`.

```
<androidx.constraintlayout.widget.ConstraintLayout xmlns:android='
  xmlns:app="http://schemas.android.com/apk/res-auto"
  xmlns:tools="http://schemas.android.com/tools"
  android:layout_width="match_parent"
  android:layout_height="match_parent"
  tools:context=".searchforcompanion.SearchForCompanionFragment">

  <FrameLayout
    android:id="@+id/viewCompanion"
    android:layout_width="0dp"
    android:layout_height="0dp"
    android:translationZ="10dp"
    app:layout_constraintBottom_toBottomOf="parent"
    app:layout_constraintEnd_toEndOf="parent"
    app:layout_constraintStart_toStartOf="parent"
    app:layout_constraintTop_toTopOf="parent" />

  <androidx.constraintlayout.widget.ConstraintLayout
    android:id="@+id/searchForCompanion"
    android:layout_width="0dp"
    android:layout_height="0dp"
    app:layout_constraintBottom_toBottomOf="parent"
    app:layout_constraintEnd_toEndOf="parent"
    app:layout_constraintStart_toStartOf="parent"
    app:layout_constraintTop_toTopOf="parent">

    <com.google.android.material.textfield.TextInputLayout...>

    <com.google.android.material.button.MaterialButton...>

    <androidx.recyclerview.widget.RecyclerView
      android:id="@+id/petRecyclerView"
      android:layout_width="match_parent"
      android:layout_height="0dp"
      app:layout_constraintBottom_toBottomOf="parent"
      app:layout_constraintEnd_toEndOf="parent"
      app:layout_constraintHeight_percent=".8"
      app:layout_constraintStart_toStartOf="parent"
      app:layout_constraintTop_toBottomOf="@id/searchField" />

    <TextView...>
  </androidx.constraintlayout.widget.ConstraintLayout>
</androidx.constraintlayout.widget.ConstraintLayout>
```

This `FrameLayout` is on the same level as a `ConstraintLayout` that has a `RecyclerView`, which ultimately displays the search results.

Also notice:

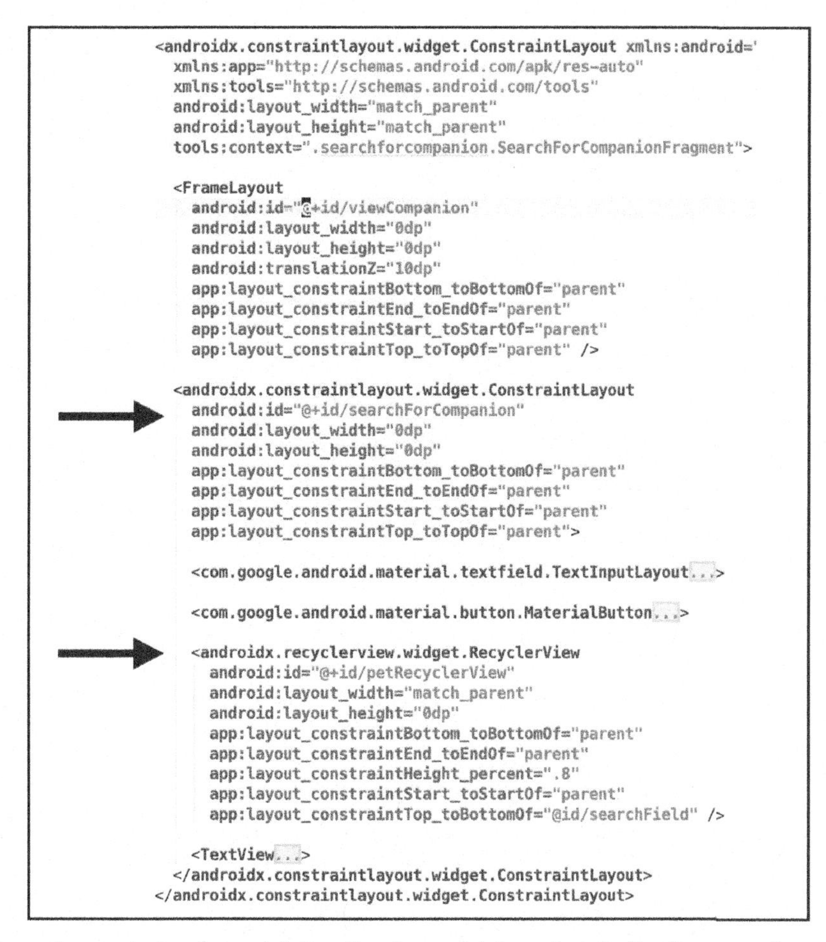

```
<androidx.constraintlayout.widget.ConstraintLayout xmlns:android='
  xmlns:app="http://schemas.android.com/apk/res-auto"
  xmlns:tools="http://schemas.android.com/tools"
  android:layout_width="match_parent"
  android:layout_height="match_parent"
  tools:context=".searchforcompanion.SearchForCompanionFragment">

  <FrameLayout
    android:id="@+id/viewCompanion"
    android:layout_width="0dp"
    android:layout_height="0dp"
    android:translationZ="10dp"
    app:layout_constraintBottom_toBottomOf="parent"
    app:layout_constraintEnd_toEndOf="parent"
    app:layout_constraintStart_toStartOf="parent"
    app:layout_constraintTop_toTopOf="parent" />

  <androidx.constraintlayout.widget.ConstraintLayout
    android:id="@+id/searchForCompanion"
    android:layout_width="0dp"
    android:layout_height="0dp"
    app:layout_constraintBottom_toBottomOf="parent"
    app:layout_constraintEnd_toEndOf="parent"
    app:layout_constraintStart_toStartOf="parent"
    app:layout_constraintTop_toTopOf="parent">

    <com.google.android.material.textfield.TextInputLayout...>

    <com.google.android.material.button.MaterialButton...>

    <androidx.recyclerview.widget.RecyclerView
      android:id="@+id/petRecyclerView"
      android:layout_width="match_parent"
      android:layout_height="0dp"
      app:layout_constraintBottom_toBottomOf="parent"
      app:layout_constraintEnd_toEndOf="parent"
      app:layout_constraintHeight_percent=".8"
      app:layout_constraintStart_toStartOf="parent"
      app:layout_constraintTop_toBottomOf="@id/searchField" />

    <TextView...>
  </androidx.constraintlayout.widget.ConstraintLayout>
</androidx.constraintlayout.widget.ConstraintLayout>
```

This `FrameLayout` also has a higher Z value, which makes it display over the `ConstraintLayout`.

Notice here:

```
<androidx.constraintlayout.widget.ConstraintLayout xmlns:android='
  xmlns:app="http://schemas.android.com/apk/res-auto"
  xmlns:tools="http://schemas.android.com/tools"
  android:layout_width="match_parent"
  android:layout_height="match_parent"
  tools:context=".searchforcompanion.SearchForCompanionFragment">

  <FrameLayout
    android:id="@+id/viewCompanion"
    android:layout_width="0dp"
    android:layout_height="0dp"
    android:translationZ="10dp"
    app:layout_constraintBottom_toBottomOf="parent"
    app:layout_constraintEnd_toEndOf="parent"
    app:layout_constraintStart_toStartOf="parent"
    app:layout_constraintTop_toTopOf="parent" />

  <androidx.constraintlayout.widget.ConstraintLayout
    android:id="@+id/searchForCompanion"
    android:layout_width="0dp"
    android:layout_height="0dp"
    app:layout_constraintBottom_toBottomOf="parent"
    app:layout_constraintEnd_toEndOf="parent"
    app:layout_constraintStart_toStartOf="parent"
    app:layout_constraintTop_toTopOf="parent">

    <com.google.android.material.textfield.TextInputLayout...>

    <com.google.android.material.button.MaterialButton...>

    <androidx.recyclerview.widget.RecyclerView
      android:id="@+id/petRecyclerView"
      android:layout_width="match_parent"
      android:layout_height="0dp"
      app:layout_constraintBottom_toBottomOf="parent"
      app:layout_constraintEnd_toEndOf="parent"
      app:layout_constraintHeight_percent=".8"
      app:layout_constraintStart_toStartOf="parent"
      app:layout_constraintTop_toBottomOf="@id/searchField" />

    <TextView...>
  </androidx.constraintlayout.widget.ConstraintLayout>
</androidx.constraintlayout.widget.ConstraintLayout>
```

Look at the `setupClickEvent` in `CompanionViewHolder`, and you'll see that you're doing a transaction to replace `R.id.viewCompanion` with a `ViewCompanionFragment`.

```
transaction.replace(R.id.viewCompanion, viewCompanionFragment)
  .addToBackStack("companionView")
  .commit()
```

The issue is most likely that two views show this information — but one is hiding below the other. One way to fix this problem might be to also match on the ID of the field.

Currently, in **find_pet_list_layout.xml**, you've given the field that contains the breeds an ID of `breed` which is displayed by the `CompanionViewHolder` in the `RecyclerView`.

```
<androidx.appcompat.widget.AppCompatTextView
  android:id="@+id/breed"
  android:layout_width="0dp"
  android:layout_height="wrap_content"
  android:paddingEnd="10dp"
  android:paddingStart="10dp"
  android:text="Breed"
  app:layout_constraintBottom_toBottomOf="@+id/sex"
  app:layout_constraintEnd_toEndOf="parent"
  app:layout_constraintStart_toEndOf="@id/sex"
  app:layout_constraintTop_toTopOf="@id/sex" />
```

It's also named `breed` in **fragment_view_companion.xml** that is displayed by your `ViewCompanionFragment`.

```
<androidx.appcompat.widget.AppCompatTextView
  android:id="@+id/breed"
  android:layout_width="wrap_content"
  android:layout_height="wrap_content"
  android:text="@string/breed_placeholder"
  app:layout_constraintBottom_toTopOf="@+id/email"
  app:layout_constraintEnd_toStartOf="@id/city"
  app:layout_constraintStart_toStartOf="parent"
  app:layout_constraintTop_toBottomOf="@+id/petCarouselView" />
```

You could change the ID of the breed in the `ViewCompanionFragment`, but a better approach is to do a full replacement of the fragment, so you don't have two simultaneous view hierarchies in the `ViewCompanionFragment`.

Since you're already using the Jetpack Navigation Components, this is a good time to do a refactor to use this. If you're new to Android Navigation Components, you can learn more about them at https://developer.android.com/guide/navigation.

Open **nav_graph.xml** inside **res ▸ navigation** and add the following inside the `<navigation>` element at the bottom:

```
<fragment
  android:id="@+id/viewCompanion"

android:name="com.raywenderlich.codingcompanionfinder.searchforc
```

```
ompanion.ViewCompanionFragment"
  android:label="fragment_view_companion"
  tools:layout="@layout/fragment_view_companion" >
  <argument
    android:name="animal"

app:argType="com.raywenderlich.codingcompanionfinder.models.Anim
al" />
</fragment>
```

This adds the `ViewCompanionFragment` to the navigation graph.

Next, replace:

```
<fragment
  android:id="@+id/searchForCompanionFragment"

android:name="com.raywenderlich.codingcompanionfinder.searchforc
ompanion.SearchForCompanionFragment"
  android:label="fragment_search_for_pet"
  tools:layout="@layout/fragment_search_for_companion" />
```

With the following:

```
<fragment
  android:id="@+id/searchForCompanionFragment"

android:name="com.raywenderlich.codingcompanionfinder.searchforc
ompanion.SearchForCompanionFragment"
  android:label="fragment_search_for_pet"
  tools:layout="@layout/fragment_search_for_companion" >
  <action
    android:id="@+id/
action_searchForCompanionFragment_to_viewCompanion"
    app:destination="@id/viewCompanion" />
</fragment>
```

This adds an action to allow you to navigate between the `SearchForCompanion` and `ViewCompanion` fragment.

Looking at `clickListener()` in the `CompanionViewHolder`, you're passing an animal object to that fragment:

```
view.setOnClickListener {
  val viewCompanionFragment = ViewCompanionFragment()
  val bundle = Bundle()
  bundle.putSerializable(ViewCompanionFragment.ANIMAL, animal)
  viewCompanionFragment.arguments = bundle
  val transaction =
    fragment.childFragmentManager.beginTransaction()
```

```
    transaction.replace(R.id.searchForCompanion,
      viewCompanionFragment)
      .addToBackStack("companionView")
      .commit()
  }
```

To pass the arguments with Jetpack Navigation, you'll use **Safe Args**. If you've not used this before, you can learn more about it at https://developer.android.com/guide/navigation/navigation-pass-data#Safe-args.

Open CodingCompanionFinder **build.gradle** and add the following to the dependencies:

```
classpath "androidx.navigation:navigation-safe-args-gradle-
plugin:2.3.5"
```

Next, open your app level **build.gradle** and add the following to the top of the file:

```
apply plugin: "androidx.navigation.safeargs.kotlin"
```

This adds in Safe Args support.

Now, open **CompanionViewHolder.kt** and replace `setupClickEvent()` with the following, fixing the imports as needed:

```
private fun setupClickEvent(animal: Animal) {
  view.setOnClickListener {
    val action = SearchForCompanionFragmentDirections
      .actionSearchForCompanionFragmentToViewCompanion(animal)
    view.findNavController().navigate(action)
  }
}
```

This is using `SearchForCompanionFragmentDirections` which is generated by Safe Args to create a navigation action with the animal as a parameter. You're then passing the action to the `navigate` method on the navigation controller to perform the navigation to the `ViewCompanionFragment`.

Finally, open **ViewCompanionFragment.kt** in the same package and add the following property:

```
val args: ViewCompanionFragmentArgs by navArgs()
```

Then replace onCreateView with the following:

```
override fun onCreateView(
    inflater: LayoutInflater, container: ViewGroup?,
    savedInstanceState: Bundle?
): View? {
  // Inflate the layout for this fragment
  animal = args.animal
  viewCompanionFragment = this
  return inflater.inflate(R.layout.fragment_view_companion,
    container, false)
}
```

This retrieves the arguments passed to the fragment via ViewCompanionFragmentArgs which is generated by Safe Args.

Open **fragment_search_for_companion.xml** and remove the FrameLayout with an android:id of @+id/viewCompanion.

Finally, execute the searching_for_a_companion_and_tapping_on_it_takes_the_user_to_the_companion_details test in **FindCompanionInstrumentedTest.kt**, and it'll be green.

Test Results	14 s 706 ms
com.raywenderlich.codingcompanionfinder.FindCompanionInstrumentedTest	14 s 706 ms
searching_for_a_companion_and_tapping_on_it_takes_the_user_to_the_companion_details	14 s 706 ms

Your first focused refactor

Now that you have proper test coverage around ViewCompanionFragment, it's time to refactor it. To get started, open the app level **build.gradle** and add the following to the dependencies section:

```
// Architecture components
def lifecycle_version = "2.2.0"
implementation "androidx.lifecycle:lifecycle-extensions:
$lifecycle_version"
kapt "androidx.lifecycle:lifecycle-compiler:$lifecycle_version"
```

This is adding the Jetpack Lifecycle components. Next, add the following to the Android section below buildTypes in the same file to enable data binding:

```
dataBinding {
  enabled = true
}
```

Following that, create a Kotlin file named **ViewCompanionViewModel.kt** in the **searchforcompanion** package and add the following:

```
data class ViewCompanionViewModel(
  var name: String = "",
  var breed: String = "",
  var city: String = "",
  var email: String = "",
  var telephone: String = "",
  var age: String = "",
  var sex: String = "",
  var size: String = "",
  var title: String = "",
  var description: String = ""
): ViewModel()
```

This creates a `ViewModel` for the data.

Next, open **fragment_view_companion.xml** and add a `<layout>` tag around the `ConstraintLayout` along with a `<data>` and `<variable>` tag for the view model, so it looks like this:

```
<layout>

  <data>
    <variable
      name="viewCompanionViewModel"

type="com.raywenderlich.codingcompanionfinder.searchforcompanion
.ViewCompanionViewModel" />
  </data>

 <androidx.constraintlayout.widget.ConstraintLayout
xmlns:android="http://schemas.android.com/apk/res/android"
   xmlns:app="http://schemas.android.com/apk/res-auto"
   xmlns:tools="http://schemas.android.com/tools"
   android:layout_width="match_parent"
   android:layout_height="match_parent"
   android:background="@color/secondaryTextColor"
   android:translationZ="5dp"
   tools:context=".randomcompanion.RandomCompanionFragment">
   .
   .
   .
  </androidx.constraintlayout.widget.ConstraintLayout>
</layout>
```

This adds the ability to bind data from the `ViewCompanionViewModel` to this view.

Now, bind each attribute of the view model to each element with a corresponding ID by replacing the text with the binding. For example, for the element with an ID of “name”, you’ll replace the text with `@{viewCompanionViewModel.name}`.

Your final **fragment_view_companion.xml** will look like this:

```
<layout>

  <data>
    <variable
      name="viewCompanionViewModel"

type="com.raywenderlich.codingcompanionfinder.searchforcompanion
.ViewCompanionViewModel" />
  </data>

  <androidx.constraintlayout.widget.ConstraintLayout
xmlns:android="http://schemas.android.com/apk/res/android"
    xmlns:app="http://schemas.android.com/apk/res-auto"
    xmlns:tools="http://schemas.android.com/tools"
    android:layout_width="match_parent"
    android:layout_height="match_parent"
    android:background="@color/secondaryTextColor"
    android:translationZ="5dp"
    tools:context=".randomcompanion.RandomCompanionFragment">

    <androidx.appcompat.widget.AppCompatTextView
      android:id="@+id/petName"
      android:layout_width="wrap_content"
      android:layout_height="wrap_content"
      android:layout_marginTop="10dp"
      android:layout_marginBottom="5dp"
      android:text="@{viewCompanionViewModel.name}"
      android:textSize="24sp"
      android:textStyle="bold"
      app:layout_constraintBottom_toTopOf="@id/petCarouselView"
      app:layout_constraintEnd_toEndOf="parent"
      app:layout_constraintStart_toStartOf="parent"
      app:layout_constraintTop_toTopOf="parent" />

    <com.synnapps.carouselview.CarouselView
      android:id="@+id/petCarouselView"
      android:layout_width="0dp"
      android:layout_height="200dp"
      android:layout_marginBottom="5dp"
      app:fillColor="#FFFFFFFF"
      app:layout_constraintBottom_toTopOf="@id/breed"
      app:layout_constraintEnd_toEndOf="parent"
      app:layout_constraintStart_toStartOf="parent"
      app:layout_constraintTop_toBottomOf="@id/petName"
```

```
        app:layout_constraintWidth_percent=".6"
        app:pageColor="#00000000"
        app:radius="6dp"
        app:slideInterval="3000"
        app:strokeColor="#FF777777"
        app:strokeWidth="1dp" />

    <androidx.appcompat.widget.AppCompatTextView
        android:id="@+id/breed"
        android:layout_width="wrap_content"
        android:layout_height="wrap_content"
        android:text="@{viewCompanionViewModel.breed}"
        app:layout_constraintBottom_toTopOf="@+id/email"
        app:layout_constraintEnd_toStartOf="@id/city"
        app:layout_constraintStart_toStartOf="parent"
        app:layout_constraintTop_toBottomOf="@+id/petCarouselView"
/>

    <androidx.appcompat.widget.AppCompatTextView
        android:id="@+id/city"
        android:layout_width="wrap_content"
        android:layout_height="wrap_content"
        android:text="@{viewCompanionViewModel.city}"
        app:layout_constraintBottom_toBottomOf="@id/breed"
        app:layout_constraintEnd_toEndOf="parent"
        app:layout_constraintStart_toEndOf="@+id/breed"
        app:layout_constraintTop_toTopOf="@+id/breed" />

    <androidx.appcompat.widget.AppCompatTextView
        android:id="@+id/email"
        android:layout_width="wrap_content"
        android:layout_height="wrap_content"
        android:text="@{viewCompanionViewModel.email}"
        android:textStyle="bold"
        app:layout_constraintBottom_toTopOf="@+id/age"
        app:layout_constraintEnd_toStartOf="@id/telephone"
        app:layout_constraintStart_toStartOf="parent"
        app:layout_constraintTop_toBottomOf="@+id/breed" />

    <androidx.appcompat.widget.AppCompatTextView
        android:id="@+id/telephone"
        android:layout_width="wrap_content"
        android:layout_height="wrap_content"
        android:text="@{viewCompanionViewModel.telephone}"
        android:textStyle="bold"
        app:layout_constraintBottom_toBottomOf="@id/email"
        app:layout_constraintEnd_toEndOf="parent"
        app:layout_constraintStart_toEndOf="@+id/email"
        app:layout_constraintTop_toTopOf="@+id/email" />

    <androidx.appcompat.widget.AppCompatTextView
        android:id="@+id/age"
        android:layout_width="wrap_content"
```

```
        android:layout_height="wrap_content"
        android:text="@{viewCompanionViewModel.age}"
        app:layout_constraintBottom_toTopOf="@id/
meetTitlePlaceholder"
        app:layout_constraintEnd_toStartOf="@id/sex"
        app:layout_constraintStart_toStartOf="parent"
        app:layout_constraintTop_toBottomOf="@id/email" />

      <androidx.appcompat.widget.AppCompatTextView
        android:id="@+id/sex"
        android:layout_width="wrap_content"
        android:layout_height="wrap_content"
        android:text="@{viewCompanionViewModel.sex}"
        app:layout_constraintBottom_toBottomOf="@id/age"
        app:layout_constraintEnd_toStartOf="@id/size"
        app:layout_constraintStart_toEndOf="@id/age"
        app:layout_constraintTop_toTopOf="@id/age" />

      <androidx.appcompat.widget.AppCompatTextView
        android:id="@+id/size"
        android:layout_width="wrap_content"
        android:layout_height="wrap_content"
        android:text="@{viewCompanionViewModel.size}"
        app:layout_constraintBottom_toBottomOf="@id/age"
        app:layout_constraintEnd_toEndOf="parent"
        app:layout_constraintStart_toEndOf="@id/sex"
        app:layout_constraintTop_toTopOf="@id/age" />

      <androidx.appcompat.widget.AppCompatTextView
        android:id="@+id/meetTitlePlaceholder"
        android:layout_width="wrap_content"
        android:layout_height="wrap_content"
        android:text="@{viewCompanionViewModel.title}"
        android:textStyle="bold"
        app:layout_constraintBottom_toTopOf="@+id/
descriptionScroll"
        app:layout_constraintEnd_toEndOf="parent"
        app:layout_constraintStart_toStartOf="parent"
        app:layout_constraintTop_toBottomOf="@+id/age" />

      <androidx.core.widget.NestedScrollView
        android:id="@+id/descriptionScroll"
        android:layout_width="match_parent"
        android:layout_height="0dp"
        android:paddingStart="30dp"
        android:paddingEnd="30dp"
        app:layout_constraintBottom_toBottomOf="parent"
        app:layout_constraintEnd_toEndOf="parent"
        app:layout_constraintHeight_percent=".25"
        app:layout_constraintHorizontal_bias="0.0"
        app:layout_constraintStart_toStartOf="parent"
        app:layout_constraintVertical_bias="1.0">
```

```
      <androidx.appcompat.widget.AppCompatTextView
        android:id="@+id/description"
        android:layout_width="wrap_content"
        android:layout_height="wrap_content"
        android:text="@{viewCompanionViewModel.description}" />
    </androidx.core.widget.NestedScrollView>

  </androidx.constraintlayout.widget.ConstraintLayout>
</layout>
```

Build and run to make sure the app compiles and that there are no errors.

With your view in good shape, go back to **ViewCompanionViewModel.kt** and add the following method to the `ViewCompanionViewModel` class:

```
fun populateFromAnimal(animal: Animal) {
  name = animal.name
  breed = animal.breeds.primary
  city = animal.contact.address.city + ", " +
    animal.contact.address.state
  email = animal.contact.email
  telephone = animal.contact.phone
  age = animal.age
  sex = animal.gender
  size = animal.size
  title = "Meet " + animal.name
  description = animal.description
}
```

This is a helper method for converting an `Animal` object to your `ViewModel`.

Now go to **ViewCompanionFragment.kt** and replace `onCreateView` with the following:

```
override fun onCreateView(
  inflater: LayoutInflater, container: ViewGroup?,
  savedInstanceState: Bundle?
): View? {
  animal = args.animal
  viewCompanionFragment = this
  // 1
  val fragmentViewCompanionBinding =
    FragmentViewCompanionBinding
      .inflate(inflater, container, false)
  // 2
  val viewCompanionViewModel =
ViewModelProvider(this).get(ViewCompanionViewModel::class.java)
  // 3
  viewCompanionViewModel.populateFromAnimal(animal)
  // 4
```

```
    fragmentViewCompanionBinding.viewCompanionViewModel =
      viewCompanionViewModel
    // 5
    return fragmentViewCompanionBinding.root
  }
```

If you find that the import for `FragmentViewCompanionBinding` is not behaving, do a build and then try again.

The code you just added does the following:

1. It inflates the view via a data-binding-generated `FragmentViewCompanionBinding` object.
2. Creates an instance of `ViewCompanionViewModel` via the `ViewModelProviders`.
3. Populates the view model from an `Animal`.
4. Assigns the view model to your view.
5. Returns the root of the view.

Finally, in `onResume`, replace the call to `populatePet()` with `populatePhotos()`.

Run your test now, and it'll be green.

Test Results 14 s 706 ms
com.raywenderlich.codingcompanionfinder.FindCompanionInstrumentedTest 14 s 706 ms
searching_for_a_companion_and_tapping_on_it_takes_the_user_to_the_companion_details 14 s 706 ms

There's still one other piece of this refactor that you'll need to do to wrap things up. With your data binding, you no longer need `populatePet()` or `populateTextField(...)`, so delete them.

Your next refactor

Swapping manual view binding for data binding in the `ViewCompanionFragment` was a relatively simple refactor. Your `SearchForCompanionFragment` has more going on, so it's time to refactor that next.

Adding test coverage

Just like you did with the `ViewCompanionFragment` test, you want to make ensure that you have enough test coverage for the `SearchForCompanionFragment`.

Three things happen in this fragment:

1. It presents the user with a screen to search for a companion.

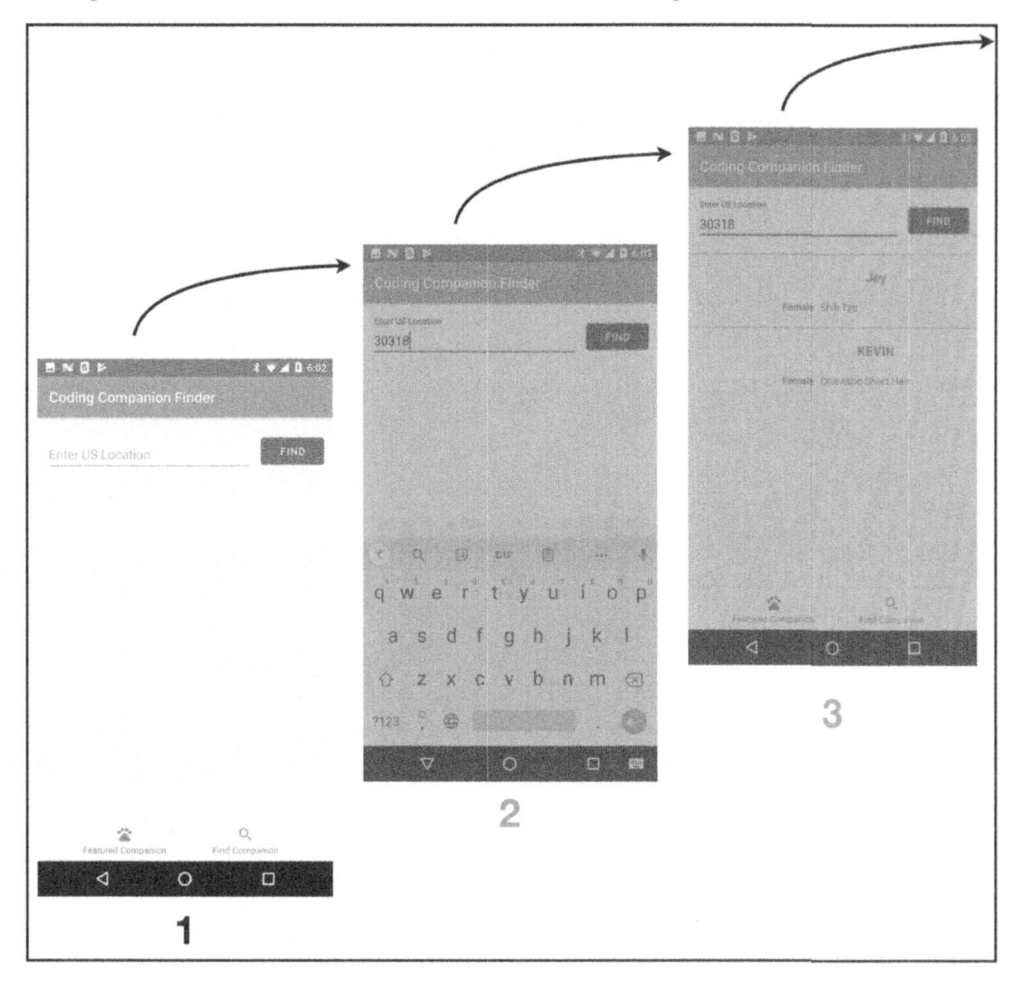

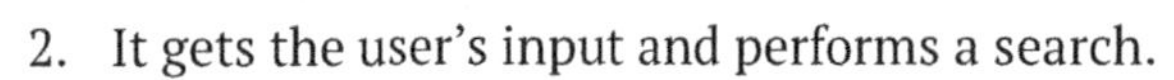

2. It gets the user's input and performs a search.

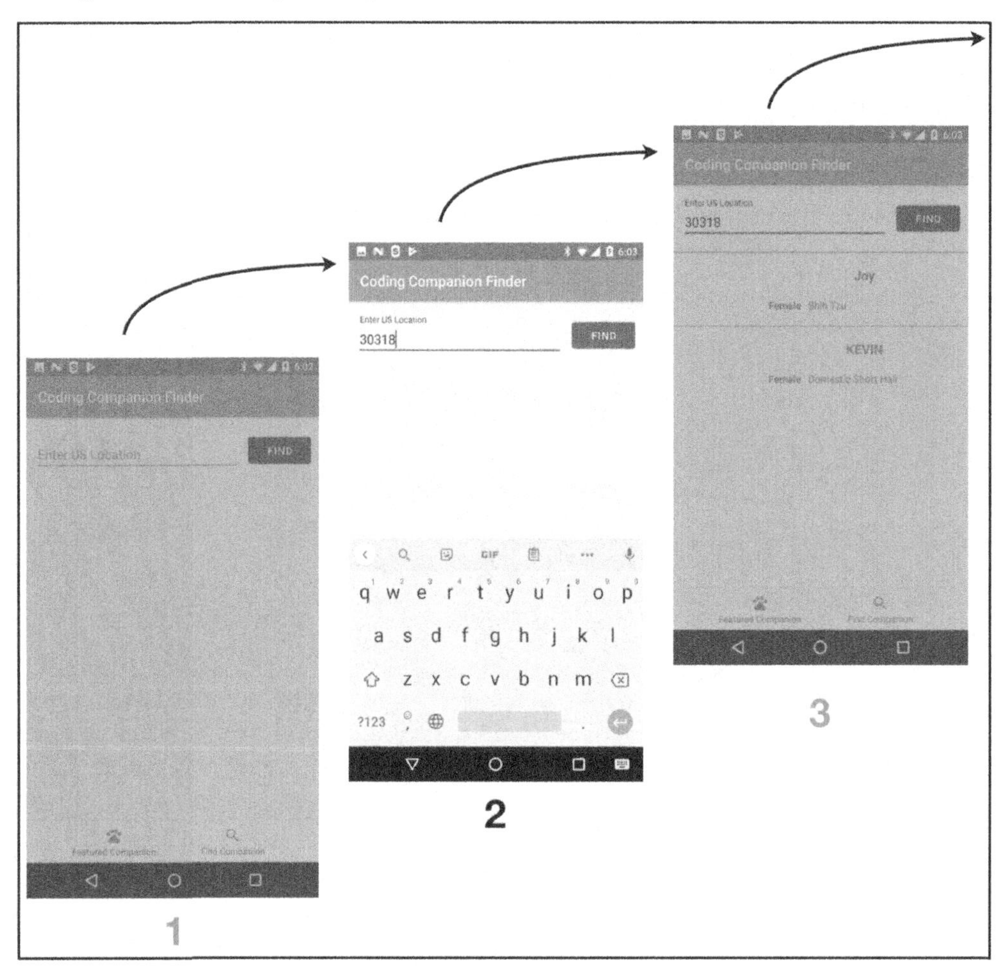

3. It presents the search results and allows navigation to the `ViewCompanionFragment`.

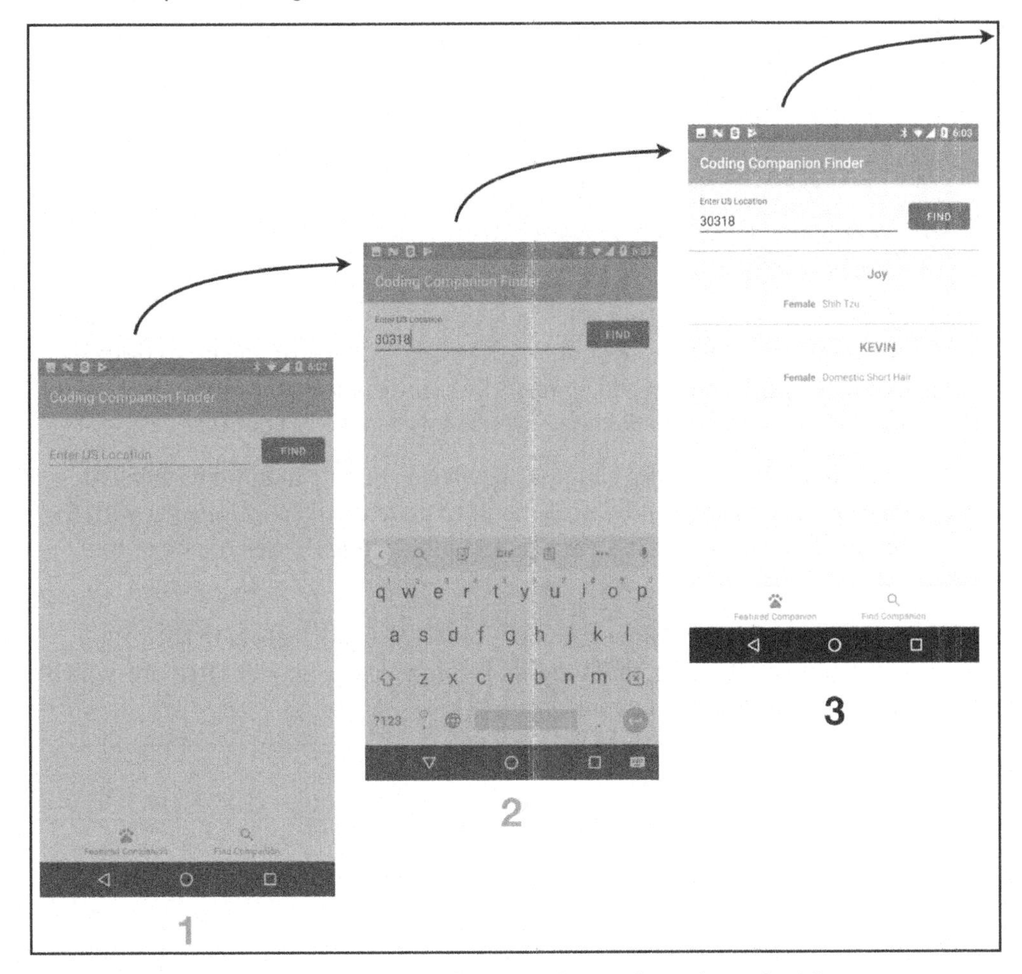

Open **FindCompanionInstrumentedTest.kt** located inside **androidTest** source set.

Looking through the tests, two of the three tests are referencing the following method:

```
private fun find_and_select_kevin_in_30318() {
  onView(withId(R.id.searchForCompanionFragment))
    .perform(click())
  onView(withId(R.id.searchFieldText))
    .perform(typeText("30318"))
  onView(withId(R.id.searchButton)).perform(click())
  onView(withId(R.id.searchButton))
   .check(matches(isDisplayed()))
  onView(withText("KEVIN")).perform(click())
}
```

This does a good job of testing most of the three scenarios with one exception: It does not verify all of the data when you list the results of a search. To fix that, you'll write a test, but there's one small change you need to make to your test data first.

If you look at your search results data, you have two animals that are both females. But earlier, you learned about it being difficult to match multiple elements with the same value/ID. To make things easier to test, you'll change the sex of one of the companions.

Start by opening **search_30318.json**, which is located inside **assets** in the `androidTest` source set. Then, find the first instance of the gender attribute, which is associated with the Shih Tzu named Joy.

```
{
  "animals": [
   {
     "id": 44543909,
     "organization_id": "GA604",
     "url": "https://www.petfinder.com/dog/joy-44543909/ga/loganville/five-fr
     "type": "Dog",
     "species": "Dog",
     "breeds": {"primary": "Shih Tzu"...},
     "colors": {"primary": "White / Cream"...},
     "age": "Senior",
     "gender": "Female",
     "size": "Small",
     "coat": "Medium",
     "attributes": {"spayed_neutered": true...},
     "environment": {"children": true...},
     "tags": [...],
     "name": "Joy",
     "description": "Joy is a docile, quiet lapdog who just wants to be held
     "photos": [
     ],
     "status": "adoptable",
     "published_at": "2019-04-25T13:45:51+0000",
     "contact": {"email": "fivefreedomsfarm@gmail.com"...},
     "_links": {...}
   },
```

Next, change the gender to **Male**.

Following that, open **FindCompanionInstrumentedTest.kt** and add the following test:

```
@Test
fun searching_for_a_companion_in_30318_returns_two_results() {
  onView(withId(R.id.searchForCompanionFragment))
    .perform(click())
  onView(withId(R.id.searchFieldText))
    .perform(typeText("30318"))
  onView(withId(R.id.searchButton)).perform(click())
  onView(withId(R.id.searchButton))
    .check(matches(isDisplayed()))
  onView(withText("Joy")).check(matches(isDisplayed()))
  onView(withText("Male")).check(matches(isDisplayed()))
  onView(withText("Shih Tzu")).check(matches(isDisplayed()))
  onView(withText("KEVIN")).check(matches(isDisplayed()))
  onView(withText("Female")).check(matches(isDisplayed()))
  onView(withText("Domestic Short Hair"))
    .check(matches(isDisplayed()))
}
```

This verifies all of the data elements for the search results without clicking on one like the other tests are doing.

Finally, run the test, and everything will be green.

Test Results
com.raywenderlich.codingcompanionfinder.FindCompanionInstrumentedTest
searching_for_a_companion_in_30318_returns_two_results

> **Note**: For the sake of brevity, you're not breaking these test conditions before making them pass. Before you move on, however, a good exercise is to try changing various data elements to ensure that each assertion breaks before setting the data back to a state that makes the test pass.

There are two other scenarios that you need to address.

Looking at `searchForCompanions()` in **SearchForCompanionFragment.kt**, there are two instances that can lead to a text view with a message indicating that no results are available:

```
if (searchForPetResponse.isSuccessful) {
  searchForPetResponse.body()?.let {
    GlobalScope.launch(Dispatchers.Main) {
```

```
      if (it.animals.size > 0) {
// No Results Text View is invisible when results are available.
        noResultsTextView?.visibility = INVISIBLE
        viewManager = LinearLayoutManager(context)
        companionAdapter = CompanionAdapter(it.animals,
          searchForCompanionFragment)
        petRecyclerView = view?.let {
          it.findViewById<RecyclerView>(R.id.petRecyclerView)
          .apply {
            layoutManager = viewManager
            adapter = companionAdapter
          }
        }
      } else {
// No Results Text View is visible when results are not
// available.
        noResultsTextView?.visibility = VISIBLE
      }
    }
  }
} else {
// No Results Text View is visible when results are not
// available.
  noResultsTextView?.visibility = VISIBLE
}
```

This displays by going to the app and searching for companions under an invalid location.

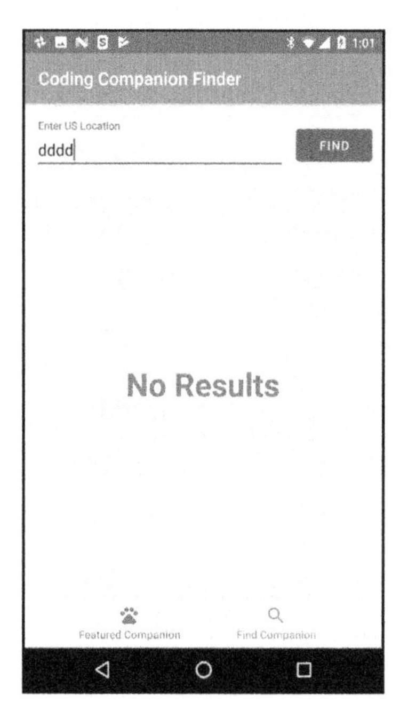

There are two scenarios for which you need to add coverage:

1. When the user enters a valid location, but there are no results.
2. When the user enters an invalid location.

You'll start with the first scenario.

Open **CommonTestDataUtil.kt** inside **androidTest** and replace `dispatch` with the following:

```
fun dispatch(request: RecordedRequest): MockResponse? {
  return when (request.path) {
    "/animals?limit=20&location=30318" -> {
      MockResponse()
        .setResponseCode(200)
        .setBody(readFile("search_30318.json"))
    }
// test data for no response
    "/animals?limit=20&location=90210" -> {
      MockResponse()
        .setResponseCode(200)
        .setBody("{\"animals\": []}")
    }
    else -> {
      MockResponse().setResponseCode(404).setBody("{}")
    }
  }
}
```

This adds a mock for a zip code location of 90210 that returns no results.

Next, add the following test to **FindCompanionsInstrumentedTest.kt**:

```
@Test
fun searching_for_a_companion_in_90210_returns_no_results() {
  onView(withId(R.id.searchForCompanionFragment))
    .perform(click())
  onView(withId(R.id.searchFieldText))
    .perform(typeText("90210"))
  onView(withId(R.id.searchButton)).perform(click())
  onView(withId(R.id.searchButton))
    .check(matches(isDisplayed()))
  onView(withId(R.id.noResults))
    .check(matches(withEffectiveVisibility(Visibility.VISIBLE)))
}
```

Since it's a good idea to have a failing test first, go into **SearchForCompanionFragment.kt** and comment out the line that sets the visibility for `noResultsTextView`:

```
if (it.animals.size > 0) {
  noResultsTextView?.visibility = INVISIBLE
  viewManager = LinearLayoutManager(context)
  companionAdapter = CompanionAdapter(it.animals,
    searchForCompanionFragment)
  petRecyclerView = view?.let {
    it.findViewById<RecyclerView>(R.id.petRecyclerView).apply {
      layoutManager = viewManager
      adapter = companionAdapter
    }
  }
} else {
// Comment out this line
//noResultsTextView?.visibility = VISIBLE
}
```

Now, run your new test, and it'll fail.

```
Test Results
  com.raywenderlich.codingcompanionfinder.FindCompanionInstrumentedTest
    searching_for_a_companion_in_90210_returns_no_results
```

Finally, uncomment that line, run the test again — and this time, it passes.

```
Test Results
  com.raywenderlich.codingcompanionfinder.FindCompanionInstrumentedTest
    searching_for_a_companion_in_90210_returns_no_results
```

For the second no results scenario, open **FindCompanionInstrumentedTest.kt** and add the following test:

```
@Test
fun
searching_for_a_companion_in_a_call_returns_an_error_displays_no
_results() {
  onView(withId(R.id.searchForCompanionFragment))
     .perform(click())
  onView(withId(R.id.searchFieldText)).perform(typeText("dddd"))
  onView(withId(R.id.searchButton)).perform(click())
  onView(withId(R.id.searchButton))
    .check(matches(isDisplayed()))
  onView(withId(R.id.noResults))
    .check(matches(withEffectiveVisibility(Visibility.VISIBLE)))
}
```

Run this test without commenting out the implementation, and you'll see a failure message that reads:

```
Test failed to run to completion. Reason: 'Instrumentation run
failed due to 'Process crashed.'. Check device logcat for
details
Test running failed: Instrumentation run failed due to 'Process
crashed.'
```

Looking at the code in `searchForCompanions` in the **SearchForCompanionFragment.kt**, you'll see the following:

```
if (searchForPetResponse.isSuccessful) {
  searchForPetResponse.body()?.let {
// This is a bug, the scope should be at a higher level.
    GlobalScope.launch(Dispatchers.Main) {
      if (it.animals.size > 0) {
        noResultsTextView?.visibility = INVISIBLE
        viewManager = LinearLayoutManager(context)
        companionAdapter = CompanionAdapter(it.animals,
          searchForCompanionFragment)
        petRecyclerView = view?.let {
          it.findViewById<RecyclerView>(R.id.petRecyclerView)
          .apply {
            layoutManager = viewManager
            adapter = companionAdapter
          }
        }
      } else {
        noResultsTextView?.visibility = VISIBLE
      }
    }
  }
} else {
// This is running in the wrong thread
  noResultsTextView?.visibility = VISIBLE
}
```

There's a bug in the app where a "no results" scenario causes the app to crash. This happens because it's trying to set a value in the view outside of the main thread.

To fix this error, move the `GlobalScope.launch(Dispatchers.Main)` line to the outside of your code block below `val searchForPetResponse = getAnimalsRequest.await()`. When you're done, it should look like this:

```
GlobalScope.launch(Dispatchers.Main) {
  if (searchForPetResponse.isSuccessful) {
    searchForPetResponse.body()?.let {
      if (it.animals.size > 0) {
        noResultsTextView?.visibility = INVISIBLE
```

```
          viewManager = LinearLayoutManager(context)
          companionAdapter = CompanionAdapter(it.animals,
            searchForCompanionFragment)
          petRecyclerView = view?.let {
            it.findViewById<RecyclerView>(R.id.petRecyclerView)
            .apply {
              layoutManager = viewManager
              adapter = companionAdapter
            }
          }
        } else {
          noResultsTextView?.visibility = VISIBLE
        }
      }
    } else {
      noResultsTextView?.visibility = VISIBLE
    }
  }
```

Now, run your test and it'll be green.

```
Test Results
  com.raywenderlich.codingcompanionfinder.FindCompanionInstrumentedTest
    searching_for_a_companion_in_a_call_returns_an_error_displays_no_results
```

Refactoring SearchForCompanionFragment

Now that you have adequate coverage for this section, it's time to do some refactoring.

To get started, create a new file named **SearchForCompanionViewModel.kt** in the **searchforcompanion** package. Give it the following content:

```
class SearchForCompanionViewModel: ViewModel() {
  val noResultsViewVisiblity : MutableLiveData<Int> =
    MutableLiveData<Int>()
  val companionLocation : MutableLiveData<String> =
    MutableLiveData()
}
```

This creates a `ViewModel` for the fragment with `LiveData` elements for the `noResults` `View` and `companionLocation`.

Next, open **fragment_search_for_companion.xml** and add a <layout> tag around the ConstaintLayout. Also, add a <data> and <variable> tag for the ViewModel:

```
<layout>

  <data>
    <variable
      name="searchForCompanionViewModel"

type="com.raywenderlich.codingcompanionfinder.searchforcompanion
.SearchForCompanionViewModel" />
  </data>

  <androidx.constraintlayout.widget.ConstraintLayout
xmlns:android="http://schemas.android.com/apk/res/android"
    xmlns:app="http://schemas.android.com/apk/res-auto"
    xmlns:tools="http://schemas.android.com/tools"
    android:layout_width="match_parent"
    android:layout_height="match_parent"

tools:context=".searchforcompanion.SearchForCompanionFragment">

    .
    .
    .

  </androidx.constraintlayout.widget.ConstraintLayout>
</layout>
```

Now bind the SearchForCompanion ViewModel's companionLocation to the searchField text attribute of the <TextInputEditText> with the ID of @+id/searchFieldText by adding:

```
android:text="@={searchForCompanionViewModel.companionLocation}"
```

Also, bind that ViewModel's noResultsViewVisibility to the visibility attribute of the <TextView> with the ID of @+id/noResults by replacing:

```
android:visibility="invisible"
```

With the following:

```
android:visibility="@{searchForCompanionViewModel.noResultsViewV
isiblity}"
```

The final **fragment_search_for_companion.xml** will look like this:

```
<?xml version="1.0" encoding="utf-8"?>
<layout>
```

```
  <data>
    <variable
      name="searchForCompanionViewModel"

type="com.raywenderlich.codingcompanionfinder.searchforcompanion
.SearchForCompanionViewModel" />
  </data>

  <androidx.constraintlayout.widget.ConstraintLayout
xmlns:android="http://schemas.android.com/apk/res/android"
    xmlns:app="http://schemas.android.com/apk/res-auto"
    xmlns:tools="http://schemas.android.com/tools"
    android:layout_width="match_parent"
    android:layout_height="match_parent"

tools:context=".searchforcompanion.SearchForCompanionFragment">

    <androidx.constraintlayout.widget.ConstraintLayout
      android:id="@+id/searchForCompanion"
      android:layout_width="0dp"
      android:layout_height="0dp"
      app:layout_constraintBottom_toBottomOf="parent"
      app:layout_constraintEnd_toEndOf="parent"
      app:layout_constraintStart_toStartOf="parent"
      app:layout_constraintTop_toTopOf="parent">

      <com.google.android.material.textfield.TextInputLayout
        android:id="@+id/searchField"
        android:layout_width="0dp"
        android:layout_height="wrap_content"
        app:layout_constraintBottom_toTopOf="@id/
petRecyclerView"
        app:layout_constraintEnd_toStartOf="@id/searchButton"
        app:layout_constraintStart_toStartOf="parent"
        app:layout_constraintTop_toTopOf="parent"
        app:layout_constraintWidth_percent=".7">

        <com.google.android.material.textfield.TextInputEditText
          android:id="@+id/searchFieldText"
          android:layout_width="match_parent"
          android:layout_height="wrap_content"

android:text="@={searchForCompanionViewModel.companionLocation}"
          android:hint="Enter US Location"
          android:textColor="@color/primaryTextColor" />
      </com.google.android.material.textfield.TextInputLayout>

      <com.google.android.material.button.MaterialButton
        android:id="@+id/searchButton"
        android:layout_width="wrap_content"
        android:layout_height="wrap_content"
        android:text="Find"
        app:layout_constraintBottom_toBottomOf="@+id/
```

```
searchField"
        app:layout_constraintEnd_toEndOf="parent"
        app:layout_constraintStart_toEndOf="@id/searchField"
        app:layout_constraintTop_toTopOf="@id/searchField" />

      <androidx.recyclerview.widget.RecyclerView
        android:id="@+id/petRecyclerView"
        android:layout_width="match_parent"
        android:layout_height="0dp"
        app:layout_constraintBottom_toBottomOf="parent"
        app:layout_constraintEnd_toEndOf="parent"
        app:layout_constraintHeight_percent=".8"
        app:layout_constraintStart_toStartOf="parent"
        app:layout_constraintTop_toBottomOf="@id/searchField" />

      <TextView
        android:id="@+id/noResults"
        android:layout_width="wrap_content"
        android:layout_height="wrap_content"
        android:text="No Results"
        android:textSize="36sp"
        android:textStyle="bold"

android:visibility="@{searchForCompanionViewModel.noResultsViewV
isiblity}"
        app:layout_constraintBottom_toBottomOf="parent"
        app:layout_constraintEnd_toEndOf="parent"
        app:layout_constraintHeight_percent=".8"
        app:layout_constraintStart_toStartOf="parent"
        app:layout_constraintTop_toBottomOf="@id/searchField" />
    </androidx.constraintlayout.widget.ConstraintLayout>
  </androidx.constraintlayout.widget.ConstraintLayout>
</layout>
```

With that done, go back to **SearchForCompanionFragment.kt**, add the foloowing two properties and replace `onCreateView` with the following:

```
private lateinit var fragmentSearchForCompanionBinding:
  FragmentSearchForCompanionBinding
private lateinit var searchForCompanionViewModel:
  SearchForCompanionViewModel

override fun onCreateView(
    inflater: LayoutInflater, container: ViewGroup?,
    savedInstanceState: Bundle?
): View? {
  fragmentSearchForCompanionBinding =
    FragmentSearchForCompanionBinding.inflate(inflater,
      container, false)
  searchForCompanionViewModel = ViewModelProvider(this)
      .get(SearchForCompanionViewModel::class.java)
  fragmentSearchForCompanionBinding.searchForCompanionViewModel
```

```
      = searchForCompanionViewModel
    fragmentSearchForCompanionBinding.lifecycleOwner = this
    return fragmentSearchForCompanionBinding.root
  }
```

Note: If you find the `FragmentSearchForCompanionBinding` import not resolving, perform a build.

Locate `searchForCompanions()` and replace it with the following:

```
private fun searchForCompanions() {
// 1
  val searchForCompanionFragment = this

  GlobalScope.launch {
    accessToken = (activity as MainActivity).accessToken
    (activity as MainActivity).petFinderService?
    .let { petFinderService ->
      EventBus.getDefault().post(IdlingEntity(1))
// 2
      val getAnimalsRequest = petFinderService.getAnimals(
        accessToken,
        location =
          searchForCompanionViewModel.companionLocation.value
      )

      val searchForPetResponse = getAnimalsRequest.await()

      GlobalScope.launch(Dispatchers.Main) {
        if (searchForPetResponse.isSuccessful) {
          searchForPetResponse.body()?.let {
            if (it.animals.size > 0) {
              // 3
              searchForCompanionViewModel
                .noResultsViewVisiblity
                .postValue(INVISIBLE)
              viewManager = LinearLayoutManager(context)
              companionAdapter = CompanionAdapter(it.animals,
                searchForCompanionFragment)
              petRecyclerView = view?.let {
                it.findViewById<RecyclerView>(
                  R.id.petRecyclerView
                ).apply {
                  layoutManager = viewManager
                  adapter = companionAdapter
                }
              }
            } else {
// 3
```

```
                searchForCompanionViewModel
                  .noResultsViewVisiblity
                  .postValue(VISIBLE)
              }
            }
          } else {
// 3
            searchForCompanionViewModel
              .noResultsViewVisiblity
              .postValue(VISIBLE)
          }
        }
        EventBus.getDefault().post(IdlingEntity(-1))
      }
    }
  }
```

This does the following:

1. Removes the `findViewById` references for the two text elements.
2. Uses the bound value from the `ViewModel` to pass the location that a user is searching for into the web API call.
3. Uses the bound value for `noResultsViewVisibility` to set the visibility of the No Results text whether or not results are found.

Run the tests in **FindCompanionsInstrumentedTest.kt**, and they'll all still be green. Great refactor!

Test Results
com.raywenderlich.codingcompanionfinder.FindCompanionInstrumentedTest
verify_that_companion_details_shows_a_valid_phone_number_and_email
searching_for_a_companion_and_tapping_on_it_takes_the_user_to_the_companion_details
searching_for_a_companion_in_30318_returns_two_results
searching_for_a_companion_in_a_call_returns_an_error_displays_no_results
searching_for_a_companion_in_90210_returns_no_results
pressing_the_find_bottom_menu_item_takes_the_user_to_the_find_page

This is a good first step at refactoring `SearchForCompanionFragment`, but there's still a lot of logic in your controller.

`searchForCompanions()` has a lot of stuff going on with its calls to Retrofit; these can be moved to the `ViewModel`. This allows you to bring the testing of this component down to a unit level, which you'll do in the next chapter.

To get started, open **SearchForCompanionViewModel.kt** and add the following:

```
// 1
val animals: MutableLiveData<ArrayList<Animal>> =
  MutableLiveData<ArrayList<Animal>>()
```

```
lateinit var accessToken: String
lateinit var petFinderService: PetFinderService

fun searchForCompanions() {

  GlobalScope.launch {

    EventBus.getDefault().post(IdlingEntity(1))
// 2
    val searchForPetResponse = petFinderService.getAnimals(
      accessToken,
      location = companionLocation.value
    )

    GlobalScope.launch(Dispatchers.Main) {
      if (searchForPetResponse.isSuccessful) {
        searchForPetResponse.body()?.let {
// 3
          animals.postValue(it.animals)
          if (it.animals.size > 0) {
// 3
            noResultsViewVisiblity.postValue(INVISIBLE)
          } else {
// 3
            noResultsViewVisiblity.postValue(View.VISIBLE)
          }
        }
      } else {
// 3
        noResultsViewVisiblity.postValue(View.VISIBLE)
      }
    }
    EventBus.getDefault().post(IdlingEntity(-1))
  }
}
```

This is a refactored version of the controller's `searchForCompanions` method; it does three things:

1. Creates some variables used to pass data between your `ViewModel`, View layout and Fragment.
2. Calls `petFinderService` to make calls to the API.
3. Sets appropriate values in the ViewModel used in your View layout.

Next, open **SearchForCompanionFragment.kt** and add the following method:

```
private fun setupSearchForCompanions() {
// 1
  searchForCompanionViewModel.accessToken =
    (activity as MainActivity).accessToken
  searchForCompanionViewModel.petFinderService =
    (activity as MainActivity).petFinderService!!
// 2
  viewManager = LinearLayoutManager(context)
  companionAdapter = CompanionAdapter(
    searchForCompanionViewModel.animals.value ?: arrayListOf(),
    this
  )
  petRecyclerView = fragmentSearchForCompanionBinding
    .petRecyclerView.apply {
      layoutManager = viewManager
      adapter = companionAdapter
    }
// 3

searchForCompanionViewModel.animals.observe(viewLifecycleOwner,
{
    companionAdapter.animals = it ?: arrayListOf()
    companionAdapter.notifyDataSetChanged()
  })
}
```

This does the following:

1. Passes the Retrofit service and access token into your `ViewModel`.
2. Sets up the `RecyclerView` for the list of companions.
3. Observes changes to the list of animals which occurs when results come back from a search. It also updates the `RecyclerView` with the new data when that happens.

Following that, in the same fragment, replace `onActivityCreated` with the following:

```
override fun onActivityCreated(savedInstanceState: Bundle?) {
// 1
  fragmentSearchForCompanionBinding.searchButton
  .setOnClickListener {
    try {
      val inputMethodManager = activity?.getSystemService(
        Context.INPUT_METHOD_SERVICE) as InputMethodManager?
      inputMethodManager!!.hideSoftInputFromWindow(
        activity?.getCurrentFocus()?.getWindowToken(),
        0
```

```
      )
    } catch (e: Exception) {
      // only happens when the keyboard is already closed
    }
// 2
    searchForCompanionViewModel.searchForCompanions()
  }
// 3
  setupSearchForCompanions()
  super.onActivityCreated(savedInstanceState)
}
```

This code:

1. Migrates the `findViewById` call to using the data binding reference to get your search button.
2. Replaces the call to the fragment's local `searchForCompanions` with a call to the same method name on the `searchForCompanionViewModel`.
3. Adds a call to the new `setupSearchForCompanions` in this fragment.

Now that you made those changes, you can remove `searchForCompanions()` in the `SearchForCompanionFragment`.

Finally, call run on all of your tests in **FindCompanionsIntrumentedTest.kt** and they'll remain green.

```
Test Results
  com.raywenderlich.codingcompanionfinder.FindCompanionInstrumentedTest
    verify_that_companion_details_shows_a_valid_phone_number_and_email
    searching_for_a_companion_and_tapping_on_it_takes_the_user_to_the_companion_details
    searching_for_a_companion_in_30318_returns_two_results
    searching_for_a_companion_in_a_call_returns_an_error_displays_no_results
    searching_for_a_companion_in_90210_returns_no_results
    pressing_the_find_bottom_menu_item_takes_the_user_to_the_find_page
```

Insert Koin

Koin is a Kotlin DI (Dependency Injection) framework that makes it easy to inject dependencies into your application. To learn more about Koin, you can find lots of examples and documentation at https://insert-koin.io/.

In the next chapter, you'll make use of Koin when you refactor some of your tests. But since you're refactoring your code now, you can add Koin now.

To get started, add the following to the app level **build.gradle**:

```
// Koin
implementation 'org.koin:koin-android-viewmodel:2.0.1'
androidTestImplementation 'org.koin:koin-test:2.0.1'
```

This brings the Koin dependencies into your project.

Next, open **MainActivity.kt**. You need to move this code:

```
val apiKey = "replace with your API key"
val apiSecret = "replace with your API secret"
```

And place it into a **companion object**. You also need to rename them to `API_KEY` and `API_SECRET`:

```
val API_KEY = "your api ket"
val API_SECRET = "your api secret"
```

Now, add another value in the companion object named `DEFAULT_PETFINDER_URL`:

```
val DEFAULT_PETFINDER_URL = "http://api.petfinder.com/v2/"
```

The final companion object should look like:

```
  companion object {
    val PETFINDER_URI = "petfinder_uri"
    val PETFINDER_KEY = "petfinder_key"
    val API_KEY = "your client id"
    val API_SECRET = "your client secret"
    val DEFAULT_PETFINDER_URL = "https://api.petfinder.com/v2/"
  }
```

Next, remove the `Intent` `String` fetch on line 3 from `onCreate`:

```
// remove these!!
intent.getStringExtra(PETFINDER_KEY)?.let {
  apiKey = it
}
```

Following that, remove the following line since it's no longer needed:

```
var token: Token = Token()
```

Open **AuthorizationInterceptor.kt** located inside the **retrofit** package in your project, and replace it with the following:

```
// 1
class AuthorizationInterceptor : Interceptor, KoinComponent {

// 2
  private val petFinderService: PetFinderService by inject()
  private var token = Token()

  @Throws(IOException::class)
  override fun intercept(chain: Interceptor.Chain): Response {
    var mainResponse = chain.proceed(chain.request())
    val mainRequest = chain.request()

    if ((mainResponse.code() == 401 ||
      mainResponse.code() == 403) &&
      !mainResponse.request().url().url().toString()
        .contains("oauth2/token")) {
// 3
        val tokenRequest = petFinderService.getToken(
          clientId = MainActivity.API_KEY,
          clientSecret = MainActivity.API_SECRET)
        val tokenResponse = tokenRequest.execute()

        if (tokenResponse.isSuccessful()) {
          tokenResponse.body()?.let {
            token = it
            val builder = mainRequest.newBuilder()
              .header("Authorization", "Bearer " +
                it.accessToken)
              .method(mainRequest.method(), mainRequest.body())
            mainResponse.close()
            mainResponse = chain.proceed(builder.build())
          }
        }
    }

    return mainResponse
  }

}
```

This changes the following things:

1. It removes the dependencies that needed to be passed into this class when it's created. It also adds a dependency on `KoinComponent` that allows you to inject dependencies into the class.
2. It injects `PetFinderService` and brings the token it needs to periodically refresh into the interceptor class.
3. It uses the companion object parameters from `MainActivity` for `CLIENT_ID` and `CLIENT_SECRET`.

Go to **MainActivity.kt** and remove the `this` parameter from the following line in `onCreate`:

```
.addInterceptor(AuthorizationInterceptor(this))
```

Change it to:

```
.addInterceptor(AuthorizationInterceptor())
```

Next, open **SearchForCompanionViewModel**, and add `val petfinderService: PetfinderService` as a constructor parameter, like this:

```
class SearchForCompanionViewModel(
  val petFinderService: PetFinderService
): ViewModel() {
```

Now, remove:

```
lateinit var petFinderService: PetFinderService
```

This makes it easier to inject the `PetFinderService` into `SearchForCompanionViewModel`.

Koin also requires a **KoinModule** that tells it what to inject.

Create a new file in the main project package named **KoinModule.kt** and add the following:

```
const val PETFINDER_URL = "PETFINDER_URL"

val urlsModule = module {
  single(named(PETFINDER_URL)) {
    MainActivity.DEFAULT_PETFINDER_URL
  }
}
```

```
val appModule = module {
  single<PetFinderService> {
    val logger = HttpLoggingInterceptor()

    val client = OkHttpClient.Builder()
      .addInterceptor(logger)
      .connectTimeout(60L, TimeUnit.SECONDS)
      .readTimeout(60L, TimeUnit.SECONDS)
      .addInterceptor(AuthorizationInterceptor())
      .build()

    Retrofit.Builder()
      .baseUrl(get<String>(named(PETFINDER_URL)))
      .addConverterFactory(GsonConverterFactory.create())
      .client(client)
      .build().create(PetFinderService::class.java)
  }

  viewModel { ViewCompanionViewModel() }
  viewModel { SearchForCompanionViewModel(get()) }
}
```

The `appModule` is creating a single instance of `PetFinderService` and allows it to be injected as needed. It's also creating instances of the ViewModels, which under the hood uses the Jetpack `ViewModelFactory` that binds to the lifecycle of the Fragment. The `urlsModule` creates a string that references the Petfinder URL and is used in `appModule`.

In the main project package, **com.raywenderlich.codingcompanionfinder** create a file named **CodingCompanionFinder.kt** and add the following content:

```
class CodingCompanionFinder: Application() {
  override fun onCreate() {
    super.onCreate()
    startKoin {
      androidContext(this@CodingCompanionFinder)
      modules(listOf(appModule, urlsModule))
    }
  }
}
```

This adds some code to initialize Koin when your app is started.

Now, open **AndroidManifest.xml** and add `android:name=".CodingCompanionFinder"` to the `application` tag so that it looks like this:

```
<application
  android:name=".CodingCompanionFinder"
  android:allowBackup="true"
  android:icon="@mipmap/ic_coding_companion"
  android:label="@string/app_name"
  android:roundIcon="@mipmap/ic_coding_companion_round"
  android:supportsRtl="true"
  android:usesCleartextTraffic="true"
  android:theme="@style/AppTheme">
  .
  .
  .
```

This tells the app to use the new Application object when starting the app.

Following that, open **SearchForCompanionFragment.kt** under the **searchforcompanion** package and change:

```
private lateinit var searchForCompanionViewModel:
  SearchForCompanionViewModel
```

To the following:

```
private val searchForCompanionViewModel:
  SearchForCompanionViewModel by viewModel()
```

This uses Koin to inject the lifecycle-aware `ViewModel`.

Finally, in the same Fragment, remove the following line from the `onCreateView` since you no longer need it:

```
searchForCompanionViewModel =
  ViewModelProviders.of(this)
    .get(SearchForCompanionViewModel::class.java)
```

Now, remove this from `setupSearchForCompanions`:

```
searchForCompanionViewModel.petFinderService =
  (activity as MainActivity).petFinderService!!
```

Run your app, and it'll still work as it did before.

While your app is working correctly, run the tests. You'll notice that most of them are broken.

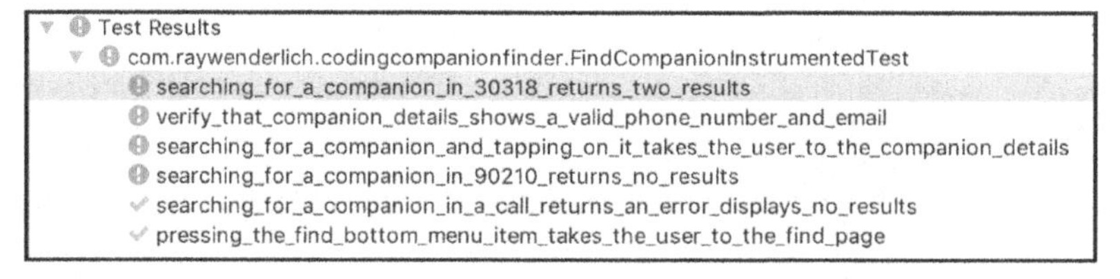

To fix them, open the **FindCompanionInstrumentedTest.kt** inside **androidTest** and make the test class inherit from `KoinTest`. It'll look like this:

```
class FindCompanionInstrumentedTest : KoinTest {
```

Next, add the following method:

```
private fun loadKoinTestModules() {
  loadKoinModules(listOf(module(override = true) {
    single(named(PETFINDER_URL)){server.url("").toString()}
  }))
}
```

This is creating a function that loads the `appModule` you defined earlier and an inline module that replaces `urlsModule` to reference the URL for your MockWebServer.

In `beforeTestRun()`, add a call to `loadKoinTestModules()`, after you launch the `ActivityScenario`. Your changes will look like this:

```
@Before
fun beforeTestsRun() {
  testScenario = ActivityScenario.launch(startIntent)
// Insert it here!!
  loadKoinTestModules()
  EventBus.getDefault().register(this)
  IdlingRegistry.getInstance().register(idlingResource)
}
```

Since Koin starts as part of the app, this stops that instance of Koin, so you can inject the test Koin modules, which is done in `loadKoinTestModules()`.

Run your tests, and they'll be green again.

Test Results
com.raywenderlich.codingcompanionfinder.FindCompanionInstrumentedTest
verify_that_companion_details_shows_a_valid_phone_number_and_email
searching_for_a_companion_and_tapping_on_it_takes_the_user_to_the_companion_details
searching_for_a_companion_in_30318_returns_two_results
searching_for_a_companion_in_a_call_returns_an_error_displays_no_results
searching_for_a_companion_in_90210_returns_no_results
pressing_the_find_bottom_menu_item_takes_the_user_to_the_find_page

Challenge

Challenge: Refactor and addition

- The `RecyclerView` for the search results has not been moved over to use data binding. Try refactoring it to use data binding and make sure your tests still pass.
- Try adding a new feature with an Espresso test and then refactor it.

Key points

- Make sure your tests cover everything that you're changing.
- Sometimes, you'll need to refactor your code to make it more testable.
- Some refactors require changes to your tests.
- Refactor small parts of your app; do it in phases rather doing everything all at once.
- DI provides a cleaner way to add test dependencies.
- Keep your tests green.
- Move slow to go fast.

Where to go from here?

You've done a lot of work in this chapter to set yourself up to go fast. Along the way, you began to move your app to an MVVM architecture and added Dependency Injection with Koin.

TDD is a journey, but there are a lot of homeless coding companions and pair-less developers counting on you. So, stay tuned for the next chapter, where you'll learn how to refactor your tests to start to go fast.

Chapter 15: Refactoring Your Tests

By Lance Gleason

Sometimes you need to slow down to move fast. In development, that means taking the time to write and refactor your tests so that you can go fast with your testing. Right now your app is still fairly small, but the shelters have big plans for it. There are lots of homeless companions and pairless developers that need to be matched up! In the last chapter you started with end-to-end UI tests, added some missing coverage, and then refactored your code to made it easier to go fast.

End-to-end tests usually run in a simulator or on a device. Because of that, they take longer to build, deploy, and run. In Chapter 4, “The Testing Pyramid,” you learned about how you should aim to have a pyramid of tests, with your unit tests being the most numerous, followed by your integration tests, and finally your end-to-end tests. Right now you have an inverted pyramid where all of your tests are end-to-end.

As your app gets larger, this will slow down your development velocity because a number of things happen, including:

- Your Espresso tests will take longer and longer for the test suite to run.
- Tests that exercise one part of the app will often be exercising other parts of the app as well. A change to these other parts can (and will) break many tests that should not be related to what you are testing.

In this chapter you're going to break down your tests into integration and unit-level. Along the way you will learn some tricks for mocking things out, breaking things down, and even sharing tests between Espresso and Robolectric. A lot of people are counting on you, so let's get started!

> **Note**: In a normal development setting, it may be considered premature optimization to refactor an app the size of your Coding Companion Finder until it gets larger. That is a trade-off we needed to make with this book. That said, there is an art to knowing when to break things down. When you are new to TDD, it is easy to slip into a rut of not testing enough and not breaking down your tests soon enough. This is because testing is hard and it is easy to say it is not worth the effort.
>
> Until you get some experience with TDD, it is better to err on the side of over-testing and over-optimization. As you get more familiar with the tools and techniques you will be in a better place to make that determination. There will always be gray areas that experienced TDDers will disagree on.

Source sets, UTP and sharedTest

With `androidx.test`, Robolectric 4.0 and the Unified Test Platform (UTP), which can be found here (https://www.youtube.com/watch?v=juEkViDyzF8), you have the ability to write tests in Espresso and run them in either Robolectric on the JVM or in an emulator/real device. One common use case is to run integration and some end to end tests using the faster Robolectric while working on your local machine. Then running the same tests using slower, but closer to real life, Espresso during less frequent Continuous Integration cycles to find potential issues on specific versions of Android.

Up to this point with your refactoring, you have been focusing on running your tests in Espresso and putting them in `androidTest`. This is how an Android project is configured out of the box. If you want to run the same test in Robolectric you would need to move that test to the `test` source set or create a new test.

This limitation negates that benefit of being able to run the same test in Espresso and Robolectric (other than the shared syntax). This is a shortcoming with the current default Android project setup. Luckily, there is a way to get around this by using a shared source set.

To get started, open the starter project for this chapter or your final project from the last one. Go to the **app ▸ src** directory. You will see three directories there – **androidTest**, **main** and **test**. Add a **sharedTest** directory, and copy all of the contents of **androidTest** to your new **sharedTest** directory, then delete the contents of **androidTest ▸ assets** and **androidTest ▸ java ▸ com ▸ raywenderlich ▸ codingcompanionfinder**. Note: you need to leave the directories in **androidTest** for Android Studio to be able to know that it has integration tests, even if all of them are currently in your **sharedTest** directory.

Next, open your app level **build.gradle** and add the following under your `android` section:

```
android {
  sourceSets {
    String sharedTestDir = 'src/sharedTest/java'
    String sharedResources = 'src/sharedTest/assets'
    test {
      java.srcDir sharedTestDir
      resources.srcDirs += sharedResources
    }
    androidTest {
      java.srcDir sharedTestDir
      resources.srcDirs += sharedResources
    }
  }
}
```

This is creating a new source set that maps both your `test` and `androidTest` to your `sharedTest` directory. It is also nesting an Android directive under an Android directive so yours should look like this:

```
android {
  .
  .
  .
  android {
    sourceSets {
```

```
      .
      .
      .
    }
  }
  .
  .
  .
}
```

> **Note**: This may look familiar from the **sharedTest** set up you did in Chapter 11, "User Interface."

Now, in your **sharedTest ▸ java ▸ com ▸ raywenderlich ▸ codingcompanionfinder** package open **CommonTestDataUtil.kt**. In the first line of your `readFile` function get rid of the `/assets` in this line:

```
val inputStream = this::class.java
  .getResourceAsStream("/assets/$jsonFileName")
```

so that it looks like this:

```
val inputStream = this::class.java
  .getResourceAsStream("/assets/$jsonFileName") ?:
  this::class.java
  .getResourceAsStream("/$jsonFileName")
```

Run your tests in Espresso (you might need to sync Gradle first) and they will be green.

> **Note**: If you find some of the tests are failing, check that `MainActivity.accessToken` is set to your token you retrieved in Chapter 13.

Test Results
com.raywenderlich.codingcompanionfinder.FindCompanionInstrumentedTest
verify_that_companion_details_shows_a_valid_phone_number_and_email
searching_for_a_companion_and_tapping_on_it_takes_the_user_to_the_companion_details
searching_for_a_companion_in_30318_returns_two_results
searching_for_a_companion_in_a_call_returns_an_error_displays_no_results
searching_for_a_companion_in_90210_returns_no_results
pressing_the_find_bottom_menu_item_takes_the_user_to_the_find_page

Now that you have your tests moved to a **sharedTest** source set, there are a few things you need to do in order to get them working with Robolectric.

First, open your app level `build.gradle` and add the following to the `dependencies` section:

```
testImplementation 'androidx.test:runner:1.3.0'
testImplementation 'androidx.test.espresso:espresso-core:3.3.0'
testImplementation "androidx.test:rules:1.3.0"
testImplementation "androidx.test.ext:junit:1.1.2"
testImplementation "androidx.navigation:navigation-testing:
2.3.5"
testImplementation 'com.squareup.okhttp3:mockwebserver:3.12.0'
testImplementation "androidx.test.espresso:espresso-contrib:
3.3.0"
testImplementation 'org.robolectric:robolectric:4.5.1'
testImplementation 'org.koin:koin-test:2.0.1'
androidTestImplementation "org.robolectric:annotations:4.5.1"
```

This is adding all of the dependencies that you had for your Espresso tests at the unit level. It is also including the Robolectric dependencies that you will need. Next, add the following to the top level `android` section of the same file:

```
testOptions {
  unitTests.includeAndroidResources = true
  unitTests.returnDefaultValues = true
}
```

These are telling Robolectric to include Android resources. Because Robolectric is not an actual emulator or device, many Android system calls do not actually do anything. The `unitTests.returnDefaultValues` makes them return a dummy default value in those instances, instead of throwing an exception.

Arctic Fox, Bumble Bee and the New Test Runners

At the time of this writing. The current, released version of Android Studio is 4.2.1. In this version, along with older versions, the test runners for both **unit** and **Espresso** driven tests are different in Android Studio than they are when running the **Gradle** build from the command line. That can cause tests to behave slightly different when running in a CI environment. To reduce that uncertainty, **Android Studio Arctic Fox** migrated the built-in unit test runner to run through **Gradle**. **Android Studio Bumble Bee** moves the **Espresso** driven integration tests to use the same runner.

The shared source sets you added are affected by this. When you run your test through gradle, running one of the gradle commands such as `test` or `testDebugUnitTest` to execute all unit tests will run all tests in your `test` directory along with all of the tests in `sharedTest`. But if you are using a version of Android Studio that is older than Arctic Fox and try running all of the unit tests under the unit test directory, it will not pick up your shared tests.

Running Your Source set in Android Studio 4.2.1 and Older

If you are using Android Studio Arctic Fox or newer you can skip ahead to the next section. Otherwise, go to your app component drop-down at the top of your IDE and select **Edit Configurations**.

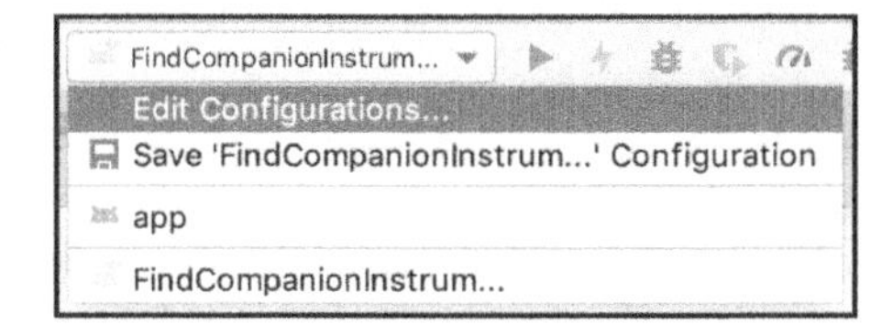

Select the + button.

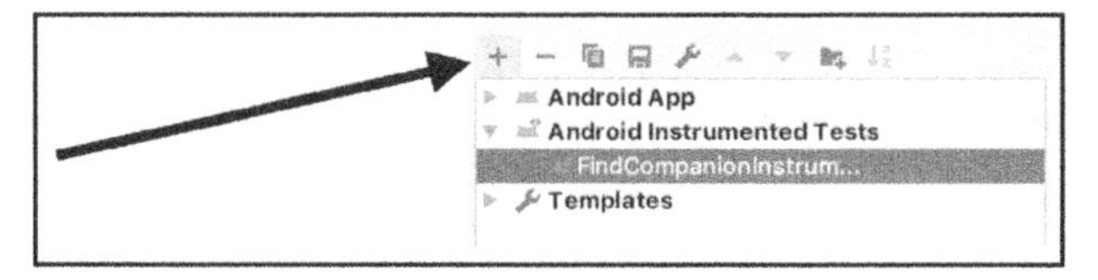

Then, **Android Junit**.

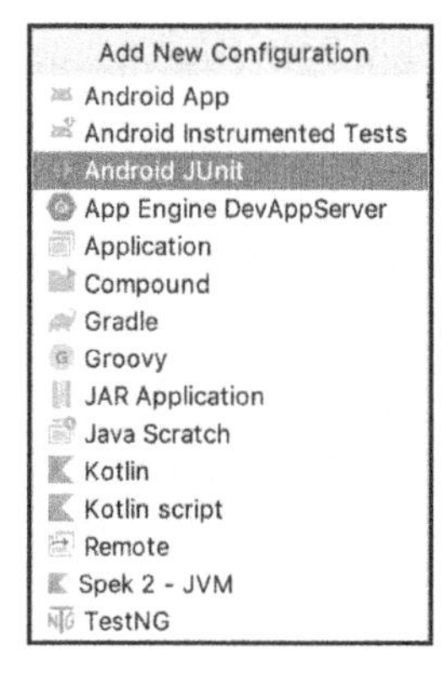

You will be taken to a screen with a fresh configuration.

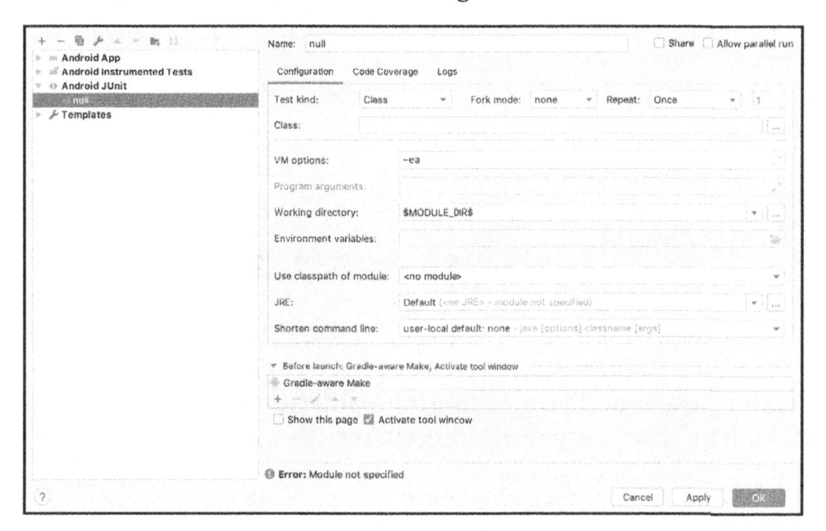

Under **Use classpath or module** select your **CodingCompanionFinder.app** module.

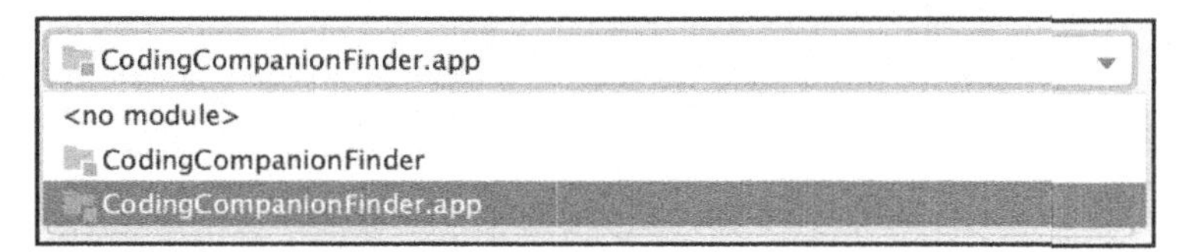

Then under **Test kind** select **All in package**.

Now, under the package select the ellipsis .... The following window will pop up:

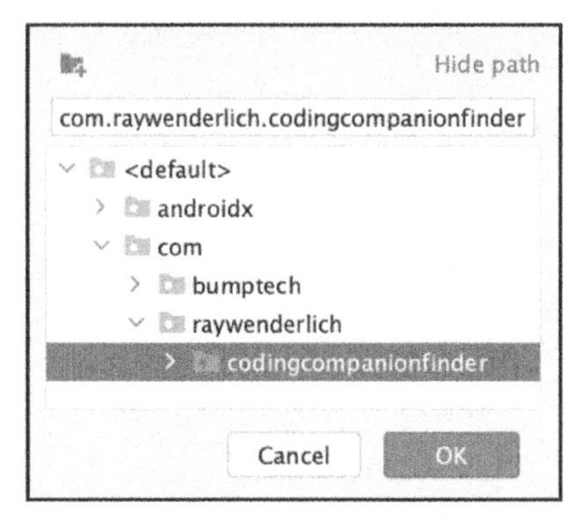

Select ▸ **com** ▸ **raywenderlich** ▸ **codingcompanionfinder** and press **OK**. Finally, it will take you to the previous screen. Press **OK** on that to continue.

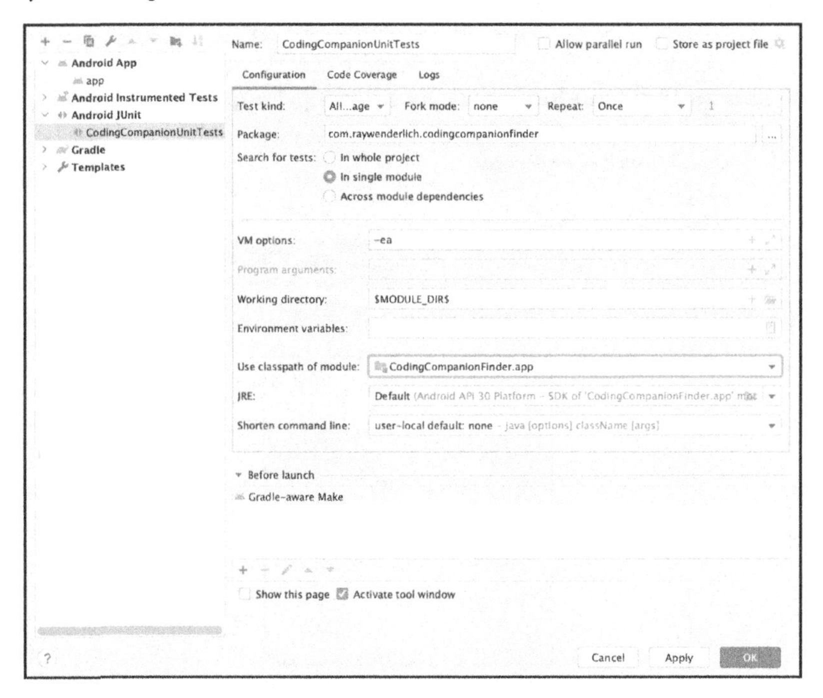

Your new test configuration will be highlighted! Go ahead and run it.

Arctic Fox and Later

If you are using Arctic Fox or later, under your **project** side tab make sure that you have it in the **Android** view mode.

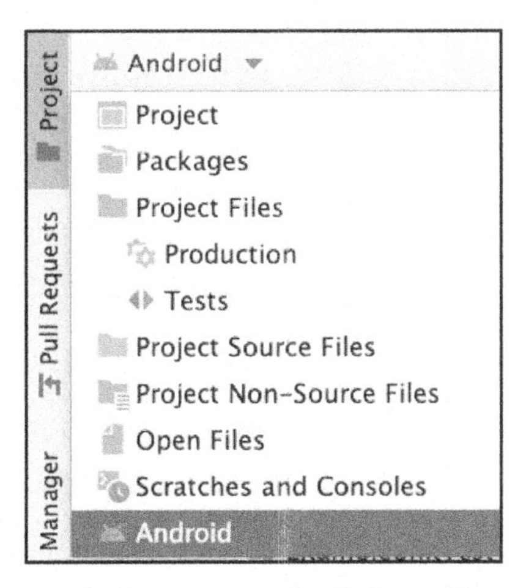

Next, right click on the second **com.raywenderlich.codingcompanionfinder(test)**. This will be the one that does not contain the files that you copied.

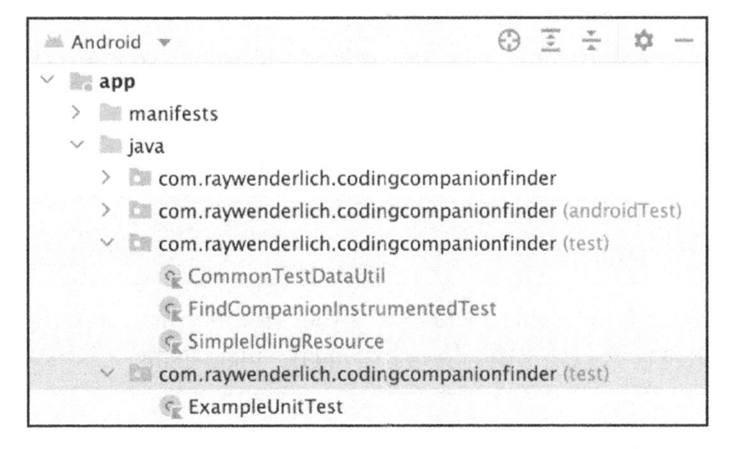

Then select the **run tests in 'com.raywen…'** option to run your tests.

Your Running Tests

After following the steps for your version of Android Studio, your tests will run and you should see the following.

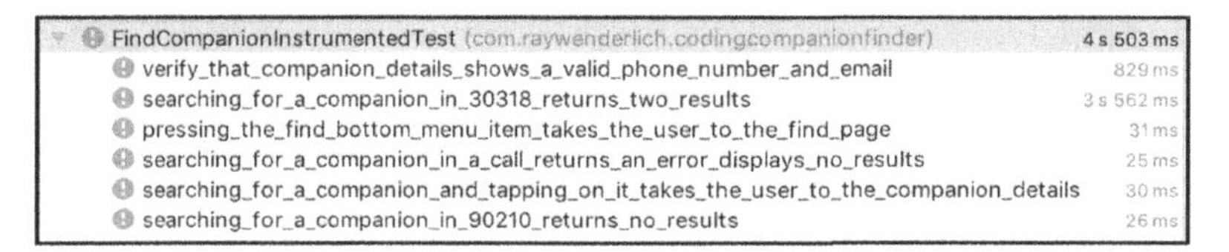

Oh no! Something is not right. If you look at the error messages you will see the following (you may need to scroll down beyond the first couple of errors):

```
kotlin.UninitializedPropertyAccessException: lateinit property startIntent has not been initialized

  at com.raywenderlich.codingcompanionfinder.FindCompanionInstrumentedTest.beforeTestsRun(FindCompanionInstrumentedTest.kt:115) <9 internal calls>
  at org.robolectric.RobolectricTestRunner$HelperTestRunner$1.evaluate(RobolectricTestRunner.java:546)
  at org.robolectric.internal.SandboxTestRunner$2.lambda$evaluate$0(SandboxTestRunner.java:252)
  at org.robolectric.internal.bytecode.Sandbox.lambda$runOnMainThread$0(Sandbox.java:89)
  at java.util.concurrent.FutureTask.run(FutureTask.java:266)
  at java.util.concurrent.ThreadPoolExecutor.runWorker(ThreadPoolExecutor.java:1142)
  at java.util.concurrent.ThreadPoolExecutor$Worker.run(ThreadPoolExecutor.java:617)
  at java.lang.Thread.run(Thread.java:745)
```

> **Note**: If you are using Android Studio Arctic Fox or later and see a robolectric error message similar to `Failed to create a Robolectric sandbox: Android SDK 30 requires Java 9 (have Java 8)` in your failed tests you will need to change your gradle jvm setting. That can be done by doing to **preferences**, selecting **Build, Execution, Deployment ▸ Build Tools ▸ Gradle**. From there change your **Gradle JDK** setting to a version that is 1.9 or greater. If you are un-sure about which version to use, the **Embedded JDK** is an option that will fix this.

Looking at your code, your `ActivityScenario.launch` is being called from here with an `Intent` that is being passed in:

```
@Before
fun beforeTestsRun() {
  testScenario = ActivityScenario.launch(startIntent)
```

That `Intent` is set up in your companion object:

```
@BeforeClass
@JvmStatic
fun setup() {
  server.setDispatcher(dispatcher)
  server.start()
// It is being set right here!
  startIntent = Intent(
    ApplicationProvider.getApplicationContext(),
    MainActivity::class.java)
  startIntent.putExtra(MainActivity.PETFINDER_URI,
    server.url("").toString())
}
```

When running Robolectric this doesn't get called before the `@Before` setup function. More importantly, this `Intent` was initially set up to pass in your **mockwebserver** URL when running your tests. In the last chapter you refactored things so that this is not needed anymore, so let's get rid of it.

To do that, get rid of the last two lines in that function so that it looks like this:

```
@BeforeClass
@JvmStatic
fun setup() {
  server.setDispatcher(dispatcher)
  server.start()
}
```

Then, change the call on the first line of `beforeTestRun` from:

```
@Before
fun beforeTestsRun() {
  testScenario = ActivityScenario.launch(startIntent)
```

To:

```
@Before
fun beforeTestsRun() {
  testScenario =
    ActivityScenario.launch(MainActivity::class.java)
```

That gets rid of the intent that you deleted. Next, replace **loadKoinTestModules**:

```
private fun loadKoinTestModules() {
  loadKoinModules(module(override = true) {
    single(named(PETFINDER_URL)){server.url("").toString()}
  })
}
```

With:

```
private fun loadKoinTestModules() {
  stopKoin()
  startKoin {  }
  loadKoinModules(listOf(module(override = true) {
    single(named(PETFINDER_URL)){server.url("").toString()}
  }, appModule))
}
```

That is needed to make sure that Koin is shut down for before executing the next test when running in Robolectric. Finally, replace the the class definition:

```
class FindCompanionInstrumentedTest: KoinTest {
```

With this:

```
class FindCompanionInstrumentedTest: AutoCloseKoinTest() {
```

This ensures that Koin is stopped at the end of a test run. Now run your tests again.

FindCompanionInstrumentedTest (com.raywenderlich.codingcompanionfinder)	15 s 242 ms
verify_that_companion_details_shows_a_valid_phone_number_and_email	11 s 15 ms
searching_for_a_companion_in_30318_returns_two_results	1 s 179 ms
pressing_the_find_bottom_menu_item_takes_the_user_to_the_find_page	901 ms
searching_for_a_companion_in_a_call_returns_an_error_displays_no_results	661 ms
searching_for_a_companion_and_tapping_on_it_takes_the_user_to_the_companion_details	738 ms
searching_for_a_companion_in_90210_returns_no_results	748 ms

Things are looking better but you still have some failing tests (or perhaps not!).

> **Note**: Depending on the speed of your machine or resources, you may end up with zero, two, or three failing tests. But even if they all pass for you, there's something wrong here that you should fix.

```
androidx.test.espresso.NoMatchingViewException: No views in hierarchy found matching: with text: is "KEVIN"

View Hierarchy:
```

These are failing with the same error message. At this point, before reading further, a good exercise is to trace through things to see if you can figure out what is going wrong here.

If you trace through this you will see that there are two tests that fail when they try to click on an element with text that contains **KEVIN**, which is the last line of the following function:

```
private fun find_and_select_kevin_in_30318() {
  onView(withId(R.id.searchForCompanionFragment))
    .perform(click())
  onView(withId(R.id.searchFieldText))
    .perform(typeText("30318"))
  onView(withId(R.id.searchButton)).perform(click())
  onView(withId(R.id.searchButton))
    .check(matches(isDisplayed()))
  onView(withText("KEVIN")).perform(click())
}
```

It would appear that data from your mockWebServer is not being loaded. The odd thing is that if you look at this test:

```
@Test
fun searching_for_a_companion_in_30318_returns_two_results() {
  onView(withId(R.id.searchForCompanionFragment))
    .perform(click())
  onView(withId(R.id.searchFieldText))
    .perform(typeText("30318"))
  onView(withId(R.id.searchButton)).perform(click())
  onView(withId(R.id.searchButton))
    .check(matches(isDisplayed()))
  onView(withText("Joy")).check(matches(isDisplayed()))
  onView(withText("Male")).check(matches(isDisplayed()))
  onView(withText("Shih Tzu")).check(matches(isDisplayed()))
  onView(withText("KEVIN")).check(matches(isDisplayed()))
  onView(withText("Female")).check(matches(isDisplayed()))
  onView(withText("Domestic Short Hair"))
    .check(matches(isDisplayed()))
}
```

It is able to load up the data and works correctly on some machines but fails on others. You may experience either of these scenarios. This is something that can cause a lot of frustration. Some tests are working correctly, other similar ones that should are not — despite the tests running correctly on Espresso. The problem has to do with how Robolectric handles threads. Unlike when you are running tests on an emulator or device, Robolectric shares a single thread for UI operations and test code.

More importantly, by default, operations run synchronously using this looper which means that many operations will not happen in the same order that they would occur on a live device. This has been an issue with Robolectric for a while, but luckily they've created a fix for it by adding a `@LooperMode(LooperMode.Mode.PAUSED)` annotation before your test class.

Add it to the beginning of our test class so that it looks like following:

```
import org.robolectric.annotation.LooperMode

@RunWith(AndroidJUnit4::class)
@LooperMode(LooperMode.Mode.PAUSED)
class FindCompanionInstrumentedTest: AutoCloseKoinTest() {
```

Now run your tests again and all of them will pass.

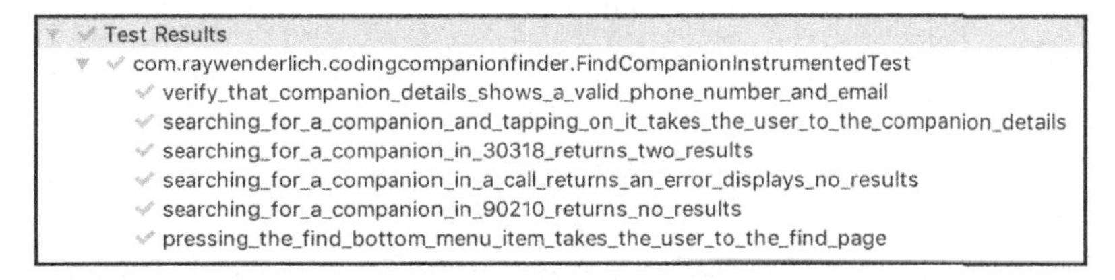

> **Note**: Your can find out more about this **PAUSED** Robolectric **LooperMode** at http://robolectric.org/blog/2019/06/04/paused-looper/.

Testing fragments in isolation

Until now your tests have been large end-to-end UI tests. That said, some of your test cases are actually testing one component that could be tested in isolation. A good example of that is your `ViewCompanionFragment`. This fragment is called via your `SearchForCompanionFragment`.

This happens after you have searched for a companion and select one to see more details.

When you refactored this fragment in the last chapter, you modified it so that all of the data it needs to display, contained in an `Animal` object, is passed into it via navigation parameters. That data is then passed into a `ViewModel` which binds these attributes to the view.

Your end-to-end test is currently testing all of this, but the shelters have a lot of changes that they are going to want to make to this page, along with the `SearchForCompanionFragment` and other fragments in your end-to-end test chain. This will begin to make your end-to-end tests fragile, so now is a good time to move this to a more focused test.

To get started, open up your app level **build.gradle** and add the following to your dependencies:

```
// Once https://issuetracker.google.com/127986458 is fixed this
can be testImplementation
// fragmentscenario testing
debugImplementation 'androidx.fragment:fragment-testing:1.3.4'
debugImplementation "androidx.test:core:1.3.0"
```

This is adding the AndroidX fragment testing dependencies.

> **Note**: At the time of this writing there is a known issue with this module. This means that you need to include it as part of your implementation. To prevent this from going to production you are limiting this to a debug build.

It is also adding the **Robolectric** annotations to **androidTestImplementation** to ensure that your `Looper` annotation does not cause compile issues with the new test you are about to add.

Now, go to your **sharedTest** folder and under the **com.raywenderlich.codingcompanionfinder** package add a class called `ViewCompanionTest`. Above the class add the following:

```
import androidx.test.espresso.Espresso.onView
import androidx.test.espresso.matcher.ViewMatchers.*
import androidx.test.espresso.assertion.ViewAssertions.matches

@RunWith(AndroidJUnit4::class)
@LooperMode(LooperMode.Mode.PAUSED)
```

This is telling it to run with **AndroidJUnit4** and sets the `LooperMode` for the Robolectric runs. Inside of your class add the following:

```
@Before
fun beforeTestsRun() {
// 1
  val animal = Animal(
    22,
    Contact(
      phone = "404-867-5309",
      email = "coding.companion@razware.com",
      address = Address(
        "",
        "",
        "Atlanta",
        "GA",
        "30303",
        "USA"
      )
    ),
    "5",
    "small",
    arrayListOf(),
    Breeds("shih tzu", "", false, false),
    "Spike",
    "male",
    "A sweet little guy with spikey teeth!"
  )
// 2
  val bundle = ViewCompanionFragmentArgs(animal).toBundle()
// 3
  launchFragmentInContainer<ViewCompanionFragment>(bundle,
    R.style.AppTheme)
}
```

This is doing the following:

1. Creating a test `Animal` object.
2. Creating a `Bundle` with your animal object.
3. Launching your fragment with the bundle that you just created.

Two and three might seem like a bit of magic, so let's break that down. The SafeArgs that are used to pass arguments to your fragment through the Jetpack Navigation components are doing some things under the hood for you (see the previous chapter for some description on SafeArgs). In your `CompanionViewHolder`, you have the following `setupClickEvent` method:

```
private fun setupClickEvent(animal: Animal){
  view.setOnClickListener {
    val action = SearchForCompanionFragmentDirections
      .actionSearchForCompanionFragmentToViewCompanion(animal)
    view.findNavController().navigate(action)
  }
}
```

If you trace into the generated `actionSearchForCompanionFragmentToViewCompanion` function you will see that it is part of the following:

```
class SearchForCompanionFragmentDirections
  private constructor() {
// 2
  private data class
  ActionSearchForCompanionFragmentToViewCompanion(
    val animal: Animal
  ) : NavDirections {
    override fun getActionId(): Int =
      R.id.action_searchForCompanionFragment_to_viewCompanion

// 3
    @Suppress("CAST_NEVER_SUCCEEDS")
    override fun getArguments(): Bundle {
      val result = Bundle()
      if (Parcelable::class.java
          .isAssignableFrom(Animal::class.java)) {
          result.putParcelable("animal",
            this.animal as Parcelable)
      } else if (Serializable::class.java
          .isAssignableFrom(Animal::class.java)) {
          result.putSerializable("animal",
            this.animal as Serializable)
      } else {
          throw UnsupportedOperationException(
```

```
                Animal::class.java.name +
                " must implement Parcelable or Serializable or" +
                " must be an Enum.")
        }
        return result
      }
    }

    companion object {
  // 1
      fun actionSearchForCompanionFragmentToViewCompanion(
        animal: Animal
      ): NavDirections =
          ActionSearchForCompanionFragmentToViewCompanion(animal)
    }
  }
```

This is doing the following things:

1. Calling the private constructor for the class.
2. Creating the new instance of the class.
3. When the navigation call is made it calls the `getArguments` function which serializes the arguments, puts them in the bundle and returns the bundle.

Your `ViewCompanionFragmentArgs` generated class provides methods to deserialize and serialize your arguments as well which you can see if you trace into them. This is what is called behind the scenes by Jetpack Navigation when you add `by navArgs()` to an attribute definition in your fragment.

At the time of this writing, Jetpack Navigation does not have testing hooks for this scenario. Because of that we needed to understand what this was doing behind the scenes to create this test. While that created a bit of extra short term work, in the long term it gives you more understanding about the framework.

By having a better understanding, when issues pop up while you are wiring up your navigation safe arguments, you will know how it works and be able to better understand how to trace it. Ultimately, this will make it easier and faster for you to fix issues surrounding navigation.

Now that you have that out of the way, add the following test to your `ViewCompanionTest` class:

```
@Test
fun check_that_all_values_display_correctly() {
  onView(withText("Spike")).check(matches(isDisplayed()))
  onView(withText("Atlanta, GA")).check(matches(isDisplayed()))
  onView(withText("shih tzu")).check(matches(isDisplayed()))
  onView(withText("5")).check(matches(isDisplayed()))
  onView(withText("male")).check(matches(isDisplayed()))
  onView(withText("small")).check(matches(isDisplayed()))
  onView(withText("A sweet little guy with spikey teeth!"))
    .check(matches(isDisplayed()))
  onView(withText("404-867-5309")).check(matches(isDisplayed()))
  onView(withText("coding.companion@razware.com"))
    .check(matches(isDisplayed()))
}
```

Even though this is a more focused test, it still will be run in Espresso. To reduce test execution time you are verifying all of the expected display fields in one test instead of breaking that up. Run the test in Espresso and it will pass.

```
Test Results
  com.raywenderlich.codingcompanionfinder.ViewCompanionTest
    check_that_all_values_display_correctly
```

Finally, following the instructions earlier in this chapter, run all of your unit tests. This, along with the others will pass.

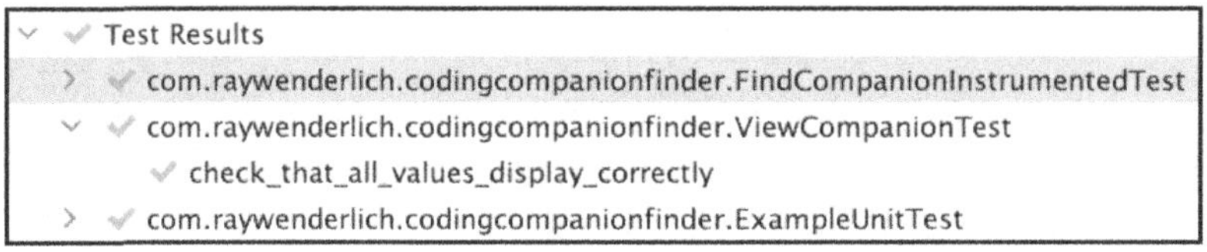

```
Test Results
  com.raywenderlich.codingcompanionfinder.FindCompanionInstrumentedTest
  com.raywenderlich.codingcompanionfinder.ViewCompanionTest
    check_that_all_values_display_correctly
  com.raywenderlich.codingcompanionfinder.ExampleUnitTest
```

Now that you have your `ViewCompanionFragment` test more focused, let's refactor your `SearchForCompanionFragment` tests.

Reviewing from the previous chapter, this fragment does the following:

1. It presents the user with a screen to search for a companion.

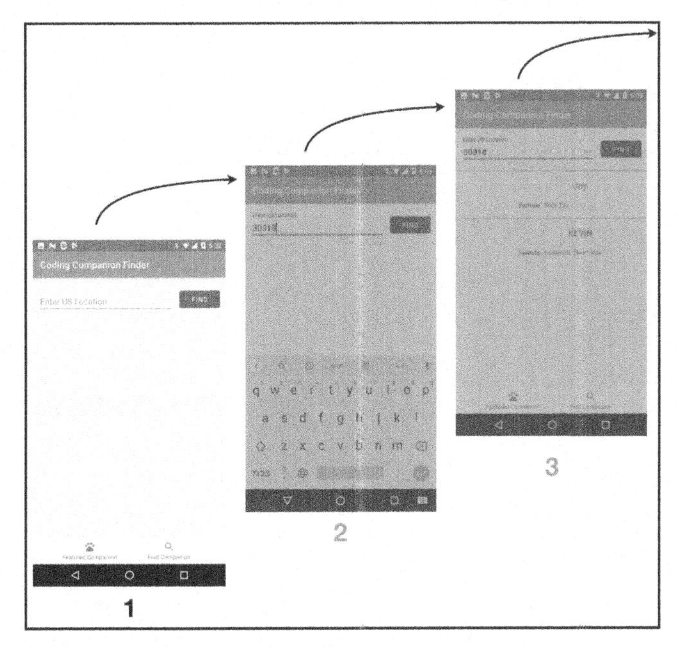

2. It gets the user's input and performs a search.

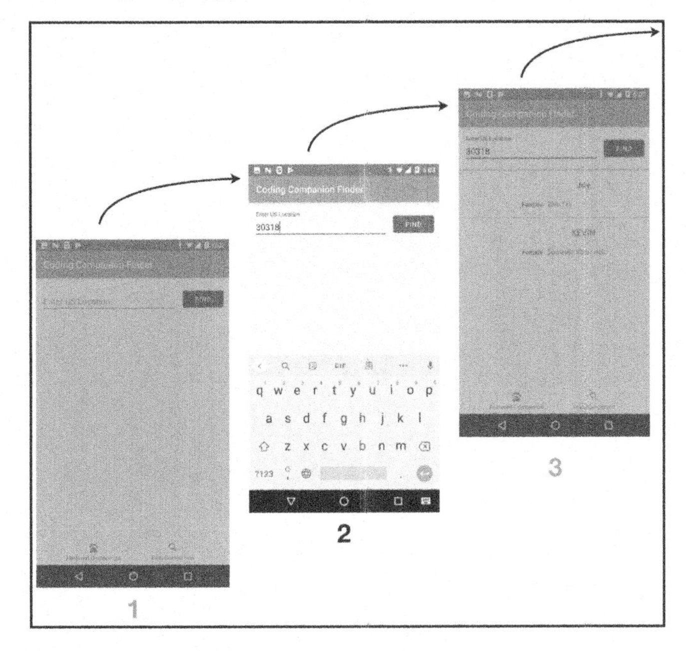

3. Presents the search results and allows navigation to the `ViewCompanionFragment`.

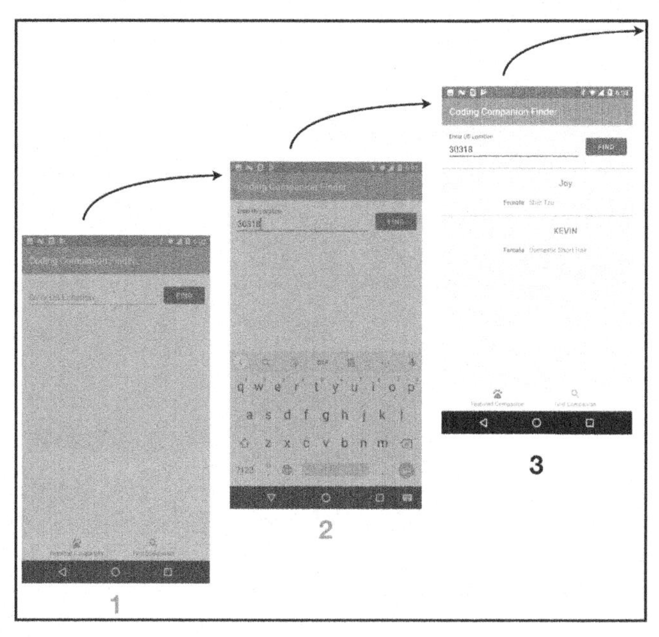

To get started, create a new file in your test package called **SearchForCompanionTest.kt**. Next, create the following class definition:

```
import org.robolectric.annotation.LooperMode
import org.junit.runner.RunWith
import androidx.test.espresso.Espresso.onView
import androidx.test.espresso.matcher.ViewMatchers.*
import androidx.test.espresso.assertion.ViewAssertions.matches
import org.junit.BeforeClass
import org.junit.Before
import org.junit.After
import org.junit.Test

@RunWith(AndroidJUnit4::class)
@LooperMode(LooperMode.Mode.PAUSED)
class SearchForCompanionTest : AutoCloseKoinTest() {

  private val idlingResource = SimpleIdlingResource()
}
```

This is inheriting from `AutoCloseKoinTest()` like you did with `FindCompanionInstrumentedTest`, adding in the `LooperMode` for Robolectric and setting up your `IdlingResource`. Now, add in the following to the body of your class:

```
companion object {
  val server = MockWebServer()
  val dispatcher: Dispatcher = object : Dispatcher() {
    @Throws(InterruptedException::class)
    override fun dispatch(
      request: RecordedRequest
    ): MockResponse {
      return CommonTestDataUtil.dispatch(request) ?:
        MockResponse().setResponseCode(404)
    }
  }

  @BeforeClass
  @JvmStatic
  fun setup() {
    server.setDispatcher(dispatcher)
    server.start()
  }
}

private fun loadKoinTestModules(serverUrl: String){
  loadKoinModules(listOf(module(override = true) {
    single(named(PETFINDER_URL)) { serverUrl }
  }))
}

private fun loadKoinTestModulesTryCatch(serverUrl: String) {
  try {
    loadKoinTestModules(serverUrl)
  } catch (koinAlreadyStartedException:
KoinAppAlreadyStartedException) {
    stopKoin()
    loadKoinTestModules(serverUrl)
    loadKoinModules(listOf(module(override = true) {
      single(named(PETFINDER_URL)) { serverUrl }
    }))
  } catch (illegalStateException: IllegalStateException){
    startKoin {
      modules(listOf(appModule))
    }
    loadKoinTestModules(serverUrl)
  }
}

@Subscribe
fun onEvent(idlingEntity: IdlingEntity) {
  idlingResource.incrementBy(idlingEntity.incrementValue)
}
```

These methods are the same as the ones with the same name in your `FindCompanionInstrumentedTest` with the addition of some `try{} catch() {}` logic for the `loadKoinTestModules` method.

Normally, at this point, you might want to consider refactoring this into a shared component (although bear in mind the Three Strikes Rule, which you can read about here: https://wiki.c2.com/?ThreeStrikesAndYouRefactor), but there are some things that may change so you are going to hold off on that. Following that, add in the following methods:

```
@Before
fun beforeTestsRun() {
  val serverUrl = server.url("").toString()
  loadKoinTestModules(serverUrl)
  launchFragmentInContainer<SearchForCompanionFragment>(
    themeResId = R.style.AppTheme,
    factory = FragmentFactory())
  EventBus.getDefault().register(this)
  IdlingRegistry.getInstance().register(idlingResource)
}

@After
fun afterTestsRun() {
  // eventbus and idling resources unregister.
  IdlingRegistry.getInstance().unregister(idlingResource)
  EventBus.getDefault().unregister(this)
  stopKoin()
}
```

This is launching your fragment, passing in a `FragmentFactory`. In your `ViewCompanionTest` you did not need a `FragmentFactory`, because you were launching your `MainActivity`. The reason you are using a factory here has to do with Koin. Your `ViewCompanionTest` did not need to set Koin up and `FindCompanionInstrumentedTest` was able to stop Koin and inject your test modules after the app started. That only worked for those tests because you are not testing anything on the Featured Companion page rendered by your `RandomCompanion` fragment. Because you set up the Koin dependencies before you instantiated a `SearchForCompanionFragment` your test Koin modules were injected.

With your refactored tests you are directly loading your `SearchForCompanionFragment` in a test activity. When that starts up, it is loading up your app-level Koin dependencies. If you want to change them over to your test modules by stopping Koin and loading your test modules after things have been injected into your fragment, there is not an easy way to do that. To solve this problem, you are passing in a factory that stops Koin itself, and initializes it with your test dependencies *before* instantiating your fragment so that you hit your MockWebServer when making API requests.

Beyond this, your code is setting up your `IdlingResource` before your tests run and tearing them down afterwards. Now, add the following test:

```
@Test
fun
pressing_the_find_bottom_menu_item_takes_the_user_to_the_find_pa
ge() {
  onView(withId(R.id.searchButton))
    .check(matches(isDisplayed()))
  onView(withId(R.id.searchFieldText))
    .check(matches(isDisplayed()))
  onView(withId(R.id.searchFieldText))
    .perform(typeText("30318"))
  onView(withId(R.id.searchButton)).perform(click())
}
```

This is the same test that you have in your `FindCompanionInstrumentedTest` except it doesn't have to navigate to your `SearchForCompanionFragment` since it is being directly instantiated for this test.

Next open `CodingCompanionFinder` and replace your `onCreate()` method with the following:

```
override fun onCreate() {
  super.onCreate()
  try {
    startKoin {
      androidContext(this@CodingCompanionFinder)
      modules(listOf(appModule, urlsModule))
    }
  } catch (koinAlreadyStartedException:
KoinAppAlreadyStartedException) {
    Log.i("CodingCompanionFinder",
"KoinAppAlreadyStartedException, should only happen in tests")
  }
}
```

This is a hook for testing that will prevent the app from crashing if koin has already been started.

Go back to your new test and run it. It will fail.

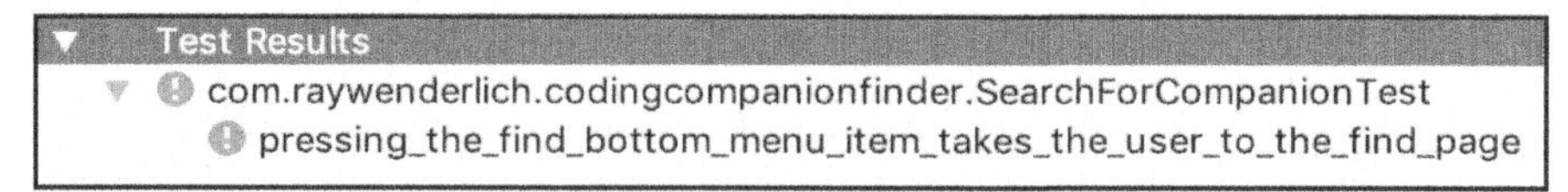

Looking at the error message you will see a message that reads `java.lang.RuntimeException: java.lang.ClassCastException: androidx.fragment.app.testing.FragmentScenario$EmptyFragmentActivity cannot be cast to com.raywenderlich.codingcompanionfinder.MainActivity`. Looking at your stack trace, the following line in `SearchForCompanionFragment` is your problem:

```
searchForCompanionViewModel.accessToken = (activity as
  MainActivity).accessToken
```

For now, remove this line. It is setting a stored access token that was being cached. For the eagle-eyed readers: this will result in extra requests without tokens being made. Later on there will be an exercise where you can fix this. Next, open up your `SearchForCompanionViewModel` and change the following line close to the top of the class from:

```
lateinit var accessToken: String
```

To:

```
var accessToken: String = ""
```

Run the test via Espresso and it will be green.

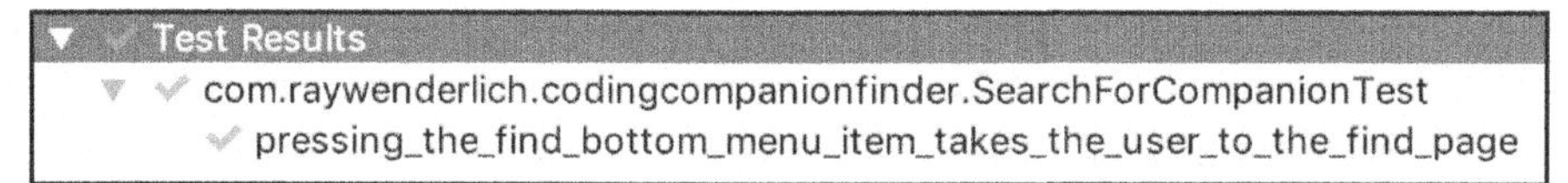

Now execute all of your unit tests using either a configuration or right clicking on the tests depending on the version of Android Studio you have. They will also be green.

Test Results
com.raywenderlich.codingcompanionfinder.FindCompanionInstrumentedTest
verify_that_companion_details_shows_a_valid_phone_number_and_email
searching_for_a_companion_in_30318_returns_two_results
pressing_the_find_bottom_menu_item_takes_the_user_to_the_find_page
searching_for_a_companion_in_a_call_returns_an_error_displays_no_results
searching_for_a_companion_and_tapping_on_it_takes_the_user_to_the_companion_details
searching_for_a_companion_in_90210_returns_no_results
com.raywenderlich.codingcompanionfinder.ViewCompanionTest
check_that_all_values_display_correctly
com.raywenderlich.codingcompanionfinder.SearchForCompanionTest
pressing_the_find_bottom_menu_item_takes_the_user_to_the_find_page
com.raywenderlich.codingcompanionfinder.ExampleUnitTest
addition_isCorrect

Next, add the following two tests:

```
@Test
fun searching_for_a_companion_in_90210_returns_no_results() {
  onView(withId(R.id.searchFieldText))
    .perform(typeText("90210"))
  onView(withId(R.id.searchButton)).perform(click())
  onView(withId(R.id.searchButton))
    .check(matches(isDisplayed()))
  onView(withId(R.id.noResults)).check(
    matches(
      withEffectiveVisibility(
        Visibility.VISIBLE
      )
    )
  )
}

@Test
fun
searching_for_a_companion_in_a_call_returns_an_error_displays_no
_results() {
  onView(withId(R.id.searchFieldText)).perform(typeText("dddd"))
  onView(withId(R.id.searchButton)).perform(click())
  onView(withId(R.id.searchButton))
    .check(ViewAssertions.matches(isDisplayed()))
  onView(withId(R.id.noResults))
    .check(ViewAssertions.matches(
      withEffectiveVisibility(Visibility.VISIBLE)))
}
```

These are also the same as your similarly-named tests in `FindCompanionInstrumentedTest` minus the navigation to your `SearchForCompanionFragment`. Run all of your tests via Robolectric and they will be green.

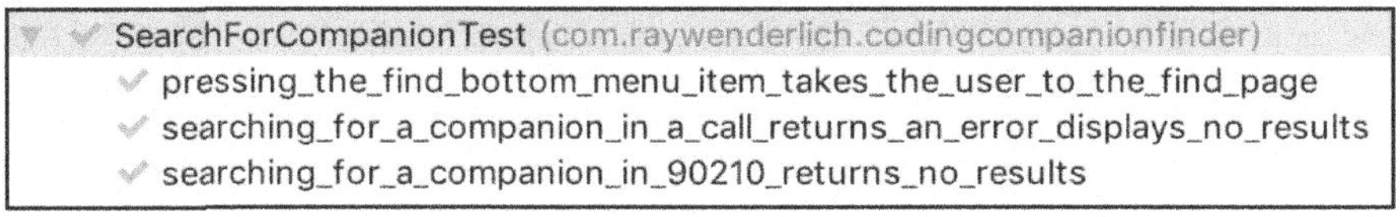

SearchForCompanionTest (com.raywenderlich.codingcompanionfinder)
pressing_the_find_bottom_menu_item_takes_the_user_to_the_find_page
searching_for_a_companion_in_a_call_returns_an_error_displays_no_results
searching_for_a_companion_in_90210_returns_no_results

Now execute all of your Espresso tests using **(androidTest)** by right clicking on the package annotated and selecting the option to run all of the tests in it.

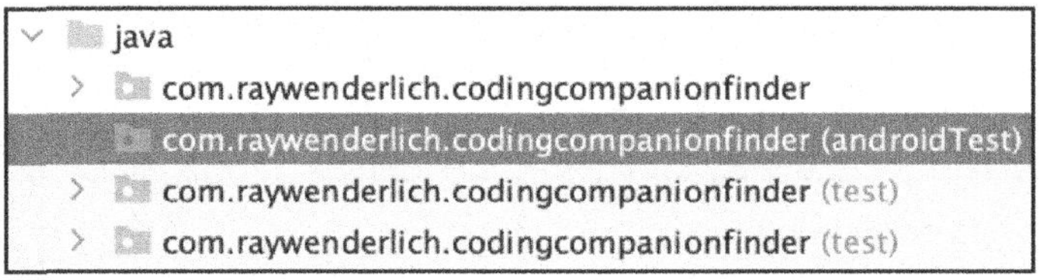

java
com.raywenderlich.codingcompanionfinder
com.raywenderlich.codingcompanionfinder (androidTest)
com.raywenderlich.codingcompanionfinder (test)
com.raywenderlich.codingcompanionfinder (test)

All of the tests will be green

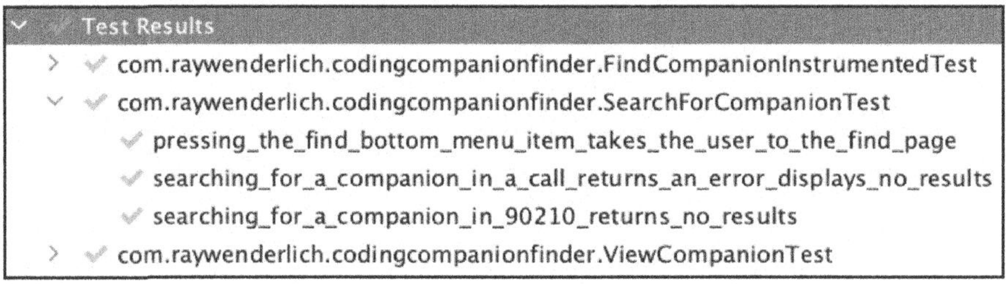

Test Results
com.raywenderlich.codingcompanionfinder.FindCompanionInstrumentedTest
com.raywenderlich.codingcompanionfinder.SearchForCompanionTest
pressing_the_find_bottom_menu_item_takes_the_user_to_the_find_page
searching_for_a_companion_in_a_call_returns_an_error_displays_no_results
searching_for_a_companion_in_90210_returns_no_results
com.raywenderlich.codingcompanionfinder.ViewCompanionTest

Now, add the following test to assert that the values being displayed after doing a search are correct:

```
@Test
fun searching_for_a_companion_in_30318_returns_two_results() {
  onView(withId(R.id.searchFieldText))
    .perform(typeText("30318"))
  onView(withId(R.id.searchButton)).perform(click())
  onView(withId(R.id.searchButton))
    .check(matches(isDisplayed()))
  onView(withText("Joy")).check(matches(isDisplayed()))
  onView(withText("Male")).check(matches(isDisplayed()))
  onView(withText("Shih Tzu")).check(matches(isDisplayed()))
  onView(withText("KEVIN")).check(matches(isDisplayed()))
  onView(withText("Female")).check(matches(isDisplayed()))
  onView(withText("Domestic Short Hair"))
    .check(matches(isDisplayed()))
}
```

Run all of your tests in Espresso and everything will be green.

```
Test Results
  FindCompanionInstrumentedTest
  SearchForCompanionTest
    searching_for_a_companion_in_30318_returns_two_results
    pressing_the_find_bottom_menu_item_takes_the_user_to_the_find_page
    searching_for_a_companion_in_a_call_returns_an_error_displays_no_results
    searching_for_a_companion_in_90210_returns_no_results
  ViewCompanionTest
```

Now execute your tests in Robolectric and they will be green as well.

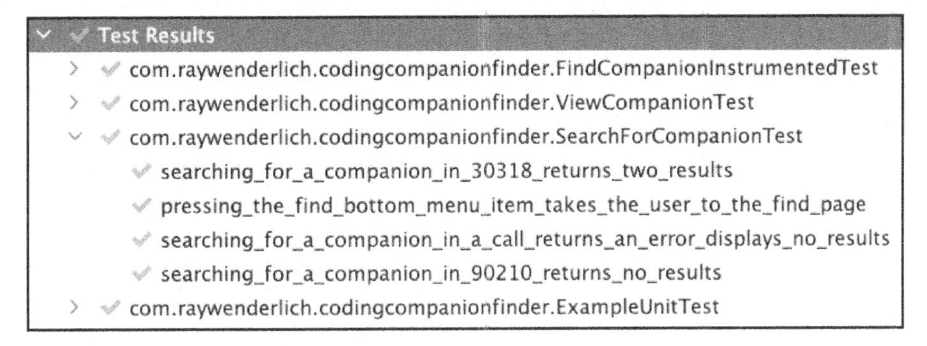

Breaking out unit tests

Up to this point your tests have had dependencies on Android. But, as we discussed in Chapter 4, "The Testing Pyramid," you should strive to have unit tests. Ideally, you will have more unit tests than integration tests and more integration tests than end-to-end/UI tests.

Some scenarios where unit tests might make sense include testing:

- Classes that focus on business logic.
- ViewModels that have logic to present, retrieve, or store/post data.
- Services that do things.
- Classes that can be tested without needing to depend on Android.

Alternatively, in the following scenarios unit testing may not make sense. These include tests that:

- Focus on Activities and Fragments.
- Depending on Android components to run.
- Cover boiler plate getters and setters, for example in data objects.
- Cover basic data marshaling that are covered at other levels of the pyramid.
- Require a significant amount of mocking.

Looking in your **searchforcompanion** package, there are only two classes that are candidates for unit testing. They are your `ViewCompanionViewModel` and `SearchForCompanionViewModel`. They are view models that can be tested in isolation.

To get started open **ViewCompanonViewModel.kt** and you will see the following:

```
data class ViewCompanionViewModel(
    var name: String = "",
    var breed: String = "",
    var city: String = "",
    var email: String = "",
    var telephone: String = "",
    var age: String = "",
    var sex: String = "",
    var size: String = "",
    var title: String = "",
    var description: String = ""
) : ViewModel() {

    fun populateFromAnimal(animal: Animal) {
        name = animal.name
        breed = animal.breeds.primary
        city = animal.contact.address.city + ", " +
                animal.contact.address.state
        email = animal.contact.email
        telephone = animal.contact.phone
        age = animal.age
        sex = animal.gender
        size = animal.size
        title = "Meet " + animal.name
        description = animal.description
    }
}
```

The variable definitions that are part of your data class are not good candidates for tests, but your `populateFromAnimal()` function could be tested.

To get started, rename your **ExampleUnitTest** to **ViewCompanionViewModelTest.kt** in your test package. Next, replace it's contents with the following:

```
class ViewCompanionViewModelTest {
// 1
  val animal = Animal(
    22,
    Contact(
      phone = "404-867-5309",
      email = "coding.companion@razware.com",
      address = Address(
        "",
        "",
        "Atlanta",
        "GA",
        "30303",
        "USA"
      ) ),
    "5",
    "small",
    arrayListOf(),
    Breeds("shih tzu", "", false, false),
    "Spike",
    "male",
    "A sweet little guy with spikey teeth!"
  )
//2
  @Test
  fun
populateFromAnimal_sets_the_animals_name_to_the_view_model(){
    val viewCompanionViewModel = ViewCompanionViewModel()
    viewCompanionViewModel.populateFromAnimal(animal)
// 3
    assert(viewCompanionViewModel.name.equals("foo"))
  }
}
```

This has the following parts:

1. An `Animal` object. This is the same data that you had in your `ViewCompanionTest` animal object.
2. A test to make sure that the animals name is set when the user calls the `populateFromAnimal()` function.
3. A focused failing assertion to start out with to ensure that we have a valid test.

This test will only run as a unit test, so go ahead and run it.

```
ViewCompanionViewModelTest (com.raywenderlich.codingcompanionfinder)
  populateFromAnimal_sets_the_animals_name_to_the_view_model
```

Now that you have a failing assertion, correct it to check for the name of your animal:

```
assert(viewCompanionViewModel.name.equals("Spike"))
```

Run the test again and it will pass.

```
ViewCompanionViewModelTest (com.raywenderlich.codingcompanionfinder)
  populateFromAnimal_sets_the_animals_name_to_the_view_model
```

You may have noticed that your test here is much more focused with only one assertion. This is intentional for a number of reasons including:

- Unit tests are intended to be more focused.
- They run faster and as such do not take as much time to spin up dependencies.
- The focused assertions lead to individual tests that are not as brittle.

Just like dancing, driving a car, or learning to speak a language, repetition and practice help to make you a better TDD'er. We could spend pages and pages writing focused tests for all of these fields. But, this is a great opportunity for you to practice.

Before you continue on, take some time to do the following:

1. Write a test function for the next field in your `ViewModel` with one assert that should fail.
2. Run the test to make sure that it fails.
3. Fix the assert expectation to ensure that it passes.
4. Go back to step one and repeat this until you have done this for all fields.

Unit testing Retrofit calls

Now that you have your `ViewCompanionViewModel` under test, let's do the same for your `SearchForCompanionViewModel`.

To get started, create a new Kotlin file called **SearchForCompanionViewModelTest.kt** in the same directory as **ViewCompanionViewModelTest.kt** and add the following content to it:

```
class SearchForCompanionViewModelTest {

}
```

Now open up **SearchForCompanionViewModel.kt** and you will see the following:

```
class SearchForCompanionViewModel(
  val petFinderService: PetFinderService
): ViewModel() {
// 1
  val noResultsViewVisiblity : MutableLiveData<Int> =
    MutableLiveData<Int>()
// 2
  val companionLocation : MutableLiveData<String> =
    MutableLiveData()
// 3
  val animals: MutableLiveData<ArrayList<Animal>> =
    MutableLiveData<ArrayList<Animal>>()
  var accessToken: String = ""
// 4
  fun searchForCompanions() {

    GlobalScope.launch {

      EventBus.getDefault().post(IdlingEntity(1))
      val getAnimalsRequest = petFinderService.getAnimals(
          accessToken,
          location = companionLocation.value
      )

      val searchForPetResponse = getAnimalsRequest.await()

      GlobalScope.launch(Dispatchers.Main) {
        if (searchForPetResponse.isSuccessful) {
          searchForPetResponse.body()?.let {
            animals.postValue(it.animals)
            if (it.animals.size > 0) {
              noResultsViewVisiblity.postValue(INVISIBLE)
            } else {
              noResultsViewVisiblity.postValue(View.VISIBLE)
            }
```

```
            }
          } else {
            noResultsViewVisiblity.postValue(View.VISIBLE)
          }
        }
        EventBus.getDefault().post(IdlingEntity(-1))
      }
    }

  }
```

At a high level, this has the following testable elements:

1. The visibility for your `noResults` view.
2. The location that you want to search on.
3. The animals that are returned.
4. A Retrofit call that uses #2 to return data for #3 and either displays or hides #1.

To start off, you are going to do a focused test that enters **30318** as your location and checks to be sure that two results are returned. Add the following to your **SearchForCompanionViewModelTest**:

```
// 1
val server = MockWebServer()

lateinit var petFinderService: PetFinderService
// 2
val dispatcher: Dispatcher = object : Dispatcher() {
  @Throws(InterruptedException::class)
  override fun dispatch(
    request: RecordedRequest
  ): MockResponse {
    return CommonTestDataUtil.dispatch(request) ?:
      MockResponse().setResponseCode(404)
  }
}

// 3
@Before
fun setup() {
  server.setDispatcher(dispatcher)
  server.start()
  val logger = HttpLoggingInterceptor()
  val client = OkHttpClient.Builder()
    .addInterceptor(logger)
    .connectTimeout(60L, TimeUnit.SECONDS)
    .readTimeout(60L, TimeUnit.SECONDS)
    .build()
```

```
  petFinderService = Retrofit.Builder()
    .baseUrl(server.url("").toString())
    .addConverterFactory(GsonConverterFactory.create())
    .client(client)
    .build().create(PetFinderService::class.java)
}

// 4
@Test
fun call_to_searchForCompanions_gets_results() {
  val searchForCompanionViewModel =
    SearchForCompanionViewModel(petFinderService)
  searchForCompanionViewModel.companionLocation.value = "30318"
  searchForCompanionViewModel.searchForCompanions()

  Assert.assertEquals(2,
    searchForCompanionViewModel.animals.value!!.size)
}
```

This test is doing the following:

1. Setting up your `MockWebServer`.
2. Setting up your `MockWebServer` dispatcher.
3. Initializing your `PetfinderService` pointing it to your `MockWebServer`.
4. Executes a test, which creates a `SearchForCompanionViewModel` with your `PetFinderService`, sets your location value, runs the search, and checks that the result has only two results.

This is not an Espresso test, but it may try to run as one due to your sharedTest setup, so use the **Edit Configuration** option to set it up to run as an **Android Junit** test. Then try running your test.

```
SearchForCompanionViewModelTest (com.raywenderlich.codingcompanionfinder)
    call to searchForCompanions gets results
```

```
java.lang.NullPointerException
  at androidx.arch.core.executor.DefaultTaskExecutor.isMainThread(DefaultTaskExecutor.java:74)
  at androidx.arch.core.executor.ArchTaskExecutor.isMainThread(ArchTaskExecutor.java:116)
  at androidx.lifecycle.LiveData.assertMainThread(LiveData.java:442)
  at androidx.lifecycle.LiveData.setValue(LiveData.java:286)
  at androidx.lifecycle.MutableLiveData.setValue(MutableLiveData.java:33)
  at com.raywenderlich.codingcompanionfinder.SearchForCompanionViewModelTest.call to searchForCompanions gets results(SearchForCompanionViewModelTest.kt:68)
```

Oh no! Your test is failing with a dreaded `NullPointerException` when it tries to set a value on your `companionLocation` `LiveData` object. I thought Kotlin was supposed to help prevent null pointers! The *actual* null pointer is thrown when it tries to determine if this task is running on the main thread.

This is because your test is trying to access the "main" thread — which does not exist in the unit test. To fix that you are going to need to add an `InstantTaskExecutorRule`. This swaps the default executor for your `ViewModel` with one that executes everything synchronously on your current thread. To add this, add the following in your app level dependencies:

```
testImplementation "androidx.arch.core:core-testing:2.0.1"
androidTestImplementation "androidx.arch.core:core-testing:
2.0.1"
```

Then add this to your test class:

```
@get:Rule
val instantTaskExecutorRule = InstantTaskExecutorRule()
```

You will also need to add this import:

```
import
androidx.arch.core.executor.testing.InstantTaskExecutorRule
```

Now, run your test again.

SearchForCompanionViewModelTest (com.raywenderlich.codingcompanionfinder)
call to searchForCompanions gets results

```
kotlin.KotlinNullPointerException
  at com.raywenderlich.codingcompanionfinder.SearchForCompanionViewModelTest.call to searchForCompanions gets results(SearchForCompanionViewModelTest.kt:76)
```

Oops! It's still failing, but this time for a different reason! Let's track this down.

Your error message is because your `searchForCompanionViewModel.animals.value` is `null`. Looking at your method body of the `searchForCompanions` method in your `ViewModel`, there are two co-routines that you are using.

```
fun searchForCompanions() {

  GlobalScope.launch {
    .
    .
    // getAnimals is a suspend function
    val searchForPetResponse = petFinderService.getAnimals(
          accessToken,
          location = companionLocation.value
    )
    .
    .
    GlobalScope.launch(Dispatchers.Main) {
      .
      .
```

```
        .
      }
    }
}
```

If you debug through the call you will see that the test exits before your call completes with your `getAnimalsRequest`. You are going to need to do something to allow this to execute your threads and wait for it until execution is done.

To get started, add the following dependencies to the `dependencies` section of your app level `build.gradle` file:

```
def coroutinesVersion = "1.5.0"

testImplementation "org.jetbrains.kotlinx:kotlinx-coroutines-
android:$coroutinesVersion"
testImplementation "org.jetbrains.kotlinx:kotlinx-coroutines-
test:$coroutinesVersion"

androidTestImplementation "org.jetbrains.kotlinx:kotlinx-
coroutines-android:$coroutinesVersion"
androidTestImplementation "org.jetbrains.kotlinx:kotlinx-
coroutines-test:$coroutinesVersion"
```

This is adding coroutine testing support, which you can read more about here: https://github.com/Kotlin/kotlinx.coroutines. Next, add the following at the class level of your test:

```
private val mainThreadSurrogate =
  newSingleThreadContext("Mocked UI thread")
```

This is setting up a thread context, owned by your test thread that will make all of your tests run under one thread.

Then add this to the top of your `setup` method:

```
Dispatchers.setMain(mainThreadSurrogate)
```

This tells the system to use this new thread context that you just created. Now run your tests.

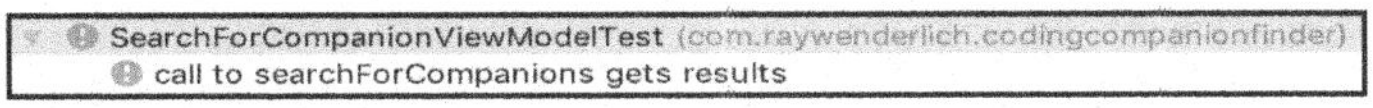

```
SearchForCompanionViewModelTest (com.raywenderlich.codingcompanionfinder)
    call to searchForCompanions gets results
```

```
kotlin.KotlinNullPointerException
  at com.raywenderlich.codingcompanionfinder.SearchForCompanionViewModelTest.call to searchForCompanions gets results(SearchForCompanionViewModelTest.kt:76)
```

Another problem?! The issue is that the `LiveData` result is coming back after you did your assert. To fix that, replace your test with the following:

```
@Test
fun call_to_searchForCompanions_gets_results() {
  val searchForCompanionViewModel =
    SearchForCompanionViewModel(petFinderService)
  searchForCompanionViewModel.companionLocation.value = "30318"
// 1
  val countDownLatch = CountDownLatch(1)
  searchForCompanionViewModel.searchForCompanions()
// 2
  searchForCompanionViewModel.animals.observeForever {
    countDownLatch.countDown()
  }
// 3
  countDownLatch.await(2, TimeUnit.SECONDS)
  Assert.assertEquals(2,
    searchForCompanionViewModel.animals.value!!.size)
}
```

This is adding a `CountDownLatch` that waits until your result comes back. There are three parts to using it:

1. Setting up your latch with an initial latch value; in this case it is one. The number is how many times `countDown` needs to be called on it before it continues after `await`.
2. Using an `observeForever` on your `LiveData` object, and, when a result is received, incrementing the value of the latch down.
3. A call to `await` with a timeout of 2 seconds to wait for the result to be returned. The timeout is important so that the test does not hang indefinitely if there is a problem that causes the latch to not fire.

Run your test again and it will be green!

> **Note**: `CountDownLatches` are useful but can make tests slow and brittle. An easy way to get around them often is to make the scheduling/threading a *dependency* of the class you're testing, so that you can put in "fake" synchronous scheduling within tests.

SearchForCompanionViewModelTest (com.raywenderlich.codingcompanionfinder)
call to searchForCompanions gets results

Since you want to verify that this is a valid test, change the expectation on your assert to another value, such as 1 and re-run your test.

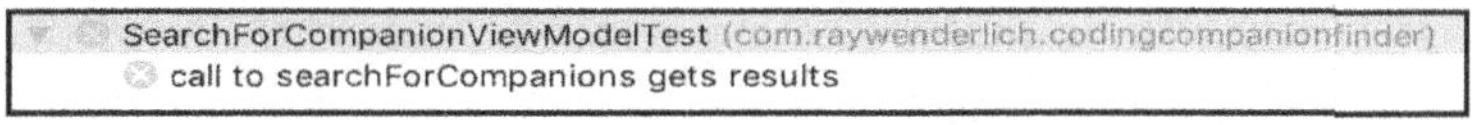

SearchForCompanionViewModelTest (com.raywenderlich.codingcompanionfinder)
call to searchForCompanions gets results

It fails, which is what we wanted. Now change the value back to 2 and make it green.

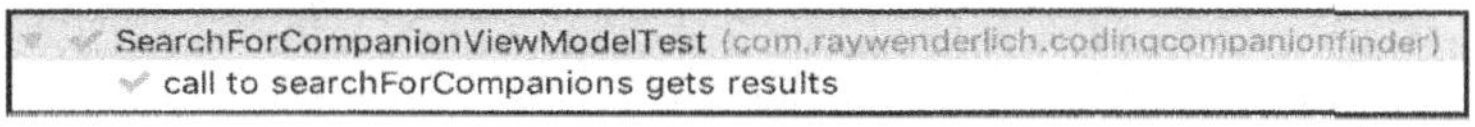

SearchForCompanionViewModelTest (com.raywenderlich.codingcompanionfinder)
call to searchForCompanions gets results

When this `ViewModel` fetches data it sets values for your view, it also sets the value of `noResultsViewVisibility` to `INVISIBLE` if there are results or `VISIBLE` if there are none. Let's add some tests for that. To get started add the following test:

```
@Test
fun
call_to_searchForCompanions_with_results_sets_the_visibility_of_
no_results_to_INVISIBLE() {
  val searchForCompanionViewModel =
    SearchForCompanionViewModel(petFinderService)
  searchForCompanionViewModel.companionLocation.value = "30318"
  val countDownLatch = CountDownLatch(1)
  searchForCompanionViewModel.searchForCompanions()
  searchForCompanionViewModel.noResultsViewVisiblity
    .observeForever {
      countDownLatch.countDown()
    }

  countDownLatch.await(2, TimeUnit.SECONDS)
  Assert.assertEquals(INVISIBLE,
    searchForCompanionViewModel.noResultsViewVisiblity.value)
}
```

Since you want to have a failing test first, go to your `SearchForCompanionViewModel` and change the following line in your `searchForCompanion` function:

```
noResultsViewVisiblity.postValue(INVISIBLE)
```

to:

```
noResultsViewVisiblity.postValue(VISIBLE)
```

Now run your test and it will fail.

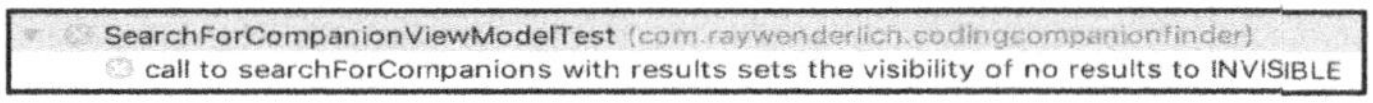

SearchForCompanionViewModelTest (com.raywenderlich.codingcompanionfinder)
call to searchForCompanions with results sets the visibility of no results to INVISIBLE

Undo the last change in searchForCompanion so that the line is back to:

```
noResultsViewVisiblity.postValue(INVISIBLE)
```

Run your test again and it will pass.

SearchForCompanionViewModelTest (com.raywenderlich.codingcompanionfinder)
call to searchForCompanions with results sets the visibility of no results to INVISIBLE

DRYing up your tests

Tests are code that you need to maintain, so let's write some more tests for your SearchForCompanionViewModel and DRY (Do not repeat yourself) them up along the way. To get started, add the following test:

```
@Test
fun
call_to_searchForCompanions_with_no_results_sets_the_visibility_
of_no_results_to_VISIBLE() {
  val searchForCompanionViewModel =
    SearchForCompanionViewModel(petFinderService)
  searchForCompanionViewModel.companionLocation.value = "90210"
  val countDownLatch = CountDownLatch(1)
  searchForCompanionViewModel.searchForCompanions()
  searchForCompanionViewModel.noResultsViewVisiblity
    .observeForever {
      countDownLatch.countDown()
    }

  countDownLatch.await(2, TimeUnit.SECONDS)
  Assert.assertEquals(INVISIBLE,
    searchForCompanionViewModel.noResultsViewVisiblity.value)
}
```

Because you want to have a failing test first, your assert is currently not correct. Run the test and it will fail.

SearchForCompanionViewModelTest (com.raywenderlich.codingcompanionfinder)
call to searchForCompanions with no results sets the visibility of no results to VISIBLE

Now change the assert to be correct:

```
Assert.assertEquals(VISIBLE,
  searchForCompanionViewModel.noResultsViewVisiblity.value)
```

Run the test again and it will pass.

SearchForCompanionViewModelTest (com.raywenderlich.codingcompanionfinder)
call to searchForCompanions with no results sets the visibility of no results to VISIBLE

Looking at this test and the previous one you did around visibility they are very similar:

```
@Test
fun
call_to_searchForCompanions_with_results_sets_the_visibility_of_
no_results_to_INVISIBLE() {
  val searchForCompanionViewModel =
    SearchForCompanionViewModel(petFinderService)
  searchForCompanionViewModel.companionLocation.value = "30318"
  val countDownLatch = CountDownLatch(1)
  searchForCompanionViewModel.searchForCompanions()
  searchForCompanionViewModel.noResultsViewVisiblity
    .observeForever {
      countDownLatch.countDown()
    }

  countDownLatch.await(2, TimeUnit.SECONDS)
  Assert.assertEquals(INVISIBLE,
    searchForCompanionViewModel.noResultsViewVisiblity.value)
}

@Test
fun
call_to_searchForCompanions_with_no_results_sets_the_visibility_
of_no_results_to_VISIBLE() {
  val searchForCompanionViewModel =
    SearchForCompanionViewModel(petFinderService)
  searchForCompanionViewModel.companionLocation.value = "90210"
  val countDownLatch = CountDownLatch(1)
  searchForCompanionViewModel.searchForCompanions()
  searchForCompanionViewModel.noResultsViewVisiblity
    .observeForever {
      countDownLatch.countDown()
    }

  countDownLatch.await(2, TimeUnit.SECONDS)
  Assert.assertEquals(VISIBLE,
    searchForCompanionViewModel.noResultsViewVisiblity.value)
}
```

The only real difference is your `companionLocation` value and your visibility assert. Let's refactor this by replacing these two tests with the following:

```
fun
callSearchForCompanionWithALocationAndWaitForVisibilityResult(lo
cation: String): SearchForCompanionViewModel{
  val searchForCompanionViewModel =
    SearchForCompanionViewModel(petFinderService)
  searchForCompanionViewModel.companionLocation.value = location
  val countDownLatch = CountDownLatch(1)
```

```
    searchForCompanionViewModel.searchForCompanions()
    searchForCompanionViewModel.noResultsViewVisiblity
      .observeForever {
        countDownLatch.countDown()
      }

    countDownLatch.await(2, TimeUnit.SECONDS)
    return searchForCompanionViewModel
  }

  @Test
  fun
  call_to_searchForCompanions_with_results_sets_the_visibility_of_
  no_results_to_INVISIBLE() {
    val searchForCompanionViewModel =
  callSearchForCompanionWithALocationAndWaitForVisibilityResult("3
  0318")
    Assert.assertEquals(INVISIBLE,
      searchForCompanionViewModel.noResultsViewVisiblity.value)
  }

  @Test
  fun
  call_to_searchForCompanions_with_no_results_sets_the_visibility_
  of_no_results_to_VISIBLE() {
    val searchForCompanionViewModel =
  callSearchForCompanionWithALocationAndWaitForVisibilityResult("9
  0210")
    Assert.assertEquals(VISIBLE,
      searchForCompanionViewModel.noResultsViewVisiblity.value)
  }
```

What you are doing here is using a common function for setting up your call, `CountDownLatch`, but keeping your assert in the test. Now, technically, you could have the assert in your common method and just pass in the expected value to this common method. This is a matter of style. Since part of the purpose of unit tests is to provide documentation about how the code works, in the authors' opinion, not having the assert in the common method makes it a little bit more readable. That said, if you find it to be more readable by putting the assert in the common method, that can be valid as well. The key takeaway is that tests are a form of documentation and the goal is to structure them to make it easier for a new person looking at the code base to understand it.

Challenge

Challenge: Test and edge cases

- If you didn't finish out your test cases for your `ViewCompanionViewModel` to test the other data elements, add tests following a red, green, refactor pattern.
- The tests you did for your `SearchForCompanionViewModel` missed a lot of data validation and edge cases. Follow a red, green, refactor pattern and try to cover all of these cases with very focused assertions.

Key points

- Source sets help you to run Espresso tests in either Espresso or Robolectric.
- Not all Espresso tests will run in Robolectric, especially if you are using Idling resources.
- As you get your legacy app under test, start to isolate tests around Fragments and other components.
- `ViewModels` make it possible to move tests to a unit level.
- Be mindful of mocking final classes.
- It is possible to unit test Retrofit with MockWebServer.
- Strive to practice Red, Green, Refactor.
- As your tests get smaller, the number of assertions in each test should as well.
- Strive towards a balanced pyramid, but balance that against the value that your tests are bringing to the project.
- Test code is code to maintain, so don't forget to refactor it as well.
- Move slow to go fast.

Where to go from here?

With this refactoring you have set your project up to go fast. It will help many homeless companions, and companion-less developers get paired up. That said, there are other tips and tricks to learn in future chapters. For example, how do you deal with test data as your suite gets bigger? How do you handle permissions? Stay tuned as we cover this in later chapters!

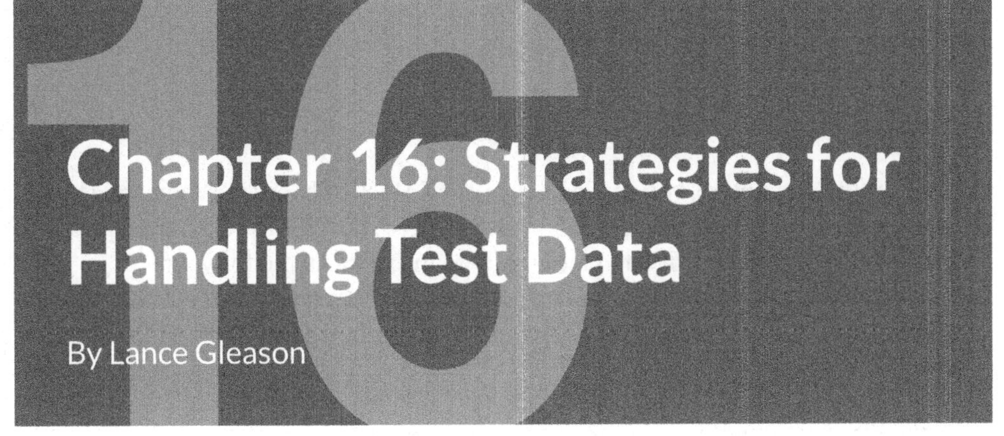

Chapter 16: Strategies for Handling Test Data

By Lance Gleason

In the previous three chapters, you learned how to move slow to go fast. Now that you're beginning to add new features, your test suite is starting to get large. Lots of homeless coding companions are being placed with developers. But, as that's happening, an inevitable problem is presenting itself. Namely, your test data is starting to get difficult to maintain. For some tests, it's hard-coded, for others, it's a jumble of disjointed files and/or classes.

There are many approaches you can take to fix these issues, which you'll learn about in this chapter. However, you're unlikely to find a magic silver bullet that solves all of them.

JSON data

In the past three chapters, you made heavy use of MockWebServer. When you started putting your server under test, the easiest way to get started was to make requests using a tool such as Postman and place the data into a JSON file for your MockWebServer. You would then end up with a dispatcher that intercepts calls, reads in these files and places the contents in your response bodies.

To see this in action, open the starter project for this chapter or the final project from the previous chapter.

Look at the **CommonTestDataUtil.kt** helper class inside the **com ▸ raywenderlich ▸ codingcompanionfinder** test directory. Looking at your dispatcher, you'll see the following:

```
fun dispatch(request: RecordedRequest): MockResponse? {
  return when (request.path) {
    "/animals?limit=20&location=30318" -> {
      MockResponse().setResponseCode(200).setBody(
        readFile("search_30318.json")
      )
    }
    "/animals?limit=20&location=90210" -> {
      MockResponse().setResponseCode(200).setBody(
        readFile("search_90210.json")
      )
    }
    else -> {
      MockResponse().setResponseCode(404).setBody("{}")
    }
  }
}
```

In this example, you're doing exact matches on the request path and specifying files based on the request. Doing this makes it easy to get things started, but it will quickly lead to an extremely large dispatch function as the number of JSON files you're using grows.

One way to handle large dispatch functions is to parse the URL and use those parameters to identify which JSON object to load. For example, with the **Coding Companion Finder** app, you might have a dispatch method that looks like this:

```
fun dispatch(request: RecordedRequest): MockResponse? {
  val fileNameAndPath = getFileNameAndPath(request.path)
  return if (!fileNameAndPath.isEmpty()) {
      MockResponse().setResponseCode(200).setBody(
        readFile(fileNameAndPath)
```

```
      )
    else -> {
      MockResponse().setResponseCode(404).setBody("{}")
    }
  }
}
```

`getFileNameAndPath(path: String)` converts the URL into a file name by replacing characters.

For example, a path of `/animals?limit=20&location=30318` becomes `animals_limit_20_location_30318.json`, and `/animals?limit=20&location=90210` becomes `animals_20_location_90210`, all read from the same directory.

Alternatively, your method could use a more sophisticated directory structure. `/big/animals?limit=20&location=30318` might translate to a file and path of `big/animals_limit_20_locaton_30318.json`, and `small/animals?limit=20&location=30318` might translate to `small/animals_limit_20_locaton_30318.json`.

Post requests

Up to this point, your MockWebServer is only dealing with GET requests. It's time to look at how to handle POST requests.

The PetFinder API used in your app requires OAuth credentials. POST requests are used to support this OAuth workflow during certain steps that — up to this point — you've short-circuited with your MockWebServer. It's time to address this gap in your test coverage.

Since you need to understand how OAuth works to test it, let's do a quick review of the OAuth flow as you're currently using it:

Open **AuthorizationInterceptor.kt** inside your apps **retrofit** package, and you'll see where these steps take place:

```
class AuthorizationInterceptor : Interceptor, KoinComponent {
  private val petFinderService: PetFinderService by inject()
  private var token = Token()
  @Throws(IOException::class)
  // 1
  override fun intercept(chain: Interceptor.Chain): Response {
    var mainResponse = chain.proceed(chain.request())
    val mainRequest = chain.request()
    // 2
```

```
      if ((mainResponse.code() == 401 ||
          mainResponse.code() == 403) &&
          !mainResponse.request().url().url()
            .toString().contains("oauth2/token")) {
        // 3
        val tokenRequest = petFinderService.getToken(
          clientId = MainActivity.API_KEY,
          clientSecret = MainActivity.API_SECRET)
        val tokenResponse = tokenRequest.execute()
        if (tokenResponse.isSuccessful) {
          // 4
          tokenResponse.body()?.let {
            token = it
            // 5
            val builder =
              mainRequest.newBuilder().header("Authorization",
                  "Bearer " + it.accessToken)
                .method(mainRequest.method(), mainRequest.body())
            mainResponse = chain.proceed(builder.build())
          } }
      }
      // 6
      return mainResponse
    }
  }
```

Here's how this code works:

1. First, a GET request is made to the server to retrieve some data on the `/animals` endpoint. An `accessToken` is passed into it. When it's the first time a call has been made after opening the app, this `accessToken` will be blank.

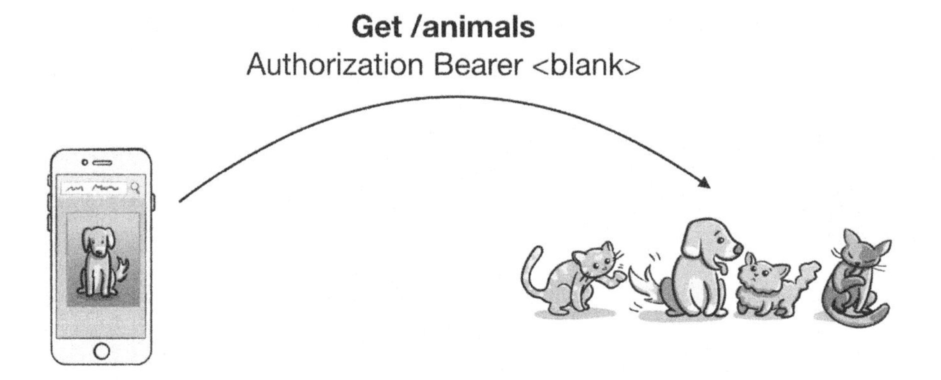

2. If the token is either blank, invalid or expired, the server responds back with a **401**, indicating that the current credentials are unauthorized.

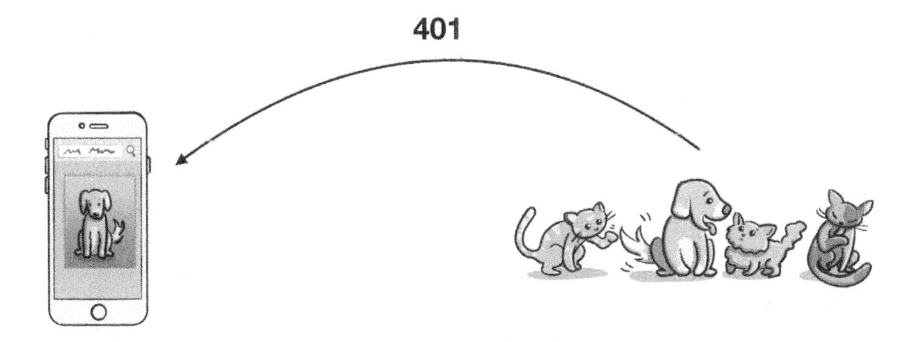

3. This **401** is caught by your apps `AuthorizationInterceptor`, which posts an `/oauth2/token` request with your API Key and API Secret.

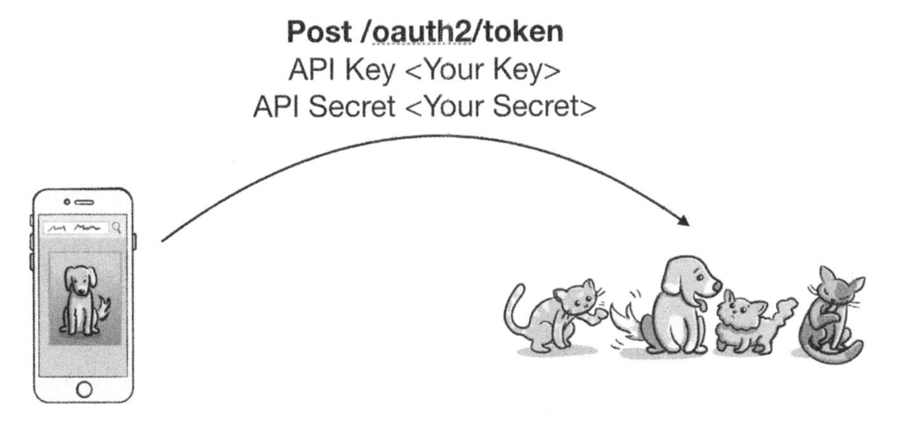

4. A token is returned to your `AuthorizationInterceptor`.

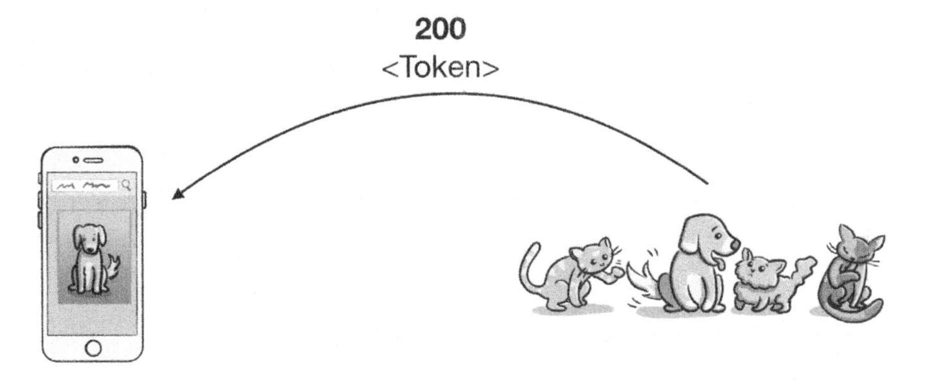

5. Your `AuthorizationInterceptor` then retries the original request to `/animals`.

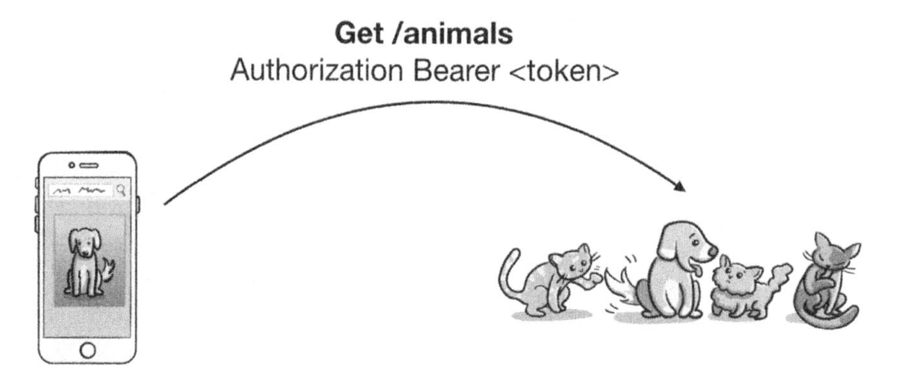

6. The response with animal records is passed to the original caller of #1.

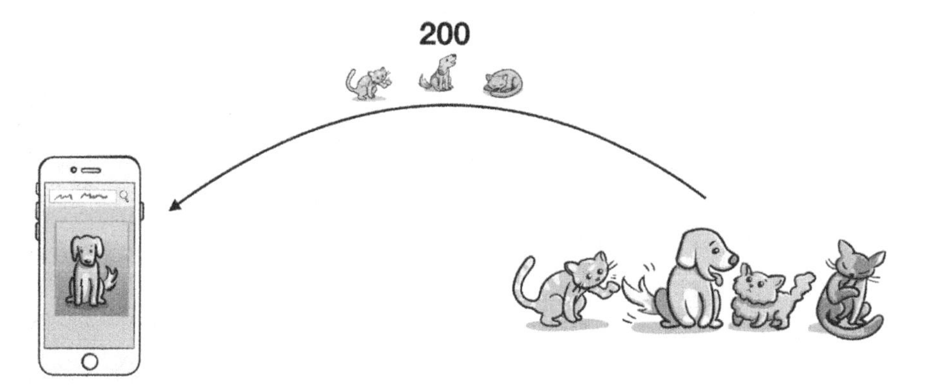

You're going to add some non-focused test coverage. This non-focused test coverage will cause your tests to fail if you break something.

Go back to **CommonTestDataUtil.kt** and replace `dispatch(request: RecordedRequest)` with the following:

```
fun dispatch(request: RecordedRequest): MockResponse? {
  val headers = request.headers
  // 1
  if(request.method.equals("POST")){
    if(request.path.equals("/oauth2/token")){
      return MockResponse().setResponseCode(200).setBody(
        "{\"access_token\":\"valid_token\"}")
    }
  }
  // 2
  val authorization = headers.values("Authorization")
```

```
    if (!authorization.isEmpty() &&
        authorization.get(0).equals("Bearer valid_token")) {
      return when (request.path) {
        "/animals?limit=20&location=30318" -> {
          MockResponse().setResponseCode(200).setBody(
            CommonTestDataUtil.readFile("search_30318.json")
          )
        }
        "/animals?limit=20&location=90210" -> {
          MockResponse().setResponseCode(200)
            .setBody("{\"animals\": []}")
        }
        else -> {
          MockResponse().setResponseCode(404).setBody("{}")
        }
      }
    } else {
      // 3
      return MockResponse().setResponseCode(401).setBody("{}")
    }
  }
```

This code adds the following things to `dispatch()`:

1. Logic to look for a post request to `/oauth2/token` and to return a token value of `valid_token`.
2. Logic to check if a valid token is on your GET request before processing it.
3. A return statement to return a **401** if the token is not `valid_token`.

Now, run your tests by right clicking on the second of the two **(test)** packages in your Android project view.

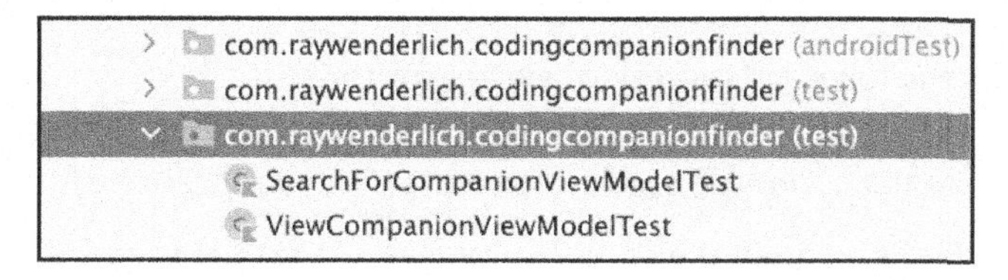

Then select **run 'Tests in 'com.raywen...''**.

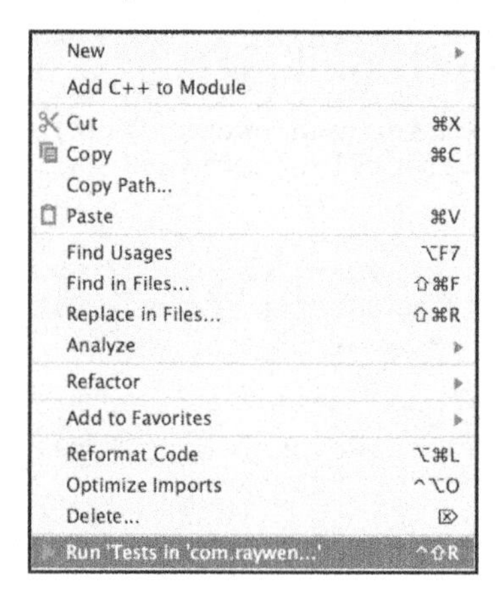

Your tests will run.

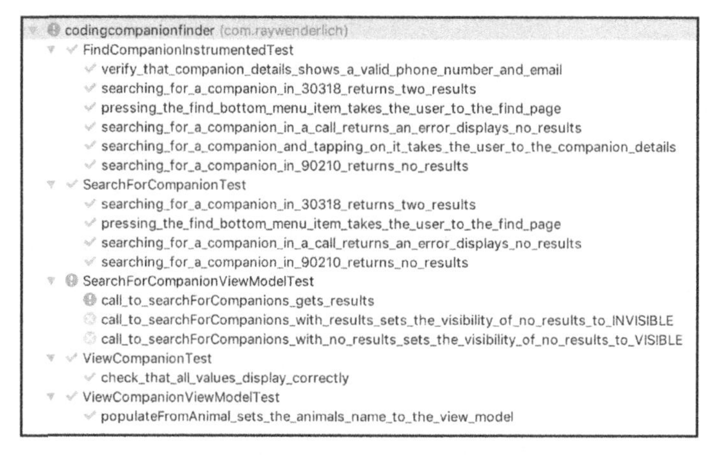

Oh, no! Most of the tests are successful except for those in `SearchForCompanionViewModelTest`. Before you changed your dispatcher, they were green. If you trace into the stack trace for these, you'll see the following error:

```
lateinit property koinContext has not been initialized
```

This ends up tracing back to the following line in **AuthorizationInterceptor.kt** (the one you looked at earlier):

```
val tokenRequest = petFinderService.getToken(
  clientId = MainActivity.API_KEY,
  clientSecret = MainActivity.API_SECRET)
```

If you look at where `petFinderService` is declared, around the beginning of the class, you'll see the following:

```
private val petFinderService: PetFinderService by inject()
```

This is using **Koin** to inject a `PetFinderService` into this class.

Open **SearchForCompanionViewModelTest.kt**. You might remember from the last chapter that you didn't use Koin in this test. There are two different ways you can fix this. One way is to configure this test to use Koin. The other is to create a second dispatcher that doesn't hit the authorization interceptor in this test. Since the first option was exercised in **FindCompanionsInstrumentedTest.kt**, you're going to use option two.

Go to **CommonTestDataUtil.kt** and add the following function:

```
fun nonInterceptedDispatch(
  request: RecordedRequest
): MockResponse? {
  val headers = request.headers
  return when (request.path) {
    "/animals?limit=20&location=30318" -> {
      MockResponse().setResponseCode(200).setBody(
      readFile("search_30318.json")
      )
    }
    "/animals?limit=20&location=90210" -> {
      MockResponse().setResponseCode(200)
        .setBody("{\"animals\": []}")
    }
    else -> {
      MockResponse().setResponseCode(404).setBody("{}")
    }
  }
}
```

This code adds a version of your dispatcher that does not end up causing your `AuthorizationInterceptor` in your app to be called.

Go back to **SearchForCompanionViewModelTest.kt**, and replace the dispatcher declaration with the following:

```
val dispatcher: Dispatcher = object : Dispatcher() {
  @Throws(InterruptedException::class)
  override fun dispatch(
    request: RecordedRequest
  ): MockResponse {
    return CommonTestDataUtil.nonInterceptedDispatch(request) ?:
      MockResponse().setResponseCode(404)
  }
}
```

This code calls your new dispatcher.

Run all of your tests again, and everything is green.

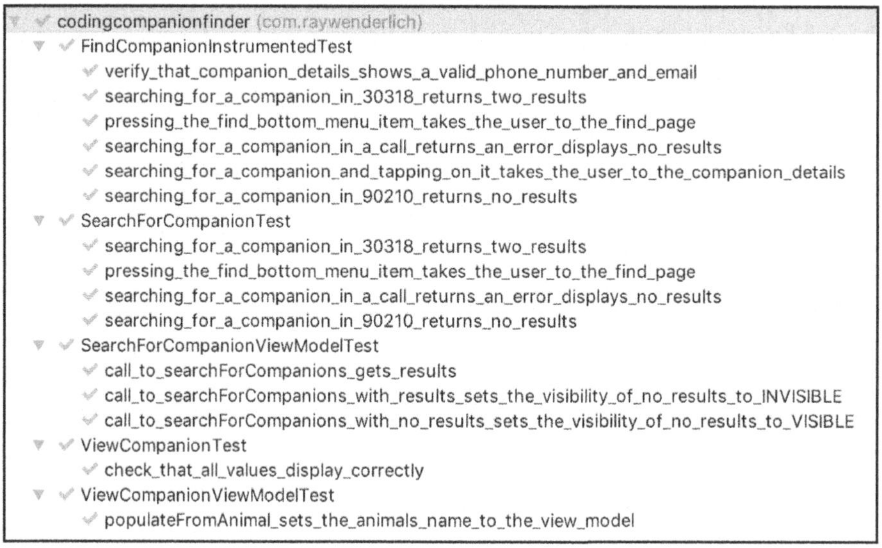

- codingcompanionfinder (com.raywenderlich)
  - FindCompanionInstrumentedTest
    - verify_that_companion_details_shows_a_valid_phone_number_and_email
    - searching_for_a_companion_in_30318_returns_two_results
    - pressing_the_find_bottom_menu_item_takes_the_user_to_the_find_page
    - searching_for_a_companion_in_a_call_returns_an_error_displays_no_results
    - searching_for_a_companion_and_tapping_on_it_takes_the_user_to_the_companion_details
    - searching_for_a_companion_in_90210_returns_no_results
  - SearchForCompanionTest
    - searching_for_a_companion_in_30318_returns_two_results
    - pressing_the_find_bottom_menu_item_takes_the_user_to_the_find_page
    - searching_for_a_companion_in_a_call_returns_an_error_displays_no_results
    - searching_for_a_companion_in_90210_returns_no_results
  - SearchForCompanionViewModelTest
    - call_to_searchForCompanions_gets_results
    - call_to_searchForCompanions_with_results_sets_the_visibility_of_no_results_to_INVISIBLE
    - call_to_searchForCompanions_with_no_results_sets_the_visibility_of_no_results_to_VISIBLE
  - ViewCompanionTest
    - check_that_all_values_display_correctly
  - ViewCompanionViewModelTest
    - populateFromAnimal_sets_the_animals_name_to_the_view_model

Using JSON data has the following benefits:

- It makes it easier to quickly get data into your app to test.
- It exercises a larger portion of your web request stack.
- By taking snapshots from requests you make from tools like Postman, you can get data that most closely resembles production data.

Some drawbacks to using JSON include:

- If your requests return large objects, the files can be cumbersome.
- Modifying data in the files usually has to be done by hand or requires a non-trivial effort to write code to read and modify it.
- As your dataset grows, managing the files and the corresponding logic can get complex.
- Asserts generally need to be hard-coded values since you don't have a reference value from an object to perform an assert against.

Hard-coded data

Another approach you've used is hard-coded data. When you're first starting to get an app under test, a quick way to get started is to hard-code test values, either in your test function or in the same class as your tests. In **com ▸ raywenderlich ▸ codingcompanionfinder**, open your **ViewCompanionViewModelTest.kt** and you'll see the following:

```
class ViewCompanionViewModelTest {
// 1
  val animal = Animal(
    22,
    Contact(
      phone = "404-867-5309",
      email = "coding.companion@razware.com",
      address = Address(
        "",
        "",
        "Atlanta",
        "GA",
        "30303",
        "USA"
      ) ),
    "5",
    "small",
    arrayListOf(),
    Breeds("shih tzu", "", false, false),
    "Spike",
    "male",
    "A sweet little guy with spikey teeth!"
  )

  @Test
  fun
```

```
populateFromAnimal_sets_the_animals_name_to_the_view_model(){
    val viewCompanionViewModel = ViewCompanionViewModel()
// 2
    viewCompanionViewModel.populateFromAnimal(animal)
// 3
    assert(viewCompanionViewModel.name.equals("Spike"))
  }
}
```

This is a classic example of hard-coded test data. Here's how it works:

1. Create an `Animal` using a series of hard-coded values.
2. Pass the object into `populateFromAnimal(animal: Animal)`.
3. Perform an assertion based on the outcome of the function call.

Advantages to using hard-coded data include:

- Test data is contained within the same class — sometimes the same functions as your tests — making it easier to see what the values should be.
- It's faster to get started writing tests.

Disadvantages include:

- The initialization calls need hard-coded values that create larger test files, which reduces the readability of a test class as it gets larger.
- A lot of effort is duplicated across test files creating the data.
- Large data sets become too verbose.

Test object libraries

One way to address the hard-coded data issues is to create a test object library. This is best explained with code.

To get started, create a new package inside the **com ▸ raywenderlich ▸ codingcompanionfinder** test package, and name it **data**.

Inside the newly created **data** package, create a file named **AnimalData.kt**, and add the following content to it:

```
object AnimalData {
  val atlantaShihTzuNamedSpike = Animal(
    22,
    atlantaCodingShelter,
    "5",
    "small",
    arrayListOf(),
    shihTzu,
    "Spike",
    "male",
    "A sweet little guy with spikey teeth!"
  )
}

object AddressData {
  val atlantaAddress = Address(
    "",
    "",
    "Atlanta",
    "GA",
    "30303",
    "USA"
  )
}

object BreedsData {
  val shihTzu = Breeds("shih tzu", "", false, false)
}

object ContactsData {
  val atlantaCodingShelter = Contact(
    phone = "404-867-5309",
    email = "coding.companion@razware.com",
    address = atlantaAddress
  )
}
```

When you import the required classes, make sure you import the correct one for `Address` — the one in your project, not the one from the framework packages. This creates test objects with the same data you hard-coded in **ViewCompanionViewModelTest.kt**.

Next, open **ViewCompanionViewModelTest.kt** and replace its contents with the following:

```
class ViewCompanionViewModelTest {

  @Test
  fun
populateFromAnimal_sets_the_animals_name_to_the_view_model() {
    val viewCompanionViewModel = ViewCompanionViewModel()
    viewCompanionViewModel
      .populateFromAnimal(atlantaShihTzuNamedSpike)
    assert(viewCompanionViewModel.name
      .equals(atlantaShihTzuNamedSpike.name))
  }
}
```

This code completely removes the hard-coded object creation, allowing you to focus on the test and specific data it's testing. As you test other functions that need an `Animal`, you'll have much more concise code and shared objects that you can reuse.

Run your test, and you'll notice it's still green.

```
ViewCompanionViewModelTest (com.raywenderlich.codingcompanionfinder)
  populateFromAnimal_sets_the_animals_name_to_the_view_model
```

Green is good; green is wonderful in TDD, so take a moment to enjoy this view!

Pros of using test object libraries include:

- Test files that are more readable with shorter data set up code.
- Test data that can easily be reused across test classes.

Cons of using them include:

- It takes a little extra effort to set them up initially.
- You have to look in another file to see details about the test data.

Faker

Up to this point, your actual test values have been hard-coded strings that are the same every time you use them in a test. Over time, you may run out of ideas for names. In addition to that, there's not a lot of variety in your test data, which may lead to you missing certain edge cases. But don't worry, there's a tool to help you address this: **Faker**. You first saw this in Chapter 10, "Testing the Network Layer."

Faker has data generators for various kinds of data, such as names and addresses. To see the full power of it, you need to add it to your app. To get started, open the **app** level **build.gradle**, and add the following to the dependencies section:

```
testImplementation 'com.github.javafaker:javafaker:0.18'
androidTestImplementation 'com.github.javafaker:javafaker:0.18'
```

This is adding the dependencies to your project. Next, open up your **AnimalData.kt** file from above and add the following at the top level of the file:

```
val faker = Faker()
```

This code gives you an instance of a `Faker`.

Next, add the following `val` to **AnimalData.kt** at the top of the file:

```
val fakerAnimal = Animal(
  faker.number().digits(3).toInt(),
  fakerShelter,
  faker.number().digit(),
  faker.commerce().productName(),
  arrayListOf(),
  fakerBreed,
  faker.name().name(),
  faker.dog().gender(),
  faker.chuckNorris().fact()
)
```

This code adds another animal object with Faker-generated data for things like the companion's name and gender. (Yes, we added the Chuck Norris fact for the description for fun. Don't worry about the code not compiling just yet. We need to add more to this file.)

Next, add the following above `fakerAnimal` in **AnimalData.kt**.

```
val fakerAddress = Address(
  faker.address().streetAddress(),
  faker.address().secondaryAddress(),
  faker.address().city(),
  faker.address().state(),
  faker.address().zipCode(),
  faker.address().country()
)
```

This code adds Faker elements for the address.

Add the following above `fakerAddress` in **AnimalData.kt**:

```
val fakerBreed = Breeds(faker.cat().breed(),
  faker.dog().breed(), faker.bool().bool(), faker.bool().bool())
```

This code fakes out the breed.

Add this above `fakerBreed` in **AnimalData.kt**:

```
val fakerShelter = Contact(
  faker.phoneNumber().cellPhone(),
  faker.internet().emailAddress(),
  fakerAddress
)
```

This code fakes out the contact information.

Now, go back to **ViewCompanionViewModelTest.kt** and add the following test:

```
@Test
fun
populateFromAnimal_sets_the_animals_description_to_the_view_mode
l(){
  val viewCompanionViewModel = ViewCompanionViewModel()
  System.out.println(fakerAnimal.toString())
  viewCompanionViewModel.populateFromAnimal(fakerAnimal)
  assertEquals("faker", viewCompanionViewModel.description)
}
```

This code creates a test that does an assert on the description. It also prints the contents of your object so that you can see what kind of data Faker creates.

Run this test and you'll see a failed test:

ViewCompanionViewModelTest (com.raywenderlich.codingcompanionfinder)
populateFromAnimal_sets_the_animals_name_to_the_view_model
populateFromAnimal_sets_the_animals_description_to_the_view_model

Your object output is on one line; however, breaking it down, so it's more readable, you'll end up with something that looks like this:

```
Animal(
  id=798,
  contact=Contact(
    phone=1-256-143-0873,
    email=malinda.hoppe@hotmail.com,
    address=Address(
      address1=09548 Wayne Dale,
      address2=Suite 523,
```

```
    city=Charitybury,
    state=West Virginia,
    postcode=30725-9938,
    country=Northern Mariana Islands
    )
  ),
  age=0,
  size=Synergistic Wool Bottle,
  photos=[],
  breeds=Breeds(
    primary=Khao Manee,
    secondary=Sealyham Terrier,
    mixed=false,
    unknown=false),
  name=Miss Linnea Hills,
  gender=female,
  description=For Chuck Norris, NP-Hard = O(1).)
```

Of course, since you're now using Faker, the information will be different each time. At the moment, your assertion is not the right value, which is reflected in the error message.

```
junit.framework.ComparisonFailure:
Expected :faker
Actual   :For Chuck Norris, NP-Hard = O(1).
 <Click to see difference>
```

To fix this incorrect value, change the assert in your test on the last line to:

```
assertEquals(fakerAnimal.description,
  viewCompanionViewModel.description)
```

You're now making sure that your assertion tests using the data generated by Faker. You want to ensure that `viewCompanionViewModel` contains the same `description` as the `fakeAnimal`, regardless of what Faker generated there.

Run your tests again, and notice they're all green.

```
✓ ViewCompanionViewModelTest (com.raywenderlich.codingcompanionfinder)
  ✓ populateFromAnimal_sets_the_animals_name_to_the_view_model
  ✓ populateFromAnimal_sets_the_animals_description_to_the_view_model
```

The pros of using Faker include:

- Random data that's more representative of actual app data.
- You don't need to come up with test data yourself.

The cons of using Faker include:

- While Faker has test data many scenarios, it doesn't include all possibilities.
- Your assertions become assertions against values in Faker objects rather than text you can read in your tests.
- Sometimes, the data generated by Faker is outside of the scope of your business logic, and you need to limit it.

Locally persisted data

If you have an app that locally persists data, you may have some tests that need to have the datastore in a certain state before you run your test.

If you've had experience doing server-side TDD, your first thought might be to:

1. Get your datastore into the state you want it to be.
2. Dump it to a file.
3. Load up that data before running your tests.

On Android, at the time of this writing, the only way to do something like this is for your app to have root access or to use **adb**, which is not practical for Robolectric tests. This leaves you with only one option: To load test data using code.

To load test data using code, you could, for example, use Faker with a series of test objects you load using a helper function *before* running the tests.

Because datastores tend to be slower, especially if you need to test with a significant number of test records, you should consider executing that set up using a `@BeforeClass` annotated function.

Key points

- There are no magic silver bullets with test data.
- JSON data is great for quickly getting started with end-to-end tests but can become difficult to maintain as your test suites get larger.
- Hard-coded data works well when your test suite is small, but it lacks variety in test data as your test suite grows.
- Faker makes it easier to generate a variety of test data for object libraries.
- Tests that need to get data stores into a certain state can be expensive because you need to insert data into the data store programmatically.

Where to go from here?

Wrangling your test data is another way that you're able to move slow to go fast. In your case, going fast means more companions in homes and programmers with higher quality code. To learn more about Faker, check out the project page at https://github.com/DiUS/java-faker.

Chapter 17: Continuous Integration & Other Related Tools

By Lance Gleason

Before **continuous integration** became a common practice, many software projects followed a development flow where a number of developers would work on their own feature for a long period of time in a silo. Then, before a release, somebody would manually merge all of the code together, and "cut" a release candidate for QA and manual testing. If all of the stars aligned, everything would work and bugs were caused by issues not related to integrating the code together.

What actually happened on a lot of projects was much uglier. Often there would be issues merging the code together. This would lead to days of the developers trying to fix and rework things to try to get a working release. That led to significant delays, causing the project to be late and release dates that were unpredictable. Instead of being a minor part of your development process, integration became a big, unpredictable multi-day, week, or event.

Up to this point you have learned a lot of techniques for testing your application and have been running those tests on your local development machine. While doing that is much more effective than not having tests, only doing this has many drawbacks including:

- Situations where the tests run successfully on one developers machine but not another.
- Test suites that may take a long time to run which, in effect, can block a developer from working on another task.
- No common build status that all developers have visibility into.

Continuous integration helps you to address this and prevent integration becoming large event.

Continuous integration fundamentals

Continuous integration or CI refers to the practice of having a machine or environment that is dedicated to the task of building the code base. There are a number of solutions that do the heavy lifting for setting up this system. You will learn more about that later on in this chapter. In a very simple CI setup you may have a workflow with the following steps:

1. When a user pushes up new changes to a Git repo, the CI server kicks off a new build.
2. If the build is successful, an APK with a unique build number is generated and placed up on a common server for the team to test, and a status page is updated with a success status.
3. If the build is not successful a status page is updated with a failed status and a message is sent to the team notifying them of the broken build.

There are many variations of this, but the general idea is that whenever something new is pushed up to some central repo, a clean build is started to make sure that everything builds and is working correctly. Many development teams with no automated tests will use this approach.

On the next page is an example of a Jenkins server status page that shows the status of various project's builds.

The green check marks indicate the last build was successful, the **!** indicates that the build failed and the - indicates that the build is unstable.

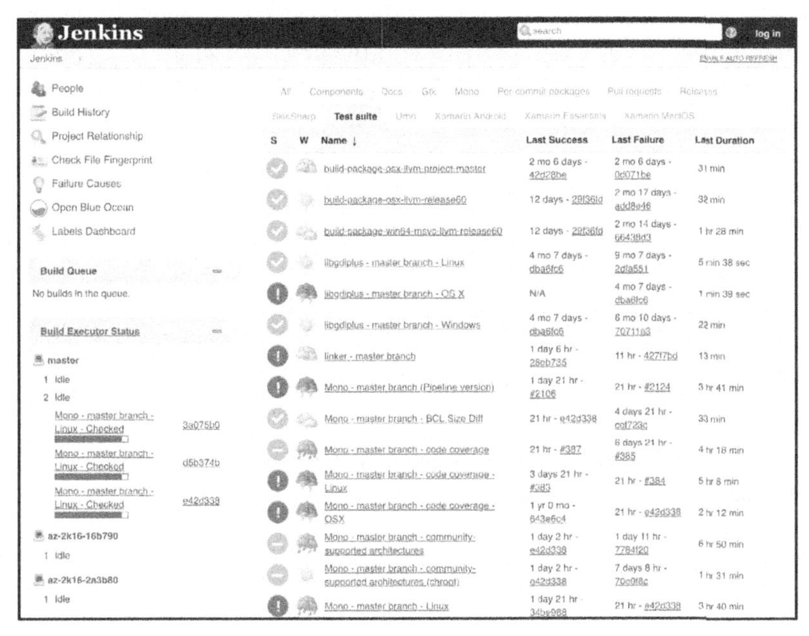

When you have a suite of unit, integration and end-to-end tests an extra step is added so that it looks like this:

1. A build is kicked off on a commit to the repo.
2. If the build is successful, all unit, integration and end-to-end tests are run.
3. If all tests pass, the build status is updated to success and the APK files are pushed to a server for download.
4. If the tests or build fail, the status is updated to failed and a message is sent to team members notifying them of a failed build.

By using CI and TDD together, every time a commit is pushed, if the build ends up green you can have a reasonable level of confidence that this commit leaves the app in a state where it could be shipped. Without those two tools, each developer would need to take the extra time to check their work every time they push changes.

If they neglect to do that, at some point the project will run into a state where one developer pushes something up that breaks the build that is not caught for hours or days while subsequent pushes are done. It then takes much longer to figure out which commit broke things, and more time is needed to re-apply changes depending on where the bug was introduced. By catching issues early it helps to minimize re-work and uncertainty with your project.

Branches and CI

Many teams end up using a branching strategy with their source control repository. One that is commonly used is called Git Flow https://nvie.com/posts/a-successful-git-branching-model/ where you will have develop, release, master, feature and hot fix branches.

If your entire test suite does not take a lot of time to run, a best practice is to have CI run whenever a new push is made to a branch.

But, if you have a large test suite that takes several minutes to run you may need to take a more sophisticated approach. To better understand this consider a test suite that has the following attributes:

- Fifty percent of tests are unit tests that run quickly on the JVM. The entire suite of unit tests take one minute to execute.
- Thirty five percent are integration tests that can run in either Robolectric or Espresso. The suite of integration tests take two minutes to execute in Robolectric and twenty minutes in Espresso.
- Fifteen percent of the tests are end-to-end that mostly only run in Robolectric. This suite takes eight minutes to execute in Espresso.

Running tests in Espresso versus Robolectric give the most realistic test results, but they take twenty nine minutes to execute. In this scenario, running this test suite using Espresso on your local development machine before pushing up changes would not be a practical thing to do.

Most development teams facing this will:

- Run tests related to a feature they are working on along with all unit and Robolectric tests locally.
- Push it up to source control and let CI run the full test suite with Espresso.

With the CI test runs you have another issue. When using a branching strategy, a good practice is to have short running feature branches. Ideally that branch is only worked on for few hours, reviewed and merged them into the development branch. Waiting for a half an hour before merging feature branches would slow down integration. Especially on a larger team. There are multiple ways you could address that, but like most things in programming, there's trade-offs for each one. Possible solutions include:

- Only running Robolectric and unit tests via CI on feature branches.
- Using a less frequent schedule, IE: once or twice a day, for running the full Espresso suite from your development or feature branches.

CI tools

CI solutions need to do a lot of things including:

- Monitoring your source code repository for changes.
- Managing and orchestrating build agents (computers or VMs that actually perform builds).
- Offering some sort of dashboard or visualization of the build status.

When looking at CI tools there are two main categories you will run across:

1. Self hosted solutions.
2. Cloud based solutions.

Self hosted CI

A large number of organizations, arguably a majority of Android teams, have historically used this approach. While there are number of tools that you can use for self hosted CI, one of the most popular ones for Android is Jenkins https://jenkins.io/. Jenkins installations have two main components:

1. A Build Server.
2. One, or multiple build executors.

The build server is what handles things such as:

- The project configuration.
- Build pipeline through checkout, build, test, deploy, etc.
- Coordinating build executors.

Build executors are the machines/VM's where builds take place. Each executor that you use needs to have the proper tools installed to be able to compile and run your project. A build executor can only run one pipeline at a time. So let's say that you have one developer working on feature branch A and another that is working on feature branch B. Developer A pushes up a commit that starts a CI pipeline. Before that build is completed a commit is pushed up to feature branch B. If your Jenkins system only has one build executor, it will not start that pipeline until the build executor is done working an the pipeline for branch A. If the test suite takes a while to run, or there are a lot of developers on the project this could cause a CI backlog. To address this you can add additional build executors which will allow multiple branch pipelines to run at the same time.

Advantages of these self hosted solutions include:

- More control over your build environment.
- Less expensive than using a cloud based solution, especially when running a lot of builds.
- The ability to add your own physical devices to perform automated tests on.
- Better security when working in a high security environment or behind a corporate firewall.

Disadvantages include:

- Significantly more work involved in managing server instances.
- Build executors need to be updated when updating versions of Android tools.
- Headless servers can provide extra configuration challenges for Espresso based tests.

Cloud based CI

Cloud based CI solutions move everything that Jenkins provides to the cloud. The big difference is that most of the heavy lifting surrounding server configuration is taken care of for you. Some of the more popular services include:

- CircleCI
- Bitrise
- Travis CI

Each service has its own nuances, but in general they have have different plans that go up in price based on the concurrency and total system build/run time that you need. All of these services also have free plans for open source software projects.

Advantages of these solutions include:

- Significantly less effort is needed to configure and manage server instances.
- Updates for build tools are often taken care of by the service.
- Scaling for more concurrency can be done by changing your plan.
- Free plans for open source projects.

Disadvantages include:

- Generally, less control over your build agents.
- Limited support for running Espresso suites on your own test devices.
- No support for high security environments behind firewalls.
- A system needing a lot of concurrency and build time can get expensive.

Device farms

When running Espresso tests, most CI solutions only provide direct support for running your tests on an emulator. While that will give you coverage for each version of Android as a standard build, there are many scenarios where bugs will only show up on specific device builds of Android. Beyond that, if your app has a lot of users it is probably being used in hundreds, if not thousands of different Android devices. Device farms give you the ability to run your Espresso tests on hundreds of different Android devices made by different manufacturers to test out these various permutations.

Depending on your needs, you can even opt to run all of your CI Espresso tests in a device farm. There are a number of device farm providers. Two popular ones are:

1. Firebase Test Lab
2. AWS Device Farm

As is the case with cloud based CI offerings, the more device time you use, the more the farms will charge you.

CI strategy guidelines

Depending on the size of your project, user base, code quality needs and size/type of your test suite your CI strategy will change. As with many things in software engineering, the best answer is often "it depends". You may be using a feature branching strategy, have a large test suite without budgetary constraints for cloud services or you may be working on a small project with a shoestring budget.

Wait time

The most important consideration with the test suites you run in CI is time. Ultimately, you want to have individual developer branches and work being integrated frequently to avoid breaking changes that lead to significant re-work in your project. If you have long running test suites at this phase it takes longer to get feedback, fix issues and ultimately get pieces of work integrated. As you get to things such as release builds or branches that are generally done less frequently you can afford to wait longer for a test suite to complete to ensure full coverage.

Here are some guidelines based on branch commit frequency:

- One or more commits per hour - test suites that run in less than five minutes.
- One to two commits per day - test suites that run in less than thirty minutes.
- Releases or less than once per day - all test suites.

Test service cost

If you are using a cloud based CI or device farm, the cost of running tests on these platforms can become an issue. Developer time is generally your largest project cost. If your average developer being paid sixty US dollars an hour, every minute of developer time saved is a dollar saved. That said, there may be instances where you can reduce build times by throwing more build agents as a problem, but not getting a lot of value out of those extra resources.

An example of this might be where you have a large, modularized application with a long running Espresso test suite. One approach that some teams have taken to reduce test execution time is to "shard" (divide up) the test runs so that they can be executed in parallel. Doing this could allow you to run a test suite that takes 30 minutes in less than five minutes by breaking the work up among multiple build agents as part a complex build pipeline. That will reduce your developer time, but if you are providing enough resources to allow all of these tests to run for feature branches it will also significantly increase you CI service cost. This will give you better coverage by executing more tests frequently, but is that extra frequency providing enough value to offset the cost?

Ultimately, you want to have all of your tests run in CI before cutting QA and Release versions of your app, but there may be times where the cost to run some of the more expensive test frequently may not be offset by the benefits.

Device coverage

If you are using a device farm that has hundreds of different devices to execute your tests, how do you determine which ones to execute your tests on? In an ideal world, the answer would be, all devices all of the time. Unfortunately, in reality that would be a very expensive proposition.

For example, lets take a look at the cost, at the time of this book writing, to run an Espresso test suite in Firebase Test Lab. This suite takes six minutes to run on a device, and you want to run it on one hundred different Android devices:

- 100 devices * 6 minutes = 600 device minutes or 6 device hours
- 1 Test lab physical device hour costs $5.00 USD
- 6 device hours * $5.00 = $30.00 USD

If you average twenty work days in a month and ran these tests once a day on work days your device farm cost would be $600 USD. For a small project that cost may not justify the benefit. If your project could justify that, but you ran these this for all daily commits it would become cost prohibitive.

There are no magic bullets on how to address this but here are some ideas to figure out the best strategy:

- Look at your applications analytics and only choose the devices that have the most users.
- Run tests more frequently on devices that have surfaced more device specific bugs.
- Run frequently executed test runs on a randomly selected device from a list.
- Only run your suite on a large number of devices infrequently, i.e. before cutting a release candidate.

Key points

- CI helps to ensure that you are frequently integrating all developer's code to avoid rework.
- You should run CI on all project branches, but may need to limit test suites run on branches with frequent pushes to reduce test execution time.
- Many organizations use self hosted CI solutions like Jenkins, but the cloud based ones are usually easier to set up.
- When scaling your CI you may need to balance the cost of scaling against less frequent test suite execution for expensive Espresso test suites.
- Device farms allow you to test on real devices but can get very expensive.
- There are no magic bullets when figuring out the best CI strategy.

Where to go from here?

- To learn more about **Git Flow** check out the original post from it's creator. https://nvie.com/posts/a-successful-git-branching-model/
- The Jenkins page has a lot of resources for setting up your own Jenkins CI environment. https://jenkins.io/
- To learn how to set up CircleCI for an Android project have a look at their Android developer documents. https://circleci.com/docs/2.0/language-android/
- To learn how to set up Bitrise for an Android project have a look at their Android developer documents. https://devcenter.bitrise.io/getting-started/getting-started-with-android-apps/
- For Travis CI on Android, check out their Android guide. https://docs.travis-ci.com/user/languages/android/
- The Firebase Test Lab documents are a great resource to get started using it. https://firebase.google.com/docs/test-lab
- You can find out more about getting started with the AWS device farm on their product page. https://aws.amazon.com/device-farm/

Chapter 18: Testing Around Other Components

By Lance Gleason

Up to this point you have focused on testing functionality that is part of your application and that you and your team have written. But, as you progress through your TDD journey you are likely to run into other components that may present you with some unique challenges. These generally fall into one of three categories:

1. **Testable**: These are components that can be easily tested and/or verified, so no problems here.
2. **Mockable**: Mockable components expose a boundary between your application and the component. Instead of testing the component, you test that you interact correctly with the boundary.
3. **Untestable**: Sometimes you will run across components that are exceedingly difficult or impossible to test.

The testable

Some components you use have been designed so that they can be tested, or have end-state values that make it easy to test with them in the mix. For example, in Chapter 9, "Testing the Persistence Layer," you learned about how to test the persistence layer in your application tests.

Some examples of Android components that are testable include:

- Local persistence, such at MySQL and Realm-based data stores.
- Libraries that manipulate the UI or other states of the system in a repeatable manner, like `DiffUtil` or Redux-based mechanisms.
- Libraries that have testing hooks built-in.

The mockable

At times you will run across circumstances where your test needs to cross a system boundary that requires mocking. For example, in Chapter 10, "Testing the Network Layer," the `MockWebServer` you are using is mocking out your `okhttp` calls that are made to a server. In this case, the mocking was taken care of for you. In other instances you will need to mock out system boundaries manually.

Permissions

Another common scenario is when working with a component that requires permissions to test. As a quick review, there are three types of Android permissions:

1. **Normal Permissions**: These only require a declaration in the manifest to grant the user permission.
2. **Signature Permissions**: The system grants these permissions at install time, but only when the app that is using it is signed by the same app that grants the permission.
3. **Dangerous Permissions**: These are permissions that are accessing things such private user data, etc. In order to request these you need to have the permission specified in the app manifest and prompt the user for it at run time.

If you are testing functionality that requires normal permissions, there is nothing you will need to do other than include them in your app's manifest. Signature permissions follow a similar pattern. Things get a little bit more involved when working with dangerous permissions. To understand this, let's look at an example that uses the `CALL_PHONE` permission.

To get started import the starter **Coding Companion** project. Once it is imported, add your device keys you generated in Chapter 13, "High-Level Testing With Espresso," and run the app:

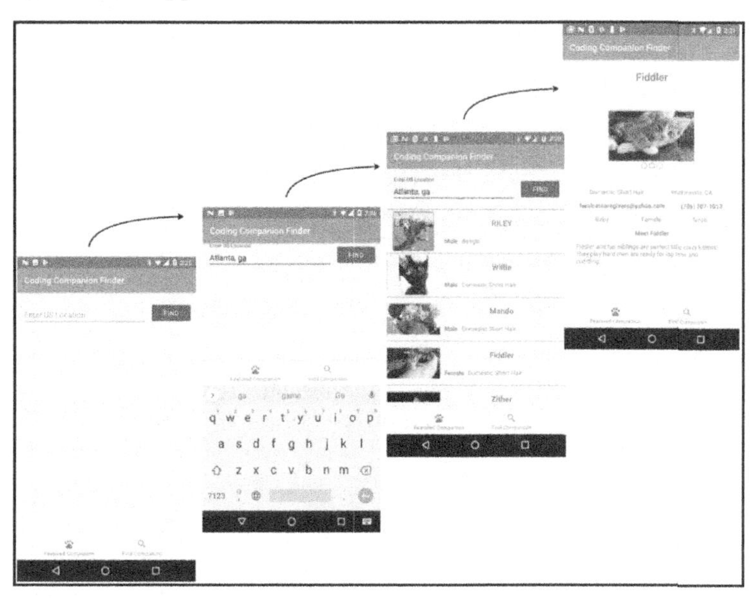

Tap on **Find Companion**, enter a location, tap on **Find** followed by selecting a companion:

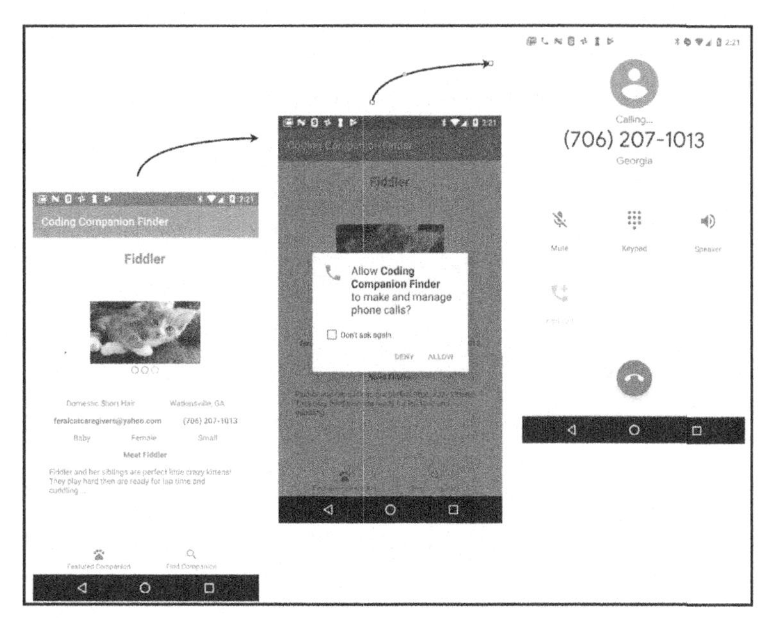

Now, tap on the phone number for the companion, select **ALLOW** to allow the permission request and then a call will begin to the shelter.

Open **ViewCompanionFragment.kt** and look at the `setupPhoneNumberOnClick()` function:

```
private fun setupPhonNumberOnClick(){
  fragmentViewCompanionBinding.telephone.setOnClickListener {
    // 1
    Dexter.withActivity(activity)
      .withPermission(Manifest.permission.CALL_PHONE)
      .withListener(
        object : PermissionListener {
          // 3
          override fun onPermissionGranted(
            response: PermissionGrantedResponse
          ) {/* ... */
            val intent = Intent(Intent.ACTION_CALL, Uri.parse(
              "tel:" + viewCompanionViewModel.telephone))
            startActivity(intent)
          }

          override fun onPermissionDenied(
            response: PermissionDeniedResponse
          ) {/* ... */}

          // 2
          override fun onPermissionRationaleShouldBeShown(
            permission: PermissionRequest,
            token: PermissionToken
          ) {/* ... */
            token.continuePermissionRequest()
          }

        }
      )
      .onSameThread()
      .check()
  }
}
```

This is doing three things:

1. It uses the **Dexter** library to check for the `CALL_PHONE` permission.
2. If permission has not been granted it shows a dialog asking for it.
3. If permission is granted it starts a `ACTION_CALL` intent to call the number you tapped on.

Note: To learn more about the Dexter library you can visit https://github.com/Karumi/Dexter.

To test this scenario you are going to need to do two things:

1. Grant `CALL_PHONE` permissions in your test.
2. Do an assert on the intent.

To get started go to **FindCompanionsInstrumentedTest.kt** and add the following to the beginning of your class:

```
@get:Rule
val grantPermissionRule: GrantPermissionRule =
  GrantPermissionRule.grant(
    android.Manifest.permission.CALL_PHONE)
```

This is granting the `CALL_PHONE` permission for all of the tests in your class. Next add the following to your app level `build.gradle` in your `dependencies` section:

```
testImplementation 'androidx.test.espresso:espresso-intents:
3.3.0'
androidTestImplementation 'androidx.test.espresso:espresso-
intents:3.3.0'
```

This adds in support for **Espresso Intents**, which allows you to assert that an intent is sent. You can learn more about Espresso Intents at https://developer.android.com/training/testing/espresso/intents.

Now add the following to the beginning of your `FindCompanionsInstrumentedTest`:

```
@get:Rule
val intentsTestRule = IntentsTestRule(MainActivity::class.java)
```

This adds a rule to use **Espresso Intents** in your test. Now add the following test:

```
@Test
fun verify_that_tapping_on_phone_number_dials_phone() {
  // 1
  Intents.init()
  // 2
  val intent = Intent()
  val result =
    Instrumentation.ActivityResult(Activity.RESULT_OK, intent)

  intending(
```

```
      allOf(
        hasAction(Intent.ACTION_CALL)
      )
    ).respondWith(result)
    // 3
    find_and_select_kevin_in_30318()
    onView(withText("(706) 236-4537")).perform(click())
    // 4
    intended(allOf(hasAction(Intent.ACTION_CALL),
      hasData("tel:(706) 236-4537")))
    // 5
    Intents.release()
  }
```

Make sure to import the `org.hamcrest.CoreMatchers.allOf` package. This is doing the following:

1. Initializes the `Intents` object.
2. Creates a mock `Intent` that will be called when the `ACTION_CALL` intent is fired in your app.
3. Navigates to a search result and clicks on the phone number.
4. Asserts that the `ACTION_CALL` intent has been sent.
5. Releases the `Intents` now that the test is finished.

Run your test and it will now be green:

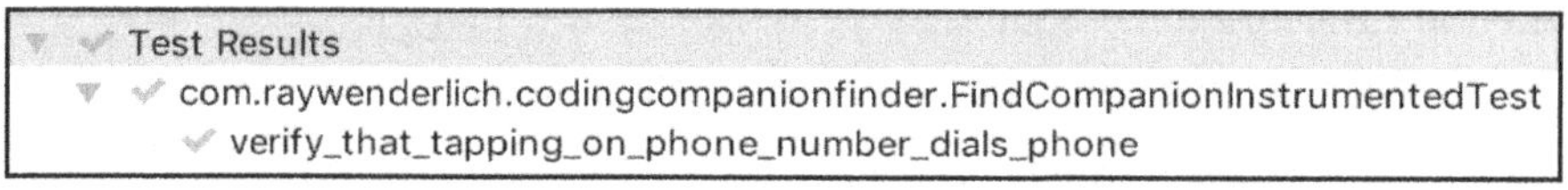

Test Results
com.raywenderlich.codingcompanionfinder.FindCompanionInstrumentedTest
verify_that_tapping_on_phone_number_dials_phone

Run all of the the tests in **(androidTest)** and **(test)** and they will be green.

Test Results 11 sec 174 ms
com.raywenderlich.codingcompanionfinder.FindCompanionInstrumentedTest 10 sec 24 ms
com.raywenderlich.codingcompanionfinder.SearchForCompanionViewModelTest 176 ms
com.raywenderlich.codingcompanionfinder.ViewCompanionTest 95 ms
com.raywenderlich.codingcompanionfinder.ViewCompanionViewModelTest 139 ms
com.raywenderlich.codingcompanionfinder.SearchForCompanionTest 740 ms

Other mockable components

There are many classes of external components where your best testing strategy will be to mock out your interaction with them. Some good candidates for this include:

- Glide
- Picasso
- Video Players
- Intents to other applications etc.
- Network calls
- Interactions with sensors and hardware

The untestable

There are some components where the best TDD option is to not test it. Determining that the component is untestable can be tricky. TDD is hard. On one hand you don't want to give up too soon on testing something. On the other hand you don't want to spend too much time trying to test the untestable.

Some traits that may make a component untestable include:

- It draws things on a graphical `Canvas`.
- There is not a testable end state after interacting with it.
- No test extensions or mechanisms are provided by the library author.
- The component is implemented primarily though the NDK.
- The library is popular, but a Google search doesn't turn up any instructions on testing it.
- You are making system calls to get device traits.

Let's look at some examples to better understand the thought process that goes into this. The names have been changed to protect the innocent, but these are actual scenarios that the author encountered in projects.

Google maps Android SDK

Google Maps Android SDK https://developers.google.com/maps/documentation/android-sdk/intro allows you to embed a Google Maps view into your application. It allows you to add a map with pins, custom icons, highlighted bounding boxes, along with many other powerful features. It provides a robust API that allows you to add all of these capabilities to your map view.

If you dive in to a view generated by it, the elements on the map are not in a structure where you can verify that a component is in a specific location because it a basically a canvas view. If you do a Google search the only solutions you will find for testing this are using a UI automator to click on a specific position on a pre-determined map. That test will work fine when you have a specific screen size, but if you are supporting multiple screen sizes and DPIs, the coordinates you use for one screen size may not work for another.

Your best bet when testing with this SDK is to:

- Test callbacks made by your map — i.e. when you click on a point on the map.
- Test the data and items being used to create things on the map.
- Rely on manual testing for the map functionality.

These will also work well for similiar libraries which are hard to test.

System setting API calls

Imagine you have an app that needs to get the values for some system attributes on your device such as the device's IP address, SIM card provider and current GPS location. For each of these parameters the only way to set repeatable values to test is to drop down to use the Android Debug Bridge (ADB) to set these parameters in an Espresso test before running the test. While this can be done in unit tests, it can be a problematic solution for multiple reasons including:

- In order to give the system time to apply the setting you will need to add `Thread.sleep()` calls which will cause much longer test execution times, and also might result in unreliable tests.
- Depending on the version of Android, some settings may not be available via ADB or be very difficult to get at.
- Some settings may only be testable on real devices, not emulators.

With enough work you might be able to create reliable, repeatable tests for these. In many cases it might be better to abstract that code into a simple library (sometimes called a **shim**) that is manually tested. In your unit tests you could then use **Dependency Injection** to mock this shim you created to test the code that depends on it.

Key points

- Testable components have hooks or inputs and outputs that can be validated.
- Many components are best tested by mocking your interaction with them.
- It is possible to test dangerous permissions.
- There are some components that are untestable.
- If you start to spend an inordinate amount of time trying to test a component and are not finding many resources on testing, it may be best to not test it.

Where to go from here?

- For a tutorial on how to get started with the Google Maps SDK go to https://www.raywenderlich.com/230-introduction-to-google-maps-api-for-android-with-kotlin
- To learn more about the `GrantPermissionRule` go to https://developer.android.com/reference/android/support/test/rule/GrantPermissionRule
- To learn more about **Espresso Intents** check out https://developer.android.com/training/testing/espresso/intents
- If your curious about permissions check out https://developer.android.com/guide/topics/permissions/overview

19 Conclusion

Congratulations on completing this book! You should have a firm understanding of Android test-driven development. Throughout this book, you learned how to write a variety of different tests for many different apps in various states of their development life cycle.

We hope this book provides you an awesome reference as you undertake making high quality apps built with TDD.

If you have any questions or comments as you work through this book, please stop by our forums at http://forums.raywenderlich.com and look for the particular forum category for this book.

Thank you again for purchasing this book. Your continued support is what makes the tutorials, books, videos, conferences and other things we do at raywenderlich.com possible, and we truly appreciate it!

Wishing you all the best in your continued Android adventures,

Victoria, Fernando, Lance and Jonathan

The *Android Test-Driven Development by Tutorials* team

Appendix

Appendix A: Other Related Techniques

By Fernando Sproviero

TDD focuses on writing tests for classes and methods *before* writing code to support the app's features. While this approach might be useful for the developers, some argue that it doesn't consider the end user since they tend to focus on the expected behavior of the app or its use cases. Writing tests for functionality may even be easier to validate with the users.

After exploring TDD and reading this chapter, you'll discover that other techniques and frameworks exist to enhance or complement TDD.

Acceptance test-driven development

In **Acceptance test-driven development (ATDD)** the entire team first defines what the acceptance criteria of a feature is before development on that feature starts.

Here's how it works: The team collaborates with the end users. Based on that collaboration, the team writes one or more acceptance tests for each requirement. After that, the development team writes the code needed for the requirement to pass those acceptance tests.

ATDD focuses on the acceptance criteria agreed upon with the users. If these tests pass, you can assume the users will be happy with your app. This process gives you an idea of the feature development progress and also avoids **gold-plating**, which means to over-develop features or add functionality that end users don't need or want.

With ATDD, you can take each requirement and write it in the user story format. Once you have that, you can write the acceptance tests for each one. That's why, sometimes, this technique is also called **Story Test-Driven Development (STDD)**.

Here's an example template you might use to write a user story:

```
As a <role> I can <capability>, so that <receive benefit>.
```

Once you have that, you can turn it into this:

```
As a seller, I can publish an item so that I can sell it.
As a buyer, I can search for an item so that I can purchase it.
```

You can write **user acceptance tests (UATs)**, also known as **Story Tests**, in a plain document or even a spreadsheet. Because these tests are not technical, any non-technical person can read and modify them. Once the team is satisfied, developers can use these tests as input to translate into test code. For example, in an app that has a login feature:

1. Open the application.
2. Log in with invalid `<username>` and `<password>`.
3. Verify an error message is shown: "Invalid `<username>` and/or `<password>`!"

Or you may have a spreadsheet with inputs and expected output, for example, in a calculator app:

```
Number  Operator   Number  Expected
1       +          2       3
2       *          0       0
```

These story tests provide the following advantages:

- You can use them to communicate between all of the roles of the team.
- They're easier to agree with the final user.
- The examples are concrete.
- Analysts, developers, testers and the end users have a more active role. They're more involved and they all work together in creating possible scenarios. They understand the stories, the examples and the acceptance criteria.

Behavior driven development

Behavior Driven Development (BDD) is an extension of TDD. You might think of BDD as an enhanced version of TDD.

BDD explains that behaviors should drive the development of an app's features. The behaviors are explained with examples in a simple language that's understandable by all of the people involved in the app. That means that developers, testers and analysts can all collaborate in BDD. Usually, BDD is used as a tool that allows creating tests in plain English and allows collaboration between technical and non-technical members of the team.

The main focus of TDD is to write tests first and to think about designing the features. BDD not only does that, but also uses a natural language to describe the tests. To begin with, it pays attention to tests method naming. For example, the name of the methods could start with `should`, or use the `given/when/then` format instead of the traditional naming, which starts with `test`. This method naming was selected to focus and better describe a behavior. The idea is to break down a test scenario into three parts:

- **given**: Describes the state of the world before you begin the behavior you're specifying in this scenario. These are the pre-conditions to the test.
- **when**: You specify the behavior.
- **then**: Here you describe the expected changes due to the behavior.

Instead of writing a test class per class of a feature, BDD suggests writing a class per requirement. It also enforces writing code that uses the same business language, so there's a **ubiquitous language**. This means that analysts and developers use the same language. For example, if you're writing a game where the analyst states that cars are racing, you should have a class named `Car` and not a class called `Automobile`.

BDD doesn't care about how the app is architected or implemented; its main focus is on the behavior.

In BDD, you can write the acceptance criteria as follows:

```
Given [a context]
When [an event happens]
Then [assert something]
```

Cucumber is a tool that supports BDD using this style for the acceptance criteria. It reads executable specifications that you provide written in plain English and it'll validate that your app does what those specifications state. The specifications consists of multiple examples, or scenarios.

For example, suppose you're writing a calculator application for Android. You could write the following feature file for Cucumber:

```
Feature: Calculate a result
  Perform an arithmetic operation on two numbers using a
mathematical operator

  Scenario Outline: Enter a digit, an operator and another digit
    Given I have a CalculatorActivity
    When I press <num1>
    And I press <op>
    And I press <num2>
    And I press =
    Then I should see "<result>" on the display

  Examples:
    | num1 | num2 | op | result   |
    | 9    | 8    | +  | 17.0     |
    | 7    | 6    | –  | 1.0      |
    | 5    | 4    | x  | 20.0     |
    | 3    | 2    | /  | 1.5      |
    | 1    | 0    | /  | Infinity |
```

Here's how this works:

You specify the name of the feature, give a description and write the scenario using the `given/when/then` format, in plain English.

You also have to translate those steps into Java or Kotlin. These steps are known as **step definitions**, For example:

```
@When("I press {operator}")
fun i_press_op(op: Char) {
  when (op) {
    '+' -> onView(withId(R.id.btn_op_add)).perform(click())
    '–' -> onView(withId(R.id.btn_op_subtract)).perform(click())
    'x' -> onView(withId(R.id.btn_op_multiply)).perform(click())
    '/' -> onView(withId(R.id.btn_op_divide)).perform(click())
    '=' -> onView(withId(R.id.btn_op_equals)).perform(click())
  }
}
```

The step `I press {operator}` is parameterized with an operator. Therefore, you create a function that handles this and translates each of the operators into an action within the UI. In this case, it's pressing the corresponding button. This type of code is often called **glue-code** because it maps the English sentences into a lower-level language such as Kotlin.

By having enough step definitions mapped, you can let a non-technical person write various scenarios.

ATDD vs. BDD

You may find that some people consider both techniques the same thing since they focus on the end user requirements, understanding behaviors and generating similar outcomes.

Here's a closer look at each technique you've seen so far:

- TDD enforces good class design, ensuring that those classes work correctly in units and collaboration with others. ATDD and BDD enforce building the appropriate app for the user.
- ATDD focuses on acceptance tests written in collaboration with the stakeholders. Sometimes these tests are written using spreadsheets and are understandable by non-technical people. However, at some point, the technical team needs to translate these tests to an automatizable test in code.
- In BDD, you try to bring the business team and the technical team closer by using a common language that's understandable by both parties. Using the `given/when/then` style, even non-technical people can write tests that can directly run in automated environments.
- ATDD and BDD both have an objective of tackling down any misunderstood requirements inside of the team. All team members should interpret them the same way.

No matter which technique you choose or if you take parts of each one, they're all great practices to explore on your team.

Key points

- In TDD, you need to write tests before adding or modifying features.
- You write tests in a technical language such as Java or Kotlin.
- The people involved in TDD need to have a technical background. But in BDD or ATDD, both technical and non-technical people on the team can get involved.
- TDD focuses on the implementation of the features. BDD focuses on the behavior. ATDD focuses on capturing the requirements and the acceptance criteria.
- Each of the techniques outlined in this chapter enforces creating tests *before* adding or modifying features. This is in contrast to traditional development.

Where to go from here?

If you want to learn more about other TDD techniques, look at the following:

- "TDD: State of the art and trends" by Carlos Fontela: http://sedici.unlp.edu.ar/handle/10915/4216
- To write tests with the `given/when/then` style using Cucumber, check its documentation: https://cucumber.io/docs

Made in the USA
Coppell, TX
05 August 2021

59984148R00234